MIDNIGHT
DIARIES

MIDNIGHT DIARIES

Boris Yeltsin

Weidenfeld & Nicolson

LONDON

First published in Great Britain in 2000
by Weidenfeld & Nicolson

A CIP catalogue record for this book is available
from the British Library.

ISBN 0 297 64678 8

Printed in Great Britain by
Clays Ltd, St Ives plc

Weidenfeld & Nicolson

The Orion Publishing Group Ltd
Orion House
5 Upper Saint Martin's Lane
London, WC2H 9EA

To my wife, Naina Yeltsina

Contents

Author's Note

My first book, *Against the Grain,* was written during the years of Mikhail Gorbachev's perestroika.* In that account I set the simple task of talking about myself—who I was, where I was born, and how I grew into politics. At that time there was a pitched battle between the old-school technocrats, who wanted to keep the Soviet Union the way it was, and the new politicians who fought for democratic values.

I was one of those new politicians. I had to follow through to the end. I had to take the country through difficult reforms, through an entire parade of political crises and upheavals. Those first steps of the Russian democracy and the crises of 1991–1993 became the material for my second book, *The Struggle for Russia.*†

This new book, *Midnight Diaries,* describes the events from my second term as president—the upheavals in the government, the financial

---

* *Against the Grain: An Autobiography* (Summit Books, 1990)—Trans.
† *The Struggle for Russia* (Times Books, 1994)—Trans.

collapse, the search for a new leader, the brutal election campaign, and the ascent of Vladimir Putin. I have tried to write as truthfully and honestly as possible. To some extent this book looks back on and sums up my entire decade in Russian politics.

The genre of the diary does not necessitate a chronological recounting of events. I would often jot things down, recording important moments in fragments over the years. I usually wrote late at night or early in the morning. Sometimes I tried to understand what was going on; sometimes I was just documenting my impressions. Since my resignation I have had time to systematize these notes, to flesh them out with more detailed accounts of the incidents and the people involved.

The main purpose of this book is to describe accurately the history of our political reforms and my personal history as the first democratically elected president of Russia. If my book helps even in some small way to make sense of recent events, it will have accomplished my goal.

BORIS NIKOLAYEVICH YELTSIN
JULY 1, 2000

Chronology

February 1, 1931:	Yeltsin is born in the Siberian village of Butka, Sverdlovsk (now Yekaterinburg) region.
1955:	Yeltsin graduates from Ural Polytechnic Institute with a degree in civil engineering.
1955–1976:	Yeltsin works in construction and industrial development.
1956:	Yeltsin marries Naina Girina.
1957:	Birth of first daughter Yelena (Lena).
1960:	Birth of second daughter Tatyana (Tanya).
1961:	Yeltsin joins the Communist Party of the Soviet Union.
1976–1985:	Yeltsin is First Secretary of the Sverdlovsk Regional Party Committee.
1985:	Yeltsin moves to Moscow and is elected First Secretary of the Moscow City Party Committee.
February 1986:	Yeltsin is elected Candidate Member of the Politburo.
October 1987:	At a Central Committee Plenum, Yeltsin criticizes the

slow pace of Gorbachev's political and economic reforms (*perestroika*) and is censured by Gorbachev.

November 1987: Yeltsin is hospitalized with chest pains and a severe headache. Gorbachev summons Yeltsin back to the Plenum of the Moscow City Committee where Yeltsin is subjected to lengthy and harsh criticism and dismissed as First Secretary. Yeltsin returns to the hospital in poor physical condition.

May 1988: Doctors in Barcelona operate on Yeltsin's spine after his plane crashes in Spain. Yeltsin will continue to suffer from serious back pain.

March 1989: Yeltsin is elected to the USSR Congress of People's Duputies (the Soviet legislature).

March 1990: Yeltsin is elected to the Russian Congress of People's Duputies (the national legislature of the republic of Russia during the Soviet era).

March 1990: Publication of *Against the Grain*, the first volume of Yeltsin's autobiography.

May 1990: Yeltsin is elected Chairman (speaker) of the Russian Supreme Soviet (parliament).

June 1990: Yeltsin presides over the Russian Congress's adoption of the Declaration of National Sovereignty of the Russian Soviet Federated Socialist Republic.

July 1990: Yeltsin resigns from the Communist Party.

June 1991: Yeltsin is elected President of Russia.

August 1991: Yeltsin leads resistance to a coup d'état led by KGB chief Vladimir Kryuchkov and other security ministers seeking to depose Gorbachev.

October 1991: Yeltsin reportedly requires two weeks rest because of heart problems.

September–
December, 1991: Authority and power steadily shift from the USSR to Russia, from Gorbachev to Yeltsin.

November 1991: Yeltsin signs a decree banning the activities of the Communist Party in Russia.

November 1991: Yeltsin is granted emergency powers by the Congress of People's Deputies as chairman (Prime Minister) of the reform government. Yeltsin appoints Gennady Burbulis as his First Deputy and Yegor Gaidar as his Deputy for Economic Reform.

December 1991:   Yeltsin, Ukrainian leader Kravchuk, and Belarussian leader Shushkevich sign the Belovezh Agreement to dissolve the Soviet Union and create the Commonwealth of Independent States (CIS).

December 1991:   Gorbachev signs a decree resigning as President of the Soviet Union and transfers his remaining powers and his office in the Kremlin to Yeltsin.

January 1992:   Gaidar's economic "shock therapy" begins, eliminating state control over most prices, beginning privatization, and reforming the market.

January 1992–
October 1993:   Mounting attacks on Yeltsin and his economic program in the Supreme Soviet led by its speaker, Ruslan Khasbulatov.

June 1992:   Yeltsin names Gaidar Acting Prime Minister of Russia.

December 1992:   After Gaidar is rejected for the post of Prime Minister by the Congress of People's Deputies, Victor Chernomyrdin is nominated and confirmed as Prime Minister.

March 1993:   A parliamentary motion to impeach Yeltsin fails by a small margin.

April 1993:   Yeltsin receives vote of confidence in national referendum.

September 1993:   Yeltsin dissolves the Russian parliament and calls for new parliamentary elections, but some deputies barricade themselves in the offices at the White House building.

October 1993:   After two weeks of mounting conflict, supporters of the Supreme Soviet break through police lines around the White House, and then, encouraged by speaker Khasbulatov and Vice President Rutskoi, occupy the Moscow Mayor's office and storm the Ostankino TV tower. Yeltsin declares a state of emergency and orders tank bombardment of the parliament building. The deputies surrender and the ringleaders are arrested. More than one hundred people are killed.

December 1993: Elections are held for the new parliament, called the Federal Assembly, consisting of the 450-seat State Duma and the 178-seat Federation Council. A new Russian Constitution, which provides for presidential government, is approved. Yeltsin orders Russian troops into the breakaway republic of Chechnya.

May 1994: Publication of *The Struggle for Russia*, the second volume of Yeltsin's memoirs.

January 1996: Yeltsin dismisses Deputy Prime Minister Anatoly Chubais.

Spring 1996: Yeltsin puts together a presidential re-election campaign team, led by Oleg Soskovets and Aleksandr Korzhakov. After scandals and infighting, Yeltsin reconstructs the team, bringing in Anatoly Chubais, Boris Nemtsov, and his daughter Tanya.

May 1996: Yeltsin meets with Chechen rebel leader Zelimkhan Yandarbiyev and agrees to end the war and grant Chechnya broad autonomy from Russia.

June 1996: Yeltsin suffers his first severe heart attack.

June 1996: Yeltsin wins the first round of the presidential race, but is forced into a run-off against Gennady Zyuganov, Chairman of the Communist Party.

July 1996: Yeltsin appoints Chubais to post of Chief of Presidential Administration. He will dismiss him several months later.

August 1996: General Aleksandr Lebed signs an agreement at Khasavyurt with Chechen commander Aslan Maskhadov granting political autonomy to Chechnya.

November 1996: Yeltsin undergoes quintuple coronary bypass surgery.

March 1997: Summit meeting of Group of "Seven Plus One (Russia)" in Helsinki; Yeltsin criticizes the expansion of NATO, warning against a new confrontation between East and West.

March 1997: Yeltsin appoints a radical, young team to top positions in the government. Led by the re-instated Anatoly Chubais as Minister of Finance, the 1997 Team is given the task of introducing much-needed economic reforms.

May 1997:	State visit of King Juan Carlos I of Spain and Queen Sophia.
May 1997:	Yeltsin signs a peace treaty with Chechen President Maskhadov.
May 1997:	Yeltsin signs friendship treaty with Ukrainian President Leonid Kuchma, settling the Soviet Black Sea fleet crisis.
June 1997:	Summit meeting of Group of Eight in Denver, Colorado.
July 1997:	Svyazinvest telecommunications auction.
November 1997:	Fishing trip with Ryutaro Hashimoto.
February 1998:	Yeltsin visits Pope John Paul II at the Vatican.
March 1998:	Yeltsin dismisses Prime Minister Viktor Chernomyrdin and replaces him with 35-year old Sergei Kiriyenko.
March 1998:	Meeting of the "troika" (Yeltsin, Jacques Chirac, and Helmut Kohl) in Bor, outside Moscow.
May 1998:	Summit of the Group of Eight in Birmingham, England.
July 1998:	Yeltsin attends the burial of Nicholas II, Tsarina Aleksandra, and their children in St. Petersburg's Cathedral of St. Peter and St. Paul.
August 1998:	The Russian stock market collapses, the ruble is severely devalued, and Russia defaults on its domestic and foreign debts. In response to the severe financial crisis, Yeltsin dismisses Kiriyenko and announces that Chernomyrdin will return to head the government. The Communist Duma rejects Chernomyrdin twice. If it rejects him a third time, Yeltsin can disband the Duma and call new parliamentary elections. In response, the parliamentarians begin impeachment procedures against Yeltsin. Meanwhile, Yeltsin gets severe bronchitis. His medical condition spurs further calls for his resignation.
September 1998:	Rather than risk impeachment, Yeltsin decrees Yevgeny Primakov to serve as Prime Minister. Primakov, an old Communist spymaster, staves off massive discontent with his Soviet-style rhetoric and rule.
March 5, 1999:	The representative of the Russian Interior Ministry, Major General Gennady Shpigun is kidnapped by

Chechen rebels at the Grozny airport and held hostage. Moscow decides not to respond militarily. Gen. Shpigun's body is found in the woods in June 2000.

March 1999: The Skuratov sex scandal erupts and the Prosecutor General is suspended from his post. Prosecutor Skuratov is eventually dismissed by the Federation Council in May 2000.

March 1999: Yeltsin appoints Aleksandr Voloshin as Chief of Administration to replace Nikolai Bordyuzha.

March-June 1999: The Kosovo crisis erupts. NATO bombs Yugoslavia under Yeltsin's protest.

April-June 1999: Yeltsin sends Viktor Chernomyrdin to handle negotiations with Yugoslav leader Slobodan Milosevic.

April 1999: Moscow meeting of the heads of the CIS states.

May 1999: Yeltsin dismisses Primakov and replaces him with Sergei Stepashin, who lasts about three months as Prime Minister.

May 1999: Five-item impeachment vote fails in the Duma.

June 1999: War ends. NATO and Russian peacekeeping forces sent into Kosovo.

August 1999: Yeltsin replaces Stepashin with former KGB bureaucrat, Vladimir Putin as prime minister.

August-September 1999: Chechen rebel Shamil Basayev leads incursions into neighboring Dagestan.

September 1999: Apartment explosions in Moscow and other locations.

September 1999: War in Chechnya begins with the first Russian airstrikes.

November 1999: Summit of the Organization for Security and Cooperation in Europe (OSCE) in Istanbul (Yeltsin's last summit).

December 31, 1999: Yeltsin resigns from office during his televised New Year's address to the nation, leaving Prime Minister Vladimir Putin as Acting President.

May 2000: Putin is elected second President of Russia.

Principal Figures
in *Midnight Diaries*

ASKAR AKAYEVICH AKAYEV
Academician at the Academy of Sciences of Kyrgyzstan. Head of department of science and education for the Kyrgyz Communist Party. President of Kyrgyz Republic of the USSR (1989–1990). President of the Republic of Kyrgyzstan (since 1990).

NIKOLAI YEMELYANOVICH AKSYONENKO
Deputy First Minister of Russian Ministry of Transportation (1994–1997). Minister of Transportation (April 1997–1999). First Deputy Prime Minister (1999). Minister of Transportation (since 1999).

HEIDAR ALIEVICH ALIEV
Deputy Chair and Chair of the Committee for State Security (KGB) of Azerbaijan Republic of USSR (1964–1969). First Secretary of the Communist Party of Azerbaijan (1982–1987). Speaker of Parliament of the Nakhichevan Autonomous Republic. Deputy Chair of the Supreme Soviet of Azerbaijan. President of the Azerbaijan Republic (since 1993).

Boris Abramovich Berezovsky

General Director of LogoVAZ (since 1989). General Director of the All-Russian Automobile Alliance (since 1994). Part-owner and chair of the board of directors of ORT, Russia's public television (since 1995). Deputy Secretary of the Security Council (1996–1997). Executive Secretary of the Commonwealth of Independent States (CIS) (1998–1999). Deputy of the Russian State Duma.

Nikolai Nikolayevich Bordyuzha

Deputy Director and then Director of the Federal Government Communications Agency (FAPSI) (1995–1998). Chief of Administration of the President (December 1998–1999). Chair of the State Customs Committee (1999). Ambassador to Denmark.

Sergei Konstantinovich Dubinin

First Deputy Finance Minister and then Acting Finance Minister (1993–1994). Vice President of Imperial Bank (1994–1995). Chair of the Central Bank of the Russian Federation (1995–1998). Vice chair of the board of Gazprom, the oil company.

Tatyana Borisovna Dyachenko

Daughter of President Boris Yeltsin. Computer programmer for Salyut Design Bureau (1983–1994). Member of Yeltsin's election campaign staff (1996). Advisor to the President on public relations (1997–2000).

Sergei Aleksandrov Filatov

First Deputy Chair of the Russian Supreme Soviet (1991). Chief of Administration of the President. Member of the Security Council (1993–1996). Deputy of the State Duma.

Vladimir Aleksandrovich Gusinsky

President of MOST-Bank and President of Media-MOST, a leading Russian company whose holdings include NTV, Russia's leading independent television station, and *Itogi*, the news magazine. President of the Russian Jewish Congress.

Islam Abduganiyevich Karimov

First Secretary of the Central Committee of the Communist Party of Uzbekistan (1989–1991). President of the Republic of Uzbekistan (since 1991).

SERGEI VLADILENOVICH KIRIYENKO
President of NORSI-OIL (1997). Russian Minister of Fuel and Energy
(1997–1998). Prime Minister (1998). Deputy of the State Duma, member of
the Union of Right Forces faction.

ROBERT KOCHARIAN
President of Nagorno-Karabakh (1994–1997). Prime Minister of Armenia
(1997). President of the Republic of Armenia (since 1998).

ALEKSANDR VASILYEVICH KORZHAKOV
Boris Yeltsin's bodyguard and chief of his personal security (1985–1996). Di-
rector of Presidential Security Service (1991–1996). Deputy of the State
Duma, member of the faction Fatherland-All Russia.

YURY VASILYEVICH KRAPIVIN
Head of the Federal Guard Service and Acting Director of Presidential
Security Service during the Yeltsin administration.

LEONID DANILOVICH KUCHMA
Prime Minister of Ukraine (1992). President of the Ukrainian Union of Industrialists and Entrepreneurs (1993). President of Ukraine (since 1999).

ANATOLY SERGEYEVICH KULIKOV
Deputy Minister of Interior. Minister of Interior (1995–1997). Deputy of the
State Duma.

ALEKSANDR IVANOVICH LEBED
Commander of the 14th Army on Transdniester of Moldova (1992–1996). Secretary of the Russian Security Council and aide to the President for national
security (1996). Governor of Krasnoyarsk Territory, member of the Federation Council.

ALEKSANDR GRIGORYEVICH LUKASHENKO
Director of the Gorodets Collective Farm (1985–1990). Deputy of the
Supreme Soviet of the Belarusian Republic (1990–1996). Chair of the Ad-Hoc
Commission on Corruption of the Supreme Soviet of Belarus (1993). Presi-
dent of Belarus (since 1994).

YURY MIKHAILOVICH LUZHKOV
Chair of the Executive Committee of the Moscow City Council (1990–1991).
Vice Mayor of Moscow (1991–1992). Appointed Mayor of Moscow by Boris

Yeltsin in 1992 after the resignation of Gavrill Popov, and elected Mayor in 1996. Member of the Federation Council, leader of the Fatherland movement.

ALBERT MIKHAILOVICH MAKASHOV

Retired Lt. General. Member of the Coordinating Council of the Working Russia movement (since 1992). Chair of the Committee for National Salvation (since 1993). Led the storming of the Mayor's Office in 1993 and an unsuccessful attempt at seizing the Ostankino TV tower, for which he was jailed and eventually amnestied. A leader of the Russian National Assembly.

YURY DMITRIYEVICH MASLYUKOV

General Director of Yugtrastinvest (1995). Chair of the State Duma Committee on Economic Policy (1996). Russian Minister of Industry and Trade. First Deputy Prime Minister (1998). Deputy of the State Duma and member of the Communist Party faction.

ASLAN ALIYEVICH MASKHADOV

Chief of Staff of the Armed Forces and Minister of Defense of the Chechen Republic. President of the Chechen Republic of Ichkeria (since 1997).

NURSULTAN ABISHEVICH NAZARBAYEV

First Secretary of the Central Committee of the Communist Party of Kazakhstan (1989–1991). Chair of the Supreme Soviet of the Kazakh Soviet Socialist Republic (1990). President of the Republic of Kazakhstan.

BORIS YEFIMOVICH NEMTSOV

Representative of the President of Russia in Nizhegorod Region (1991), then Governor. First Vice Premier and Minister of Fuel and Energy (1997). Deputy Chair of the State Duma, member of the Union of Rights Forces faction.

SAPARMURAD ATAYEVICH NIYAZOV

First Secretary of the Central Committee of the Communist Party of Turkmenistan (1985–1991). Chair of the Supreme Soviet of the Turkmen Soviet Socialist Republic (1990). Prime Minister of Turkmenistan (1991–1992). President of Turkmenistan for life.

VLADIMIR OLEGOVICH POTANIN

President of Interros, a financial industrial group (since 1991). Vice President then President of the International Finance Company (1992–1993). President of ONEKSIMbank (1993–1996). First Deputy Premier (1996–1997).

Yevgeny Maksimovich Primakov

First Deputy Secretary of the Committee for State Security (KGB) of the USSR and then Director of the Central Intelligence Service (1991). Director of the Russian Foreign Intelligence Service (SVR) (1991–1996). Russian Minister of Foreign Affairs (1996–1998). Prime Minister (1998–1999). Deputy of the State Duma and leader of the Fatherland-All Russia faction.

Emomali Sharifovich Rakhmonov

Director of a collective farm in Dangarin District of the Kulyab Region of Tajikistan. Chair of the Supreme Soviet of Tajikistan (since 1992). President of the Republic of Tajikistan.

Igor Nikolayevich Rodionov

Chief of the Military Academy of the General Staff (1996–1997). Minister of Defense.

Ivan Petrovich Rybkin

Held various offices in the Communist Party (1987–1992). Deputy of Russian Parliament (1990). Chair of the State Duma (1994–1996). Secretary of the Security Council (1996–1997).

Nikolai Ivanovich Ryzhkov

Chair of the Council of Ministers of the USSR (1985–1990). Deputy of the State Duma. Chair of People's Power, a deputies' group in parliament.

Gennady Nikolayevich Seleznyov

Deputy Chief of Propaganda of the Central Committee of the Soviet Communist Party, then Editor in Chief of *Komsomolskaya Pravda* (1980–1988). Chair of the State Duma.

Igor Dmitriyevich Sergeyev

Deputy Commander in Chief and then Commander in Chief of the Russian Armed Forces. Minister of Defense. Marshal of the Russian Federation.

Eduard Amvrosiyevich Shevardnadze

Soviet Minister of Foreign Affairs (1985–1991). Member of the Soviet President's Political Consultative Group (1991). President of the Republic of Georgia.

Vladimir Nikolayevich Shevchenko

Chair of the Protocol Office of the President's Administration (since 1992). Awarded the title of ambassador (1993).

ALEKSANDR ISAYEVICH SOLZHENITSYN
Nobel Peace Prize laureate (1970). Author and former political prisoner stripped of his citizenship and expelled from the Soviet Union in 1974. Lived in exile in Vermont, USA, until his return to Russia in 1994, after the treason case against him was dropped in 1991.

OLEG NIKOLAYEVICH SOSKOVETS
Minister of Metallurgy (1991). President of Roschermet, a state corporation, and then Vice Premier and Minister of Industry of the Republic of Kazakhstan. Chair of the Russian government's Committee on Metallurgy (since 1992). First Deputy Prime Minister (1993). Chair of the board and president of the Association of Financial and Industrial Groups of Russia (since 1996).

SERGEI VADIMOVICH STEPASHIN
First Deputy, then Director of the Russian Federal Counterintelligence Service (1993–1995). Russian Minister of Justice (1997). Minister of the Interior (1998). Prime Minister (1999). Deputy of the State Duma, member of the Yabloko faction.

YEGOR SEMYONOVICH STROYEV
Held various offices in the Soviet Communist Party (1963–1991). Governor of Orlov Region (since 1993). Chair of the Federation Council (since 1996).

MOVLADI SAIDARBIYEVICH UDUGOV
First Vice Premier of the Chechen Republic of Ichkeria (since 1996). Minister of State Policy and Information and Minister of Foreign Affairs.

VLADIMIR VIKTOROVICH VINOGRADOV
President of Inkobank (1993–1998) and Chair of the Moscow Bank Union (until 1999). Member of the board of the Russian Union of Industrialists and Entrepreneurs.

SERGEI VLADIMIROVICH YASTRZHEMBSKY
Director of the Department for Information and Press of the Russian Foreign Ministry (1992–1993). Russian Ambassador to Slovakia (1993–1996). Press Secretary to the Russian President (1996). Deputy Chief of Administration of the President (1997). Assistant to the President in the Yeltsin administration.

GRIGORY ALEKSEYEVICH YAVLINSKY
Chair of the Center for Economic and Political Research (since 1993). Deputy of the Russian State Duma and head of the Yabloko faction.

NIKOLAI DMITRIYEVICH YEGOROV
Russian Minister for Nationalities and Regional Affairs and Deputy Premier
(1994–1995). Chief of Administration of the President (1995–1996). Governor
of Krasnodar Territory (July-December 1996). Died in 1997.

VALENTIN BORISOVICH YUMASHEV
Deputy Editor in Chief of *Ogonyok*, a leading Russian magazine, and then
General Director of the Ogonyok Publishing House (1987–1996). Advisor to
the President on government-media relations (1996–1997). Chief of Administration of the President (1997–1998).

VLADIMIR VOLFOVICH ZHIRINOVSKY
Chair of the Liberal Democratic Party of Russia (since 1992). Deputy Chair
of the Russian State Duma.

GENNADY ANDREYEVICH ZYUGANOV
Chair of the Russian Communist Party (since 1992). Deputy of the State
Duma. Chair of the Communist Party faction in parliament.

BORIS YELTSIN'S WORLD

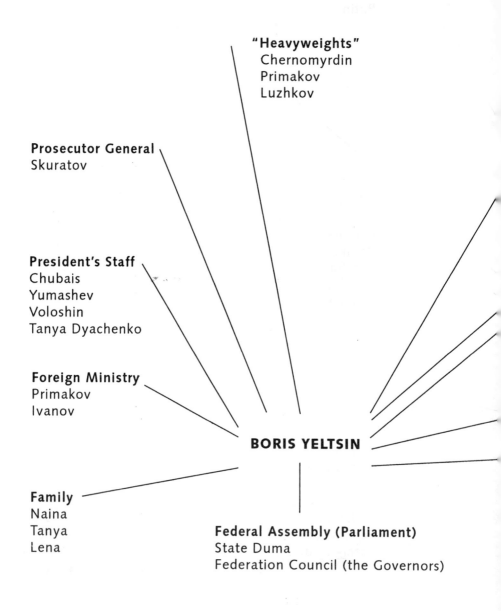

"Heavyweights"
Chernomyrdin
Primakov
Luzhkov

Prosecutor General
Skuratov

President's Staff
Chubais
Yumashev
Voloshin
Tanya Dyachenko

Foreign Ministry
Primakov
Ivanov

BORIS YELTSIN

Family
Naina
Tanya
Lena

Federal Assembly (Parliament)
State Duma
Federation Council (the Governors)

Prime Ministers
Chernomyrdin
Kiriyenko
Primakov
Stepashin
Putin

Generals
Lebed
Korzhakov
Barsukov
Grachev

Oligarchs
Berezovsky
Gusinsky
Potanin
Khodorkovsky
Vyakhirev
Smolensky
Vinogradov

Reformers
Chubais
Nemtsov
Kiriyenko

Power Ministries & Security Agencies
Defense Ministry
Interior Ministry
Justice Ministry
Federal Security Service
Federal Guard Service
Foreign Intelligence Service

MIDNIGHT DIARIES

· 1 ·

December 31, 1999

It is December 28, 1999, and President Boris Yeltsin is taping his annual New Year's address to the Russian people. Suddenly he stops the cameraman and announces that the speech must be rewritten. His flustered aides have three days to come up with something better. Little do they know that Yeltsin has already decided to resign. Only one other person knows the secret: Vladimir Putin, his designated successor. But Putin doesn't know the timing, and Yeltsin doesn't dare tell anyone else about his decision—not even his wife. His resignation must be swift and sudden. No one can steal his thunder. We witness Yeltsin's last three days in office, as he strategically relinquishes the reins of the second most powerful nation on earth.

· ·

ON DECEMBER 28, 1999, as usual, the president's New Year's address to the nation was being taped. The setting was the reception hall of the Kremlin, with a decorated tree, gilded grandfather clocks, and customary ritual; the speech was to include the standard New Year's greetings.* A camera crew from ORT, Russia's public television station, worked briskly and attentively. There were just a few people—the producer, the cameraman, and the sound and light men.

I wished Russians a happy New Year and got up from my desk. The lighted text on the teleprompter grew dim.

"So, here's the story," I said dryly. "My voice is hoarse today, and I don't like the text. So we're going to retape the speech."

My speechwriters' faces fell. I hadn't commented on the text before

* In the Soviet era, New Year's Eve replaced the traditional religious holiday, complete with a decorated fir tree and presents. The Russian Orthodox Christmas Eve falls on January 6, yet the custom of gift-giving on New Year's Eve has been retained. — Trans.

then, and my announcement came as a complete surprise. "Why, Boris Nikolayevich?" they asked.*

"More work has to be done on the text. I'm giving it three days," I told them. "We'll tape it on December 31."

The television crew was upset. "Boris Nikolayevich, why December 31? How will we have time to edit the tape before it airs? What if you have some changes, or, God forbid, there is some kind of technical mishap? Why such a late deadline?"

"Let me repeat: The retaping will be on December 31."

And I left the room.

I couldn't reveal the real reason for my apparent capriciousness. Thank God my staff had grown used to my nature, to my impromptu remarks and surprises. They were no longer truly fazed by anything. They were just a little upset. But what if one of them suspected something? Thinking of this possibility, I slowed my step, causing my adjutant to stumble and glance at me in surprise before slowing down behind me.

The long Kremlin corridors always give me time to calm myself and collect my thoughts. I had a lot to think about. I had never kept such an important decision secret for so long, even from my close aides in the presidential staff.

I have always liked to make decisions in private and implement them rapidly. Once a decision is made, I cannot tolerate the red tape, the conversations, and the delays. With each hour the decision loses its force and effectiveness. That is why I usually turn on the conveyor belt immediately. The implementation machine—first my chief of staff, then my aides, the analysts, the lawyers, and the office staff—goes straight to work. The press secretary, television reporters, wire services, and others follow. With each passing minute, more and more people learn the news. It's as if waves are spreading out from the decision.

That's how it always has been in my eight years in the number-one post in the country, the president of the new Russia. But today it's completely different. Today I'm carrying the burden of a decision I

---

* Russians commonly refer to colleagues by first name and patronymic or last name only. Throughout the book, there will be instances where Yeltsin omits first names.—Trans.

have made in private. I am completely alone—almost. Besides me, there is only one person who knows about this decision. I cannot share this information with anyone else. If the news were to leak, the whole effect would be lost. The emotional, human, and political point of my gesture would be gone. The energy of the decision would dissipate.

I had decided to resign from the office of president.

I was leaving deliberately, of my own volition. I was putting all the force of my political will into this act. Therefore any leak, any advance talk, any forecasts or proposals would put the impact of the decision in jeopardy.

Today I would have to include two more people in the tight circle of those who knew. I had invited the head of the administration, Aleksandr Voloshin, as well as the former head of my administration, Valentin Yumashev, to my residence at Gorki-9, outside Moscow, for a meeting at 6:00 P.M.*

They waited in the living room. To be honest, I was nervous. Very nervous. Here it was, the moment when I would launch my project. It was like firing a rocket from the Baikonur Space Center.

I asked my adjutant to invite the guests into my office. They came in, greeted me, and sat down.

"Aleksandr Stalyevich, Valentin Borisovich," I said, "listen to me carefully. I want to inform you about my decision. On December 31, I will resign."

Voloshin stared at me, not blinking an eye. Yumashev also froze and waited for what I would say next.

"You must draft the appropriate decrees and the text of my speech," I continued.

Voloshin kept staring at me, paralyzed.

"Aleksandr Stalyevich," I said. "You must have nerves of steel! The president has just announced to you that he is resigning, and you don't even react. Do you understand what I just said?"

Voloshin snapped out of it. "Boris Nikolayevich, I always keep my

---

* *Gorki* means "the hills" in Russian. Gorki-9 was one of the numbered residential areas for Russian leaders in the suburbs of Moscow.—Trans.

stormiest reactions inside. Of course I understood you. As chief of administration, I should probably try to talk you out of this move. But I won't do this because your decision is right, and very powerful."

Later Voloshin told me that he had become so flustered at that moment that he almost lost his composure. He had a lump in his throat. I guess Stalyevich really did have nerves of steel.*

I felt relieved. Now there were four of us who knew the secret. Yumashev couldn't refrain from saying a few ecstatic words. A creative person, he immediately appreciated the beauty of the event.† It was a new century! A new president!

Then we got down to the nuts and bolts—when we would prepare the text of the speech, what letters needed to be written, what decrees and other legal documents needed to be drafted for the morning of December 31. There was no precedent for a voluntary resignation by Russia's head of state, so everything had to be legally verified in full.

We sketched out an approximate plan of action for December 31, noting when the television address would be made, the decrees would be signed, and the letters sent out to the Duma and the Federation Council. We figured out whom we had to meet with and whom we had to telephone. This all had to be thought through in advance.

I don't think they expected this from me. Yumashev had known me for a long time, for more than ten years, and he had no inkling it would happen. When we finally seemed to have worked everything out, Valentin suddenly said: "Boris Nikolayevich, it's not right that Tanya‡ doesn't know anything about this. It's not right, and it's not fair. She has been working with you for the last four years. Please tell her."

"All right, I'll think about it," I replied. We said good-bye. As I returned to my desk, I felt as if cats were scratching at me. I generally didn't tell my family about my decisions. But this was something else. My decision was too bound up with their lives.

---

* Voloshin's patronymic is based on the name "Stal," which means "steel" in Russian.—Trans.
† Yumashev is a writer and former head of the Ogonyok publishing house.—Trans.
‡ Tatyana Dyachenko is Yeltsin's daughter.—Trans.

I called Tanya in and told her to be seated across from me. She looked at me expectantly. "Yes, Papochka?" she said.*

"Tanya, I'm going to resign," I told her.

She looked at me in surprise then threw herself toward me, crying. I gave her a handkerchief.

"Papa! Forgive me. Forgive me, please. Don't think... It's just that it's so unexpected. You didn't tell anyone. Let me give you a kiss."

Then she and I sat for a long, long time talking. She told me what an interesting life we would now have. We would be able to walk down the street and meet people and visit people, and it would all be without a protocol and without a schedule. But the whole time her eyes kept welling up. "Daughter, you're driving me to tears," I said, waving my hand as if to say, "Go on, now."

Then Tanya asked me almost frantically, like a child, why Mama didn't know anything about this. "Later. Everything will come later," I said. We went downstairs for dinner. Naina, my wife, noticed that Tanya had been crying. She looked at me inquisitively but didn't say anything.

Now it was important not to have any slipups or leaks. If the news got out, there wouldn't be a resignation. I would have to delay it to a later time. But I didn't think anything would happen. With my reliable team, there wouldn't be any explosions. In fact, I was the one who struggled to keep the secret. In the comfortable, calm atmosphere of my home, I couldn't help but sometimes blurt out "Now, after the 31st..." or "Well, after the New Year, everything will be clear." I would drop a hint like this, and then watch people to see if there was any reaction. Naina was calm. Lena, my other daughter, didn't seem to notice anything. They suspected nothing.

Now it was too late for doubts. The countdown had begun. The bomb was ticking.

There was only one other important hurdle: my conversation with my prime minister, Vladimir Putin. This would be our second talk

---

* Russian names have many diminutives and nicknames that designate degrees of familiarity and affection. Boris Nikolayevich would be called "Borya" or "Papochka" by his family. —Trans.

about my decision. I assumed it would be very short. My first conversation with Putin had taken place about two weeks earlier, on December 14, five days before the parliamentary elections. We met in the office of my Gorki-9 residence. The conversation had not been brief. When I told him that I intended to make him acting president, Putin's first reaction made my heart sink. "I'm not ready for that decision, Boris Nikolayevich," he had said.

No, it wasn't weakness on his part. You wouldn't call Putin weak. It was the doubts of a strong person. "You see, Boris Nikolayevich," he explained. "It's a rather difficult destiny."

I didn't want to have to twist Putin's arm. Instead, I told him about myself, how I had come to work in Moscow. I was a little over fifty at that time, older than Putin by about seven or eight years. I was an energetic, healthy person. I told myself that if I got fed up with these Moscow bureaucrats, I would do something different. I would get out of politics. I would go back into construction. I'd move back to Sverdlovsk or somewhere else. Life seemed like a wide field, full of possibilities.

But there was only one path into the field. How could I explain that to Putin?

"I want to step down this year, Vladimir Vladimirovich," I told Putin. "This year. That's very important. The new century must begin with a new political era, the era of Putin. Do you understand? At one time, I, too, wanted to live my life in a completely different way. I didn't know it was going to turn out this way. But I had to... I had to choose. Now you have to choose."

Putin turned the conversation to something else. "Russia needs you, Boris Nikolayevich. And you help me a lot. Remember the summit in Istanbul? If I had gone, it would have gone one way, but you went, and it was a different situation.* It's very important that you and

---

* In a later chapter, Yeltsin recounts his meeting with U.S. president Bill Clinton in Oslo prior to the Istanbul summit of the Organization for Security and Cooperation in Europe, of which Russia and the United States are members. Knowing that the Chechnya conflict would be on the agenda for the fifty-four-member regional body, the Russian government expected a tough reaction from the West. Yeltsin contemplated sending Putin, then prime minister, in his place but ultimately attended himself. —Trans.

I work together. Maybe it would be better if you left at the end of your term."*

I was silent for a while. I looked out the window. Two people were sitting and talking. It was a typical Moscow day, an ordinary morning. It was so simple, so open. But unlike Putin, I was in the iron grip of a decision already made. Once made, it wouldn't let me go.

"Well, what do you think? You haven't answered me," I prodded Putin.

"I agree, Boris Nikolayevich," he said.

That had been almost two weeks ago. Putin had had the opportunity to calmly think over everything that we had talked about at our last meeting. On the 14th we had discussed this issue in general, and now we had to get down to the details. Ready or not, he would have to take the reins of power immediately.

At 9:00 A.M. Putin came into my Kremlin office. I immediately had the impression that he was a different man. I suppose he seemed more decisive. I was satisfied. I liked his demeanor.

I told Putin how I planned to arrange things on the morning of December 31, what events would take place one after another: the television address, the signing of the decrees, the handing over of the nuclear suitcase, the meetings with the power ministers, and so on. Then we made some insignificant changes in what was now our joint plan.

I really liked Putin. I liked how he reacted, how he corrected several points in the plan—everything was clear and precise. I love this moment in my work, when I leave the realm of emotions, feelings, and ideas and move to the hard plane of a decision's realization. It was simple, really: One president was leaving, and another (as yet only acting president) was coming in. Strictly by the law, accurately, and dryly, we were implementing the article of the Russian constitution concerning the transition of power. Since we were doing this for the first time, it was important not to forget anything.

Finally, we were finished. Our meeting was taking place in the Kremlin. The official setting wouldn't allow for a display of feelings. But here

* Under the Russian constitution, Yeltsin had a five-year term starting in 1996.—Trans.

and now, for the last time, I was sitting next to Putin in the role of president, and for the last time he was not first person of the country.*
There was a lot I wanted to tell him. I think he had a lot to say to me, too. But we didn't say anything. We shook each other's hand. We hugged good-bye. Our next meeting was to be on December 31, 1999.

On December 30 Yumashev brought me the text of my televised speech. I read through it several times then took out a pen and began to make corrections. I added a line about how no one should think that I was leaving because of illness or that someone had forced me into this decision. This was my own decision, and I realized that I had to do it right away.

Yumashev started arguing with me. He said that no one had ever thought that they could force me out because of my illness or for any other reason. What kind of illness, with the elections six months away? "That line weighs down the whole speech," he said.

I thought about what he said, read it again, and decided that he was probably right.

On December 31 I woke up earlier than usual. After my normal family breakfast, while I was getting ready to leave for work, Tanya reminded me: "You'll tell Mama?"

Once again, I had my doubts. Perhaps I shouldn't worry her now? "Papa, I beg you," said Tanya.

I stood in the front hallway, undecided. I slowly buttoned up my coat.

"Naina, I've made a decision," I said. "I'm retiring. My televised address is this afternoon. Be sure to watch the TV."

Naina froze in place. She looked first at me, then at Tanya. She couldn't believe her ears. Then she turned like a whirlwind and began kissing and hugging me.

"How wonderful! Finally!" she cried. "Borya, is it really true?"

"That's it now. I have to go."

---

* Just as Americans call the president's wife the "first lady," so Russians call the president the "first person." PublicAffairs has published a book of interviews with Putin titled *First Person* (2000).—Trans.

Tanya had been right. It was wrong not to warn my wife, the person closest to me, about such a decision. It wasn't human. But now it seemed as if I was growing sentimental, turning from a politician back into a regular human being. Thank heavens!

A car drove up to the doorway. There was that distinctive whoosh of the tires that bullet-proof cars make. Tolya Kuznetsov, head of the security service, opened the door for me as usual. He surely assumed that he and I would be setting off for the Kremlin like this every morning for another six months. I said nothing. I would have a heart-to-heart with Tolya later, after I retired.

8:00 A.M.: Voloshin summoned Brycheva, head of the legal department of the administration, and Zhuykov, Voloshin's aide on legal matters, to his office. He told them to prepare the decree on the resignation of the president and to draft two letters, one to the Duma and one to the Federation Council.

8:15 A.M.: I walked into my Kremlin office. On my desk, as usual, was my schedule of the day's activities: the taping of the New Year's address, a meeting with Prime Minister Putin, meetings with the deputies of the head of administration, a discussion of the January calendar, and then, finally, several telephone calls.

I no longer needed the calendar.

I got out my real schedule from my inside jacket pocket. It was the schedule I would be living by from now on. The piece of paper had gotten crushed in my pocket. I simply can't stand crumpled papers. I put the sheet on my desk and tried to smooth it out with my hand. I covered it with a folder, just in case, so no one would see it. But what was there to hide? Minutes were left before the countdown.

At 9:00 A.M.: Valery Semenchenko, office manager, came into my office, and put the usual presidential mail on my desk. By the end of the day I was supposed to have reviewed this pile of papers (coded telegrams, different reports from the power ministries*, telegrams from the Foreign Ministry, and so on). I was also supposed to sign

---

* The power ministries, so called because they represent the might of the state, include the Defense, Interior, and Justice Ministries and the Federal Security Service, Federal Guard Service, and Foreign Intelligence Service.—Trans.

several documents (a veto of some laws, several assignments to various agencies, and some telegram greetings). I looked at one more document, a draft outline for my message to the Federal Assembly.* "I won't be needing that," I thought to myself.

Semenchenko wished me a happy New Year and left.

All the documents that lay on my desk didn't mean anything anymore. There was only my crumpled schedule. But where were the main resignation decrees? I pushed a button on my console and asked for Voloshin.

He came in carrying a red folder, his expression agitated. Well, it seemed that Aleksandr Stalyevich of the steel nerves was beginning to crumble. "Boris Nikolayevich, everything is apparently ready, but...," he began timidly.

I looked at him sternly. "What? Have you suddenly begun to have doubts? Just follow the plan!"

Voloshin looked at me in surprise. "No, no. What are you saying, Boris Nikolayevich? We're going according to the plan."

Once again, I pushed a button on the control panel. I asked that Putin be summoned by 9:30 A.M.

I opened the red folder with the decrees: "1. In accordance with Part 2, Article 92, of the Russian Federation constitution, at 12:00 midnight on December 31, 1999, I terminate the exercise of the powers of the office of the president of the Russian Federation. 2. In accordance with Part 3, Article 92, of the Russian Federation constitution, the chair of the government of the Russian Federation will temporarily exercise the powers of the office of the Russian Federation president from 12:00 midnight on December 31, 1999. This decree enters into effect the moment it is signed." Well, thank God.

---

* Russia has both a parliamentary system of government and a presidential system. In 1991, Boris Yeltsin became the first freely elected president of Russia. In 1993, a new constitution gave Yeltsin the power to override and dissolve the Russian parliament (also called the Federal Assembly), which consists of the Federation Council (upper house) and the State Duma (lower house). The Federation Council consists of 178 governors, representing the legislative and executive branches of power in each republic and region. These governors review laws passed by the Duma; appoint judges to Russia's constitutional and supreme courts; must approve the introduction of martial law; and can impeach the country's president. The State Duma consists of 450 members, elected for four-year terms. These parliamentarians pass federal laws, approve the presidential nominee for prime minister, and can bring impeachment charges against the president. — Trans.

With a great sense of satisfaction and with a thick scratch of my pen, I signed the decree.

At exactly 9:30 A.M., Putin entered my office. We greeted each other. I asked him to summon Vladimir Shevchenko, head of protocol, and Dmitry Yakushkin, press secretary, along with Georgy Muravyov, the Kremlin cameraman, and the photographer, Aleksandr Sentsov.

I looked at everyone carefully and then read the decree aloud. Shevchenko was the first one to break down. "Boris Nikolayevich," he groaned. "Let's not sign that decree yet. Let's wait for a week. We have the trip to Bethlehem coming up."

I looked at Putin. He gave a slightly embarrassed smile. I shook his hand. "Congratulations."

My aides were in shock: Anatoly Kuznetsov, Valery Semenchenko, Aleksei Gromov, Andrei Vavra, the secretary from the outer office—I can't list them all now. I just remember their amazed expressions. And their silent question: "Why?" I had known that this would come as a surprise to them, but I hadn't supposed it would be such a shock.

I went into the reception room, with its familiar New Year's decorations. The same camera crew was there. They didn't have happy holiday expressions on their faces. They already knew that I was resigning. Half an hour ago, in accordance with our plan, Voloshin had brought them the text of my television address. It was already typed into the teleprompter.

I walked decisively over to the desk and then sat down. I heard the voice of the producer, Kaleriya Ivanovna. "Camera! Action!" I cleared my throat, but my voice came out as a croak. I stopped, took a sip of water, and then calmly and firmly began my speech: "My dear fellow Russians!"

I got through the speech with almost no trouble. Almost. At one point a speck got in my eye, and I rubbed it away with my hand.

When I finished the last word, there was absolute silence. I could hear the clock ticking in the room. And then suddenly somebody clapped, and then another person, and another, and I raised my eyes and saw that the entire television crew was giving me a standing ovation. I didn't know what to do. The women didn't try to hide their tears, and I cheered them up as best I could. I asked that champagne be brought in, and the women gave me flowers. We clinked our glasses and raised a toast to the New Year and to that day. To my surprise I realized that I was in a good mood—a very good, cheerful mood.

The cameraman took the cassette out of the camera. I took it in my hands. A small black plastic box. That was it. It was probably more important than any of the decrees or the letters to the Duma. Here, on this tape, I was announcing my decision to the people. From the moment this speech went on the air, my presidential term would be over, and the term of Vladimir Putin as acting president would begin.

I searched for Yumashev, and nodded to him. He took the cassette and left. An armored car was parked at entry number 6 of the Kremlin, at the Borovitsky Gates. The car was accompanied by the traffic police. That was how the cassette would be delivered, under escort, to Ostankino, where the television studio was located. And there Yumashev would personally see to it that at exactly 12:00 noon, the televised speech would go on the air.

What came next on my crumpled paper? A meeting with Patriarch Aleksy. I returned to my office. The patriarch slowly entered. I told him about my decision. He looked at me attentively, pausing for a long time. "A manly decision," said the patriarch, using an expression that was not the least bit clerical. Then he blessed me. We talked for a while, the patriarch, Putin, and I. I noticed to my satisfaction that Putin was developing nice personal relations with his holiness. Putin, too, would need the help of this wise man. Aleksy wished him every success and bowed to him as he left.

The next item on my schedule was the transfer of the nuclear suitcase. Since the public would be most interested in this historic moment, Dmitry Yakushkin asked that it be filmed by our cameraman. The procedure itself was fairly dull. Yet another aspect of presidential power was taken from my shoulders and transferred to those of Vladimir Putin. Now I was no longer responsible for the nuclear suitcase and the nuclear button. Maybe I would finally get rid of my insomnia.

11:30 A.M.: Meeting with the power ministries. A ceremonial farewell lunch. A table was set in the presidential apartments on the third floor. This was our farewell, my farewell to my faithful comrades and their farewell to their commander in chief. We would watch my resignation speech on TV together.

At about 11:50, in the middle of lunch, Naina telephoned Tanya. "Tanya," she said. "I've been thinking that the resignation shouldn't be announced today. Why upset people? Why get them worried? Can you imagine? People have to celebrate New Year's and here the president is leaving. Why couldn't he wait for a few days? He can leave after the New Year. Think about it. Talk to Papa again."

Tanya answered in a steely voice, "Mama, that's not possible. Don't worry; everything's going to be fine. Go and watch TV."

In fact, there was a mix-up with our TV viewing at the lunch. Five minutes before the show was to go on the air, it turned out there was no television set in the hall where we were meeting. People searched around frantically. The closest TV was in Tanya's office. We dragged it out of there and just barely managed to turn it on a half minute before the speech began.

I hardly looked at the TV. I wanted to close my eyes and bow my head, but instead I stared directly ahead. The ministers and the generals watched in complete silence. Some of them had tears in their eyes. If these were the toughest men in the country, how would others react?

We drank champagne. An enormous bouquet of flowers appeared from somewhere. The chandeliers, the crystal, the windows—everything glittered with a New Year's glow. Suddenly, for the first time that day, I realized that it was actually New Year's Eve. Some present I was giving to everyone!

After lunch, I retreated to my office. At about 1:00 P.M., I got up from my desk, said good-bye and headed toward the door. My soul was light and airy. There was only an unusually loud thudding of my heart, the tension of these days making itself felt. I stopped in the hallway near the elevator. I had almost forgotten. I took my presidential pen out of my pocket—the pen I had used to sign my last decree—and gave it to Putin.

That was it. That was all. Everything I wanted to do that day I had done.

I went downstairs. My car drove up to the door. It was snowing. A nice, soft, clean snow surrounded the Kremlin.

I wanted to say something important in farewell to Vladimir Putin. What a hard job he would be facing. How I wanted to help him in some way.

"Take care . . . Take care of Russia," I said to him. Putin looked at me and nodded his head. The car slowly circled. I closed my eyes. I was tired, very tired.

On the way to the dacha, a telephone rang in the car. My adjutant said, "Clinton wants to speak with you." I asked the president of the United States to call back later, at 5:00 P.M. Now I could indulge a little. Now I was retired.

Naina and Lena greeted me, kissed me, and congratulated me. My granddaughter Katya called. "Wow, Grandpa! You're really some hero!"

There were dozens of calls. Tanya couldn't get off the telephone. I told her I was going to take a nap. I asked her not to wake me for an hour or two.

That New Year's Eve, as always, I played the gift-giver, Father Frost. I took presents for people out of my sack. My family gave me a handsome watch. Then we all went outside. We looked at the stars, the banks of snow, the trees. The night was pitch black. My family and I hadn't been so happy in a long time. In a long, long time.

· 2 ·

Tanya

We jump back to 1995, when Yeltsin suffers the first of several serious heart attacks. Not only is Yeltsin's health failing, but he finds himself increasingly isolated politically. It's time to prepare for the upcoming presidential elections, but Yeltsin's cabinet, administration, and campaign team are in total chaos. Yeltsin grows desperate. He needs someone on the inside, someone who can report honestly on the scandals and intrigues surrounding him. He needs someone he can trust. Who is that person? Tanya, his smart, young, and media-savvy daughter. Indeed, by her very presence in Yeltsin's entourage, Tanya changes the course of the presidential campaign, the day-to-day operations in the Kremlin, and history.

* *

IN LATE 1995 I had my first severe heart attack. I didn't attach much significance to it. It meant I had to rest in the hospital for a while and then plunge back into the fray. Most leaders typically disregard their health. There's a particular human type among them—flabby from a sedentary lifestyle, potbellied from bad habits, eyes reddened from chronic lack of sleep, heavy expressions. I always thought of myself as an exception among them. I played sports; I didn't have a big belly; I went swimming in icy water; I went skiing, played volleyball and tennis, and loved to take walks. And I had good genes—both my father and my grandfather lived to a grand old age, as if they were made out of seasoned oak. And that's why I always counted on my own body. I figured it would heal itself. I was wrong. After age forty or forty-five, the human heart, especially in men, tends to give out, regardless of whether you are a great athlete or a sybarite, a monk or a sinner.

New Year 1996 arrived with everything in disarray. It was right after my heart attack and right after a terrible defeat in the Duma elections. The bloc of the leftist parties, mainly the Communists and agrarians, had gained more than 40 percent of the seats, that is, about 200 votes, in the Duma in the December 1995 parliamentary elections. And the so-called party of power—the Our Home Is Russia Party, headed by Viktor Chernomyrdin—had barely managed to garner 10 percent. And we still saw no breakthrough in the Chechen war. With such a burden of moral responsibility, it was very difficult to go into a second term.

That was the state I was in when I rang in the New Year. It was a year in which not only the country but I myself would have to make a big choice, whether or not to run for a second term in the June presidential elections and face the runoffs in July.

Naina, my wife, was categorically opposed to my running for office again. I, too, felt as if the constant stresses were completely wearing me out and squeezing me dry. And perhaps for the first time in my life, I felt as if I were almost completely isolated politically. It wasn't just a question of my 3-percent approval rating in the polls, which was described as an "almost negative rating" at the time. Rather, I stopped feeling the support of those with whom I had begun my political career, the people with whom I had embarked on the first parliamentary elections and then the presidential race. The intelligentsia, the democratic politicians, the journalists—my allies, as my unyielding bastion of support—all seemed to have left me. Some disapproved of the war in Chechnya; others frowned on the abrupt firing of prime ministers; still others felt dissatisfied with the general course of development in our country. Everyone had reasons. All those reasons were seemingly logical and fair. But I had an intuitive sense that these people were prepared to unite. They were still my allies, just as they had always been, but they longed for a central idea to solidify their union.

In late 1995 people in my closest circles—informally led by Aleksandr Korzhakov, head of my security service—began to discuss an idea: My successor should not be Viktor Stepanovich Chernomyrdin, who had lost the Duma elections as the candidate of the Our Home Is Russia Party, but Oleg Nikolayevich Soskovets, the first vice premier.

Soskovets was a handsome man with an honest, open Russian expression. Former head of an iron and steel plant, he was a real manager and quite a worthy, representative figure who was essentially already the number-two man in the government. At that time I didn't realize how dangerous Korzhakov was in his role as "savior of the fatherland" or why he was so zealously protecting his close friend Oleg Soskovets.

Nobody said anything to my face, but Korzhakov was pushing me toward dismissing Chernomyrdin. I could see the events that would unfold: Riding the wave of Chechen separatism and the "Communist threat," a semimilitary team of post-Soviet generals would come to power—Aleksandr Korzhakov; Mikhail Barsukov, director of the Federal Security Service; and Oleg Soskovets, who was their powerful protector.* Others would be found as well.

At that time my whole life seemed under assault, battered about by all sorts of storms and strife. I stayed on my feet but was almost knocked over by the gusts and blows. My strong body had betrayed me. Like wolves that gradually turn to a new leader of the pack, my closest friends had already found themselves a replacement. Even those upon whom I had always depended, who were my last resort, my resource, the spiritual leaders of the nation, even they had abandoned me. And the people could not forgive me for economic "shock therapy" or for the humiliation of Budyonnovsk and Grozny.† It seemed as if all were lost.

But just then a strange, final clarity came over me. I told myself, "If I run in the elections, I will win them without a doubt. I know that for sure! Despite all the prognoses, despite all the polls, despite my political isolation. I will win." The idea of leaving and thus enable the Communists to come to power was intolerable. Most likely I was saved at that moment by my eternal passion, my will to resist all circumstances. I had made my choice by the end of December.

---

* Soskovets was considered the most powerful man in government after the prime minister. He supervised the Energy, Transport, Construction, Health, and Nuclear Power Ministries.—Trans.

† Budyonnovsk is a Russian city attacked by Chechen rebels in the first Chechen war in 1995. Chechen warlord Shamil Basayev took hospital patients hostage, killing hundreds of them before a police raid to rescue the hostages. Grozny is the capital of the Republic of Chechnya.—Trans.

And then Tanya appeared.

Don't misunderstand me. Lena and Tanya, my two daughters, had never disappeared from my life. They were the people I loved most in the world. But I had one firm rule: No politics at home. And I had never violated it. That is, not until 1996.

Everybody has their habits, their quirks, their way of life. It is well known, for example, that Mikhail Gorbachev never kept secrets from his wife. And of course he was right, in his own way. But I had the opposite situation in my family. For many years, I never spoke about politics at home. Not a word! My wife and daughters learned practically all the news from television. I would listen to all their opinions and responses and keep my mouth shut. "Borya, how can you go on not paying people their pensions! When will the government finally get this right?" I kept silent, my face motionless. Or I would try to change the subject: "Isn't the weather wonderful today?" They learned to guess my opinions about people and situations from a hint, a gesture, a reaction. That's how it continued for many long years. I refused to give them long and complicated lectures about politics, and I didn't want to chitchat about serious matters.

But at the moment of the most severe political crisis, my family suddenly rallied to my side. Relief came in the person of my daughter Tanya.

Tanya was a total techno-whiz. She had never thought about politics. She was already over thirty by that time, an independent, formed person. She had graduated from the faculty of computer science and cybernetics at Moscow State University and had been working for the Salyut Design Bureau. She was a good programmer. Her work involved ballistics and in particular calculating the trajectory of space vehicles. It always seemed to me that she viewed my stormy political career with respect and probably with some amazement, fright, and pity. "Papa, where have you been blown away to?" she seemed to wonder.

Tanya's personal life had worked out nicely. Her husband, Aleksei Dyachenko, was an aeronautic engineer and the son of an aeronautic engineer. He and Tanya worked in the same office. By this time their son Borya was already in high school and their younger son, Gleb, had just been born. Tanya was on maternity leave, taking care of little Gleb.

In early January I announced my decision to run in the elections. I immediately put together a campaign team, headed by Soskovets. I figured if Soskovets had any political ambitions, I should know. I wanted to see what kind of politician he was and what kind of political will he possessed.

The scandals in my campaign headquarters began almost at once. The first had to do with the ballot signatures needed by law to support a candidate for the presidential election. The newspapers immediately spread the story that the rail and steel workers were being forced to sign up when they got paid. They were sent to two windows—one to get their pay packet and the other to support President Yeltsin. I asked that the story be checked out, and it turned out to be true. This blew up into a worldwide scandal. My campaign manager had "forgotten" that we were already living in another country and not the old Soviet Union, where politicians could buy voters so crudely.

Nowadays we talk in terms of "political planning" and "campaign technology." But back then we were not so sophisticated. Instead, there was a constant, total, and shameful pressure on Russia's regional governors. The governors had to back us and guarantee voters for us. The governors, ashen with fright, would meet with us and argue that there was no point—there were no comprehensible campaign slogans and no coherent strategy. I remember once when Soskovets shouted rudely at some television journalists over some trifle, something he didn't like in the top news program, and practically started a quarrel between our campaign and the TV people. All of this type of manipulative behavior came from the old Soviet mold. It all reminded me of the old meetings of the bureau of the regional Communist Party—the same methods, expressions, and attitudes, as if from the deep, dark past. When you talked to people in the hallways, they seemed normal, animated people, but when you saw them in the meetings, they were buttoned-down "suits."

That's when I knew that I needed a new person in my campaign. I needed someone who would impartially and honestly tell me about what was going on, someone who could help me look at the situation from the outside. Most important, this had to be a person who was free from group prejudices, free from the struggle of different interest groups, above the fray. The campaign had too much of that already.

But where could I find such a person? And what's more, where could I find someone who wouldn't provoke suspicion and intrigue, who would come into the campaign calmly, without shaking things up? I needed someone who would be practically invisible.

One day Valentin Yumashev came to visit me in Barvikha.* I shared my thoughts with him: I felt I couldn't control the campaign. I could see from the gloomy expressions of my aides, in particular Viktor Ilyushin, that the situation in the campaign was getting worse by the day. Slowly but surely we were sinking into a swamp. The headquarters was filled with quarreling; there was no strategy; there was Soviet-style communication; and it looked nothing like a gathering of like-minded people.

"I need to have my own person in the campaign," I told Yumashev. He listened, nodded his head, and thought for a while. But who? Who could that be?

"What about Tanya?" he blurted out.

At first I didn't even know what he was talking about. "What has Tanya got to do with this?" I asked. Then I realized what he was suggesting. I was immediately engulfed in doubts: How would the public perceive this? What would the journalists and the politicians say? How would Tanya be received in the Kremlin?

Still, Tanya was the only person who could report all the information to me. People would tell her things that they weren't able to tell me to my face. And she's an honest, intelligent person without bureaucratic complexes. She wouldn't conceal things from me. She's my daughter. She has my nature. She has my attitude toward life.

At about this time, I had my first-ever meeting with representatives of the major banks and media groups: Boris Berezovsky, Vladimir

---

* Barvikha is the area outside Moscow where the dachas of the president and other top officials are located. — Trans.

Gusinsky, Mikhail Khodorovsky, Vladimir Potanin, Mikhail Fridman. The meeting took place at their initiative, which I initially regarded rather cautiously. I understood that they had nowhere to go, that they had to support me, and I thought that the conversation would probably be about the funding of my campaign. But the conversation was about something completely different.

"Boris Nikolayevich," they said. "What's going on in your campaign headquarters and in your entourage means almost certain failure. This situation is forcing some businessmen to make deals with the Communists or to pack their bags. We don't have anyone to make a deal with. The Communists will hang us from the lampposts. If we don't turn this situation around drastically, in a month it will be too late."

I hadn't expected such tough talk. They offered all their resources— media, regional contacts, and funding. But most important, they offered me people. They suggested I bring their best people into my campaign, and that's when the "analytical group" was formed, consisting of the sociologist Aleksandr Oslon; Igor Malashenko, head of NTV; Sergei Zveryev; Vasily Shakhnovsky; and other young and very capable political analysts.

But what amazed me most was that they all agreed that I needed Anatoly Chubais in the campaign. Chubais had been dismissed recently from the government, and the Korzhakov-Soskovets group had managed to stir up a quarrel between Chubais and me.

But we were able to put our differences aside. Chubais was appointed head of our analytical group. And soon I saw how Tanya could fit into their work. They would make a wonderful team.

In mid-March I created a new campaign council, which I headed until Viktor Chernomyrdin took over. With my heart in my mouth, I introduced Tanya at the meeting: "I would like to introduce to you a new member of the campaign team, Tatyana Dyachenko."

At first no one understood what was going on. Here was a new face, a woman who was willing to work late hours, who came very early in the morning, who sat in on all sorts of meetings day and night, who talked to everyone, and who asked naive questions. Maybe she was some sort of whiz? And suddenly it became clear: With her there, certain negative conduct was simply impossible. The atmosphere of intrigue and intense, selfish, macho power struggles evaporated. I was told about this only later. I didn't attend all those endless meetings.

The fact is, Tanya entered the world of the Kremlin from a completely different life. Her simple, natural reactions threw the most jaded bureaucrats off balance. She just kept asking: "But why?" And people's stupidity, which had been covered up with a certain arrogant aplomb, was immediately exposed. And the problems became abundantly clear.

At several meetings, Tanya had spoken utterly frankly and without embarrassment about things that shocked her listeners. "Listen," she had said, "Who are we electing here?! Why is Papa meeting only with top officials? What, there aren't any regular people around? That's not going to fly at all."

What does a father feel when his daughter finally becomes a full adult? It is very hard to put into words. It's a different kind of love, no less strong than what he experienced previously, when she was a baby, then a child, a teenager, a woman, a young mother. It's different at different stages. But now I found in my grown-up daughter a remarkable female charm, a tenderness, an intellect, a sophistication. At the same time, with some surprise, I found in her some of my own traits. And yet she was the same person who could tell me, sometimes even sharply, the whole truth.

Of course I didn't realize all of these things at once. At first they were only feelings, conflicting but usually good feelings. Tanya was always nearby now. How much calmer I began to feel! She would come in, straighten my tie and button my shirt, and my mood would improve. And the psychological condition of a candidate for president is very important. Before Tanya joined the campaign, I often thought that I couldn't physically carry the load of the presidential race. All the trips and speeches would put me into a state of stress. I was afraid I was going to break down. What could I do?

But with Tanya there I began to think that I wouldn't break down. I could do it. And most important, it seemed that all the most unsolvable problems were beginning to be resolved. For the first time in many years, I felt a light surge of optimism. I could glimpse some hope for the future, and I thought that I didn't have to jump through the hoops of the previous years—performing gestures for effect, making abrupt moves, demonstrating my will for power, and showcasing my strength. I saw that I had to tap a different resource—young people with clear heads and straightforward language, unburdened by the heavy weight of the past. These young people would not push the interests of their group or clan but would work simply because it was interesting and profitable for them.

You have to remember, Russia is a country of very highly educated people, where, despite all the difficulties, there is something for young minds. There is the opportunity for them to show what they're made of, to earn money, to build their futures on their own. I had to rely on such people from Tanya's generation. Despite my age and my long Party biography, even though they made jokes about me and laughed, I was *their* president. And they were *my* voters. If they wanted to keep their standard of living, they would have to turn out to vote. They were my hope. They were my helpers.

The young people of the analytical group started working furiously, the atmosphere in the campaign improved, and the tone of the press changed. By the end of March, my ratings had nudged up a little. But I kept thinking, "It's late—too late. It will take too long to make all these changes."

There is no point in hiding it: I had always been inclined toward simple, effective decisions. It had always seemed to me that chopping through the Gordian knot was easier than spending years untying it. At some stage, when I compared the two strategies proposed to me by two teams, one headed by Chubais and one by Soskovets, different in their mentality and their approach, I came to the conclusion that we couldn't wait for the results of the June elections: We had to act now.

Korzhakov was also still searching for his election strategy. "It is senseless to struggle when you have a 3-percent approval rating, Boris Nikolayevich," he said to me. "If we lose time with all these electoral games, then what?"

I had to take a radical step. I told my staff to prepare the documents. Decrees were written to ban the Communist Party, dissolve the Duma, and postpone the presidential elections. These formulations contained the verdict: I had not been able to manage the crisis within the framework of the current constitution. But this is how I saw the situation at the time: By outlawing the Communist Party, true, I would pay a very heavy price in credibility for going beyond the constitution's limits. But I would fix one of the main problems I'd had since the beginning of my presidential term. After the ban, the Communist Party would be finished forever in Russia.

On March 23 I held a closed meeting with Chernomyrdin, Soskovets, Chief of Administration Nikolai Yegorov, and some of those in the Security Council and the power ministries. I acquainted them all with this plan, then said, "Here's the idea. Let me hear your opinions. What do you all think?"

There was an awkward pause.

Anatoly Kulikov, the interior minister, spoke out unexpectedly sharply against the plan. The Communist Party, he said, controlled the local, legislative, or representative branch of government in more than half of the regions of Russia. The Party could get people out on the streets. He couldn't vouch for all of his subordinates in such a situation. What would we do if some police units were for the president and others against him? Would we fight? Chernomyrdin expressed the same position, saying that he didn't understand why there was a need for such abrupt and irreversible actions. But others spoke in support of the plan.

Finally, I said, "All right. The majority are for postponement of the elections. The meeting's over. Go on; I'll think it over by myself."

Alone, I thought through all sides of the matter. I had to decide within twenty-four hours. Such things cannot be put off, otherwise information starts to leak. Once again I felt that internal chill: I had to make a decision, and I alone would be responsible for it.

While I was in my office, Tanya called Chubais and summoned him to the Kremlin. "Papa, you must listen to another opinion. You simply must," she said.

When Chubais is worried, his face instantly flushes scarlet. "Boris Nikolayevich," he said. "This is not 1993. The difference between that moment and now is that now, the one who goes beyond the constitutional boundaries will fail first. It doesn't matter that the Communists were the ones to go out of bounds back in 1993. It's a crazy idea to get rid of the Communists in this way. The Communist ideology is in people's heads. A presidential decree can't put new heads on people. When we build a normal, strong, wealthy country, only then will we put an end to communism. The elections cannot be postponed."

We spoke for about an hour. I objected. I raised my voice. I practically shouted, something I rarely do. And finally I reversed a decision I had *almost* already made. To this day, I am grateful to fate, and grateful to Anatoly Borisovich Chubais and Tanya, that at that moment another voice was heard, and I, who possessed enormous power and strength, became ashamed before those who believed in me.

The political situation was complicated at the time. The Communists had experienced the sweet taste of near victory. Power was right there. They just had to reach out and grab it. Their tactic was to take power by storm. The "leftist" Duma had tried to rouse nostalgic feelings in voters by voting to annul the Belovezh agreements of 1991, essentially resurrecting the former Soviet Union. Calls had been made in the Duma to try, convict, and imprison those who signed the documents of December 1991 that had ended the Soviet Union. It had been a real provocation.

I responded instantly. Immediately after the next formal Security Council session, I made some harsh remarks about the Duma to reporters, saying that I was outraged by their decisions and that I would not allow anyone to commit unconstitutional acts. It was clear that a war of nerves was beginning.

Regardless of what they had thought about banning the Communist Party outright, the majority of the those who had attended the closed meeting on March 23rd had still supported the idea of postponing the elections. "Boris Nikolayevich," they had said. "You're not canceling the elections; you're just postponing them for two years, so you can't be accused of violating democratic principles. The people don't want any elections. Everyone has grown used to you. And you can get rid of the Communists only with decisive measures. How long will they go on confusing people and poisoning their minds? Maybe now is the right moment to do this. Your rating is up; everyone will get behind you."

But in the end, that is not what we did. After the important psychological and ideological victory in advising me on the campaign and stopping the radical move of banning the Communist Party, the analytical group headed by Chubais became the main center for making all political decisions. Soskovets's campaign headquarters ceased to exist. The Chubais team was now fully launched.

Step by step the sociologist Aleksandr Oslon began to draw a demographic map for the elections. It wasn't the portrait of the statistically average Russian, among whom I had only a 2- to 3-percent credibility rating, but an exact picture of the various segments and sectors of society. It turned out that most Russians didn't see things the way our political model of the "average" Russian did. Civil servants and "shuttle traders,"* students and young professionals, people over forty with families and working pensioners, residents of the south and the north, the large and small cities—everyone had different expectations about the elections. While we were discussing an idea, when everyone asked the question, "And what do the people think?"—all eyes would turn to Oslon. And digging into his notebooks, he would deliver the final verdict on whatever it was the people thought.

There was one very telling moment when Igor Malashenko conducted an experiment: He laid before me two photographs from the two election campaigns—the current one and the 1991 campaign. In the more recent photograph from the 1996 campaign, I was pictured with a crowd of officials. A group of frightened people were cordoned off behind a rope, waiting for us. (I think the scene was in Krasnodar.) In the photo from 1991, there was a huge crowd of people with lively expressions and gleaming eyes. I noticed the happy face of one woman who was reaching her hand out to me, another Yeltsin, and I almost

---

* "Shuttle traders" are individuals who travel to big cities or abroad and purchase cheap items in bulk for re-sale at home. Much of the Russian consumer economy is driven by such dealers. —Trans.

yelped in pain. It made a strong impression on me. It had only been five years ago. I remembered how I felt back then when I met people, and everything fell into place.

We began to look for a target audience for the campaign. We needed a new tone, a new style. We scrapped the stilted government lexicon for lively, idiomatic language. "Yeltsin's different," people started saying in surprise. And as a result, starting about mid-April, my ratings began to climb rapidly. Of course the media played a great role. The journalists realized that if they didn't want Communist censorship, they would have to work in coordination with us. Malashenko created a firm vertical chain of command for work with the television reporters and journalists.

We had achieved the main thing—we had come up with a strategy for the elections. Here was the idea: Boris Yeltsin was not just the president but one of several candidates in the race. Together with the others, he was fighting for the electorate's votes. For the most part, I would travel around the country, meeting with people and conducting an active campaign with an aggressive youth focus, concerts for supporters, posters, and media advertising. In the grand scheme of things, the election was a big, life-affirming game. No one was forcing anyone else to play in the game. No one was pressuring or intimidating anyone. No one was threatening, "If you don't vote for Yeltsin, you're done for." They were just being told to go and vote.

I later realized that just at the right time, my youthful team had moved the pointer away from the ideology everyone was sick of to a new game: "choose or lose." The entire active part of society was drawn into this new game. It was like one of those television game shows. If you push one button, you'll get one result; if you push the other, you'll get just the opposite.

There was another game element we introduced, an ad campaign called "Choose from the Heart." In the ads ordinary people would say what they thought about me. Now it's hard to imagine the effect this ad campaign had. The interest in the president's personality grew. It forced people to think about how their stereotype of the president differed from this new image.

It was as if the voters woke up. Sure, they could bet on Grigory Yavlinsky from the liberal opposition, or Aleksandr Lebed, or Zhirinovsky from the conservative opposition. But were those candidates prepared to guarantee Russia's prosperity? Were they prepared to defend people from the new social upheavals? No, they probably weren't. But what about the "new Yeltsin"? Had he revived? Had he shaken himself off? Maybe it was time to bet on him again.

Political scientists would later describe the results of the vote as "deferred choice." That is, people voted against harsh changes, against a turning backward, against a split and shake-up of the elites. Still, I would emphasize the second word in this phrase: *choice*. It was their conscious choice.

In principle this was a normal electoral process. The campaign met with all the influential groups in society. We would say to them: "Do you want to survive? If so, help us. Do you want to continue your banking business? Help us. Do you want to have freedom of speech and private TV channels? Help us. Do you want freedom to create, freedom from censorship, freedom from Communist ideology in culture? Help us." And so on.

And once they saw what a powerful and youthful team was working for Yeltsin, all the big shots of business were drawn into the election headquarters. They "made investments"—some in logistical support, some in conceptual thinking, and some financially.

What prevented Communist Party leader Gennady Zyuganov from offering these very same influential business groups his own guarantees and his terms? Nothing. But he didn't think that the middle class and the intelligentsia would decide the race. There were too few of them. He bet on the poorest class, on the unemployed in the regions suffering from economic crisis, and on rural residents. And he was wrong. Even in these districts there were people who did not want to part with the good things they had earned, even if those things were tiny. They wouldn't give up their new lifestyles and their new opportunities to travel, see things, and save money. I am not a sociologist, but I'm absolutely certain that these modest people—the class of "shuttle traders" —would swing the pendulum to my side.

In fact, after the elections we would try to incorporate the best ideas from the presidential campaign into the everyday life of the president. Hence the president's radio addresses to Russians; hence the constant analysis of public opinion polls; hence the completely new approach to the work of the administration; hence our victory in the parliamentary elections of 1999 and the presidential elections of 2000.

I set myself the task of making the presidential administration a real brain trust. The best analysts in the country should work for the government and for the future of the country. They should be invited to serve in any post. If they didn't want to be bureaucrats, that was all right. We would let them work as advisers or just participate in the regular meetings. They could be used in any capacity.

That summer of 1996, I set my campaign and my administration staff one main task: the succession of power through the election of 2000. This was a historic task. In 2000 the new president of Russia had to be a person who would continue democratic reforms in the country, who would not turn back to the totalitarian system, and who would ensure Russia's movement forward, to a civilized community. Thus the team that came to work in the Kremlin in the summer of 1996 was given their assignment. They had four years until the presidential elections.

Back then Korzhakov had missed the danger. He was convinced that he could "swallow up" Chubais. He simply didn't pay attention to Tanya. And when he did pay attention, he tried to kick her out of the campaign. People began to talk in the Kremlin. Why is she coming here as if she's going to work? What, is she getting a salary?

Korzhakov forbade Tanya from coming to the Kremlin in pants. God knows where he got that idea, but he probably hoped that she would get upset and come running to me. And I don't tolerate such things. But Tanya just reacted with humor and continued coming to the Kremlin in pants. Another time Korzhakov kept her lingering in his waiting room for three hours.

Finally, the atmosphere of rumors—Tanya had supposedly taken a lavish office in the Kremlin far above her stature (it was all lies)—put me out of sorts. I phoned Korzhakov to call his bluff and said that it was all right and that he shouldn't let her in the Kremlin anymore. Korzhakov summoned Tanya and said tenderly, "Tanya, as an old friend of the family, of course I can't keep you out of the Kremlin. But watch out; the gossip is going to continue."

He knew our family relations and our Yeltsin nature very well. But Tanya wasn't affected by any of this. Her rational mind and firm character showed her an easy way out of the stifling, unbearable situation of pressure and petty annoyances: Just don't pay attention to it. The goal is more important.

Korzhakov, Barsukov, and Soskovets reacted rather peculiarly to the work of the analytical group, the pollsters, the television people— essentially their rivals. They decided not to talk to them at all. They locked themselves up in their offices and refused to see anyone. What they talked about among themselves I don't know.

Meanwhile, the first round of elections was around the corner. Practically every campaign trip turned into an occasion for me to be a proud father. Tanya worked like the dickens. She could get along with only three hours of sleep a night, and she displayed an incredible persistence. Together with the speechwriters, she could rewrite a speech ten times. She could go over the scenario for meetings or a concert a dozen times. I will never forget how the text of the veterans' letter was written. In honor of Victory Day on May 9, the president sent a personal letter to each participant in World War II. There were no comprehensive lists of veterans, but we got hold of the computer database of the Ministry of Defense and all the draft boards. Tanya would not give me a single draft to read until she had involved practically every single journalist and writer she had ever known. Ironically, a version of the letter written by Aleksandr Minkin, a journalist who was perhaps my harshest critic, served as the basis for the final text. It was a powerful and moving document. To this day Tanya nearly cries when she takes this letter out and reads it. I began to understand what an incredibly capable person Tanya is. And what's more, she is faithful and devoted to her father and to her friends.

I kept firmly steering the whole campaign team toward the assumption of victory in the first round. When aides tried to bring me schedules of trips and speeches after June 16, which implied a runoff in the second round, I would return them without comment. "If someone is thinking about a second round, you can forget about it!" I would say. "There's not going to be a second round." Probably some of them thought I didn't understand the reality of the situation. Nothing of the sort. It was important for me to convey how charged up I was and to get my campaign in the same mood. You have to throw everything you've got into a challenge. Then you'll get results.

The first round was held, and I came in first place. Zyuganov was slightly behind me, and Aleksandr Lebed came in third. A runoff had to be held between Zyuganov and me. At 7:00 A.M. on June 17, I held a meeting with my analytical group in the Kremlin. I came into the office and saw that everyone was waiting with tense expectation to see what I would say. Would I be annoyed and upset? Would I snap at them? I looked at them and smiled. "Well, that was a pretty good job. Report to me now on your plans for our actions in the second round. We're going to win."

On the eve of the second round of the presidential elections, Korzhakov decided to deal his final counterstrike against the analytical group. At 5:00 P.M. on June 19, in the foyer of the White House, the presidential security service detained two of Chubais's aides in the campaign. They were carrying a huge sum of cash in a cardboard box —half a million American dollars. Korzhakov had been spoiling for a scandal, and now he had found one.

At 8:00 A.M. on June 20, I scheduled a meeting with Korzhakov and Barsukov, head of the Federal Security Service (FSB).* At 9:00 A.M. I scheduled a meeting with Chernomyrdin, to be followed by an appointment with Chubais.

Early that morning Tanya had told me what had happened that night. She had learned about the arrest of Chubais's aides from Valentin Yumashev. Then Chubais and Ilyushin called her. At midnight she called Korzhakov herself. Korzhakov advised her to "wait until morning and not to interfere."

---

* During the Soviet era, the security police were called the Committee for State Security, or KGB in its Russian acronym. The KGB's sucessor is the Federal Security Service, or FSB.—Trans.

But Tanya left home at about 1:00 A.M. to go to the offices of Logovaz (Berezovsky's company), where most of the analytical group members had gathered, as well as people who simply sympathized—Boris Nemtsov, Gusinsky, journalists, and TV reporters. When she got there, the guards told her that snipers were deployed on the roofs and the building was surrounded by security service agents. It seemed to everyone that Korzhakov and Barsukov were not going to let anyone out of there.

Tanya stayed there until 5:00 A.M., drinking coffee and reassuring everyone, telling them not to be afraid and that nothing would happen to them. She was right. As long as Tanya was in the office, they wouldn't arrest or otherwise provoke anyone.

I often recall this episode. If only the people whom Tanya had protected that night—Berezovsky, Gusinsky, and Malashenko—could remember her kindness later. If only they could forgo their own interests. But unfortunately, people in politics usually have a short memory.

That was when I realized that Korzhakov had finally arrogated to himself the functions of both prosecutor and judge and, in fact, all law-enforcement agencies. On his orders people in masks were ready to tell anybody Korzhakov didn't like to lie down with their faces to the ground. He could destroy anybody who violated some rule that only he knew about. Enough complaints about Korzhakov had accumulated. He had long since crossed all the lines permitted for the head of the security service.

That morning I made a final decision. At my order Korzhakov, Barsukov, and Soskovets all wrote their resignations. A later investigation proved that there was no evidence of any crime in the actions of Chubais's aides. All the accusations turned out to be false. But the firing of Korzhakov, Barsukov, and Soskovets was not the only consequence of this scandal. The long-simmering opposition between the sane forces in my campaign and those who were spoiling for a fight in order to seize power in the campaign had finally come out into the open. And I had resolved it.

After I won the elections in the second round in July 1996, Tanya continued to be invited to the meetings at the Kremlin. Chubais, who was by then head of the presidential administration, came to me and asked that we define Tanya's status and her job at the Kremlin.

And what *was* her status? Of course the complicated machinery of the state did not allow for any liberties. Traditions of "family" rule were appropriate for Russia. I had a clear contract with the government, prescribed by the constitution. I would serve out my term, and then say good-bye. But what about Tanya? My heart was heavy. I did not want to part with her support.

A normal person, I thought, keeps work and family life separate. But in the final analysis, that Party style of housekeeping was also part of the Soviet way of life. And my views had probably grown out of date. What was wrong with Tanya's desire to help and defend me? It was normal human behavior. It was the normal inclination of a daughter to her father. Why was I obliged to reject her? And suddenly I recalled that there was such a precedent in Europe. There was Claude Chirac, daughter of French president Jacques Chirac. She was the one who became his image adviser during the presidential elections. She helped him get rid of his tendency to be verbose and certain mannerisms, and she found him the right image makers. I immediately phoned Chirac and asked him to arrange for Tanya to meet with Claude "to exchange experiences." He reacted warmly, and even said something like, "Boris, you won't regret this."

Tanya and Claude met in the Chirac residence. They are almost the same age and understood each other quickly. Claude asked Tanya in detail about the 1996 election campaign and the work of the analytical group. Some details surprised Claude. It turned out that in some matters—for example, in our extensive use of demographic polling—we were more advanced than the French. Our pollsters would conduct surveys in a region both before and after I visited there. They measured the reaction of listeners after a presidential radio address, and so on.

In turn, Claude told Tanya about her work as a public liaison in the office of the administration of the French president. She and her colleagues prepared Chirac's trips. Tanya was interested to find out how the French people had responded to Claude's appointment to an official post. As it happened, the daughter of the French president, too, had been tormented by the same problems and doubts. Claude Chirac also sensed the negative reaction of public opinion, and some unfair, critical articles had been written about her in the press. "But don't pay attention," she advised. "They always pick on the women who are near the president. Do you think my mother has an easy time of it? They'll get used to it, and that's it."

At the end of the conversation, Claude suddenly said to Tanya, "Let's go say hello to Papa." Tanya hadn't been expecting that. She thought that she would just discuss her problems with Claude.

But the conversation with the French president was surprisingly warm. Chirac talked about his upcoming meeting with me. Tanya noted that Chirac struggled to say "Boris Nikolayevich" in the Russian style. (In fact, that's what Chirac has always called me, barely getting out the consonants so awkward to the French. "You can call me 'Jacques' if you want, but I'll call you 'Boris Nikolayevich,'" he insists stubbornly.)

"Let's get a picture of the three of us," Chirac proposed. They opened up a small balcony and took a photograph against the emerald lawn. I really like that photograph, with a smiling Chirac and two bright-haired, happy girls, Claude and Tanya.

After the trip, Tanya decided that we were doing the right thing by keeping her in the Kremlin. And that was how Tanya became an adviser, an "image adviser," as the newspapers wrote. I think that Tanya herself was surprised when they began calling her that.

Having Tanya join my team was one of the best decisions I made in years. With her subtle presence and careful advice, Tanya truly helped me. I ceased to be an aggressive president who was always breaking through all the barriers, boldly running toward any conflict, toward any aggravation. On the whole I think that the phenomenon of Tanya forced me to reflect: Wasn't it time for women, for a women's politics in Russia, for a wise and creative politics? Feminists shouldn't start rejoicing—I'm not for feminism. But I am for a calm, bright future for Russia, a future without upheavals.

And one final point: I am very grateful to Tanya for never playing politics. She just helped her father.

The Operation: Before and After

Shortly before the second round of the presidential elections, Yeltsin has a second major heart attack. There is no choice: He must undergo coronary bypass surgery. Tanya and Yeltsin's other advisers urge the president to keep the operation secret or risk losing the race. We witness firsthand what it's like for a stubborn and vigorous man to suffer the searing pain of a heart attack and to lie in bed, beset with anxiety about the affairs of state that so heavily depend on his personal intervention.

· ·

IT HAPPENED on June 26, a few days before the second round of elections. I came home to the dacha from work about 5:00 P.M. It had been a stressful and difficult day. I took a few steps down the hallway and then sat down in an armchair in the living room. I thought I would rest a little right there, then go upstairs and change my clothes. But suddenly a very strange sensation came over me, as if somebody had picked me up under the arms and was carrying me away—someone big and strong. At first I didn't experience any pain, just felt this overwhelming fear. I had just been sitting here, and now I was being dragged away somewhere else. I felt as though I was encountering some sort of other reality, a realm about which we know nothing. There is another reality, after all . . .

Then the pain sliced straight through me, an enormous, crushing pain. Thank God Anatoly Mikhailovich Grigoryev, the doctor on duty, was nearby. He immediately understood what had happened to me and within minutes began to give me medications for a heart attack. They laid me down right there and brought a bed into the living room. Dr. Grigoryev set up the necessary medical equipment. I looked up at the faces of my women. They were so frightened. I must have looked pretty awful as well. But right from the first moment, all I could think was: "Lord, why am I so unlucky? It's almost the second round. There are only a few days left!"

The next day, with a tremendous effort of will, I forced myself to sit up. And once again I could talk about only one thing: "Why, why now?"

Naina kept saying, "Borya, I beg you: Calm down. Everything's going to be fine. Don't worry."

The day after my heart attack, June 27, Tanya and Chubais met at the campaign headquarters in the President Hotel. My entire schedule of meetings between the first and second election rounds—the appearances, visits to factories, trips around the Moscow area—had to be canceled. Our face-saving pretext was a change in tactics: The president's victory was assured. We also had to try to prevent any leaks about my illness and hold back information from everyone. Outside of my family, only my doctors and my immediate circle of guards and aides knew about the heart attack. Of course my aides and I were walking a tightrope. And was it really permissible to hide this kind of information from the public? To this day I'm sure that if we had given the victory away to Zyuganov or had postponed the elections, Russia would have suffered the far worse evil.

I decided not to cancel a meeting previously scheduled with General Aleksandr Lebed. Lebed had garnered 15 percent of the votes in the first round. On June 18 I had appointed him secretary of the Security Council. Our agreement before the second round was that right away, without waiting for the vote counts and the formation of the new government, Lebed was to take on the issue of Chechnya, which was vital to both of us. This brief meeting at Barvikha, on the eve of the second round, was fundamentally important for me and for him. I could not cancel it.

So on the second day after my heart attack, June 28, we turned the living room, where they had put my bed, into something like an office. The cameraman (our Kremlin video man) spent a long time figuring out how to get everything out of the picture that would betray its unusual setting, especially the piano, which had always been there, and the bed. He covered up the medical equipment. Naina kept begging me over and over: "Borya, just don't get up. Stay seated in your armchair. You can't stand up!" But I couldn't resist and forced myself to stand in order to greet Lebed.

Lebed was very happy with the meeting. He was told that I had a cold, and he didn't ask any extraneous questions. For some reason, I distinctly recall his unusual appearance. He was wearing black shoes, white socks, and a loud checked jacket. A rather unpolitical thought flashed through my mind: "He's in his summer attire."

Hour by hour my strength returned. Still, my doctors categorically forbade me to walk around, and now there were only a few days before July 3 and the second, decisive round of the elections. The question arose: Where would the president and his family vote? Naina insisted that I, as a "proper invalid," could have the ballot box brought to my bedside. "It's legal!" she cried. "Yes, it's legal," I answered. "But I want to vote along with everyone else."

I called Tanya, and we discussed various options. The first, voting on Osennaya Street in the district near our Moscow address, was immediately rejected. The building had stairs and a long hallway, and it was a long walk back to the street. Even I, for all my obstinacy, knew that this wasn't possible. The second option was the sanatorium in Barvikha, not far from our dacha where I was staying. People always voted at the sanatorium. There was a polling station there. We could even invite reporters, although we'd have to keep their numbers down.

I continued to worry. "What kind of voting is it if I'm in my bathrobe and slippers?" I asked.

"Papa," Tanya answered. "There won't be quite as many reporters, but there will still be plenty. And the major TV channels and wire services will be there, just as usual."

"And how are you going to explain that I went to Barvikha on the eve of the elections?" I asked.

"Everyone knows how much you've been traveling around the country and how much effort you have put into the campaign. No one will be surprised that you took a short break between the first and second tour. You have to rest, too."

"It's not very persuasive," I grumbled. But in the end I agreed.

We realized that Zyuganov and I were running practically neck and neck and everything depended on Lebed's and Yavlinsky's voters. Who would they vote for now, in the second round? Would they turn out at all? These voters could become my constituency. That was what concerned public opinion, not my health. The press was focused on these swing voters.

If my health problems had taken place just a month earlier, the election results would probably have been different. We would not have been able to maintain the pace and intensity of the election campaign. Zyuganov could have won. It was a horrible prospect. I tried not to think about it. I rested, took my medicine, talked to my doctors and my family, and counted the hours until the vote.

On Sunday, the day of the second round, I went to the ballot box with Naina. The Russian TV networks ORT, RTR, and NTV, newspaper and wire reporters—about twenty members of the media in all—followed my every move intently. With an immense concentration of will, I gathered my strength and smiled and said a few words. "Listen," I said, "I've already answered all your questions so many times..."

Confined to bed once again, I awaited the results of the vote. I won. It was a fantastic, amazing accomplishment. At the beginning of the year, not even my closest aides believed I could do it, but I had proved them wrong. I had won despite all the forecasts, despite the low ratings, despite the heart attack and the political crises that had haunted the entire first term of my presidency. Although I wanted to jump up and dance, I lay on my invalid's cot, staring tensely at the ceiling. Fortunately, I had my loved ones and friends around me. They embraced me and gave me flowers. Many of them had tears in their eyes.

The victory had the aftertaste of medicine for me. I had had a tough time of it during those campaign months. The physicians had tailed me everywhere. They were worse than my bodyguards with their bulging doctors' bags and their pale, frightened faces. I kept hearing the same thing, "Boris Nikolayevich, what are you doing? You've got to cut back on this overload. Boris Nikolayevich, what are you doing?" They followed my every move. They were always standing behind every corner or behind my back, ready with an injection or some tablets. And they had good reason to hover, as my heart was constantly seizing up. It was always a major spell. A choking sensation grabbed my throat, and the room began to tilt—all the classic symptoms.

I heard that among the general public people were saying that Yeltsin had danced his last dance and leapt his last leap in these elections. Actually, I did have one infamous incident when I twirled a few dance steps.* No heart condition and no warnings from my doctors could dampen my emotional enthusiasm, my overwhelming determination to win this battle. It was probably the first time I had ever taken part in such an extensive campaign: I flew around the country. I met with huge numbers of people every day. I spoke at stadiums, sports arenas, and concert halls filled with the noise, uproar, whistling, and applause of youthful audiences. And this charged me up incredibly. Right before that ill-fated concert in Rostov-on-the-Don, Tanya had begged me, "Papa, I ask you, just don't start dancing!" But I couldn't help myself and joined the singer Zhenya Osin on stage.

Now the exhaustion and stress had taken their toll. It was time to rest a little and think about what was happening to me. When did this start? And where was it all headed?

Even that spring, before the elections, my doctors had written a collective letter to Korzhakov in which they directly mentioned the catastrophic state of my heart and insisted on my having an immediate operation. I wasn't shown this letter. Neither was my family. I saw it much later. It read:

It is the conclusion of this physicians' consultation that in the last two weeks negative changes have occurred in the state of health of Russian Federation president Boris Yeltsin. All of these changes are di-

---

* The press speculated that Yeltsin was drunk at the time of this incident. — Trans.

rectly connected with the sharp increase in the level of burdens, both physical and emotional, that he is carrying. The constant change in climate and time zones when flying great distances is playing a substantial role. His sleep time has been cut to the extreme—only three to four hours per twenty-four-hour period. Such a work regime constitutes a real threat to the health and life of the president.

Ten doctors signed the statement. Korzhakov constantly hinted to Tanya that if something happened to me, she would be to blame. But he did not show the document to anyone.

Lying in my hospital bed, I recalled another letter my doctors had written about a year and a half before, advising me to have an examination of my blood vessels, a CAT scan. Besides my doctors, only Korzhakov and I knew about that letter; it wasn't shown to my family either. If only I had heeded that letter! If only they had taken care of my heart a little earlier, and not during an election year! As a result, here I was, an invalid. And though they were fairly experienced in performing these coronary bypasses, the surgeons could not guarantee 100-percent recovery. There were a number of risks, leaving a 50-percent chance of success. They told me that I could have the procedure done abroad, where there were good clinics that saw a steady stream of bypass patients, unlike those in Russia. Then again, I might feel more comfortable in Russia. And surely Russian doctors should operate on the Russian president. And if I refused to have the operation? There was a pause. "Then your health will steadily deteriorate. You will need the continual assistance of doctors. Your ability to work will constantly decrease. We can't tell how much longer you have to live—maybe a year, two, three, maybe less. We can't say exactly."

No, I couldn't live that kind of life, that was for sure. I had to face this decision. I had to have the heart operation. "When?" I asked the doctors.

"No earlier than September. First you have to restore your strength and go through all the tests." That was good news. That bought me some time to think things through and weigh the advantages and disadvantages.

The preparation for the inauguration began. Anatoly Chubais and I racked our brains about how to make the ceremony shorter. It was not easy—many of the foreign correspondents and diplomats were quite familiar with the Kremlin rituals. They would notice if we cut the ceremony short.

On August 9 I arrived at the Palace of Congresses to take the solemn oath to uphold the Russian constitution. The stage was covered with flowers—scarlet, violet, blue, all kinds. Despite the air-conditioning the room was stuffy. My eyes stung and I felt very tense. It had never been easy for me to accept honors, to perform rituals, but especially today. Although I had been given some pain shots, I felt terrible.

Yegor Stroyev, head of the Federation Council, handed me a bouquet of flowers and the presidential medal, the symbol of authority. Patriarch Aleksy II, standing next to me on the stage, seemed worried, along with everyone else in the hall. I sensed it with every nerve. "Well, don't worry," I thought. "Yeltsin is holding up. He's made it through worse things." Then there were the solemn, exalted words of the oath. For me, they were a hundred times more difficult, a hundred times more dear than ever before.

What would come next?

It took me a fairly long time to restore my strength before the operation. First I went to Zavidovo* to visit my favorite haunts. I wanted to be able to breathe that wonderful sweet air before I had to go into the hospital for surgery. I felt terrible. I was weakening with each passing day. I didn't feel like eating or drinking. I just wanted to lie down. I called in the doctors. Was this the end? "Oh no, Boris Nikolayevich. It shouldn't be. Everything is going according to plan." But they were looking rather pale themselves. Tanya, Lena, and Naina were all in

* Government official residence area outside of Moscow.—Trans.

shock. In just a few days, I had lost weight. It turned out that my he-
moglobin levels had fallen and I had become anemic. It was the first
preoperational crisis. The operation had to be postponed for a month.

The doctors were keeping me in shape, but I still suffered from
something. My mood plummeted. I realized I couldn't keep this up.
Now, at last, I would have to go public with my ailments. I had to tell
the whole country and the whole world—something I really didn't
want to do. It was yet another difficult test. Finally, in early August, I
made a hard decision: I agreed to "release my doctors from their duties." I brought a new team in from the Cardiology Center. They
scheduled an appointment for a CAT scan. Dr. Renat Akchurin and
Dr. Yury Belenkov were in charge. During our very first conversation,
I instinctively trusted Dr. Akchurin, who was to be my surgeon. He
spoke politely, but he was brutally frank and clear.

As he explained to me, the CAT scan is a fairly serious test for a
heart patient. An iodized liquid is inserted into the vein through an IV.
The dyed blood travels through the arteries to the heart. Doctors
watch the screen to see how and where the dyed blood pulses its way
through. It must be a beautiful sight, but it is a dangerous test because
it can provoke a new heart attack. I was prepped very carefully and
thoroughly.

I tried to imagine my heart, to picture how the blood was coursing,
how it was hurtling through my ventricles. I even looked at the pictures and the diagrams, but I couldn't really imagine it.

"What color will my blood wind up, and then where will it all go?"
I asked. But my doctors were in no mood to joke. The test showed that
the damage was worse than they had expected. The blood circulation
was obstructed, the arteries were blocked, and as the doctor put it, this
was a "life-indicative" operation.

"What does that mean?" I asked.

"It means that your life depends on the operation," he answered.

There was a problem with the Cardiology Center: It was headed by
Yevgeny Chazov, former minister of health of the USSR, a Nobel laureate and former head of the fourth directorate, the special health department at one time in charge of all the members of the Soviet

Politburo. Chazov was an excellent specialist, but we had shared one unfortunate experience. In 1987, at the plenary of the Moscow City Committee of the Communist Party, I was hospitalized at the Cardiology Center. I went to the hospital right after I had said some controversial things at the plenary of the full Central Committee and had been thoroughly trounced by all the other members of the Politburo and Central Committee. No one came to my defense. At issue was the Moscow City Party Committee's attempt to remove me from my post as head of the city. Although I was ill, I was forced to attend the plenary session where they discussed my dismissal.

Chazov came to visit me at the hospital and said: "Mikhail Sergeyevich Gorbachev asked that you leave the hospital and come to the Moscow City Party Committee plenary. It's necessary." They were going to remove me from office. It didn't matter whether I died or not after that. They pumped me up with medicine and put me into a car. At the plenary I felt so awful that I thought I was going to die right on the spot, in the meeting hall.

Naina said at the time, "Borya, how can it be? He's a doctor!" And what if he was? A doctor was also a subordinate. No one was just a doctor or just a teacher in those days. Everybody, in one way or another, was a soldier of the Party and a soldier of the state. Several years later, when I ran into Chazov, he smiled and shook my hand. It took some effort. And now here I was facing Chazov again. Odd, isn't it? Life is a strange thing.

For many, many years, I had kept the spirit of a ten-year-old boy. I thought I could do anything. Yes, absolutely anything! I could climb a tree or float on a raft down the river. I could hike across the taiga. I could stay up for days on end without sleeping. I could spend hours in the steam bath. I would defeat any opponent. I could do anything I wanted. But a person's omnipotence can disappear in a flash. Somebody else—his family, his doctors, his fate—takes power over his body. Was this new "me" really needed? Needed by the whole country?

I still hadn't gone public with my health problems. I was an advo-

cate of a hard-line position (widespread in Soviet times): The less the
people knew about the illness of the head of state, the calmer they
would be. Life is hard enough as it is. Hysteria would start in the press
and then spread to the people, who would want to know what was
what. A president's ailments are his personal business. I didn't take an
oath to show my X-rays to people.

Tanya tried to persuade me otherwise. "Papa," she said, "It will
seem strange if you leave the scene for such a long time and no one
knows where you are."

Tanya brought me a translation of the letter Ronald Reagan wrote
to the nation when he announced that he was already feeling the serious effects of Alzheimer's disease and that there had been irreversible
changes in his brain. Essentially, Reagan was saying good-bye to the
American people. He was never going to be the same again. He used
very simple words. It was as if he had written a note on a scrap of
paper from his hospital room. It was casual and intimate.

I pondered the question for a while—did I have the right to speak so
openly, so humanly, so absolutely frankly with the people of my country? Those close to me tried to persuade me that I had to do it. After I
had run such an open and honest election campaign, I could not hide
my operation. "This is not the personal affair of Boris Yeltsin and his
family," wrote the new press secretary, Sergei Yastrzhembsky, in a letter to me. Tanya brought me the letter in Zavidovo. My aides couldn't
trust the usual presidential courier system with this sort of message.
So far, no one knew about the operation, and the information was absolutely confidential. And here in Zavidovo, I made the final decision:
Yes, I would tell everything like it was.

I gave an interview to Mikhail Lesin. We sat in our winter garden in
Zavidovo. I remember I was wearing a casual cardigan. I stuttered and
had trouble saying the phrase "an operation on my heart." When I
later saw the clips on television, a thought flashed through my mind:
"Well, here we go. A completely new life is starting. But what kind of
life will it be?"

While I was getting ready for the operation, Lena and Tanya were
hatching a scheme to celebrate Naina's and my fortieth wedding an-

niversary in September. Early one morning they came to my room with a little dish. In it were two rings—one was new, with a jewel, for Naina, and there was a gold band for me. I had never had a wedding ring. I had borrowed a brass ring from my grandfather for the wedding bureau ceremony, so I had been without my own wedding band all these years.

"Bride and groom, sit down next to each other!" the girls said. Naina probably realized what was going on right away, but I didn't understand. I thought they wanted to tell me something very important or propose something to me. But when I finally realized what it was all about, I felt a warmth spread through my chest. "Well, Mama and Papa. Go ahead and kiss! Exchange your rings!" they said. Sunlight came streaming through the window. How good life was at that moment. How good, in spite of everything. We didn't know whether to laugh or cry. But we didn't cry, even though we couldn't raise a toast to the health of the "newlyweds."

There is nothing special to write about my operation.

It took place on November 5. We got up very early. I went by myself and left my family at home. Tense and worried, they saw me off at 6:00 A.M. They intended to follow me to the Cardiology Center later. For some reason, I was absolutely calm. No, not just calm: I felt a powerful surge of strength. Tanya noticed it first. "Papa, you're something else," she said. "We're all nervous and upset, and you're so cheerful. Good for you."

It was still dark as we drove to the hospital. I didn't ride in my usual presidential car but in the "leader," the first car in the entourage. "Why?" asked my granddaughter Masha.

"So no one knows. Otherwise there will be a crowd of journalists. There's nothing for them to film so far. And really, I don't want too much fuss," I replied.

We passed through the gates quickly. It was 6:30 A.M. The weather was damp and gray. I think it was drizzling. Wind was blowing in my face. In the foyer of the hospital, a whole crowd of people in white smocks were waiting for me. Quite frankly, their expressions didn't look good. They were pale. I remember that I tried to relieve the tension in the atmosphere. I said to Dr. Sergei Mironov, head of the consultation group, "Did you bring your knife with you?" Everybody relaxed a little bit and smiled.

The operation began at 7:00 A.M. It was over at 2:00 P.M. That was it.

Not four bypasses were needed, as originally thought, but five. Arteries were stitched into my heart from vessels taken from my legs. An American surgeon, Dr. Michael DeBakey, and two German coronary surgeons sent by Chancellor Helmut Kohl, Thornton Wallers and Axel Hawerik, followed the operation on a video monitor. And of course there were our own Russian doctors: Belenkov, Chazov, a whole brigade. They didn't let Naina and my daughters on to the "observation deck," thank God. I don't know if my women could have survived that experience. But my heart went to work immediately, as soon as I was taken off the equipment.

I had prepared and signed two decrees in advance: the transfer of all presidential powers to Viktor Chernomyrdin during the time of the operation and the return of powers to me immediately following the procedure. As soon as I woke from the anesthesia, I filled in the time on the second decree: 6:00 A.M. The press had a field day with that. They reported that I had demanded a pen and signed the decree reclaiming the presidential powers as soon as I regained consciousness. They said that I had clearly demonstrated my pure instinct for power. But that was just a journalistic cliché. I wasn't afraid of losing power. I just wanted everything to go according to plan. The moment I woke up, I needed a sense of order and precision.

After the operation someone brought me a bright red pillow—a present from an American society for patients of open-heart surgery. I read the letter that accompanied it: "Dear Boris Nikolayevich, we heartily wish you the quickest..." I almost broke down and cried. Honestly.

I don't like to be sick for long. My family knows it; my doctors as well. Fortunately, the progressive method for rehabilitation coincided perfectly with my mood. By November 7, I was already in a wheel-

chair, and on the 8th I began to walk with the help of nurses and doctors. I walked around my bed for about five minutes. My rib cage hurt
terribly. It had been sawed open during the operation and then closed
with metal staples. I had huge sutures on my chest. They were a visual
reminder of exactly how the operation had taken place.

The incisions in my legs hurt, too. I was incredibly weak. But despite all this, I felt an enormous sense of freedom, lightness, and joy. I
was breathing! My heart didn't hurt! Hurrah!

On November 8, I was already on my way to the Central Kremlin
Hospital, bypassing a special postoperative unit, despite all the original
nay-saying by my doctors. I was recovering with remarkable speed. I
cannot thank all my doctors, nurses, and attendants in this book, but I
remember all their faces. I will never forget my surgeons, my team of
doctors headed by Renat Akchurin. It had been the right choice to
have the operation at home in Russia. Seeing familiar faces helps,
that's for sure. And I will never forget, Dr. DeBakey, either. After the
operation I joked around with him. How I would like to be like him
when I'm eighty-five years old! He is lively, cheerful, an absolute opti-
mist, who is in demand everywhere and who knows everything about
this life. His very presence was like a goal before me—I had to make it
to his fortunate old age.

During my recovery at the hospital, I had time to reflect. Such disasters with my health had happened throughout my whole life.
There had been ulcers, the trauma to my spine after a plane accident
in Spain, the heart attacks, and various operations. But the periods of
illness and feeling bad always ended. They were always followed by
twenty-hour workdays, moments of extraordinary activity, and
heavy burdens. I would fall down then get right up and run farther.
That's what I needed to do. I couldn't live any other way. Lying in the
hospital bed, I realized that things would be different but that soon I
would be back to work. I was healthy again and that was the main
thing.

On November 20 the postoperative stitches were removed. For the
first time in quite a while, I went out to the park. I took a walk with
Naina, Tanya, and Masha, trailed by the press. I said several words to

the television reporters and promised to get back to work soon. The park was damp, quiet, and cold. I slowly moved along the path and looked at the brown leaves, at the November sky. It was autumn. The autumn of a president.

On November 22 I went to Barvikha. I pestered my doctors to hurry up. When? When could I get back to work? The doctors thought I could return to the Kremlin after the New Year, in early January. My mood immediately improved. I joked and teased everyone. I still could not get used to the feeling that my heart didn't hurt. How many months—no, years—had I lived with this compressed heart, as if someone were squeezing, squeezing from inside, harder and harder, but couldn't crush it completely?

If things kept on this way, everything would be back to normal and I would be able to escape the custody of the cardiologists in a year. Dr. Belenkov, who analyzed all my symptoms very carefully, made one request: "Boris Nikolayevich, don't force things. It won't turn out well. Don't go raring off anyplace."

On December 4, I moved from the sanatorium to the dacha at Gorki-9—home, one could say. My family noticed that I had changed drastically. I was joyful for the first time in a long while.

"You've changed, Grandpa," said Masha.

"How have I changed?" I asked.

"You're so nice now," she laughed.

"What, was I mean before?"

"No, it's just that you've started noticing everyone around you. You look around in a different way. You react to everything in a new way."

And I noticed the change in myself. The world around me suddenly became clear, large, and detailed. Everything became precious to me.

On December 9 I flew by helicopter to Zavidovo, where I was to finish my recovery. Helmut Kohl came to visit me. It wasn't a diplomatic visit; Kohl simply wanted to see me, to check on me after the operation. I'm really grateful to him for that. I invited him to lunch, and I noticed that he seemed to want to infect me with his appetite for life. He tasted every dish and tried some Russian beer. Kohl was great; he behaved naturally, smiling heartily from cheek to cheek.

On December 23 I returned to the Kremlin, two days ahead of my doctors' most "accelerated" schedule. Everybody around me noticed I had lost weight and moved more lightly. I didn't walk; I ran. I began to talk faster. I didn't even recognize myself in the mirror. I had gained a new sense of my body. I had a new face. It was a strange feeling, as if I had come home after a long trip. I had an almost physical sensation of impatience, a desire to work. I went out to meet the television cameras and said: "Look what's going on in the country! Look what's become of everything!" The country was exactly as it had been. It was I who had changed. I was another person. I could cope with any problem.

Things were so busy we almost didn't notice New Year's Day creeping up on us. On December 31 we went to the tree-trimming party, as we call the formal reception in the Kremlin that the Moscow mayor, Yury Luzhkov, usually hosts.

My doctors had advised against it. Naina was also opposed. But I ignored everyone and ordered my aides to get ready. The escort car raced through the city of Moscow, all decorated and twinkling for the holidays. From the very first seconds at the Grand Kremlin Palace, I felt something new and strange. After such a long absence from public life, I had almost a physical sensation of a thousand people staring at me. The rosy-cheeked, smiling Luzhkov loomed toward me. Naina looked on in alarm. Since the operation my sensitivity had evidently increased. It was as if my skin had become much thinner. I hadn't anticipated it. After so many years in politics, a kind of invisible armor grows up around you. You get used to everything—to the backs of your bodyguards, to the doctors constantly hovering nearby, to the crowds of people, to the hundreds of hands, to the aura of expectation that surrounds you, to the space around you that must always remain empty. Habit saves you from any clumsy movements or expressions.

It seems that after the operation, I lost this habit. I felt awkward and uncomfortable with everybody looking at me. It was only with great difficulty that I took the goblet of champagne, stood for the pre-scribed amount of time, and made a speech.

I wanted to see not just the usual Kremlin crowd but normal peo-ple on the street. I wanted to see what the people were doing, how they were getting ready for the holiday. It was a very light and bright and sincere feeling, a sense of the moment.

"I'll go to the store and buy my grandchildren some toys," I thought to myself. We stopped at the store called Aist on Kutuzovsky Avenue. The salespeople surrounded me, calling out their suggestions in chorus, describing things to me. I hadn't been in a toy store in a hun-dred years. Lord, how wonderful this was. There was so much for little kids, for any taste. I bought a large children's car for Gleb. I love large presents because of the impact they make: "Wow, look at that!"

A few days later, after New Year's Eve, I went to the *banya*. I tried to convince myself that I had put on enough of a Lazarus act. I was a normal person now. I could go to work, drink champagne, go to the *banya*. So I undressed and got into the steam bath. But the *banya* hadn't been warmed up yet.

On January 7 I was hospitalized in the Central Kremlin Hospital. I had a case of pneumonia. To this day, Naina can't forgive herself for not watching over me better.

· 4 ·

The Generals of Russia

Generals have always had a powerful influence in the governing of Russia. In the recent decade of turmoil, they made several lurches toward power. Yeltsin describes the generals around him—Lebed, Dudayev, Grachev, Korzhakov—and the threat of military takeover and civil war that constantly looms over Russia. Yet behind their bluster and bravado, Yeltsin finds these military men to be surprisingly meek and mild. Only Vladimir Putin, who carried the rank of colonel in the KGB, seems to have the steely smarts, quiet authority, and inner calm that true leadership requires.

·   ·   ·

RUSSIA HAS ALWAYS taken pride in its generals. There were the generals of the War of 1812, the generals of the Crimean campaign (although it was lost), General Mikhail Skobelev, General Aleksei Brusilov, and the great field commanders of World War II, or the Great Patriotic War: General Georgy Zhukov, General Konstantin Rokossov, and General Ivan Konev.

Even such controversial figures as the heroes of the civil war—Mikhail Tukhachevsky, Vasily Blyukher, Iona Yakir—have gone down in history as heroes. To this day we continue to speculate about how our life would have changed if Stalin had not jailed or executed these military leaders. Perhaps fewer people would have perished in the Great Patriotic War.*

---

* The "Great Patriotic War" is what Russians and others in the former Soviet Union call World War II, in which more than 20 million compatriots died defending their homeland. Scholars debate whether Stalin's execution of the top military commanders in the years before the Germans invaded weakened the country's defense.—Trans.

There is a startling moment in *Burnt by the Sun,* the famous film by Nikita Mikhalkov: A Red general is being taken to Lubyanka, KGB headquarters. He has been beaten and has a broken nose. Just half an hour before, this man had been a national hero, but now it's all over—he's crushed. He cannot restrain his sobs. Blood, mucus, and tears are pouring from him. And who has done this to him? Three hefty secret police thugs. They rammed their giant fists into his mouth several times, and that was it—a strong bear of a man was broken. I remember watching the film and wondering how that could be. What sort of era was that? A man who wasn't afraid to command huge units and armies, who didn't fear world war and even yearned for it—in a second he became nothing, a nonperson. His only hope for survival was to reach Stalin personally to plead his case.

I thought: If earlier in the century the famous Red generals hadn't executed the civilian population, if they had not declared total terror against rebellious peasants and Cossacks, if they hadn't purged and eradicated entire social classes—maybe they would not have had to ride in shame in the paddy wagon in the 1930s.

Why am I going into so much detail about this? Right up until the 1996 elections, a new wave of Russian generals-turned-politicians had a very strong influence on our lives. Judge for yourself: General Pavel Gravchev, defense minister; General Dzhokhar Dudayev, president of "independent Chechnya"; General Aleksandr Lebed, presidential candidate and secretary of the Security Council; General Aleksandr Korzhakov, head of my security; and General Mikhail Barsukov, director of the Federal Counterintelligence Service (FSK). Each one had a story, and there's a story for me to tell about each of them.

My previous book, which I wrote in hot pursuit of history, ended with the tragic events of the autumn of 1993. At that time I thought that communism was finished once and for all in our country. Nobody wanted things to disintegrate into mass conflict. But once the Supreme Soviet,* headed by Ruslan Khasbulatov, threatened the presi-

---

* The Supreme Soviet was the upper chamber and the Congress of People's Deputies was the lower chamber of the first relatively democratically elected parliament in the late-Soviet period under Gorbachev. — Trans.

dent and the country with civil war, swift and harsh action had to be taken. These were terrible days for Moscow.

Still, my main achievement was that we managed to avoid wide-scale bloodshed and civil war throughout Russia between supporters of the Communist Supreme Soviet and supporters of lawful presidential power. After that experience I began to reflect deeply on this phenomenon of the general-politician. It was the first time I'd encountered this type of general, a general without convictions.

These were men who were stern on the exterior, as if made from iron. They were determined, precise, loyal to oaths and to duties, and they wanted to appear that way. Yet upon closer inspection, they turned out to be just the opposite. I have often found that modest civilians, shy and bookish types—the most vivid examples being Andrei Sakharov, Dmitry Likhachev, Anatoly Sobchak, Galina Starovoitova—have firmer convictions and take more decisive actions.

I'm absolutely convinced that all this time, from 1990 to 1996, the shadow of a Time of Troubles,* a civil war, hung over Russia. Many Russians believed with utter despair that everything would come to this: a new military coup, a junta, the breaking up of Russia into numerous small republics—in short, a Yugoslav debacle or, to take an example closer to Russian history, the civil war after the 1917 revolution. It was a terrible prospect. And it was possible. The objective circumstances pushed us to precisely such a turn of events. Many people left the country for this reason.

The Soviet empire, spanning one-sixth of the earth's surface, was built over the course of many years according, without the shadow of a doubt, to an ironclad overall plan. The internal contradictions were ignored. No one proposed a scenario that allowed the empire to abandon some of its territories or yield to the formation of new states. They didn't even think of it. The economy was not custom-built to local needs and lifestyles but force-fitted on top of everything. After

---

* The term denotes the turbulent period in Russian history after the death of Ivan the Terrible and is used to describe any troubled era. — Trans.

the fall of the Soviet Union, an enormous number of Russian speakers found themselves stranded in the republics where they had instilled the empire's industry, science, and culture for decades. Because of the collapse of the internal market, there was a near economic disaster in the cities and regions. Food was brought into those areas where the only industries were steel, tanks, missiles, and appliances. Unemployed officers were added to the unemployed civilians from these industries. Our army rapidly left Europe.

Back in 1991, during the days of the foiled August coup, when the Soviet government collapsed, I personally thought that whatever else happened, everything would be fine when it came to ideology. Everybody vehemently hated communism and the Communists, and everybody denounced the false regime.

Our Russian people very much believe in the power of the word. The need for propaganda, the need to believe in eloquent words, is inexhaustible. We were rattled around too long in the years of Gorbachev's perestroika. After its collapse, too many politicians were on television. But no one could evoke the image of a peaceful, prosperous, positive Russia. The image was blurred by the putsches, the upheavals in daily life, the economic "shock therapy," the breaking down of the old way of life.

The sense of injury engendered a new generation of politicians. On the one hand, there were the hysterically furious deputies who relied on the idea of national victimhood. On the other hand, there were charismatic generals who were always prepared to stand at the head of the latest "events." Take Chechen president General Dudayev, for instance. He seemed like a real army general, a prominent Soviet military leader. He commanded a subdivision of the strategic air command and held the chief cards of Europe in his hands. It would seem he was an educated man. But back in 1991, when he returned home to Chechnya, did he not intend to leave the Russian Federation and to declare it an Islamic republic? Did he not give kudos to Ayatollah Khomeini and Muammar Qaddafi? I could not believe it. But that's exactly how it was. This man, obsessed with insane ideas, returned to his "historical homeland."

During the terrible, epochal events of 1991, we overlooked the little national disaster brewing in Chechnya. We didn't believe it could happen. We couldn't imagine it was possible. The scale of violence that swept over the republic in the first years of Dudayev's rule was simply incredible. At first tens and then hundreds of thousands of people, both Russians and Chechens, left Chechnya under curses and threats. But the main danger was not even in this invisible escalation of barbarism. A black hole of criminality had opened within Russia. Here the Chechens looked no worse and no better than other people — every nation has its bandits. But it was only in Chechnya that this banditry became a virtually legal form of income and a matter of civic pride. It's one thing when a state tries to fight organized crime in its cities and its territory where the law enforcement agencies have some sort of authority. It's another matter when the local government helps the bandits, and they can disappear with their cash, hostages, and weapons into that black hole.

In the autumn of 1994, before the onset of the first Chechen war, people were frightened by various coup attempts and did not want any more conflicts. But Dudayev threatened Russia, blackmailing it with terrorist acts and explosions at military bases and nuclear plants. On principle, a person who proclaims such things should not and cannot be negotiated with.

Chechens are very proud of the fact that they have fought against greater Russia for so long and so frequently—in the nineteenth century, with the tsar; during the civil war, against the White generals; and after the war, against the Chekists.* Dudayev manipulated this national myth, emphasizing that since ancient times the Chechens have been hostile to the other mountainous tribes surrounding them. Nothing in his dandyish, provincial appearance—the hat, the tie, the mustache—suggests today's warlords who have come in his place to terrorize. But it was Dudayev who was the godfather of these people.

Dudayev was aided in his effort by another myth, the myth of Islamic revolution. It is a dangerous myth. And the saddest thing is that

---

* The Bolsheviks' first secret police, known as Cheka, for the Russian initials for the words "Extraordinary Commission." Chekists are its agents. —Trans.

the crude policy of the Soviet Union led to the emergence of worldwide Islamic extremism. For so many years, we in the USSR fought Zionism, condemned Israel, and did not flinch at terrorism, helping the Palestinians and other Arabic movements. We fought in Afghanistan many years. As a result, imported socialism and the terrorist methods that had been instilled by our very own security agents were combined with the most radical and terrible Islamic sects and with their hatred toward Russia and Russians, which intensified during the Afghan war.

Terrorists and radical Muslims have at various times directed their hatred at different countries—the United States, Britain, France, India, Israel, and Russia. All of these countries, possessing nuclear weapons with highly developed technologies, planes, missiles, and computers, have suddenly invoked another, barbaric civilization—a medieval primitivism—and have found it incredibly hard to deal with this problem. This primitivism places in doubt our values, our world, our very existence. It's as if civilization is standing distraught before the "field commanders," before guerrilla warfare, before the seizure of hostages, before terrorist acts and saying, "How can we deal with this?" We do not know how to fight this bane, which seems to have crawled out of some deep historical underground from past centuries. We're only learning how to combat this.

And every country is doing so in its own way. The Israelis respond to a strike with a counterstrike. The Americans and British create a huge network of agents to hunt down the warlords. At the same time, they pursue foreign policies and international economic methods to link the Islamic countries to their common priorities. The French, at the height of the war with the Algerian rebels, resorted to mass oppression, deporting thousands of people from the country and simultaneously trying to maintain friendly ties with their former colonies, something they do to this day.

We Russians encountered this very same problem, and, as I indicated, it was completely unexpected for us. Now we have to recall how it all began. And we have to recall it honestly, despite the mistakes

made in those days, despite the heartache that accompanies these rec-
ollections.

In the summer of 1994, we became intensively engaged in the
Chechen problem. At that time there was a theory making the rounds
of the government. Dudayev's authority in Chechnya was extremely
unstable. The new regime in the republic was dependent on the influence of the *teypy*, the clans, and although Dudayev was supported by
the elders, there was terrible hostility among the *teypy*. Consequently,
a war for influence and power was under way. Armed conflicts constantly erupted in Chechnya—sometimes in Grozny, sometimes in the
region above the Terek River known as Nadterechny District. Industry
had ground to a halt, no one was working, nothing was functioning,
and people were already fed up with Dudayev's promises. Everyone
wanted some kind of stability. It was time for Russia to intervene with
the help of anti-Dudayev forces inside the republic.

Events in Georgia illustrate that when a leader becomes erratic and
out of control, the respected national intelligentsia is prepared to support alternative political groups, as a rule those oriented toward Russia.* So we decided to create some kind of body in Moscow, where
many prominent Chechens live, that could head up this movement.
There were quite a few appropriate candidates—Avturkhanov,
Gadzhiev, Zavgayev.

The stages of the plan were as follows: First we would gradually
but steadily introduce anti-Dudayev sentiments and forces into Chechnya; then we would encourage the people themselves to kick Dudayev
out; if armed conflict broke out, we would not tolerate bloodshed.
Peacemaking forces always enjoy the support of the people. We knew
this from the experience of Tajikistan and the Transdniester region in
Moldova.

I agreed to this plan.

* Zviad Gamsakhurdia, the leader of neighboring Georgia, imposed tyranny, was ousted, and
eventually committed suicide.—Trans.

There was a strong argument in favor of this plan: If we declared war against crime in one place and won, this would help break up the criminal world in Russia. We had to start with Chechnya. We had to remove the bandits' sense of impunity and deliver not just a surgical strike but a really powerful blow against the criminal world, which had occupied an entire republic.

Some have claimed that I aggravated the Chechen situation in order to strengthen my own authority and make the presidential regime more brutal. But that's nonsense, total delirium! I know that society is afraid of war and doesn't want it. The chief feature of the first Chechen operation was exactly this: I tried to stop the escalation of the military conflict without linking it to a specific tactical advantage. But the war didn't end. It broke out again. It spun out of our hands and reemerged in a new form. That's how it was in Budyonnovsk, in Krasnoarmeysk, and in Grozny in the summer of 1996.*

The Security Council passed a decision to launch a military operation. The press wrote a lot about this, asking who gave the order, how, and why, and claiming it was all covered in a cloud of mystery. I supposedly evaded responsibility. But once again it was all lies. I never shirked responsibility in the course of the Chechen campaign, even when other people gave the orders. I took responsibility upon myself. And I continue to take responsibility—for the storming of Grozny, for the bomb attacks, and for their cessation.

It is true that at the session of the Security Council when the decision was made to begin the campaign, minutes were not taken. I had some reports on the table before me—there were dozens of such reports then, prepared by various ministries—with the motivations and reasons to start the operations. There were also other analyses presented that said that we should not intervene in Chechnya's affairs. I laid out the arguments and asked: What are the arguments for and against? What can we expect? And the general position was unanimous: We cannot stand idly by while a piece of Russia breaks

---

* Yeltsin is referring to hostage crises in the cities of Budyonnovsk and Krasnoarmeysk and the Russian storming of Grozny in August 1996.—Trans.

off, because that would be the beginning of the collapse of the country.

One of the people who believed firmly in a lightning strike military operation was Pavel Sergeyevich Grachev, Russia's defense minister from 1992 to 1996. I must say a few words about him here.

Pavel Grachev is a real army general. I once said that he was the "best minister of defense." What did I mean? Unlike many of his colleagues, Grachev always disdained politics. This was a valuable trait, for it guaranteed the government a certain calm. Grachev always strove to be the right person for the job. In principle, running a defense ministry and running combat missions are different types of jobs—the storming of Grozny on the night of January 1 is proof of that. It remains etched in our memory. Hundreds were killed, and rebel resistance worsened. Later the combat generals fought normally under Grachev's leadership and waged a normal campaign. But the jumble of the first two months cost us very dearly. First there was the army's monstrous lack of preparation; then there was complete disarray in the actions of the power ministries. And journalists and the general public obstructed and misunderstood our actions. Consequently, the country exploded with the brutal bungling of the lightning war, and this "local" Chechen crisis could be compared to the events of 1991 or 1993.*

At the same time, Russia parted with an exceptionally dear and dangerous illusion about the might of its army, its degree of training, its combat readiness, and its ability to prevail. Back then people said, "What's Chechnya? What's there? Maybe five, ten, twenty thousand rebels? But our army is huge and powerful. It's the strongest." It soon became clear that the army had not been trained for this kind of war. It's a famous mistake that generals make. The war turned out to be horribly bloody.

I remember what a psychological effort I had to mount to meet with Sergei Adamovich Kovalev, who in the first days of the military

---

* The August coup against Gorbachev and the Parliamentary rebellion, respectively.—Trans.

operation took the side of the separatists.* He then went to Chechnya and came back to Moscow to describe at a press conference all the violations and victims he had seen in Grozny. What terrible internal contradictions beset me! Here a worthy person sat before me, a democrat, a human rights advocate, the president's commissioner for human rights. How could I explain to him, what words could I use to say that Russia's very statehood, Russia's very life was now at stake? He wouldn't listen to my arguments anyway.

So I listened to him silently, took his report, and thanked him for his work. If during those days—and they were critical days, when my aides viewed every antiwar report on television as betrayal—we had declared emergency measures and limited freedom of speech, the split in Russian society would have been inevitable, with the public taking a completely different route from the government.

I forced myself to ignore the excessive, unfair criticism. And gradually a commonsense opinion began to prevail among the general public, the middle road. People understood that it was our army fighting over there, our people. The military took care of its business, and the civilians took care of theirs. And there were no violent clashes (though perhaps some were counting on them).

It was then, in 1995, that Russia was infected by a new disease: a total negativity, a complete lack of confidence in ourselves and our strengths. We Russians had come to dislike ourselves. And that is a historical dead-end for a nation.

How did it happen? At the root of these complexes was naivete, a childish belief in the omnipotence of the government, instilled in people by the Soviet government. And when the government made a mistake, when the president, like an ordinary person, became hostage to some stereotype (including the stereotype of the might of the Russian army), the public was engulfed in total, destructive hysteria. We are coping with its aftereffects to this day.

---

* Sergei Adamovich Kovalev is a former Soviet political prisoner, former Russian human rights ombudsman, and presidential human rights commissioner who resigned in protest against the first Chechen war. He is currently a liberal parliamentary member and a vocal critic of the second Chechen war. — Trans.

In the summer and fall of 1996, fate once again linked me to one of the Russian "politicians in epaulets." Actually, by that time he had removed his epaulets, but that didn't change his modus operandi; in his heart he remained a general. I mean Aleksandr Lebed.

I can still recall Lebed's powerful voice in August 1991, when he spoke to me in the White House office. He said that one tank salvo and the entire building would explode and all my heroes would jump out the window. At that time this major general of the Soviet army had my greatest respect.*

But with the passage of time I began to understand that behind that booming voice and bearlike demeanor, behind that bravado, hid the profound insecurity of an army man who was torn out of his usual element. At one time Lebed was close friends with Pavel Grachev (although later their paths sharply diverged). Grachev was a typical general who didn't want to go beyond the bounds of regulations, army etiquette, the customary military life. He liked it there. Lebed, his former subordinate, was a completely different type of person. He was the kind of Russian officer who had found himself outside the grandiose system in which he had been an important cog his whole life and suddenly, at the age of forty, realized that life was beginning anew.

I treat this human drama very seriously. And I feel guilty about the officers dismissed from the army to whom the new Russian government did not give what they promised—an apartment, interesting work, and job security. But that is another matter.

General Lebed was in some sense an emblem of that fate, that human drama, that crisis of personality, that desperate search for oneself in new circumstances. The man plunged into politics as if making an attack. He was asked questions about the international financial situation, and he roared in reply that it looked bad for Russia to chase after loans like a goat after a carrot. He scattered jokes and aphorisms everywhere. He demonstrated what a tough and unbeatable guy he

---

* Yeltsin and his supporters remained in the White House in August 1991 for several days and nights while surrounded by tanks sent against them by the Soviet coup plotters. General Lebed and some others in the military opposed the coup and took Yeltsin's side, thereby risking their military careers. But they warned Yeltsin that he and his unarmed liberal supporters could be easily defeated "by one tank salvo."—Trans.

was. He threw journalists off balance and enraged them with his arrogant tone. But at least he provided a lively, honest, human voice and didn't play games. That's how it seemed to me at the time.

I sensed that this extraordinary man was racing back and forth, searching for the certainty, precision, and clarity to which he'd been accustomed and couldn't find in our new life. Not only did I sense this, but I empathized with him. Journalists noticed my sympathy and hastened to anoint Lebed as my successor. But of course there was no way he could become my successor.

On June 18, 1996, early in the morning at the Kremlin in the presence of journalists, I signed a decree about a new appointment. Lebed became the secretary of the Security Council. I gave the general a wide spectrum of functions, including security of the country and the war against crime and corruption. But the main issue, of course, remained Chechnya. Before the elections I had promised to end the war. The entire territory of the Republic of Chechnya, including the mountainous part, was under the control of our troops. But the flames of conflict continued to burn. People were dying.

The problem is that no one knew how to end the war. Normal negotiations had not yet led to anything. The last talks in 1995 had resulted in the abduction of Russian General Romanov. In order to conduct negotiations now, we first had to ask with whom, about what, and on what legal basis?

No one knew. Except Lebed. Under total secrecy, he flew to Chechnya, where he met with Aslan Maskhadov and Movladi Udugov at night.* It was effective, done like a general.

On August 14, the day after these talks, Lebed had me sign the decree on the settlement of the crisis in Chechnya. The Security Council assumed strategic leadership for the entire complex of Chechen problems. And two weeks later the statement by Lebed and Maskhadov on the principles for ending the war was signed in Khasavyurt. Among other things, this statement decreed that the question of the status of

---

* Maskhadov was subsequently elected president of the Republic of Chechnya. Udugov was vice president. — Trans.

Chechnya would be postponed until the year 2001; meanwhile, there would be a complete withdrawal of forces, and a joint interim governing commission would be created. Essentially, Russia acknowledged the legitimacy of the self-proclaimed Chechen republic. Russia renounced its previous aims—to establish control over the territory of Chechnya, to restore Russian law, and to disarm the unlawful army.

The Russian military called this decision treason. The newspapers called it a capitulation. The Duma called it opportunism. But Russian society greeted this settlement with enormous relief. Everyone had grown tired of the war, which was like a bloody meat grinder. Everyone wanted peace.

We didn't know yet that there would be no peace. We didn't know how this rapid and effective resolution of the Chechen problem would turn out.

At a press conference, Lebed made a statement: "An impoverished country with a half-collapsed economy and the same kind of armed forces cannot permit itself the luxury of waging war."

I listened attentively to the tone of his speeches. For a time, I had the impression that a very strong fellow had come to power and that his energy would hasten the resolution of our most acute problems. I even wondered whether I had underestimated him—perhaps he was that selfsame young politician fit to lead Russia into the future whom I had searched for and had not found.

But Lebed soon put me straight. "I wouldn't make a good bureaucrat," he said. "My spine isn't flexible enough, and the rules that are pushing the country into the abyss, they aren't for me. I didn't play by them then, and I won't play by them now. There are 11 million people behind me, and the sons of these people are dying today in this insane war."

That Lebed wouldn't be satisfied with the role of an apparatchik I had known all along. And I had also surmised that he would solve the problem of a Chechen peace in his own style—noisily, with lusty speeches, emphasizing his special position in every way. But I didn't know how the general would behave after that.

I made the changes in the power ministries in June 1996, even before the elections. The unpopular ministers who were responsible for the outcome of the Chechen campaign were fired, Grachev included. At Lebed's insistence I fired seven of Grachev's deputies and appointed General Igor Rodionov as defense minister. But even after Lebed had brought the Defense Ministry under his control, he didn't stop. He began an attack on the Ministry of the Interior and went after Minister Kulikov who, as the commander of the Interior Ministry troops for the entire year previous, bore the brunt of the responsibility for the combat actions in Chechnya. Lebed was looking for a conspiracy, a putsch, or even a minicoup, and it was here that he exposed enemies and saboteurs. Lebed and Kulikov butted heads in public. Lebed said bluntly, "Birds of a feather can't get along in the same bear cave."

Any rivalry between two agencies is always dangerous for the state. When generals fight each other, civilians as well as law and order can suffer. The generals no longer care about the constitution at that point. It was impossible to go on tolerating this situation.

Finally, the raucous foreign policy statements began. Lebed threatened the countries of Europe with "economic sanctions" if NATO were expanded to the East (although no one knew what he had in mind). He said that even though they were rusty, the Soviet missiles were in full combat readiness. He demanded that the city of Sevastopol, located now on Ukrainian territory, be returned to Russia. He didn't clear a single one of these statements with anyone, of course. The general's actions provoked such harsh criticism that I could not help but react.

Lebed didn't have any friends among the civilians, either. His quarrel with Chubais also went far beyond the bounds of decency. It was through Lebed's doing that the media began to call Chubais "the regent." Supposedly the president was so ill that everything was being run by the "regent" Chubais. Regency is a concept from monarchy; it had nothing to do with our reality. But the idea spread through the Duma and the Federation Council and took on the dangerous hue of a political label. While Lebed openly hinted at the need to dismiss Chubais, Chubais made sarcastic cracks about the intellectual capacity and knowledge of the general. The press followed the scandal developing around the new secretary of the Security Council with growing interest.

Everything that happened during those months at the Kremlin was closely connected to one very definite circumstance: my heart disease. Lebed wasn't clattering so noisily around the corridors of power just by accident. With his entire demeanor, he was illustrating his point: The president is doing badly, but I, the general-turned-politician, am ready to take his place. Besides me, there are no decent people here. I alone am able to communicate with the people at this difficult moment.

I was frightened most of all by Lebed's absolute inability to come to an agreement, to find allies, to make decisions in concert with others. It seemed for a time that this would pass, that we would teach Lebed, that soon he would be able to direct his energy toward finding an effective solution to our efforts in Chechnya. But after the Khasvyurt peace agreement, it became clear: Lebed was not going to get involved in the fine points of the Chechen problem. I assigned the working part of the negotiations with the Chechens to Chernomyrdin.

On October 3 I signed a decree stripping Lebed of his fairly serious powers of influence over the military. I turned over the leadership of the presidential commission on high military ranks and posts to Yury Baturin, head of the Defense Council. For those who understand the mentality of Russian generals, the point of this purely bureaucratic decree was obvious. Lebed no longer had control over all the stars on all the generals' epaulets. He could no longer manipulate the generals the way he wanted to.

Lebed quickly understood what I intended. Almost the same day he asked to visit me in Barvikha. There was only a little more than a month remaining before my operation.

"Boris Nikolayevich," he said, "your decision is wrong. The Defense Council is not the body that should decide the highest appointments in the army. It is now led by a civilian. The army won't understand that."

I explained to Lebed that my decision was not subject to discussion. "You need to get to work," I said. "You need to work with the premier and the others more consistently. You can't quarrel with everyone in our government."

Lebed huffed and puffed and said that in that case he would resign. He turned on his heel and walked out with his heavy general's tread. I caught myself thinking that Lebed was not as decisive and hard as he would like to seem. I had worked for so long in big politics and in various leadership posts that Lebed's lack of resolution was obvious to me from certain intonations and mannerisms. But perhaps I was mistaken? We would see.

I waited. A memorandum of resignation didn't follow. On October 7 Lebed traveled to a meeting at NATO headquarters in Brussels. He continued to give raucous, scandalous press conferences and to make startling announcements. Meanwhile I assigned my staff the job of preparing for his resignation. The issue was not as simple as it might now seem. Lebed's authority in the armed forces and other power ministries was enormous. His credibility rating with the public was reaching 30 percent, the highest rating among politicians. But the main thing was that Lebed, as I have said, had the Defense Ministry almost in his pocket. A new minister, Igor Rodionov, had just been appointed at his recommendation. (Rodionov would subsequently become a fierce ally of the Communist opposition.)

My administration was discussing the worst-case scenario of a military coup with absolute seriousness: paratroopers landing in Moscow, the buildings of the power ministries being seized, and so on. The paratroopers were the most mobile and well-trained type of ground troops. They idolized Lebed. Apparently Lebed can perform all the paratroopers' basic moves—run, stretch, parachute out of planes, and hit targets with short bursts of fire.

I didn't ascribe any importance to this talk. It was clear to me that Lebed wouldn't dare do any such thing under any circumstances. I read a completely unexpected expression in his eyes. He had the look of a C student who had forgotten the lesson he had memorized and didn't know what to do.

Still, I had some doubts about his dismissal. Was it the right moment now, when the internal political situation could become so aggravated? But what if something were to happen to me? My operation loomed ahead. I didn't want Lebed to be in the Kremlin at the moment of the operation. He was uncontrollable; he had enormous ambitions; he was rent by internal contradictions; and he was a weak politician. That last point was the worst. A strong person might work everything to his own advantage, but at least he would contain the situation. But Lebed? In order to prove something to somebody, like a little kid, he would stop at nothing. Such a person should not be given even a slim chance of running the country.

Lebed sensed his dismissal coming on. Once he came to Gorki-9 in a nervous state without any warning. He wasn't let in—I hadn't made an appointment with him. He stood outside the gates for a long time, yelling at the guards. He began to call on the city telephone lines, shouting into the handset that he wasn't being allowed to meet the president. And he claimed it was none other than Chubais who was preventing him, public enemy number one! There Lebed stood outside the gates, and the guards were getting nervous. To be honest, it was a funny feeling, something I hadn't felt in years. It was like having someone banging down your door. They won't go away even if you call the police. But I didn't have to call the police. Lebed eventually went away, apparently to contrive some new plan of action.

The situation reached the boiling point. Chernomyrdin was forced to call an emergency meeting of the power ministries. Lebed was deliberately not invited. The ministers could no longer tolerate the escapades of the secretary of the Security Council and intended to speak from a united position: Lebed could not be kept inside the government. But Lebed found out about the meeting and crashed it. A fight began. Lebed shouted. The ministers were silent. Only Kulikov gave him a harsh rebuttal.

All of this went so far outside the bounds of the permissible, the decent, and the commonsensical that I was forced to sign a decree dismissing him that very day. Most likely Lebed should have been fired earlier. But strange as it may sound, Aleksandr Ivanovich Lebed reminded me of someone: myself. Only he was a caricature of me, as if I were looking in a fun house mirror.

I went into the hospital with a heavy heart, both literally and figuratively. And my attitude toward Lebed remained strange and ambiguous. On the one hand, I was grateful to him for taking the responsibility upon himself publicly and establishing a rapid peace in Chechnya. Although this peace was short-lived and piecemeal, I had neither the moral right nor the political backing to continue the war. On the other hand, Lebed turned out to be a very noisy and very weak politician. Perhaps it is our good luck. Today he is no longer a general but a governor. I would like to believe that life will teach him something. After all, he is quite a vivid, extraordinary person.

I fear that by making broad statements about generals in this chapter I will offend many decent military people. Many generals know how highly I have valued and continue to value their services to the fatherland. They know how I have trusted them. But I cannot refrain from writing about the other, less pleasant side of the history of our relationship. Too often, it seems to me, during this slice of history from 1993 to 1996, the country depended on the decisions of generals, on both their public and their behind-the-scenes behavior. Russia went head-to-head with the generals' logic and the generals' aplomb. To a certain extent it was probably my fault.

One particularly ugly example of this problem came in the person of General Korzhakov, the chief of presidential security. Korzhakov played a special role in my personal story. This was a man who for many years was close to me, both personally and as a comrade. I long considered us to be of like mind.

Korzhakov wrote a book about his time in the Kremlin. I am told that it contains much untruth and sleaze. I decided not to read it because I couldn't overcome my revulsion. I know only one thing: For ten years, it was Korzhakov, my former bodyguard, who surrounded me with care, who swore his loyalty to me, who literally shielded me with his body, who shared all my difficulties, and who tirelessly tracked down and exposed my enemies. In fact, it was that zealousness that would destroy us. It was Korzahkov who during the most difficult moment of my life decided to trip me up.

Why did it happen? Korzhakov skipped from major of the ninth (the ninth directorate of the KGB's security service) to the rank of general within a few years. Along the way he acquired functions outside the purview of his service. He created a mighty power structure and planted his friend Barsukov, who had no direct relationship to counterintelligence, in the FSK. With all of these moves, Korzhakov concentrated more power into his hands than he could handle. And that is what eventually broke him.

In order to become a real politician, you need completely different qualities, not the ability to sniff out enemies and divide the entire political spectrum into "mine" and "yours." That Korzhakov began to influence the appointment of people in both the government and the power ministry is, of course, entirely my fault. Korzhakov was a person from my past, from the past of dramatic victories and defeats and high praise, where I was carried aloft and brought down with incredible speed. And it was very hard for me to part with this past.

When the all-powerful KGB collapsed, there was an unprecedented level of freedom on our political stage. People in uniform exploited it in their own way. That the real threat of a military coup and a civil war existed in the early 1990s was obvious to me, as I've indicated. So what prevented a coup from happening? As strange as it may sound, it was the inner persistence of the society. The young democracy had rapidly acquired an internal immunity to the generals' viruses—posturing, populism, and the desire to command everyone immediately. Freedom of speech and the political institutions of the new Russia created a counterweight to this threat. With each year I saw the influence of the generals become less and less dangerous. Therefore, when people say that in Russia there exist no democracy, no civil society, and no legal system, I disagree. They may make them out of the best of intentions, but they are wrong. If you look at our recent history, you will understand everything.

At some point in 1993, I first thought to myself that something was wrong with some of our generals. They were missing something important, perhaps a certain nobility, sophistication, or some sort of inner resolve. After all, the army is an indication of the internal culture of a society, especially in Russia—a litmus test. I was waiting for a new general to appear, unlike any other. Or rather, a general who was like the generals I read about in books when I was young. I was waiting...

Time passed, and such a general appeared. And soon after his arrival, it became obvious to our whole society how really courageous and highly professional our military people were. This "general" was named Colonel Vladimir Putin. His story follows.

· 5 ·

Chubais and the 1997 Team

In 1997, at the beginning of his second term as president, the reinvigorated Yeltsin gathers together a young team of bright minds to bring emergency economic reforms to Russia. This green team, headed by the fiery Anatoly Chubais, works night and day to strengthen the weakened economy, but they encounter all sorts of social and political disasters along the way. The Russian public, weary of the ruinous effects of rapid privatization, finally demands Chubais's head.

· · ·

ON JANUARY 7, 1997, I went into the hospital with pneumonia. Ten days later the Duma placed the question of the president's health on the agenda. The public responded to the news with a new wave of worried anticipation.

We had a problem on our hands. The constitution is not clear about how and when a president can be considered incompetent. Taking advantage of this, the Communists in the Duma tried to pass a law mandating a medical commission that would place the president under strict regulations. The president would be permitted only a certain number of sick days, and he would be allowed to remain at his post if he suffered from certain diseases but not others. It was as if I were supposed to have certain medical procedures by certain deadlines. I practically had to turn blood samples over to the Communist Duma.

The law's opponents cited numerous counterexamples: In such-

and-such a country the president had had this or that operation; in another country a president had spent many years in a wheelchair; in yet another a leader had incurable cancer. But in no other country did the parliament discuss their leader's health so cynically.

If a president senses that he isn't going to make it, he himself should raise the question of early elections. If physicals are to be mandatory, they should be performed only *before* elections. Otherwise an enormous room for intrigue, manipulation, and political instability opens up. Isn't that logical? I thought so. But the Duma has an entirely different logic. No sane arguments would sway the deputies. Ever since 1991, or even 1990, the Communists had been obsessed with one idea: getting rid of Yeltsin. My health was their latest point of attack.

In early 1997 the bright red section of the Duma—that of the Communists—was again storming down the well-worn warpath. They were out for blood, my blood. That may be just a figure of speech, but it isn't a pleasant image for someone who has just recently had his rib cage sawed open. Unfortunately, it's all too accurate.

On January 17 the Duma voted on the question of my health. Deputies from the faction called Our Home Is Russia left the hall in protest. The liberal Yabloko faction didn't support the resolution sponsored by Viktor Ilyukhin, a Communist. The agrarian parties were split. The resolution didn't pass.

How did I feel at that moment? I was mad—mad at myself, mad at my doctors, mad at anyone who crossed my path. How had it come to this? How could I not have taken care of myself after such an operation? Everything had been going so well—my heart had started working right away; I had gotten out of my hospital bed quickly; I started walking and was making a rapid recovery; it had become so much easier for me to breathe; I returned to work ahead of schedule. And then, all of a sudden, pneumonia. Perhaps I had been too hasty in going outside, or I had picked up a virus, or I had caught cold in the *banya*. I hadn't thought my body was so weak. I shouldn't have risked it. As a result, I was put out of commission for at least another month and a half and my parliament openly questioned my ability to lead the country.

Postoperative pneumonia is an interesting thing. I had lost 57 pounds while I was preparing for the operation. Now I was weak and had a high fever. It was if my body was not my own; it felt light, almost transparent. My thoughts floated away. I felt as if I were being born anew. I was already a different "I," a different Boris Yeltsin. I had suffered a lot, as if I had returned from the land of the dead. I couldn't go on solving problems as I used to, by mustering all my physical strength or charging head-on into sharp political clashes. That wasn't for me anymore.

My temperature hovered around 104 degrees for several days. Then, very slowly, it began to go down. My doctors were worried about complications. Had the infection spread? Was it affecting other organs? Finally, around my birthday, I began to feel like my old self again. February was around the corner. Winter had already passed.

On February 23, Armed Forces Day, I went out in public for the first time. There's an old Kremlin ritual: the laying of a wreath at Post Number One on the Tomb of the Unknown Soldier. Post Number One used to be at the mausoleum on Red Square, where Lenin is buried. The Kremlin guards used to change on the hour, goose-stepping back and forth in front of the tomb, which contained the mummified remains of the "leader of the world proletariat." It was by my decree that Post Number One had been moved to the Tomb of the Unknown Soldier. Now the guards march here, at the symbolic grave of all our soldiers who have died for the motherland.

It was at the tomb on this stormy February day that I would finally be able to articulate what had been bothering me for so long. I went up to a group of reporters. They were all old, familiar faces. They waited expectantly for me to say something. It was very important for them to catch my first words after such a long break. About the Duma, I said, "They'll find it hard talking to me like that. I can give as good as I get." I got those first words out with difficulty. Still, I felt much better. Nobody could think that Yeltsin had deflated like a pricked balloon. Yet there was a certain annoyance in the air. The public was expecting action, something serious. This ritualistic appearance before the television cameras only made me feel as though more was expected. The public wanted to see the old Yeltsin again.

The president's annual address to the Federal Assembly was scheduled for March 6, 1997. It was to take place in a cool, spacious, marbled hall at the Kremlin. An enormous crowd of people—hundreds of journalists, members of parliament, senators, and the entire political elite —would be present. The annual presidential address is of enormous political significance, as it lays out a concept for the development of the country.

My text had been prepared for a long time. I considered it highly important, as it was the first time since the elections that I would be presenting my program of action to the Federal Assembly and to the nation. Moreover, it would be my first appearance for a major public speech after such a lengthy absence for my operation and my postoperative recuperation. How would it turn out? Few of those in the hall wanted to see a healthy Yeltsin. My appearance alone was enough to irritate them. When I entered, there was a rumble in the crowd. Some people shouted. I didn't pay any attention. The Communists always had their repertoire. That wasn't important. What was important was that I was speaking in full confidence to my country.

I had titled my message "Order in the Government; Order in the Country." The main thesis was that the government, not circumstance, should rule the country. It was time to bring order to the government and elsewhere. I would impose it. The government had proven that it was unable to work without being shouted at by the president. Most of the promises that had been made to the people, primarily regarding social issues, had not been kept. Therefore the structure and composition of the government had to be changed. Competent and energetic people had to be brought in. We also needed legislative reform. The legislature was passing laws that served only narrow group interests. Though the majority of deputies realized that certain laws would damage Russia, they passed them anyway.

Finally, I described how I had once received a letter from the very Federal Assembly I was addressing about the need to build a parliamentary complex costing about 10 trillion rubles.* Those funds would be enough to pay the back wages of all the teachers and doctors in the country.† I couldn't agree to such a needless expenditure.

My speech was half an hour long. With each word, it got a little bit better. I was finding my voice once again. I was almost certain that I had discovered the type of bold political moves that were needed. I had been thinking this over for months. I was almost sure. Just a little bit longer . . .

Earlier that winter I had heard a speech by Patriarch Aleksy, the Russian Orthodox Church leader. In a Christmas sermon addressed to all Russian Orthodox believers, he took a sudden tangent into politics and called the nonpayment of wages and pensions a sin. His unexpected use of the word cut me to the quick. Aleksy and I had always had the most friendly, even warm relations. The word *sin* resounded like a bell in the back of my mind. Yes, back wages were a real problem, a calamity. I acknowledged there were economic difficulties. But suddenly there it was, direct and abrupt: "a sin." Another question implicitly followed: Whose sin? Mine?

While I was laid up with pneumonia, I kept thinking about the second echelon of politicians. They had to come to power sooner, much sooner, than I had anticipated. If other people didn't step into the political arena right then, it would be too late. The sin wasn't that reforms were under way in the country; the sin was that they were moving too slowly.

* The ruble fluctuated dramatically throughout Yeltsin's presidency. In 1995 and 1996, the exchange-rate fluctuations were limited by the government, and reset several times at between 4 and 6 rubles to the U.S. dollar. On the day of Yeltsin's address (March 6, 1997) the official exchange rate was approximately six rubles to the dollar. Yeltsin introduced "new" rubles in November 1997 so that as of January 1, 1998, the Bank of Russia central exchange rate for a three-year period (1998–2000) was to be 6.2 rubles to the dollar. However, in August 1998, the Bank switched back to a floating exchange rate. Because of these complicated exchange-rate fluctuations, all amounts have been left in rubles throughout. At the time of publication, 1 dollar was equivalent to approximately 28 rubles. — Trans.

† Immediately after my speech, Yegor Stroyev and Gennady Seleznyov disassociated themselves from this letter and were highly embarrassed, saying that it was an incomplete draft that had reached me accidentally. — Author.

I met with Prime Minister Chernomyrdin in the Kremlin to discuss these matters. I told Chernomyrdin that I considered the social sector to be in a crisis and that the nonpayment of wages was a prolonged illness of the government. Although Chernomyrdin said all the necessary words and made all the right promises, I sensed from his response that he was tired. He was exhausted by the constant tension and the inability to solve the accumulated problems. Chernomyrdin never stuck his head out. He never tried to play his own game. That was his strength. All these years he had stood behind me as an exceptionally decent, conscientious, and devoted person. He had tried to distance himself from the behind-the-scenes Kremlin intrigues. He was involved only in the economy, but when it was necessary—during 1993, at the beginning of the Chechen war, and during the events in Budyonnovsk—he had resolutely supported me. Probably at some earlier point, I had not given him the opportunity to blossom as an independent politician. But it was too late to regret it now. With his bulky Russian figure, his folksy, direct way of talking, his dazzling smile, his hearty humor and native wit, Chernomyrdin had managed to grow roots in the political landscape. He was the indispensable premier in the era of political crises. But it seemed to me that after the elections of 1996 that era was over. A new era had begun, an epoch of construction, of economic breakthrough.

I really wanted to help Chernomyrdin create the kind of government that would turn the economy around. The Chechen war, which had sapped away so much of our strength, was over. The elections, both parliamentary and presidential, were behind us. Now we needed a breakthrough. The country was tired of waiting, tired of uncertainty, tired of the lack of serious efforts to change the situation for the better.

I couldn't reproach Chernomyrdin personally for the fact that the economy was spinning its wheels. But I also couldn't ignore what was going on in the country. The old productive capacity of Russia—the dysfunctional manufacturing sector and the collective agricultural system—didn't fit into this new life of ours. Yet Chernomyrdin's base was mainly in the so-called directors' corps, the people who ran those defunct areas of the economy. He couldn't understand that only new managers with new ways of thinking could drag our socialist economy out of the swamp. So it was a vicious circle: Russian investors didn't want to put money into obsolete production, and only a narrow sector of the economy ran on market principles. This in turn drastically narrowed the opportunities for the economy to develop, including the banking business.

It wasn't all bleak. Thanks to domestic and foreign loans, the sale of raw materials and metal, the rise of an enormous domestic consumer market, and the emergence of a class of tradespeople who created jobs, the country had reached so-called stabilization. But in Russia's case stabilization didn't mean stability.

The Chernomyrdin government, formed in August 1996, immediately after the elections, massaged the economy for more than half a year. Unfortunately, the professionals Chernomyrdin selected for key posts seemed to be looking in completely different directions from one another. It was a government of bold projects, hearty encouragement, and good intentions, but it was hard to call it a team of like-minded people, linked by one concept and one plan for reform. By Soviet standards it was a well-meaning, thoughtful, and quite intelligent government. But all of these virtues could emerge only in a stable economic situation. In reality, everything was different. An avalanche of debt obligations and budget deficits was mounting. Moreover, the state could not buy up the products of the defense plants; the workers remained without pay; local government budgets couldn't cover the costs of doctors and teachers, health care, and assistance to the elderly.

It became more and more clear that the first Chernomyrdin government was not capable of solving the country's onslaught of economic and social problems. To use a metaphor with which I was intimately familiar at the time, the patient needed a definite surgical procedure. For one thing, we could no longer justify our original idea of attracting nongovernmental executives and professionals to serve in the government. Vladimir Potanin, who had accepted the post of first vice premier for the economy and planning in the summer of 1996, was supposed to establish long-term rules of the game for regulating

Russian businesses and their relations with government. Potanin was the first person from big business who went to work for the government. (This practice is now common; everyone has forgotten how hard it was for the first businessmen in politics.) No one knew how to combine—on one desk and in one head—the tasks of governance and the interests of the enormous private enterprises, which were also tied to the government economy with a thousand strings.

Potanin displayed great courage and persistence. Over in ONEKSIM, his own bank (his own home, as it were), he made decisions, and they were implemented within twenty-four hours. But in the Kremlin, because of the cumbersome government machinery, months would be spent coordinating a single decision. Potanin used his own funds to hire high-class, expensive specialists who prepared the necessary documents for the government—laws, resolutions, instructions. It was torture for Potanin to change his methodology and his customary way of solving problems. He even had to alter his lifestyle, abandoning his fine cuisine for the lousy White House cafeteria. In some ways the government met him halfway, letting him ride around in his own private car and bring in his own security service from the bank. Still, it was hard.

Chernomyrdin never got along with Potanin because he thought the new first vice premier was too actively defending the interests of his own bank. Finally, Chernomyrdin insisted that Potanin be fired.

By early March Chernomyrdin and I agreed that Chubais, then head of the presidential administration, should return to the cabinet of ministers. On March 17 I signed a decree concerning his appointment as first vice premier. Chubais was champing at the bit to return to the economy. He had worked all right in the post of chief of administration, but he had always said, "This isn't for me." I had always thought that having just one Chubais in the government was not enough, so I decided to find another deputy for Chernomyrdin. I needed a vivid political figure. Boris Nemtsov seemed quite appropriate for this role.

Nemtsov, the governor of Nizhegorod region, was a rather popular figure, both in his native Volga region and in Russia at large. Just by coming onto the Moscow scene, he could provide the government with a fresh reserve of credibility and improve the political climate in the country.

It was perfect: I needed to bolster Chernomyrdin from two sides, to get him moving, to show him that he had backup. Our political stalemate, which the public was sick and tired of, had to be shaken. As someone said, we needed a change of scenery. The usual Chubais with the usual Chernomyrdin—that was one scene. But two young, pushy, and aggressive (in the good sense) vice premiers who instantly surrounded Chernomyrdin with a system of high, constant, positive pressure—that was something completely different.

For a long time, young people had categorically refused to go into the government or the Kremlin. They actively resisted public service.

Right after the second round in the elections of 1996, Chubais had said to me: "That's it, thank you. I have a lot of business affairs to attend to. I'm getting a lot of interesting offers, and I don't intend to go back into the government. Thanks for your faith in me, but no thanks." And here I had wanted to invite Chubais to work as chief of the presidential administration. Then I had a novel idea: to invite Igor Malashenko, head of the television station NTV, to serve in the post. But he, too, politely but firmly refused. Perhaps personal circumstances played a role. His wife, who lived in London, had just had a baby, and Igor wanted to go there to be with his family. I didn't want to try to talk him out of his decision.

Once again we returned to the candidacy of Chubais. Chubais was well aware that we wouldn't manage to change anything in the country if this fighting among various groups inside the Kremlin kept up. We needed a tough vertical line from the president on down, and not from someone who was trying to gain influence. Chubais understood this, but he continued to hesitate.

At last I told him that I was going to have an operation and that I had to be absolutely sure that there weren't going to be any emergencies during my absence. Chubais got it. He agreed to accept the post.

Incidentally, there was another member of the young generation of politicians who refused my invitation to come work in the government: Grigory Yavlinsky. In the summer of 1996, when Chubais headed the analytical group with the election campaign, he had actively held discussions with Yavlinsky. It's possible that if Yavlinsky had agreed at that moment to support me in the second round of the elections and had overcome his own caution in selecting allies, the entire history of our reforms would have been different. But keeping himself politically pristine was far more important to Yavlinsky. He did not see this as an opportunity to prove to all his opponents that it was possible to live by your conscience. I didn't want to bargain with the premier's post, but I was prepared to look at Yavlinsky's program.

Boris Nemtsov turned out to be hardest of all. "Why do you need me in Moscow?" Nemtsov asked Chubais in the spring of 1997. "I would be of more help to you here in Nizhny Novgorod."

No matter what we told him about reforms, he kept stubbornly replying, "But who will take care of reforms in Nizhny?"

Chubais almost shouted at Nemtsov: "If you're so smart and you criticize us, then at least take part of the responsibility."

But Nemtsov returned home. What a stubborn nature. Reminds me of myself.

Then we got the idea of persuading Nemtsov by sending Tanya to see him in Nizhny. She understood the subtext of what I was saying. I didn't have to spell it out to her: This is your team of young upstarts; you go and work it out among yourselves.

Tanya wanted to set out immediately. But at that time of day there weren't any planes or trains going to Nizhny Novgorod. Tanya announced that she would go in the car. Valentin Yumashev called Nemtsov to warn him that Tanya was already on her way. Apparently Nemtsov either didn't believe it or didn't get it—after all, not everybody would dare to take a seven-hour drive on our roads at that time of night. So he was shocked when the phone rang late that night and it was Tanya.

"Tatyana Borisovna," he said in surprise. "Where are you?"

"I'm at the Kremlin."

"What Kremlin?" asked Nemtsov.

"In your Kremlin here in Nizhny," said Tanya.*

When he saw the president's daughter in his office, Nemtsov realized the proposition wasn't a joke. He finally agreed to take the job, but only after a long conversation.

With Chubais's transfer from the presidential administration to the government cabinet, we had to find his replacement within a matter of days. That's when I decided to have a talk with Valentin Yumashev.

"Boris Nikolayevich," Yumashev said. "First of all, I don't have sufficient political weight. Second, I have never been in public office. Everyone knows I am your friend and a friend of your family. The appointment will seem strange."

I listened carefully to Yumashev and then said I'd think about his argument. I didn't have long to think, though, because the decree concerning Chubais's appointment to the cabinet had already been signed. Although I wanted Yumashev to take the job, I was worried. Of course he was a talented journalist and a marvelous analyst. He had been right alongside me since 1987 and was prepared to work for days on end. Still, the apparat of the administration was an enormous office with its own traditions and procedures. It was fairly bureaucratic.

Yumashev resisted quietly, not as violently as Nemtsov or Chubais. But he was stubborn. He did not want to part with his beloved freedom. As far as I understand it, Tanya and Chubais finally put him up against the wall and said that he had given enough advice from the sidelines. It was time for him to get his hands dirty and join the fray.

Each of the young politicians had his own reasons to refuse my offers. Chubais found it psychologically difficult to return to power after his scandalous resignation in 1995. Neither Nemtsov nor Oleg Sysuyev, the former mayor of the city of Samara who eventually became vice premier, wanted to leave his regional starting gate, where

---

* *Kreml*, rendered as *Kremlin*, means "fortress" in Russian. Nizhny Novgorod has the same type of Kremlin for the seat of government as the Kremlin in Moscow. — Trans.

he had been so successful. For both personal and professional reasons, they didn't want to rush their transfer to Moscow. Valentin Yumashev was not ready to take on the role of a public politician.

But there was another generational reason for their hesitance. All of these people who grew up in the 1970s and matured in the 1980s could never have dreamed that they would some day fly so high. Power seemed to them to be the prerogative of a completely different class of people—the gray and bald-headed old men with big guts, the Party bosses who had gone through years of schooling in the Central Committee of the Communist Party or the regional Party commit-tees. Perestroika could not change this attitude. After all, Gorbachev had not hastened to part with his old apparat. The Soviet complex of the intelligentsia, of people engaged in intellectual work, was at play here as well; they thought that only people with thick skin and nerves of steel could run things. I tried to convince them that this wasn't the case. But the young Yeltsin team could not rid itself entirely of this unease. I remember how Yumashev once joked to me: "You know, Boris Nikolayevich, this life isn't really for me. I feel like I'm the hero in Mark Twain's novel *The Prince and the Pauper,* when he was given the state seal. I'm not going to use it to crack nuts, but I sometimes wish I could."

When it finally came together, the 1997 team was not just a con-glomeration of disparate ministers, vice premiers, and other top lead-ers. After several months of brutal, intense work, these individuals had turned into a real single-minded team. Sometimes on Sundays they would have something like a picnic out at Yumashev's dacha, cooking shish kebabs and singing songs around the campfire. They tried not to talk about politics and the economy—they had more than enough of that during the workweek. Sysuyev and Yumashev played guitar duets and sang folk songs by Russia's famous bards, Okudzhava, Vizbor, and Gorodnitsky: "The Atlases hold up the sky/In their stone arms." They sang this song and, it seemed, somewhere in their subconscious, felt as if they themselves were these Atlases. Chubais, a real romantic, knew the words to absolutely all the songs. But since he had a tin ear, he would just recite the words to music. Chubais's wife, Masha, always beautiful and stern, couldn't tolerate these songs at all and sat through the campfire sing-alongs only out of love for her husband.

At these picnics the wives of the senior Moscow officials would give advice to the wives of the new men from out of town—how they could get settled in Moscow, to which schools they should send their children, how they would fix the deluge of problems, and other womanly secrets.

Maksim Boyko, the vice premier responsible for privatization, usually wouldn't stay until the shish kebabs were served. His wife had just had a baby, so he hurried home to his family. Boris Nemtsov came along with his whole family, including his charming thirteen-year-old daughter, Zhanna. She didn't have any friends in Moscow, as she had just moved from Nizhny. Her papa brought her everywhere with him so that she wouldn't be sad.

They all happily told me in detail about their Sunday get-togethers. They invited me to join the cookouts, to sing along with them and relax for a while. But I didn't want to interfere with their fun on their only day off.

Anatoly Chubais was the engine of campaign '97. He brought a lot of new people into the government and galvanized them all into a single force of intellect and will. He was able to achieve harsh discipline within the team. He was the one to generate the ideas.

But the link between the Chubais team and me was Tanya. Tanya kept me informed of all the ideas, disputes, and nuances of every position. She organized informal talks and brainstorming sessions to discuss the most complex political and economic problems. I watched the whole process from the sidelines, and I liked how the team worked together. I was their patron, and I sincerely sympathized with them. I liked their youthful energy and their hunger for results.

Although Chernomyrdin had taken part in the campaigns to persuade Nemtsov to join the government, privately he was very cautious about the entire affair. He knew Chubais well, but he didn't know Nemtsov. In my television address about the young reformers being put into the government, I included this comment, directed at Chernomyrdin: "Don't be afraid, Viktor Stepanovich. They're not going to unseat you!"

Chernomyrdin grew agitated and began to call the speechwriters, demanding to know where this line had come from. They were just as shocked as he was. The line had not been in the final, agreed-upon text. Of course I wrote it in myself right before my speech, over the objections of my aides. I'm afraid that Chernomyrdin suspected some sort of Kremlin intrigue. He didn't believe that the phrase had come from me, but it really had. I had wanted to get this simple idea across to him: Don't be afraid, Viktor Stepanovich. Just don't be afraid. That's it.

Gradually, Chernomyrdin came to accept this position. He realized that the leap to reform couldn't be made without these bold, unaccommodating (and at times even unpleasant) young people. The economy, caught between the Scylla and Charybdis of the market and the permanent political crisis, needed radical transformations and totally new approaches. I realized that this new government could be unstable, subject to various storms and passions. But we had to take risks in order to pull ourselves out of our economic bog. The "Rangers' Team" was ready. They were just waiting for my signal to launch their grandiose plans. I didn't know which of them would survive in the government or prevail in the skirmishes ahead. I didn't know who would husband his resources and who might be forced to part with them. I did believe in their intensity and in their passionate desire to win.

When the "young reformers," as the newspapers dubbed them, first began working in the government, the public harbored enormous hopes. Everyone from the wily businessman to the village grandmother listened attentively to what "this red-haired guy and that curly-haired guy" were saying. In the public opinion polls, Nemtsov, who always spoke simply and animatedly, with a joke or a quip at the ready, quickly overtook Lebed, Luzhkov, and even Zyuganov. Nemtsov even beat out the leader of the Communists in some rural areas. "Boris Nemtsov is attacking Zyuganov in the villages!" exclaimed Chubais happily.

I noticed that when the four of us would get together in meetings

—Chernomyrdin, Nemtsov, Chubais, and myself—the two first vice premiers behaved quite differently from each other. Chubais spoke politely, cautiously, and tried to show total solidarity with Chernomyrdin, as two people who understood the economy. Nemtsov didn't acknowledge any rules. His slightly impudent tone ruffled Chernomyrdin. Chernomyrdin became nervous and looked at me in confusion. His expression spoke volumes: "I don't think Nemtsov is right."

We held meetings like this regularly, almost every week. If I was on vacation, Nemtsov or Chubais would come directly to my residence along with their team of specialists and would acquaint me with drafts of the latest decisions. I tried to understand how they were able to combine such youthful zeal with such a mature awareness of their purpose. Chubais and Nemtsov complemented each other perfectly. They seemed to be a totally unbreakable tandem.

At that time we drafted several long-overdue decrees and resolutions for the government. One of them was about establishing a system of competition among the private firms that delivered goods to the state, whether sugar for hospitals or food for the army. Now the companies would have to compete to get such state contracts, proving the quality of their goods and bidding the lowest price. Only those companies that provided the best terms to the state would win the contracts. With this decree, we closed off a very important loophole for abuse.

Chubais and Nemtsov made their main priority getting rid of leeches on the state treasury, making the flow of money transparent, and protecting government decisions from side deals and double bookkeeping. The energy with which the young reformers tackled these tasks was amazing. But it was natural that they made some missteps. There were the infamous white pants, hardly in keeping with protocol, that Boris Nemtsov wore to meet Azerbaijani president Heidar Aliev. Those pants went down in the history of the new Russian diplomacy.

One rather comical failure involved the plan to make all bureaucrats ride in Russian-made cars. Of course Nemtsov had the best intentions. Why spend money from the Russian budget on German or

Italian auto giants? Why buy Audis or Fiats for Russian bureaucrats if we could buy our own domestic Volgas and Moskvichi? Nemtsov got this idea when he returned to his hometown of Nizhny Novgorod and saw a Russian Volga next to some imported Mercedes and BMWs. He suddenly realized that if we didn't help our domestic automobile manufacturers through our own personal example, no one else would.

The bureaucrats were appalled. They didn't want to switch to Russian cars, which were always breaking down. And you couldn't blame them. Our domestic cars don't start in the winter, and they overheat in the summer. It was a beautiful idea, but it was about to be squashed. Nemtsov himself moved from a Mercedes to a Volga and came to me for support. I said I would support him in both word and deed.

At that time I was preparing a radio speech on the theme "Buy Russian." I wanted to tell people that there are Russian-made goods of which we could be proud. And the state had to do everything possible to help those Russian enterprises that produced high-quality products. I asked my speechwriters to put in a line about Nemtsov's car initiative that said the government's budget would be spent on our own Russian products in cases where Russian industry produced goods comparable to those imported from other countries.

Then I told my head of security that from now on I would be driven in a ZIL instead of a Mercedes. To be honest, when I stepped out on the Kremlin porch and saw that painfully familiar ZIL, I cursed myself. Ever since the days of the Politburo, I haven't liked these particular ZIL models, which people nicknamed "member-mobiles" because only members of the Politburo were driven in them. But there was nothing I could do; I had to support the young reformers.

Nemtsov's coworkers at the presidential administration and the government continued to sabotage his undertaking. Worse, he couldn't inspire his friends with his personal example. His Russian car broke down, and he constantly had to exchange it for another. The apotheosis of this story came when Nemstov's Volga overheated and broke down right on the street. Nemtsov got out of his car. Drivers rushed by, ridiculing him. By that time the whole country recognized him. There he stood by his smoking, overheated car.

For my part, I honestly rode for a while in that ZIL. Then I decided not to torture myself anymore and switched back to my Mercedes with relief. The idea was good, but the Russian-made cars weren't—yet.

In 1997 the economy finally began to show some tendency toward growth. It was our first victory, and although it was hardly permanent, it was a victory nonetheless. The Chubais team of young economists had formulated their goals very clearly and precisely. These were the so-called seven tasks of the government: to pass and implement a new tax code by January 1, 1999; to gradually reduce the budget deficit and to pass a budget code; to form a class of effective property owners with the help of privatization; to establish procedures for declaring bankruptcy; to begin reform of the pension systems; to slow the growth in price increases; to lower the profitability of state securities; to introduce land reform; and so on.

Boris Nemtsov undertook one other important project: reforming the public utilities. This may sound rather dull, but it affected practically everyone and was an extremely important step in establishing a normal economy. The problem was that since the days of socialism, the costs of the heat, gas, and electricity people received in their homes were subsidized by the state. Where did the state get the funds to subsidize utilities? It would slap unbearable taxes on enterprises. Because of such heavy taxation, Russian enterprises were not competitive. Nemstov's idea was simple: Subsidies would remain only for the needy (pensioners, large families, and so on). For the rest of the citizens, utility rates would gradually but definitely rise.

Oleg Sysuyev took on another project: reforming social services. We had inherited from our Soviet past a very widespread but poor system of social subsidies that was not needs-based. The government was readying for a transition from a system of social aid for everyone without distinction to a system of targeted social support for the genuinely needy.

Alas, for many reasons, many of these chief tasks were not taken care of. The main barrier was the furious resistance of the leftist Duma. It suited the Communist deputies who controlled the parliament to keep the country poor. They wanted the state to dole out everything so that people, like cogs in a machine, were totally reliant on the powers that be. When people are poor and unsettled, they will always vote for the Communists. When they are strong and free, they will never vote for them. Unfortunately, almost all the government programs required changes in legislation, and that meant the support of the Duma. And here I could do nothing to help Chubais. We encountered major obstructions to all our initiatives.

Still, the new government did what was in its power. A lot of new young people came to work in the White House. Chubais brought in a seasoned team of young economists: Kudrin, Ignatyev, Boyko, and others. Nemtsov brought in some of his own people from Nizhny Novgorod, including the young managers Brevnov and Savelyev, and of course Sergei Kiriyenko. Most of them were barely older than thirty. I followed all their careers. Now I can see clearly that most of them could not withstand the test of a high post with such immense responsibility. But back then everyone was filled with hope, myself included. I hoped that by the second half of 1997 and in early 1998 we would sense that something in the country was changing.

Then something happened that I could never have expected: the war of the banks over the auction to privatize the telecommunications company Svyazinvest. This played itself out in the news. The auction filled the headlines of all the newspapers as the media chose sides in the competition. Every day the television stations ORT and NTV aired obscure bulletins that seemed to say, "Death to our enemies and competitors." The newscasters made a sorry sight. They sat frightened in front of the cameras, glancing at the teleprompters, trying not to mix up the insane choice of words.

At first I didn't pay any attention. Auctions were already common practice. There were always winners and losers and somebody who was left unhappy. But here was something quite out of the ordinary. With somewhat pale faces, my aides tried to convince me that nothing special was happening. It was competition. It was normal. Two groups were fighting for influence, a classic feature of business.

"But why is our entire press divided into two camps?" I asked. "Why are they talking about Svyazinvest every night on *Vremya*?" It was time to get to the bottom of this conflict.

Vladimir Gusinsky* was the person most interested in buying stock in Svyazinvest. He had long been in talks with people inside the government who were involved in the auction. He had also been talking to the military, the FSB, and FAPSI, the state communications agency, to get them to turn over military frequencies for civilian use. With the help of Western investors, he wanted to create a powerful, modern company to produce and service telecommunications.

On the one hand, Gusinsky had every reason to stake a claim to purchase Svyazinvest. On the other, if we let him have it, the auction wouldn't be an auction but a giveaway. "It will be a mockery of the very idea of an auction!" Chubais exclaimed. "There are other financial groups, other investors who also have a full right to stake their claims to Svyazinvest. Our only criteria for evaluation of the winner of the auction should be the person who pays the most." Chubais's tone was peremptory and his arguments were ironclad, eloquent, and logical. As always, he defended his position with the utmost energy. Still, I sensed that the "father of Russian privatization" was concealing something from me. But what?

Later, after I read Chubais's book *Privatization in Russia*, I understood the essence of the conflict better. I saw that Chubais had been wrong, or at least not entirely correct, even proceeding from his own formal economic logic. A system as complex as the Russian economy, a system without precedents or analogies, could not be so abruptly thrown out of the frying pan and into the fire. According to Chubais, the transition from the first stage of privatization, when the state was forced to sell state property at a discount to Russian banks and companies, to the second stage, when real market mechanisms would kick in,

---

* Gusinsky is the owner of Media-Most, which includes major media holdings such as the television station NTV and the weekly news magazine *Itogi*.—Trans.

was supposed to happen instantly, almost without warning. And now the players in the auction who had become used to this scheme suddenly ran headlong into a wall.

"Perhaps we shouldn't start with Svyazinvest, since it is provoking such a storm of controversy," many people said to Chubais back then. But Chubais held firm to his position. He tried to prove to me that this was the only way the Russian economy would come to life. "Boris Nikolayevich, without investments—moreover, without foreign investments—without the creation of companies with foreign capital, we cannot fill our budget; we cannot solve social problems; and there will not be the leap you're expecting. Investors will come to us if they can be certain of the transparency and the honesty of the auctions held in Russia for the sale of state property."

Chubais continued: "If the state changes the rules of the game, the banks must obey because the state controls the national wealth and is responsible for the very welfare of its citizens. But our bankers think they're the bosses. Even after the elections, they will want to keep taking advantage of us. We need to sock them in the teeth for once in our lives! We won't achieve anything if we don't do this."

But in time it became obvious that Chubais was a hostage in this war. He used some financial groups in the struggle against others, playing on the tensions among the business elite. He didn't know how to keep a distance. He was using the new rules of the game as a political club.

Chubais was particularly enraged at the desperate resistance of Gusinsky and Berezovsky. Many people got the impression that they were using the Svyazinvest auction to assert their own superiority and politically crush those bankers. But it was Gusinsky and Berezovsky who had been the ones in February 1996 to propose to Chubais that he head the election campaign. Together with him, they had created a powerful team of intellectuals who had helped bring about our common victory. "It doesn't mean anything, Boris Nikolayevich," Chubais told me, dismissing my arguments. "Just as they came crawling to you back then because they had nowhere else to go, so they'll come crawling to you now." Although a market reformer in his worldview, Chubais was an absolute Bolshevik in his temperament and approach. That's what bothered me. I was also dismayed by the irreversible consequences of such a scandal within what had been essentially a single team.

Each new nasty article against Chubais and Nemtsov, each fresh bout of mudslinging on television irritated me tremendously. "Do they really not understand that such strong-armed tactics against the president will achieve nothing?" I thought, as I opened up the daily batch of morning newspapers. I was astounded by their blatant attempts to divvy up the pie by wielding these powerful news media.

Looking back on this period, I now see fairly clearly why the bankers' war caught us unawares. The young reformers were trying to overcome a gigantic economic slump in one single bound. They wanted to change the rules of the game. But usually new economic regulations are introduced little by little. There's a good reason for this. New taxes, new tariffs, new fees are announced ahead of time so that the market can adapt to them, and then they are put into effect. But the reformers wanted to do everything right away.

During the elections, financial capital turned into political capital. The banks tried to influence the government unabashedly and directly. They tried to run the country behind the backs of the politicians. We had just barely managed to eradicate the threat of a coup and a Communist revanche and had just started seeing normal institutions of civil society when this new and dangerous challenge appeared.

In today's Russia and in the world at large, the word *oligarch* refers to Russian business representatives who are involved in criminal dealings.* In fact, these people don't have any links to the criminal world. These are not robber barons and not the heads of mafia clans. These

---

* Russia's so-called oligarchs are tycoons who got rich from privatizations after the collapse of the Soviet Union. There are at least seven leading oligarchs: Boris Berezovsky, Vladimir Gusinsky, Rhem Vyakhirev, Aleksandr Smolensky, Vladimir Potanin, Mikhael Khodorkovsky, and Vladimir Vinogradov. Most are bankers, though they also have extensive interests in oil, gas, metals, and the media. During the first round of privatization in the mid-1990s, the oligarchs bought state companies at bargain prices at insider auctions. When the Russian government was strapped for funds for the budget, the oligarchs bailed out the government and bought up Russia's biggest assets. In the infamous "loans-for-shares" auctions, the leading Russian banks lent the government less than $1 billion in return for big equity stakes in the best industrial companies. The oligarchs have considerable political influence, and some have served in government positions at various times. —Trans.

are representatives of big capital who have entered into close and complex interrelations with the government. This is exactly what attracts the public's scrutiny and the fire of criticism; this is exactly what forces both journalists and law-enforcement agencies to study their lives and activities under the microscope. The influence of major capital on the government is inevitable in practically any country. The whole question is what form this influence takes. I'll try to explain how I see these processes.

When Russia became an independent state and embarked upon economic transformations, it first had to complete two extremely important tasks. For one, prices that had been fixed by the state had to be set free; we had to forcibly introduce a real marketplace, just as potatoes were introduced under Catherine the Great. Second, we had to create private property. State property had to be privatized. This was simultaneously a political and an economic task. Without it no reforms would ever become possible. It had to be done quickly. And it had to be done despite the outcry of unhappy people—with any divvying up of property, you will never leave everybody satisfied—in order to create a class of property owners and private property itself.

If the new owner of former state property turned out to be weak, he would eventually be forced to resell his property to another person who was a more skillful and capable manager, and that's how it worked in Russia.

People say that when our property was sold, it was undervalued. They say it was sold at fire-sale prices and that artificial barriers were created to prevent Western capital from entering the market.

That's absolutely true. Property was sold at bargain-basement prices. But it's all relative. If all of these companies—oil, steel, chemical, and so on—were in Western Europe or in America, they would sell for much more. And yes, Western money really did have difficulty getting into our market. But if it had been easier, Russia would not have seen the emergence of its own Russian capitalists, its own Russian property owners. Within five years after the collapse of socialism, domestic businesses obviously couldn't compete with Western capital.

But even the money that was paid for privatizing companies (relatively small amounts) was simply not available in Russia. Where did the money come from? It came in the form of loans that Russian entrepreneurs could obtain on the Western financial market. That is, once again it was Western money.

So the question arises: Why couldn't our entrepreneurs take out larger loans, so the state could have sold its factories for more? And the reason is simple: Nobody would give them more. A factory costs as much as Russian entrepreneurs could pay at a given moment. No more, no less. So in that sense there was real competition, and the prices that were paid were fair market prices.

Before 1996 almost all the state enterprises were privatized. Only a few were sold afterward, including the famous Svyazinvest. By then, the West was afraid of investing more money in Russia. It was afraid of lending more money to Russian business. Our entrepreneurs took a risk, and a big one. If the Communists had won the elections in 1996, of course the first thing they would have done would have been to nationalize all property. Having paid out hundreds of millions of dollars, Russian businesses were vitally interested in the stability of the government and its succession.

That's the point of reference. That's the answer to the question, How did government and big business wind up so closely tied together?

In March 1996 the businessmen came to me to help my election campaign. Nobody asked them to do this, and nobody undertook any obligations with them. They came to defend not Yeltsin but themselves, their businesses, their lost hundreds of millions of dollars, which they would soon have to return to their creditors.

Again, the privatized enterprises purchased from the state were worth less than if they had been located in another, more stable country. So what were our businessmen interested in above all? Political stability. The more stable the society, the higher the capitalization of the enterprise and the richer the entrepreneur. If society was not stable or the elections were unpredictable, their enterprises might turn out to be worthless. Therefore, businessmen were willing to invest money in political stability, and that meant in politics. That explains their extensive involvement in the political processes of Russia.

After the elections the value of the entire Russian market and our enterprises increased manyfold. The world market reacted to the political stability in Russia. The value of all the large companies purchased for hundreds of millions now ballooned to a billion or more. So those who try to depict the Russian oligarchs as primitive money-launderers who give bribes and make a fortune are thinking very one-dimensionally.

Nevertheless, the time had come when the oligarchs' influence upon politics, the government, and society was harmful to the country. It was necessary to set some clear boundaries. The Svyazinvest auction was one of those attempts.

I probably didn't understand the scale of this phenomenon right away, nor its danger. But I did understand one thing: Big money had entered into the political arena. It was this "political" money that constituted a serious threat to Russia's development. It was not the Communists or civil war or a Time of Troubles or local separatism or our homegrown Napoleons in generals' epaulets. No, our greatest threat came from the people with big money, who gobbled each other up and thus toppled the entire political edifice we had built with such difficulty.

The business elite tried to run government affairs in different ways. Some banks brought in bureaucrats from the mayor's office in Moscow; others worked with governors; still others (like Berezovsky and Gusinsky) threw all their resources into the creation of powerful television companies and publishing holding companies and essentially tried to monopolize the media. I remember what a battle raged over the ownership of *Izvestia,* the oldest newspaper in Russia. Representatives of two competing companies chased after the editors in order to be the first to buy the shares.

These new, illegitimate centers of power that had unexpectedly emerged in quiet bankers' offices threatened to drastically change the entire configuration of civil society. Russia had never encountered such a situation. Democratic values cannot be bought and sold, but many thought that's exactly what could and should be done. Some journalists began to work for these new property owners. At first they worked reluctantly, then with passion. It is all rather hard to admit.

Even before the Svyazinvest auction, Valentin Yumashev met with Vladimir Potanin and Pavel Gusinsky at my request. After he left the government, Potanin considered himself free of moral obligations to his colleagues and fought for the new business class by any means. Yumashev proposed that they resolve the problem peacefully, without the news wars and without planting bombs under the government. "As a last resort, you could come to an agreement among yourselves. You could invest in Svyazinvest fifty-fifty. The war you are waging is deadly for you but even more dangerous for all the others." Yumashev's proposal was not received warmly.

Two envelopes were opened at the auction on July 25, 1997. Both investors had brought in foreign partners. On Gusinsky's side were some Spaniards; on Potanin's side stood the famous American financier George Soros. Gusinsky's envelope contained a smaller sum than Potanin's envelope. The difference between those two sums cost us two brutal government crises and possibly one financial crisis. This harsh warfare without rules inside the business elite not only threatened to topple the whole economy but took hold of politics and undermined the stability of the entire political system.*

At the time one of my aides said, "Don't be surprised if within a year you have a general at the head of the administration and a Communist at the head of the government." This forecast seemed excessively grim to me at the time. Later I learned that both Gusinsky and Berezovsky had tried to prove to Chubais that the government had deliberately placed Potanin's bank, which was essentially stuffed full of government money and customs fees (just as in the case of Norilsk Nickel), under more favorable conditions in the auction. But what

---

* Potanin won the auction with a $1.9-billion bid. Gusinsky claimed that the auction had been rigged. A sleaze campaign began in the Berezovsky- and Gusinsky-controlled media, accusing members of the government of taking bribes from Potanin and leaking crucial information to him. Over the next several months, it escalated into a full-fledged war among major players in the Russian economic and political arena. —Trans.

about Berezovsky's Sibneft? And what about Gusinsky's NTV? He had been given the most lucrative VHF frequency for his station. Didn't the state offer privileges to the satellite signal? It was an endless quarrel.

Although many people wanted a review of the auction results, I was adamantly against it. The journalists' pens were poised against Chubais. There were speeches from the militant deputies, and Interior Minister Kulikov and Justice Minister Sergei Stepashin spoke out in favor of reviewing the Svyazinvest and Norilsk Nickel auctions. Even Chernomyrdin expressed some serious reservations. In a word, all the most diverse political forces managed to get in on this war, and every-one tried to exploit the situation to their own advantage. I considered it my duty to publicly declare the government's support. "The dis-putes are over," I told journalists inquiring about Svyazinvest. I insisted that the economic bloc of the government had the priority over all others in this matter.

But the sense of alarm didn't pass. The fierce tone of the press and the mutual recriminations verging on insult left us with no illusions. After the auction the war between the government and the financial elite raged on. In fact, it was just entering a new phase. The open in-tercession of the president was necessary. I needed to pressure both sides of the conflict directly. So I decided to meet with the bankers.

On September 15 we held a roundtable at the Kremlin. In atten-dance were Fridman from Alfa-Bank, Aleksandr Smolensky from SBS-AGRO, Gusinsky from Most-Bank, Mikhail Khodorovsky from Rosprom, Vladimir Vinogradov from Inkombank, and Potanin from ONEKSIM. It seemed to me to be a favorable time and place for the meeting. The Kremlin halls never fail to impress. Visitors realize that they have come for an audience with the government and not a chat with some kind uncle. The bankers listened tensely. Some of them took notes. My message to them was simple: If you think you can go on getting discounts from the state treasury, you're wrong. If we want to survive, the role of the government has to be strengthened in all areas. Business must be separated from the government. You should not be afraid of financial oversight on our part.

The bankers appeared to agree fully. They all said that they were fed up with this conflict. They said they were ready to play by the new rules. But they said these rules had to be long-term; they couldn't change every month or every quarter. "Let's work as a team; let's stop this pressure on the government," I said.

"Yes, of course, Boris Nikolayevich," they answered.

Despite their assurances, I sensed that these men had not really become my allies. Potanin seemed to stick out from all the others. I couldn't rid myself of a hunch that he had his own agenda. After the meeting there was an unfamiliar silence in the room. I had led such meetings hundreds, even thousands of times in the past. In the end I had always achieved some sort of needed result. The most diverse people had been forced to make concessions. I didn't give them any choice. But with these bankers I felt that behind all these promises and smiles there was a silence. It was as if I were dealing with people of a different race, people made not of steel but of some kind of cosmic metal. Not a single side considered itself guilty. There was no area for compromise. There were no concrete concessions. We parted supposedly satisfied with one another.

Chubais and Nemtsov decided to forestall more trouble. On November 4 they came to visit me at Gorki-9. Chubais opened the meeting by saying, "Boris Nikolayevich, a powerful attack is being prepared on the government. It will be a major political crisis. That's why we've come to you. All the reins of the crisis are in the hands of Berezovsky and Gusinsky. We have to put an end to the news wars. If you remove Berezovsky from the Security Council, he will immediately lose his clout. No one will be interested in his opinion, and the conflict will end."

I looked at Chubais and remembered how only a year ago he had come to me and tried to convince me that Berezovsky had to be appointed deputy secretary of the Security Council. He told me how important it was to invite such intelligent people to work in the government, even if they were difficult and out of the ordinary, like Berezovksy. And I had agreed with him at the time. What had happened in a year? Had Berezovsky become less intelligent or perhaps more ordinary? I didn't remind Chubais of our conversation of a year ago. I knew that he remembered it all too well himself.

My vice premiers continued to try to persuade me that Berezovsky had to be dismissed from the Security Council. They argued that a person who mixes business with politics could not occupy this post. They cited examples of how Berezovsky was undermining the authority of the government in the country. This was impermissible.

I summoned Yumashev to take part in this meeting. He listened attentively but didn't argue. Then he said frankly that he was against the dismissal. It wouldn't quell the conflict but only aggravate it further.

I hesitated for a moment, then said to Yumashev: "Your position is clear, Valentin Borisovich. Thank you. Prepare the decree."

Why did I fire Berezovsky in November? My motivations are probably more difficult to explain than it might seem at first glance. I never liked Boris Berezovsky, and I still don't like him. I don't like him because of his arrogant tone, his scandalous reputation, and because people believe that he has special influence on the Kremlin. He doesn't. I never liked him, but I always tried to keep him on my team. A paradox? Perhaps. But those who are professionally engaged in politics or governance will understand. We who are the representatives of this profession are at times compelled to use people for whom we don't have particularly warm feelings. We are forced to use their talent and their professional and business qualities. That was the case with Berezovsky.

Berezovsky was unquestionably an ally. In fact, he had been a long-time, tried-and-true ally of the president and of democratic reform in general. But he was a difficult ally. As he himself said in a television interview, "I've seen Yeltsin only a few times in my life." And that was the truth: There were a few fleeting meetings, a few brief conversations, always official. Even so, people considered Berezovsky my constant shadow. The hand of Berezovsky was seen behind the Kremlin's every move. No matter what I did, no matter whom I appointed or dismissed, people always said the same thing: "Berezovsky!" And who was creating this mysterious aura, this reputation of an éminence grise? Berezovsky himself.

Yes, I was aware that Berezovsky gathered some influential people in his club at the Logovaz office building—media moguls, politicians, and bankers. The conversation was always interesting. Berezovsky always had an unexpected and trenchant observation to offer. We should all be so gifted. Some bold ideas would emerge in these back-room discussions. And each time they would rearrange the pieces on the political chessboard. Most likely these discussions created a certain image and added authority and weight to Berezovsky's words. But it was just speculation. He had no other influence. There weren't any mechanisms through which Berezovsky might have exercised influence over me, the president.

But as soon as the situation would heat up, Berezovsky would go on television and say: "I'm personally dead set against this, I believe . . . I'm certain . . . " Each time he would get a lot of airtime with his spec-ulations. And people would think: "There's the person who's really running the country." I had grown sick and tired of even the mention of Berezovsky's name. Chubais and Nemtsov gave me the excuse to get rid of my hated "shadow."

It wouldn't be easy. I had the feeling that Chubais was about to get his head chopped off. My intuition did not fail me. Berezovsky didn't wait long to react. In a few days he launched the newest attack on the young reformer's government. Berezovsky's news team did everything it could to turn Chubais into a rogue and a parvenu in the eyes of the public. Only a few people in the country knew that in reality Chubais suffered merely for his principles, which he had defended with energy and conviction, as appropriate for the most liberal "Bolshevik."

Events unfolded rapidly. On his desk Interior Minister Kulikov had information about a book called *Privatization in Russia*. A copy of the contract for the book had been quietly filed at Segodnya, a publishing house. The authors of the book—Chubais, Boyko, Mostovoy, and Kazakov (first deputy chief of administration)—were supposed to re-ceive $90,000 each as an honorarium. The press was shouting: bribes and graft! I demanded that Kazakov be fired immediately. Then came the others' turn.

Chubais wrote me a letter that essentially stated that although the book was quite real—it had already appeared in bookstores—and the contract was legal, he considered himself guilty. He had not consid-ered the public's reaction to the size of the honorarium. He accepted moral responsibility for the incident. After that my meetings with Chubais became much less frequent.

The book scandal was a heavy blow, for me and for the government. The entire Chubais team resigned from both the presidential administration and the White House. Chubais was stripped of the post of minister of finance, but he did remain as vice premier. Nemtsov was replaced by Sergei Kiriyenko as minister of fuel and energy, but he, too, kept his post of vice premier. With all the attention drawn to the book scandal, hardly anyone noticed.

And now it was time for me to reflect on Anatoly Chubais. In a matter of days, weeks, and months, Chubais had displayed a fantastic ability to make implacable enemies. This was impossible to explain rationally. Neither Chubais's nature nor his involvement in privatization, which for the whole post-Soviet public was like waving a red flag, explained this phenomenon. Chubais's subsequent career illustrated that no matter what business he went into (the electrical company, for example), he would get into fights. But here's the strangest thing: That's why people respected Chubais. They hated him, they feared him, but still they respected him. He was fired upon from all sides; he was the most desirable target for the Communists, for the liberal journalists, for a certain part of the intelligentsia, and for some businessmen. But it was precisely his intensity, his obsession with ideas that made him so attractive to me. I know from my own experience that a politician cannot suit everybody; he cannot be graciously accepted by everyone. If a politician is real, if he is a major figure, he will always provoke some kind of desperate fury in someone, whether a forty-year-old or an eighteen-year-old. Chubais easily combined within himself both mature intensity and youthful energy. I will never forget the kind of absolute, almost ominous silence that would reign in the meeting room after one of Chubais's speeches. I looked at him, and it seemed to me that he wasn't just an obnoxious redhead, a liberal economist who was out to infuriate everybody. He was a representative of the generation that would come after me.

The book scandal was the banana peel on which the whole team of young reformers slipped. It was painful and awkward. Chubais's political reserves were undermined to a significant extent. I realized that it would take him a long time to restore his authority. But the more pressure I got from public opinion, the press, and the bankers, the more clearly I realized that I would not give up on Chubais. I simply did not have the right to submit to such blatant blackmail, to such outrageous pressure. I was obliged to resist for the sake of preserving some stability in society. Yes, I knew that Chubais had to be removed from the government. I had already made that decision. But how and when this would be done was my decision and no one else's. There was no time for us to lick our wounds. Our economic attack had to continue without a break.

· 6 ·

Kiriyenko

Faced with a deepening economic crisis, persistent roadblocks from the Communist parliament, and constant criticism in the press, Yeltsin realizes that he must dismiss Chubais and the team of young reformers. He also needs a new prime minister to replace the loyal but stodgy Chernomyrdin. A series of dismissals and forced resignations follows. Having purged his staff, Yeltsin brings in a fresh face: the young and hugely popular energy official from Nizhny Novgorod, Sergei Kiriyenko. Kiriyenko holds no connection to the Moscow elite or the oligarchs. He is just what Yeltsin thinks he needs.

·   ·

IN THE SPRING OF 1998, I made a final decision: Another person had to become the head of the government. I had to part with Viktor Chernomyrdin.

Chernomyrdin's main strength was his unique ability to compromise. He could reconcile everyone with everyone else. No conflict was too terrible for him. But that was also the problem. All these years Chernomyrdin had sat through the compromise between the market system and the Soviet directors' corps. It could no longer continue; the compromise had exhausted itself. We had to move on.

And there was something else, purely political in nature. After my departure in 2000, Chernomyrdin would not be capable of keeping the country under control. For that, we needed someone younger and stronger. That was the main reason he had to go.

But that wasn't all. In the last months of 1997, Chubais's relationship with Interior Minister Anatoly Kulikov had become particularly strained. Kulikov actively opposed privatization and the entire liberal economy. He frequently appeared at government meetings not only to criticize economic reforms but also to make open accusations. He would say that the policies of the young reformers were fostering abuse, creating poverty, encouraging criminality, destroying the country, and so on. Chubais gave it right back to him.

At some point I realized that I had to put an end to this growing conflict. Kulikov, who had got his start during the Chechen events, did not suit me at all in the role of the economy's main savior. His methods and his economic ideology could only bog down progress. But Chubais was gradually running out of steam. Stripped of his duties as minister of finance, he could still promote reform, but he would no longer serve as its motor. And a motor was exactly what I needed. That's how I developed the idea that the Chernomyrdin government should be dismissed and the two vice premiers, Chubais and Kulikov, dismissed along with it. By removing the two volatile chemicals, I would prevent the whole laboratory from blowing up.

I have often had to use such tactical maneuvers in my political career, sacrificing chess pieces and moving my castle laterally. My frequent personnel changes had become the talk of the town for news reporters. But allow me to mention several details: Not a single Soviet leader ever had to work around such dogged parliamentary obstruction, with such brutal openness in the press, and the constant threat of free-form political crisis. In order to preserve the status quo, I had to bring in new figures from time to time. I had to promote some people and sacrifice others. But any sacrifice, any dismissal, any change of the political configuration could not be accidental or merely tactical. In each of my moves, I had to keep the overall strategy and main purpose in mind.

In connection with the dismissal of the Chubais government, I contemplated who should complete the economic reforms begun by Gaidar. Who would finally achieve that breakthrough in investments, the budget, the tax system, and land reform? Who would be the new engine of the government's young team?

Bear in mind that to this day I have not grown disenchanted with Gaidar. I am confident that in 1991 he was right to free consumer prices and to introduce the entire project of liberalization known as "shock therapy." It is true Russia suffered through the shock with great hardship. Some people weren't able to find their way in this new life. Some are still searching. And of course the reforms were far from ideal. They often proceeded at an uneven pace, and there was no normal, authoritative, vertical leadership in the country to implement difficult economic changes. The directors' corps went underground and waged guerrilla warfare.

But for me it was paramount that we reject the path of the Communist economy in one swoop. Gaidar achieved the most important thing: He taught everybody, from the minister on down to the truck loader, how to think in market terms and how to count money. And I'm convinced that if we could have let his team work another year, the economy would have charged forward, normal processes would have begun in industry, and we finally would have attracted the Western investment our government dreamed of for so long.

Today, as a generation comes of age that simply doesn't remember the details of everyday life in the late 1980s, it is easy to criticize Gaidar's economic reforms. I was a candidate member of the Politburo, the head of the enormous city of Moscow, and I remember all too well what a desperate position the country was in. Sure, all the factories were running. But what was the point? All the stores, even in Moscow, were totally empty. People had to buy sugar and other staples with ration cards. And we can hardly forget the main image from that era: lines, lines, lines. Lines for everything. The hidden inflation of the Soviet era was much more powerful than today's open inflation. The country was rapidly eating up the humanitarian aid of the West, which had cost hundreds of millions of dollars. In the Politburo we seriously discussed opening our military warehouses and releasing the "strategic military stores"—grains, canned meats, and so on—into the market.

The transition to free trade and the release of prices filled the commodities market in one stroke. But this economic program required the consolidation of forces in the entire society, all segments of the population, all political movements. That's how it was done in the Eastern European countries. And that's how it was done in vast China, where the reforms were implemented by decision of the Communist Party and not one single person dared disobey.

In our case everything was different. No Gaidar law could pass through the Supreme Soviet, and not a single reform that would be painful for the population got through without encountering fierce political hindrances. Instead of common efforts and patience, we encountered stark dissatisfaction and vehement resistance. In 1991 or 1992, after the most serious political upheavals and the fall of the Soviet Union, it would have been impossible to disband the Supreme Soviet, which was severely impeding reforms. A reform government could not work together with a Communist parliament. That was the price of political freedom, which didn't result in an automatic free economy at all. On the contrary, political freedom and economic freedom were very often at odds with each other. So I was forced to say good-bye to the Gaidar government.

Gaidar handed reforms over to Chernomyrdin, and a completely different era began, a slow, careful, and rather contradictory era of economic reform. This era cannot be characterized as marching in place. The banking and loan systems started to function, privatization began, a market of goods and services emerged, and the first class of Russian entrepreneurs appeared. This was a real revolution for our country, where people had spent decades fearing the bosses and were completely devoid of initiative and competition. It was a revolution not only in the economy and politics but also in people's consciousness.

The five years that Chernomyrdin served as my first prime minister constituted a momentous historical period. These were packed years. We experienced several monetary reforms. We survived major political crises. There were huge projects and huge hopes. And there were also huge defeats. We didn't manage to overcome the monopolization in the economy, the fall in production, and the decrepit system of mutual payments that fostered corruption and theft. We didn't manage to invest major funds in industry. And the most discouraging thing: We didn't manage to improve people's lives.

On Saturday, March 21, 1998, Chernomyrdin came to visit me in Gorki-9. It was the usual, grim conversation: the unpaid back wages, the budget struggles. After a pause in the conversation, I took a deep breath and said, "Viktor Stepanovich, I'm not happy with your work."

"In what sense, Boris Nikolayevich?" asked Chernomyrdin.

He looked at me with the doomed expression of an old, experienced apparatchik who understood everything. I enumerated my complaints.

"I'll think about it, Boris Nikolayevich," he said after hearing me out. The heavy door closed slowly behind him.

Am I fair to the people who leave? Each time, with each resignation, that question torments me. Firing staff is perhaps the most unpleasant part of my job. Looking someone in the eye and saying, "You have to go," is the severest kind of stress. Letting the most intelligent, devoted, honest people go is the president's heaviest cross to bear. The people I'm firing usually seem to comprehend that there's nothing personal about it, that it's as hard for me as it is for them, if not even harder. They understand it intellectually, but the emotional hurt is stronger. Because each time, someone else leaves and I remain.

There's another side to these dismissals. Even a few years ago the political stage of the new Russia was empty. By giving a politician the chance to occupy the premier's or the vice premier's seat, I made him instantly famous. I made his actions significant; his personage important. Thus I created an entire cast of political actors for Russia. Gaidar, Chernomyrdin, Kiriyenko, Primakov, Stepashin, Chubais, and others came onto the political stage precisely because of those unexpected, sometimes annoying personnel decisions, which at times provoked so much outcry and dispute. Sometimes I think that I simply don't know of any other way to bring new people into politics.

Chernomyrdin's dismissal was probably the most difficult one for me. Viktor Stepanovich had rescued me and helped me out many a time. Getting rid of a reliable prime minister who had helped me out in such times of crisis was total madness. And wasn't I undermining the position of the young reformers? But now was not the time to succumb to pity or fear. I had to transfer power into other hands. Why? How can I formulate it exactly? As I said, Chernomyrdin is a very strong person, whose chief attribute is his ability to adapt to circumstances. At one time this may have been a most valued trait, but we were already living in another era. The future president, it seemed to me, should have another way of thinking, another view of the world. He should be firm and decisive.

Many people had written about my supposed growing "jealousy" of Chernomyrdin. Apparently, the United States had received him too warmly as a future president, and I had had a "fit of envy." It's true that not long before our conversation, Chernomyrdin had gained confidence in his future political prospects. He was aiming higher than prime minister. But I have never felt jealous toward the strong people who have worked beside me. On the contrary, I've always sought and found aggressive, bright, decisive people. In fact, the situation was exactly the opposite. If I had really believed that Chernomyrdin could become the future president—that he would conduct painful and unpopular reforms in the social sphere and achieve an economic breakthrough—I would certainly have relinquished part of the presidential powers to him and made every effort to help him prepare for the elections. But I saw that Chernomyrdin wasn't going to win the elections. His political method of eternal compromise had taken its toll, the hallmark of cautious rule, and people had grown tired of the same old faces in politics.

I had prepared for Chernomyrdin's dismissal very carefully, bit by bit. Looking for a candidate to replace him, during the three preceding months, I had used various pretexts (usually a discussion of some specific problem) to meet with potential candidates. I wanted a man who could provide a new impetus to the reforms, simply through his own personal energy and mentality. I eliminated a priori the familiar names of famous politicians like Yavlinsky and Luzhkov. I didn't want a person who had the burden of debts and obligations to his party or "his" section of the political elite. I wanted to find a prime minister free from group interests and political ties. That meant that my new prime minister would be "technical," or to be more precise, a technocrat. He would be a manager, an economist. Who did I have around like that?

There were two very strong economic planners in the government. Nikolai Aksyonenko, minister of transportation, was one of the "state monopolists" who had undertaken drastic reforms of his branch and had managed to leap into the market. It was very significant that he had been able to make some difficult and precise steps in the social sphere. For example, he removed the hospitals, clinics, and sanatoria from the railroad budgets. That immediately took a huge weight of debt off the rail companies. The second thing he did was to reject the system of mutual payments. He allowed companies to develop normally by forcing them to pay with real money, and he prevented anyone from putting money into their own pockets under the guise of writing off debts.

Then there was Vladimir Bulgak, who was in charge of communications. Bulgak's sector was economically the most successful. It was stocked with powerful, high-tech companies that were making their entree into the world market. Perhaps Bulgak would do as prime minister?

I stayed late at work, my office dark except for a pool of light from my desk lamp. Everyone else had probably gone to bed. I simply could not make the final decision. I took a pen and I crossed out two names: Aksyonenko and Bulgak. Which candidates remained? One was Sergei Dubinin, chair of the Central Bank. During a reflective conversation at the Kremlin, we had discussed not only the banking business but also a wider spectrum of questions—problems with the economy and the political situation in the country. Dubinin is a real specialist, an interesting and distinctive man. But the Central Bank is the kind of financial instrument where too much depends on the personality of the chair. I didn't want to create new problems in this contentious area. Moreover, I had the impression that during times of crisis Dubinin would display excessive excitability. He didn't seem stable.

Then there was Andrei Nikolayev, former head of the Federal Border Service, one of the breed of generals from the intelligentsia. But Nikolayev suffered from the same flaw as Dubinin: He was too excitable. He wrote a resignation request, hoping that I wouldn't authorize it. He wanted to resolve his conflict with the other power ministers in this manipulative fashion. But in fact I accepted Nikolayev's resignation. I don't like it when people pressure me in this way.

Another no. That left two candidates.

Boris Fedorov seemed to have everything: experience, knowledge, firmness, and decisiveness. Yet other economists of Gaidar's persuasion—Fedorov had worked under Gaidar for a while—had proven to be too politicized and ambitious. One of them, Chubais, had just left the government. No, there would be no logic in such a choice. There wouldn't be any novelty either. It would be a reshuffling of the old figures, and I didn't want that.

That left Sergei Kiriyenko. I had arrived at his candidacy by process of elimination, but now I saw clearly that he had the most possibilities. He would be an unexpected appointment. Kiriyenko came from Nizhny Novgorod along with Boris Nemtsov. They were friends. For several months, Kiriyenko had worked as the first deputy minister of fuel and energy. He had just recently been appointed minister. He was only thirty-five years old. In speaking with him, I was struck by his style of thinking—calm, tough, and absolutely consistent. Kiriyenko displayed the utmost politeness and absence of emotion. He was restrained in everything. He had a very keen and efficient mind. His attentive gaze observed everything from behind round glasses. There was something of the A+ graduate student in him. He wasn't Gaidar, an armchair academic and a revolutionary democrat. This was a different generation, another brand—a manager, a director, a young administrator. What made him so attractive was that he was absolutely free of the influence of any political or financial groups. And precisely because of his youth, he wouldn't be afraid of clashes or unpleasant consequences. He was a real technocrat prime minister, just what the country needed.

Was it a risk? Yes, but a calculated one. If we didn't pass some literate laws and continue these difficult, painful reforms in the tax, land, and social sectors, the country would stay stuck. Russia would have an incomprehensible, contradictory economy. I could no longer justify waiting. I needed Kiriyenko.

None of my opponents, from the Communists to the oligarchs, would expect such a move. But I would give the second echelon, the young team, one more chance. I would strengthen and renew the team. New people would come in along with Kiriyenko. The press and the public were still willing to give them the benefit of the doubt. Kiriyenko could invoke hope and positive emotions. This was very important now. Everybody needed a new figure, not someone who would lobby for the interests of some against others, not someone from some sort of camp, not someone who had already appeared in Moscow's echelons of power. We needed a clean figure. And Kiriyenko was just such a figure.

On the evening of March 21, the same Saturday that I met with Viktor Chernomyrdin, I asked Valentin Yumashev and Sergei Yastrzhembsky, my press secretary, to come see me. I announced to them that I had decided to dismiss Chernomyrdin. Along with him, I would also dismiss Chubais and Kulikov. I asked Yastrzhembsky to prepare the public presentation of these resignations and asked Yumashev to prepare the decrees. Yastrzhembsky sat there, his eyes wide. Yumashev was also visibly agitated. For my young administration, this was the first serious government crisis.

Both Yumashev and Yastrzhembsky asked me to postpone the dismissal from Saturday to Monday. Their rationale was rather simple: It was the weekend; the country was relaxing; many people were at their dachas; it was hardly prudent to create a crisis atmosphere on a Saturday or Sunday. And Chernomyrdin's resignation was a serious political crisis.

I don't like to hesitate in implementing a decision once I've made it. Politics is a subtle thing. Decision-making requires a special, almost surgical precision. A decision should not wait. With any leakage of information, the decision ceases to be a bold, unexpected move and turns into the opposite. There is powerful pressure from the outside, and circumstances change rapidly.

In the end Yumashev and Yastrzhembsky managed to persuade me that the resignation must appear calm and businesslike in the eyes of the public. We would wait until the beginning of the workweek.

"Boris Nikolayevich, who should we prepare the second decree for?" Yumashev asked cautiously at the end of the discussion. He wanted to know who would replace Chernomyrdin.

There was a brief pause. Two people already knew this strategically important information. That was already too many. A third would really be excessive. "I'll tell you on Sunday," I said. "Let's meet again tomorrow, in the latter part of the day."

The next evening I summoned Yumashev: "Prepare the decree for Sergei Kiriyenko."

I woke in the middle of the night and went into my office to think. At night my doubts are always more acute. The finality of a decision becomes more visible. Was I really dismissing this faithful and loyal prime minister, who had passed through fire and water to help me prevail in the most critical situations? Lord, Chernomyrdin had been with me since 1992. I remember how hard we had worked together to bring about political and economic stability in the country. He always tried to lighten my load and take more responsibility onto his shoulders. Perhaps I had made a mistake?

Any faithful ally in politics is worth his weight in gold. It really was dangerous to dismiss the loyal Chernomyrdin. Had I sufficiently calculated the political risk? After all, I was parting with my two strongest and most faithful allies, Chernomyrdin and Chubais. I was leaving myself in almost total political isolation. Many wise words would later be said and written about this "isolation" and my loneliness.

I have a particular relationship with risk. I don't mean that I'm afraid of nothing or that I don't react to danger as other people do. Not at all. I experience the same thing: a coldness in the chest, a certain shocked numbness, a racing heart (which wasn't a very good thing at that time). But in each episode of danger there is one moment of self-awareness. It's a moment when a thought begins to work itself out automatically, looking for an escape. And it usually finds a completely unexpected solution. Risk, including political risk, goes hand in hand with calculation. The most precise calculation is sometimes borne in the most extreme situation. That's how it was here.

I had to force myself to sleep. After all, everything was already done. Everything was already decided.

Monday, March 23, the Kremlin: The hands on the table clocks turned. The polished surfaces gleamed indifferently. But inside I felt enormous tension.

I had scheduled my meeting with Kiriyenko for 7:00 A.M., before my meeting with Chernomyrdin. A government person should know how to get up early.

"If you assign me, Boris Nikolayevich, I'm ready," Kiriyenko said almost immediately. Then he left to collect himself and make sense of it all. His reaction was good. He was a fighter.

8:00 A.M.: my meeting with Chernomyrdin. This breakup was very hard. Learning of his dismissal, Chernomyrdin became very upset. He kept asking "Why?" But what could I tell him? How could I explain the thing, which had given me no peace all these months? We needed another generation, Viktor Stepanovich! Another generation!

I said that 2000 was right around the corner, that I wanted him to concentrate on the coming elections. We had to begin working right away. Chernomyrdin grew flustered again. It was obvious that he was psychologically unprepared to resign. His face reflected a mixture of anger and depression. Faithful, decent, honest, intelligent Viktor Stepanovich. But not president for the year 2000.

With some sort of sixth sense, I suddenly realized this wasn't the last dismissal I would have to make. Far from it. I knew that I had done a very hard thing and that more hard times were coming. But still I felt an unusual rise in spirits, an enormous wave of optimism. I was full of hope. Russia finally had a young government in place, the very thing that I had dreamed of only a year ago. For the first time, a thirty-five-year-old would become head of the country. For the first time, a full-fledged, powerful chance was given to a completely different generation of politicians. For the first time, a leader came to head the government who understood the economy in the way that was needed now, today. Everything was for the first time.

Everything had come true. It had all come true.

· 7 ·

Working with the Documents

A day in the life of the president of Russia. We witness firsthand how Yeltsin functioned at the height of his political powers, determining who should be executed and who should be pardoned, who should be promoted and who should be demoted, which law should be passed and which vetoed. We tour Yeltsin's presidential desk and peruse the elaborate folder system, that helps him to implement his grand decisions of state. As we follow the president through a typical workday, we experience the vast complexity of the Kremlin bureaucracy and glimpse the psychology of contemporary Russian leadership.

·   ·

I GO INTO my office. A few steps and I'm at my desk. I know this desk by heart, like the back of my hand, like the poetry I memorized in school.

On the left side of the desk is the presidential control panel, with direct communication lines to all the leaders of the country (or for that matter, any person in the country). On top of the desk are file folders in three colors: red, white, and green. They are in a specific order that has been established by long practice. They may look light and easy to move, but they are actually very weighty. In fact, these aren't just folders, but something much more. The folders—ordinary paper folders—are another kind of control panel. Not for communication but for something immeasurably more important: for my strategy, for my decision-making. If these folders are moved or rearranged, something happens inside me. I know that for sure. At a minimum, I experience alarm.

You see, my job isn't just making dismissals and appointments or making speeches and visits. In this chapter I describe the everyday details of my work.

The red folders are the most important. These are documents that need to be read or signed immediately.

They are mainly decrees and letters to official agencies such as the Duma or the Federation Council. When a decree comes out of a red folder, a dismissal or an appointment occurs. If it doesn't come out, the decision isn't made. Sometimes several people wait for these decrees; sometimes, the whole country waits. There is a thin pile of decisions for today: Immediate. Urgent. One way or another, the contents of these red folders will be in the news by tomorrow, possibly in the national news and possibly in the world news. But I know one thing for certain: What lies in these folders today will be the landmark, the main event. If a muddled or ill-thought-out decision is made, that means that something is wrong with the entire system, with the whole mechanism for making decisions. Something is wrong inside of me.

To the right of the red folders are the white folders. They contain the inner workings of the government. The government is a machine, if you will, with a motor and moving parts. You can understand how this machine works from these white folders. You can tell whether the engine is coughing or the wheels are falling off.

The white folders hold documents of various offices and ministries awaiting consent. These are not my decisions, not my orders, not my direct responsibility. Behind each line of every document is a complicated interaction of administrative rule. It may be a secret report, a request from a government official, accounts from the Defense Ministry or the FSB or the financial programs. Much of this information remains off-camera, out of the political news. But the inner workings of Russia's enormous governmental machine consist exactly of the papers in these white folders, out of the public's sight. Each one of these documents requires my signature.

Then there are the green folders. As a rule, these contain the laws regulating the lives of citizens. My signature under a law will make it the norm for every Russian citizen for years, decades, or even whole historical epochs to come. Should I give these laws life, or should I veto them? In making decisions about the documents from the green folders, I draw on my entire personal experience, my own understanding of our time. This can be much harder than making political or personnel decisions.

Here is the story of just one green folder: After the fall of the USSR, a flood of missionaries from various countries of the world came pouring into the new Russia. Among them were some wise, worthy people, but there were also religious hucksters and people who would stop at nothing to possess young, undeveloped souls. Religious sects filled the halls of the empty movie theaters and palaces of culture. Pseudomissionaries recruited enthusiastic adherents from among high school and college students. Some sects caused human tragedies—people left their families, jobs, and studies; children ran away from their parents and began to beg on the streets. It caused terrible damage not only to their spiritual growth but to their mental condition. I knew about such instances. The Russian Orthodox Church was referring to exactly such semicriminal or outright criminal cases when it called on the government for tough restrictions on the constitutional articles concerning freedom of conscience. The church wanted restrictions that would essentially prohibit new confessions—new, unheard of religious denominations—from appearing in Russia.

After the law was passed by the Duma in September 1997, a public discussion raged. The intelligentsia, the right-wing parties, and the liberals all demanded that the president veto the law, since it contradicted a fundamental norm of civilized society: freedom of conscience. The pope, President Clinton, leaders of the world's religions, the parliaments of practically all countries, and even my own aides thought I should reject the law.

But Aleksy II, patriarch of all Russia, wrote:

> The law entirely, justly distinguishes religious associations according to the degree to which they have a presence in Russia, the number of their followers, and the time since their formation. It creates serious foundations to protect the individual and society from destructive

pseudoreligious and pseudomissionary activity causing evident damage to the spiritual and physical health of a person, to the national
identity of our people, and to the stability and civic peace in Russia.

That was our church's position.

I was faced with a very subtle and very complicated question of
spiritual freedom. It was easy to use religious freedom for harm. For
many decades, our people had been forcibly denied religion, and now
thousands, tens of thousands of new converts who barely understood
the traditions of our country and the differences between various faiths
were eager to find personal salvation. The church said that it was unfair
to exploit their naivete and ignorance about religious issues, as foreign
"prophets" were now doing. We had to put up some sort of barrier to
this unrestrained exploitation of our Russian gullibility.

Was the church right? Yes, it was. But the Russian constitution is
not a mere formality. Its articles reflect the complexity of relations between the individual and society. Does the state have the right to interfere and dictate what an individual may or may not believe in? Would
we be turning our citizens into obedient sheep? The right of the *minority* was clearly laid down in the constitution—the right to disagree,
the right to be in the opposition, the right to express one's own opinion, the right to be different from everybody else.

Even if there were only a few thousand Catholics in our country, I
could not sign a new law if it created real obstacles to their spiritual
life. I recall how members of sects were brutally persecuted in the Soviet era and how easy it was to become an object of the KGB's perse-
cution if you went to a prayer house rather than a regular church.
Would we resume this practice today? No, never.

So what was I to do? If I signed the law, the entire civilized world
would turn away from Russia and we would once again find ourselves
in political isolation. But if I vetoed it, it would be a heavy blow to the
Russian Orthodox Church and to the traditional Russian denominations, which lacked resources. The Western religious groups, backed
by billions of dollars, would then have legal grounds to rush into the
country immediately and simply annihilate the Russian churches.

I found the solution where it usually can be found: in the middle. Yes, I would veto the law. But in vetoing it, I would make some amendments. These would reflect the proposals of the Russian Orthodox Church and other traditional faiths. Pseudoreligions and pseudomissionaries would not be allowed to corrupt the vulnerable souls of our people. Islam, Buddhism, Judaism, other religious traditions in our country, and the representatives of all kinds of world churches would be clearly protected under the law and state guarantees. I rejected the law in the form passed by the Federal Assembly. On July 22, 1997, I signed an appeal to the citizens of Russia in connection with my rejection of the law; I called it "On Freedom of Conscience and Religious Associations."

"This was a difficult decision," I wrote in my appeal. "The law was supported by 370 deputies of the state Duma, the Russian Orthodox Church, and ten other religious organizations of Russia." I sent my proposals for improving the law to the Federation Council and the state Duma. Soon the amended law was passed with the presidential amendments. That was how the saga of the summer of 1997 ended.

The green files also contained requests for pardons for those convicted of capital crimes. I dreaded those files the most. How to decide a question of life or death? How, with one stroke of the pen, to determine the fate that only God knows? These were terrible documents, chilling to the soul. A person could wind up in front of the firing squad for a crime he didn't commit. Maybe he was an awful person; maybe he was horrible. But what if he hadn't committed murder? For me, this was yet another indication of how foolproof the judicial system must be. The death sentence is utterly irreversible. If a mistake is made, it can't be fixed, and a life is on our consciences.

At times it was actually the dryness of these documents, their calm enumeration of the facts, that really horrified me: "Citizen B., born 1971, only known family: a mother. No previous convictions. Sentenced to the death penalty for shooting and killing a guard, Lieutenant P., with an automatic weapon and causing heavy bodily injury to Private D." I remember this episode well. A soldier had shot his superior. He was a very young fellow and he was guilty; he had taken the life of a young officer who was most likely a father, the head of a family. But who knew what had happened in this young man's mind? What breakdown had occurred in this immature soul? I agreed with the arguments of the commission: He should be pardoned, especially because we didn't have amnesties under this article in the criminal code and he was facing a fifteen-year sentence.

Another one: "Citizen M., born 1973, unmarried. No previous convictions. Sentenced to death for the rape and murder of a girl and also the rape of three minors." This was another difficult case. It seemed impossible to let this beast live. Still, I understood the arguments of the commission and I commuted the death penalty to twenty-five years in prison. Later it was established that the accused had not committed the rape and murder of the girl. That portion of the sentence was removed, and the punishment was reset at fifteen years of imprisonment.

Justice cannot be restrictive or selective. Of course I believe that harsh punishment for rape is required. But under pressure from the Council of Europe, we declared a moratorium on the death penalty for several years. Many people were against this measure. They did not want to leave such monstrous crimes unpunished. Investigators and courts, prosecutors and the public, for understandable reasons were often absolutely ruthless to maniacs, criminals with mental deviations. Their actions, after all, were blood-chilling and terrible. But let us remember the story of the most terrible maniac, Chikatilo. How many innocent suspects were tried before they found the real "butcher of Rostov"?

It's also wrong to rely only on the opinions of specialists and the statements of experts. What about one's human conscience, one's reason? It was difficult. I would tell myself that the remorse of these people could still help. But my hand would sometimes reach toward my pen of its own accord to refuse the request for clemency. Perhaps the green folder was responsible for troubled nights when I could not sleep. Everyone has to bear his measure of responsibility. Everyone.

Thankfully, there was yet another folder with completely different stories and completely different lives. These were recommendations for awards. Although it would seem to require little reflection or work on my part to sign them, these were my favorite documents. Why? It's very important for the government to recognize excellent citizens.

Several awards come to mind from 1997: The writer Viktor Astafyev was awarded a Second-Degree Order for Services to the Fatherland. (This is the most widely granted award in the country. The First-Degree Order for Services to the Fatherland is a state treasure and was only given out once.) I had met with Astafyev many times. Once we had dinner in the Kremlin; I also visited his hometown near Krasnoyarsk, the village of Ovsynka, where he had built a library. He is an amazingly sincere, open person, and he might be called a latter-day Lev Tolstoy. That comparison doesn't seem inappropriate to me. It is absolutely on target. I was thinking something like that when I signed the document for Astafyev's award.

Academician N. G. Basov, one of the inventors of the laser and a Nobel Prize winner, also received a Second-Degree Order for Services to the Fatherland. And the inventor Mikhail Timofeyevich Kalashnikov, a modern Levsha who designed the unique Russian rifle, was awarded the highest Order of Andrei of the First Rank.*

You would think that it's a simple matter to hand out honors. What could be complicated? You take them and sign them. But I have always believed that there is the possibility of risk or unexpected surprise in any affair. One such complex situation occurred when the directors of the film *White Sun of the Desert* were awarded the State Prize. At one time this film, the most popular in the country, had been stripped of the prize because of its supposedly "casual" attitude toward the theme of the revolution. Now the twenty-fifth anniversary of this remarkable film was approaching. But the film professionals felt it was too late to bring back what was lost. Giving the directors an award twenty-five years after the fact would be awkward and strange.

But I went for broke. I was absolutely convinced I was right. If such a beloved national film didn't get an award, then why have awards at

---

* Levsha, the "left-handed craftsman," is the hero in a famous nineteenth-century Russian story by Nikolai Leskov. Levsha wins a village contest by creating and shoeing a miniature iron fly. —Trans.

all? This was one of those rare instances when I thought to myself that it was a good thing that I was president. So I introduced an additional prize by my decree, one especially for the film *White Sun of the Desert*. The winners of the State Prize for 1997 were the director, Vladimir Yakovlevich Motyl, the actors Anatoly Kuznetsov and Spartak Mishulin, and other wonderful artists who brought us this brilliant film. It was wonderful to shake Motyl's hand in the George Hall of the Kremlin. I wasn't offended on behalf of my country. On the contrary, I was pleased.

Things don't always go so smoothly with these awards. Russia wanted to honor the great Russian writer Aleksandr Isayevich Solzhenitsyn with its highest Order of Andrei of the First Rank. Solzhenitsyn had been exiled from the country in the 1970s and had recently returned home to Russia. The writer's eightieth birthday was approaching and was to be widely celebrated by the Russian public. It was clear to me that Solzhenitsyn's life was a real civic achievement. Russia should bestow on him its highest honor. At the same time, intuition told me that it was not going to be easy dealing with Solzhenitsyn. He had grown used to being in the opposition. And though he had returned home, he was cautious and critical about everything that was going on in Russia. In fact, my advisers had reported that he would likely reject the award if it were offered to him.

I recall that I became flustered. What was I to do? It seemed that I *had* to give the award to Solzhenitsyn. But if he were to refuse it, it would create a very awkward situation. How would past and future honorees react? And if we knew for a fact that he was going to turn down the award, should we artificially create some sort of public agitation about it? Or should we simply ignore Solzhenitsyn's birthday?

But something prompted me to say, No, it would be wrong and unfair not to honor this writer. He may have been in a harsh mood, and certainly his outlook was colored by emotions and old wounds. That was his nature. But it is the same nature that also helped him survive all the injustices and burdens that befell him.

I signed the decree to award Solzhenitsyn the Order of Andrei of the First Rank. And along with the decree, I wrote him a personal letter in which I said that the award was being conferred upon him not by me personally but by all the grateful citizens of Russia. Only time will tell whether Solzhenitsyn will ever appreciate this national sign of respect. But even if he never does, I am convinced that I did the right thing in giving it to him.

So what did a day in the life of Russia's president look like? I devoted a certain amount of time to the urgent decrees and letters in the red folders. I had Valery Semenchenko, head of the presidential office, to help me. As a rule, Semenchenko never let documents stamped "Special Importance," "Top Secret," or "Confidential" leave his hands. All those stamps meant one thing for him: The documents had to go directly from hand to hand. Semenchenko would enter my office holding a document. He would report on its contents. I would read the document carefully and sign it if necessary. (In fact, these confidential documents were never supposed to lie open, even on my presidential desk.) Semenchenko would then retire to the outer office and send the document by courier to the addressee, first notifying the recipient on the classified telephone line.

There were some documents that were never sent by courier. They didn't go through the usual procedure of preliminary review by my advisers and aides. They came directly to my desk. Only Semenchenko and I knew about them. These were secret reports from intelligence, references to new types of weapons, and reports about acute situations related to the government's international activities.

Semenchenko had been with me since my days on the Moscow City Communist Party Committee. He was expelled because of his proximity to me, the first secretary who fell from favor. In 1990 I called on Semenchenko to dig out the piles of documents and letters from the Communist Supreme Soviet of Russia. He was the one who, at the end of each workday, put the files away in my presidential safe and sealed it with his own personal seal. He was the one who vigilantly kept track of the documents on my desk. Any notation or resolution I made was immediately brought to the person for whom it was intended. And that's how it was for ten years without a single slipup or delay. Semenchenko is a selfless, decent, and faithful person. He's very conscientious—just what is required of a person in that job.

After the emergency mail was signed and the documents in the white and green folders approved, Semenchenko would leave and I would summon the head of the Kremlin protocol office, Vladimir Shevchenko. We would discuss my agenda for the next workday. Here is a typical schedule:

Wednesday, September 3

10:00 Taping of radio broadcast
10:45 Farewell ceremony for Roman Herzog, president of Germany
11:35 Telephone conversation with Leonid Kuchma
11:45 Meeting with Krasnov, aide on legal matters
12:00 Meeting with Interior Minister Stepashin
13:00 Meeting with Kokoshin, secretary of the Security Council
15:00 Opening of the square by the Cathedral of Christ the Savior
19:00 Opening of the new Boris Pokrovsky Opera House

The schedule was set at least a month and a half in advance. I could not permit myself any leeway, even by five minutes, because I can't stand being late—I know how agitated people can get when they are kept waiting—and because the schedule simply didn't allow for it. I couldn't be late for the taping of the radio broadcast or it wouldn't go on the air at its usual time on Friday. That's unacceptable. Furthermore, the taping had to be finished on time, because I had to talk to Kuchma on the telephone not a minute too early and not a minute too late. The president of another country should not be kept waiting on the telephone. I couldn't be late to see off such a high-ranking guest as the German president. Neither international protocol nor simple politeness would stand for this. Also, any lateness could result in profound dissatisfaction among the protocol services, who would have to look for a reason for my sudden ill will. I couldn't permit myself to do that. I didn't want to disappoint people in my own country.

Fifteen minutes to an hour had to be set aside for meetings with aides, ministers, or the secretary of the Security Council. This meant a lot for both the power ministries and my whole administration. It was important to start and end the meeting on time. I never had to look at my watch because I have an internal sense of time. It helps steer the conversation in the right direction. I remember that Tanya would try to catch me off guard: "Papa, what time is it?" she would ask me suddenly. And without looking at a clock, I would always reply correctly, to the exact minute. "How do you do it?" she would ask. I don't know how I do it. It's just something I sense.

In the Kremlin, a sense of time undoubtedly helped, but the chief of the Kremlin protocol office, Shevchenko, always let me know if there was a delay. It required some fancy footwork. Shevchenko is like a living chronometer. Of course his job description was far broader. Since 1991 he served as my guide in the labyrinth of protocol and as a faithful assistant at all official meetings. He was always near me. He remembered those hundreds and thousands of seemingly minute details that are so telling for any professional diplomat. And his help with ninety-eight official international visits with the president was priceless. Even as his American or French colleagues retreated into the shadows, Shevchenko would interrupt my talk with Clinton, Chirac, or other world leader to remind us that only a few minutes remained before the next event. He was not shy and I respected his persistence.

Where everybody should stand, how the meeting would begin and end—these were all Shevchenko's responsibilities. Any dissatisfaction, any blunder, was not only a violation of protocol but also a loss of status and prestige. Shevchenko took an unusually serious attitude toward his work. In all the years he was with me, he never let me down. He is a unique person, responsive, pleasant, and fantastically punctual.

The papers were signed. The schedule was coordinated. Before my meetings and telephone calls began, I definitely had to turn my attention to yet another part of my desk: the newspapers, magazines, press digests, and summaries of opinion polls. I can't even imagine the start of my workday without them.

September 19, 1997: The Fund for Effective Policy sends me its weekly monitoring of the Russian press, both in Moscow and in the regions, including the electronic media. Here are several lines from their report:

> "The President acknowledged that a strong economy equals
> the market plus a strong state." *(Nezavisimaya gazeta)*
> "The state cannot tolerate more pressure from business."
> *(Russkiy telegraf)*
> "Yeltsin has announced a rollback of the free market."
> *(Kommersant)*

I take a look at the headlines and note the main trends of the week. And what do people think about this? Ordinary people?

October 11–12, 1997: The Public Opinion Foundation provides me with its regular polls.

"Which politicians would you personally nominate today as candidates for president?" In August Zyuganov had increased his rating by two points, from 15 percent to 17 percent. Meanwhile, Lebed's rating had fallen two points, to 9 percent.

"If the Duma passes a no-confidence motion against the Chernomyrdin government, how would you view this?" Of those who replied, 35 percent were for such a motion, 16 were neutral, 25 were against, and 24 were undecided. There were a lot of people on the fence. So there was a reserve. We had to fight to win their confidence.

"How do you usually spend your free time?" A total of 65 percent "watch television"; 57 percent "do housework"; 30 percent "read newspapers and magazines"; 5 percent "work out or do sports." Our whole country, with all its habits and preferences, was spread out before me. Even such a simple question gave me something to think about. I made notations in the margins. I jotted down some ideas that came to me.

My day could not start without taking the pulse of the time, without the fresh newspaper headlines, without reflecting on the mood of the people. And this work culminated in the preparation of Friday's broadcast, when I looked into the black microphone in the Kremlin studio and imagined millions of people listening to me in their kitchens and their cars, at their dachas and in their backyards.

Since 1996 I had been doing this every week. There were troublesome broadcasts, especially when the government was changing, and there were others that were pleasant and calm shows, especially during the holidays.

One of the broadcasts I recall the best was about the middle class. It was a painful subject. Is there really a middle class in Russia? Who makes up this class—what social segments and groups? Is the middle class going to survive in the crisis economy? Is it really the social base for the president, as sociologists say it is?

This is what I said at the time:

Now our citizens decide for themselves: to go on living on their modest pay or to take a risk and open up their own small business—an auto repair shop, a photo shop, an apartment repair service, a private childcare center. Of course, this is difficult. You have to register the business; you have to get the raw materials; you have to look for orders; you have to fight to get clients and elbow aside the bigger competitors. But many people, starting from nothing, have already reached their goals. They have found their way in this difficult but interesting life. They deserve respect.

Yes, it was a good subject. But reading the transcript over now, I see that I could have said things very differently. I should have supported the private entrepreneurs more actively. I should have made tougher demands on the bureaucrats to give entrepreneurs room to breathe. And I shouldn't have offended anybody by calling it "small business," because those small businesses were large when taken together.

On the day in question, I was to meet with the Security Council after the taping. The permanent members and invited guests gathered in the council meeting hall. The topic for today was Russia's defense strategy.

On the way to the meeting hall, I would have five minutes to walk along the long Kremlin corridor, five minutes to collect myself and remember the details in those colossal documents, packed with technical information, that I had studied the night before. What kind of army did we need? As before, one that was prepared to wage a world war with strategic missiles, counterattack weapons, and warheads targeted at fixed geographic quadrants? Or should all our means and resources be thrown into creating rapid-response forces, of which we have few, and which are not as well trained as we would like? The bitter lessons of Chechnya forced us to pay attention to the second option. But our defense strategy is approved too far in advance to reflect the realities of today.

I got up from behind my desk, with its enormous control panel and rows of colored folders, the stern and tranquil presidential work desk. I walked down the long Kremlin corridor. As always, Shevchenko walked slightly behind me. Columns of text swam before my eyes. Numbers. Individual sentences. The documents stayed alive in my mind's eye. A great deal would depend on how clearly I could see and recall them.

Someone once described me as a machine for decision-making. It was very accurate. But this machine must think and feel and must perceive the world in all its interconnections. It must be a *living* machine. Otherwise it's not worth much.

· 8 ·

The Group of Eight and Its Leaders

Yeltsin departs from the dramas of domestic politics to give us a look at Russia's relations with the rest of the world. He works hard to obtain Russia's membership in the G-7, proudly turning it into the Group of Eight. He relates in detail the inner workings and complex relationships of the group as the members conduct summit meetings on the most pressing global issues. We witness Russia's first steps on the international stage as a "normal country," a country that can make deals and reach agreements with other nations in a friendly manner, without the dramatic confrontations of the cold war era or the cautiousness and skepticism of the Gorbachev era.

· ·

BIRMINGHAM, England, May 1998: the summit of the Group of Eight. We were having a discussion. Suddenly Tony Blair slammed his file shut and announced, "All right! It's 4 P.M. I won't make it to the stadium, but at least I can watch the football match on TV. It's Arsenal against Newcastle today—the English Cup finals!"

Everyone in the room understood. The prime ministers of Italy, Canada, and Japan; the presidents of Russia and France; and the chancellor of Germany all stood up in unison and moved toward the TV, chatting with one another as they walked out of the room.

I don't believe that we managed to finish our discussion that day. Soccer turned out to be more important. I still smile when I recall how during the game Italian premier Romano Prodi ribbed Blair, saying "Look, Tony! What a wonderful Anglo-Saxon nose that player has!" The fact was that Italian players were taking over the strongest clubs in the British league. But Blair just joked back. Sitting silently behind him was his "sherpa," as they called the aides at these summits. Sherpas were usually specialists on economic issues. This sherpa sat and watched the soccer game as well.

I have deliberately begun my account about summits of the Group of Eight with this anecdote so that the reader can sense the spirit of the club. And the Group of Eight was indeed a club. It was a club for informal meetings among the heads of the eight strongest industrial nations in the world. All the leaders tried strenuously to maintain the relaxed, friendly club atmosphere. The leaders would change, but the style remained the same.

The Eight had begun in 1975 as the Six in order to facilitate this casual communication. Several heads of the most influential countries of the world gathered by the fireside to have a heart-to-heart. As the years passed, these cozy meetings became an important instrument of world politics. Their spirit of openness and candor provided the leaders with an opportunity to discuss old and new problems on another plane, to bring their positions closer together outside the framework of international protocol.

International visits during which joint or bilateral documents are signed tend to be highly choreographed affairs. The schedules of these meetings and the agendas of the visits are determined by the Foreign Ministries approximately six months in advance. Documents, references, texts of statements, and drafts are all scheduled and regulated well before the meeting. But the world is developing too fast for us to continue to depend entirely on this heavily orchestrated mechanism of problem resolution. Thus was born the format of the Six (now Eight), absolutely solid, compact, and closed. Delegations were kept to a minimum and discussions were entirely open. Nothing from these meetings reached a broader public; only short, general communiqués were issued.

When he was president of the USSR, Mikhail Sergeyevich Gorbachev had already started to talk about the need for the Seven to become the Eight. But it was only in the 1990s that Russia began to be invited to the summits, at first as a "special guest," the financial-economic discussions closed to us. It seemed that this "Seven plus

One" format suited many of the members, as it allowed them to get closer to us. But it kept Russia feeling like a student taking an exam. This was unacceptable. I thought that there should be no double standards. We were either members of the club or we weren't.

When the question of NATO's expansion came up in 1997, we were required to make coordinated decisions with Western countries on the issue. (The conditions of our dialogue with NATO were stipulated in a special document adopted in Paris.) Japan suddenly began to make strong arguments against Russia's full entry into the Seven. Although Japan based its position on the differences in economic potential and financial systems, it was clear to me that the real issue was political: the status of the southern Kuril Islands. It appeared to the Japanese that we were selling our position on NATO in order to gain entry into the Seven. They wanted to extract political advantages. But our joining the Seven was one problem, and political agreements with Japan were an absolutely different one. We didn't feel the two should be linked.

Russia was finally granted full-fledged status in June 1997, at a summit in Denver, Colorado. Our delegation participated in almost all the meetings. Paradoxically, I think that our tough stance on the eastern expansion of NATO, a position I had elaborated at the Russian-U.S. meeting in Helsinki several months earlier, played a role in gaining us this new status. At Helsinki I had declared that NATO was making a mistake that would lead to a new confrontation between the East and the West. (And unfortunately, I wasn't wrong.) The Russian press criticized me for this extreme stance as it was not supported by military and political resources and would only weaken our position in the world. Insofar as Russia had nothing with which to oppose NATO, my threatening statements held little weight. But I soon saw that I hadn't made a mistake. When we were invited to Denver, we were included in the club of Eight.

The bilateral summit in Helsinki was memorable for another detail: U.S. president Bill Clinton had to get around in a wheelchair, as he had slipped on some steps and pulled a tendon not long before the summit. I had very recently undergone a heart operation, so everyone was expecting to see an enfeebled Yeltsin and a Clinton in splendid health. The opposite was true. At one point, I wheeled Clinton in his wheelchair a little. It seemed to make him slightly uncomfortable, but he smiled for the cameras. These pictures were shown all over the world. The image was symbolic: It wasn't a healthy America that was pushing sick Russia around in a wheelchair; instead, Russia was helping the United States. The image recalled as well the postwar Yalta agreements negotiated by the great U.S. president Franklin Roosevelt, who was also in a wheelchair.*

Bill Clinton is a notable figure in U.S. history. America's economy strengthened steadily during his administration. Clinton brought the country into the computer era, expanding its enormous intellectual potential and turning it into the undisputed leader in communications technology. The United States is now the leader among the great powers.

One would expect that Clinton would be a national hero. After all, he fulfilled practically all the tasks that his predecessors had left unfinished. Clinton brought to life the political legacy of all the U.S. presidents of the second half of the twentieth century; he achieved economic prosperity while also providing guarantees for the needy members of society. Clinton did all this. What more could one dream of? What else could one strive for?

Yet Americans seem to regard Clinton not through the prism of all these indisputable accomplishments but through the story of Monica Lewinsky. By the end of his second presidential term, Clinton was forced to undergo the impeachment process. Fortunately, he was not removed from office. But the interrogations and testimony of the president became public knowledge. That is the price of power. Every step

---

* Toward the end of World War II, Winston Churchill, Franklin D. Roosevelt, and Joseph Stalin met in Yalta in Crimea, part of the Soviet Union, and on February 11, 1945, signed an agreement on "common policies and plans for enforcing the unconditional surrender terms which we shall impose together on Nazi Germany after German armed resistance has been finally crushed." The Yalta agreement essentially divided Europe into Soviet and Western spheres of influence.—Trans.

you take and every word you say is examined under a giant magnifying glass. God forbid you should stumble or make a mistake. Nothing is forgiven. There can be no mistakes.

But the highest job in the country is filled not by a machine but by a live human being, with human responses and the ability to take independent action. Voters hardly take into account that such individual autonomy means making mistakes, normal, human mistakes. The scandal surrounding Clinton underscores a simple fact: A politician's top priority is to observe the moral and ethical norms. Ordinary people cannot bear the thought that their ruler could be under the power of some chance variables. A candidate going into a presidential election must always remember this. Clinton did not want Americans to know about the Lewinsky scandal. Later he realized that keeping it secret was impossible. American morality (and along with it the justice system) did not forgive him for these hesitations and doubts.

Of course, I empathize with Clinton because I, too, suffered through an impeachment process, but it is practically impossible to compare the American and Russian impeachments. They are two entirely different stories. However I do consider their simultaneous occurrence as a sign of fate, a kind of warning that aggressive moralizing, which can be played as a political card, can be powerfully destructive.

In my case, our leftist Russian parliament blamed the Russian president for the collapse of the Soviet Union. But behind the smokescreen of ideology there was the same kind of settling of scores that occurred in Clinton's scandal. The political establishment (or the leftist segment of it in Russia) could not forgive either Clinton or me for our toughness, decisiveness, and finally our stubborn focus on our goals. Clinton had so confounded his political rivals that they had nowhere to go. So they turned to exposure and provocation.

I could say the same thing about our Russian impeachment. After losing the first and second presidential elections, the Communists began to look for any means to destroy the president, any way to remove him from his post. They exploited everything—the fall of the USSR was declared a "conspiracy"; the mistakes of the first Chechen campaign were called a crime; economic difficulties were called "the genocide of the Russian people." Every move I made, every word I spoke, all my health problems, from my heart operation to my bronchitis, became a pretext for a major political scandal and for obstruction in the Duma.

Still, I think history will set everything straight and give everyone his due. To some extent, both my impeachment and Clinton's impeachment became turning points for social development in Russia and the United States. We may be different countries with completely different political cultures, social mores, and histories, but we share certain common patterns.

On the threshold of the new century and the new millennium, modern society has become open and transparent because of glasnost, freedom of speech, and mass communications.* Heads of state who want to maintain their posts and conduct effective policy are simply obliged to respond to any challenge. They must directly and honestly answer any question, even if public opinion is trying to intrude upon their personal lives. Presidents must display courage and dignity even in these painful confrontations. And I think in the final analysis that's what Clinton did.

I recall my first meetings with Clinton in 1993. I was completely amazed by this young, eternally smiling man who was powerful, energetic, and handsome. For me, Clinton was the personification of the new generation in politics. He lent hope to the idea of a future without wars, without confrontations, and without the grim ideological struggles of the past.

I understood that this personal, human contact with me was important for Clinton, too. In his view my political steps were connected with the fall of communism, which had been the main threat to America in the twentieth century. Clinton was ready to meet me halfway. No other U.S. president came to Moscow so many times. (And as Bill

---

* Gorbachev's reforms in the mid-1980s began under the slogan *glasnost*, often translated as "openness." The word comes from the Russian word for "voice" (*glas*) and was usually used to refer to giving voice to something previously kept silent or making public something formerly undisclosed. —Trans.

said, probably none will do so in the future.) No other U.S. president engaged in such intensive negotiations with the leaders of our country or provided us with such large-scale aid, both economic and political.

Sometimes it seemed to Clinton and me that we were establishing a new world order, a new future for our planet. These were not delusions, but life turned out to be far more complicated. It would take a long time for democratic institutions to take root in Russia. Society's adjustment to democratic values would be far more painful and difficult than we predicted. International financial institutions alone could not create the conditions for economic improvement in Russia.

As it turned out, Russia and the United States viewed few conflicts in the world in the same way. We had different interests. We had to take a sober approach after the illusions of the early 1990s, for every new disappointment would put Russian society almost into shock. Then the Americans' euphoria about Russia passed; eventually, with the help of a targeted information campaign, the ordinary American saw Russia as a country of bandits and corrupt people. Americans who were dissatisfied with the "pro-Russian" policy of the White House and Russians who were trying to disrupt the Kremlin joined forces.

In some sense the previous accomplishments of the Russian-U.S. dialogue were lost. But in my view this setback was temporary and cannot be compared to the gigantic step forward already made in the era of the "Bill and Boris" contacts. This was truly a historic step. No scandals, intrigues, or political jockeying could destroy this new Russian-American interaction. The United States and Russia ceased to be potential enemies. They had turned into potential friends.

In late 1996 after Clinton's reelection, Russian intelligence sent me a coded report containing a prognosis of how the Republicans would resolve the major political problems emerging for them and noted that Clinton had a particular predilection for beautiful young women. In the near future, the report said, Clinton's enemies planned to plant a young provocateur in his entourage who would spark a major scandal capable of ruining the president's reputation. I remember shaking my head and saying, "There's some morals for you!" But the prediction seemed too far-fetched. It seemed to me that if something like this were in the works, Clinton, with his firm grasp of reality and his staff of brilliant aides, would be able to figure out the cunning plot.

During my last meeting with Clinton, I thought I might give him the text of this coded dispatch as a souvenir. But then I decided not to traumatize the man; he had already suffered too much during this episode.

During the Denver summit of June 1997, a suffocating heat of over 100 degrees hung in the air as a cavalcade of black limousines drove the heads of state through the city. Denverites aren't used to such scenes. There were traffic jams as people stopped on the highway and climbed on top of their cars to stare at us as we drove past. Our Russian-made ZILs, which we had brought with us, apparently made them wild with delight: They yelled and waved their hands. The ZILs must have reminded them of the 1950s, when huge, powerful automobiles like tanks on wheels were in fashion.

The meeting caused enormous excitement in the American press. The Seven had turned into Eight. (The name changed thanks to Russia's initiative, against the wishes of some countries.) Russia had been accepted into the elite club of states! At home, other, more skeptical voices could be heard in the newspapers: Why "the Eight"? What would we discuss? Russia had entirely distinct problems. But despite their grumbling, the papers acknowledged that this was a great step forward.

Of course it was a step forward. The only real difference was that the economies of the other seven countries were improving while ours was only just emerging from crisis. In Denver we weren't invited to the finance ministers' conference on regulating currency values. Because the ruble wasn't formally convertible, there was nothing for us to discuss. It would have been senseless for us to have sat and listened to the lengthy talks between the Americans and the Japanese about whether to raise the yen in relation to the dollar.

I read the critical articles in the Russian press and wondered when we Russians were going to start to consider ourselves normal. After all, it was absolutely clear that the Eight was simply the way it was because of political interests. Russia is one of the most influential countries in the world. Its makeup is unique. We have huge reserves of natural resources, advanced technology, an unbelievable internal market, a highly qualified labor market, and a dynamic society. That is why we were included in the Eight. Why consider ourselves a poor relative? We weren't the eighth ranked member of the club. On the contrary, we were truly respected.

That's why, right from the start, my position at the summits was that the Eight were not to make any special statements on Russia. If the others thought that it was too early for Russia to participate in some special roundtables, that was their privilege. But they could not isolate Russia from the other participants in order to make separate decisions. That wasn't right. This situation came up in Cologne in 1999, when the Eight wanted to discuss their position on Russia's financial crisis. Because of pressure from me, a general statement was adopted on the overall results of the global crisis and the security of national financial systems. In the statement there were several points regarding Russia. It's possible that my persistence appeared strange to some, but I believe that Russia must not be treated as a country that needs help or a country whose problems can be decided by others.

Technically, the work of the Eight is carried out like this: There is a discussion table at which the state leaders sit. Directly behind each leader sits a "sherpa," who has access to a direct line to staff headquarters, where specialists from the finance ministry, external affairs, defense, intelligence, and other power ministries are ready. My sherpa at the meetings of the Eight was Aleksandr Lifshits.

The discussion usually proceeds around the circle. Every leader has his own theme, and the discussion goes from there. My own prepared theme is always outlined on a paper in front of me, but the situation can change at any moment. The sherpa must be able to react within seconds, obtain information from headquarters, quickly deliver it to me, and suggest various approaches to the issue at hand.

Lifshits had some unpleasant moments. At the summit in Cologne, for example, there was a dramatic incident. Helmut Kohl's sherpa informed us that Pakistan had just blown up a nuclear site. Lifshits immediately contacted general headquarters chief Kvashniny. In one minute he received information to the effect that our intelligence service had confirmed the explosion. But Clinton got even more precise information that the explosion had *not* occurred: It was only a demonstration of an explosion in order to frighten Pakistan's neighbors. The real explosion would happen several days later. Lifshits, my economic adviser and an especially civil fellow, was thus caught in a tug-of-war between two intelligence services, ours and the Americans'. I had to rebuke him severely; he in turn vented his anger at our security ministries.

I would divide the issues discussed at summits of the Eight into three categories. The first is economic and financial. Here our strategic goals are clear: to obtain the removal of all restrictions on trade with Russia, its final recognition as a state with a market economy, and its entry into the World Trade Organization and the Paris Club. This, however, was a paradoxical situation. On the one hand, the International Monetary Fund gives us loans and supports our financial stability. On the other hand, the Jackson-Vanik amendment, passed by the U.S. Congress in 1974, still prevents Russia's access to the U.S. market. It was adopted based on the argument that the USSR didn't allow its citizens to leave the country freely. Immigration has long since opened up, communism has fallen, and the Soviet Union no longer exists as a country, but the amendment still stands. We could have earned a lot of money on the world market long ago. We have powerful export items, including high-quality steel, other metals, uranium, technology, and arms. But our hands are tied. Similar barriers and duties exist in the European Union on Russian textiles.

It's worthwhile for us to sign a big contract with a third country— one with aerospace firms for example—as a way of circumventing this problem. In this situation, however, the Americans start quietly, sometimes openly, to put pressure on that country's government. When we tried to penetrate Latin America's arms market to sell helicopters and airplanes, the U.S. embassies began to hold briefings and organize campaigns in the local press. In some fields we have long been competitors. And it's high time we recognized this. I am convinced that all these barriers are temporary. Our industries' recession is only temporary as well. Our financial crisis and its consequences are not eternal. Continual negotiations with the Eight will certainly bear fruit.

The second group of issues concerns security and current politics. I recall an extraordinary summit on nuclear security that took place in Moscow at the beginning of 1996. It was the first summit held in Russia; that alone was of tremendous political significance. I have already written about how my 1996 electoral campaign started up with great difficulty. This unprecedented step by the leaders of the Eight was an invaluable show of moral support. They made their decision a lot sooner than many of the distinguished political elite of Russia.

In the recent past, the Eight have become more and more preoccupied with nuclear security. Countries that had never before joined the nuclear club now threatened to shift the race for nuclear arms in a new direction. That great nightmare of the 1960s and the 1970s—remember the James Bond films?—is turning into reality; nuclear technology has fallen into the wrong hands. This creates entirely new tasks for the "big" countries.

In general, the resolution of complex international problems, including those related to security, is the prerogative of other international organizations. But the Moscow and Cologne summits showed the whole world that the Eight could help NATO, Russia, and the whole European Union find their way out of a dead end. It was the consultations of the Eight that gave a second wind to the negotiations among Strobe Talbott, Slobodan Milosevic, Marti Ahtisaari, and Chernomyrdin, aimed at resolving the Yugoslav conflict.

Finally, the third set of issues always discussed by the Eight involved the global problems of human development. In fact, the club originally came into being because of these problems. Its mission was to prevent the world community from dissolving and to keep wedges from being driven between countries.

Ecology and demographies are at the top of this list. Germany, for example, is very worried about the conservation of forests. Every year the Green Party gains more political influence in German society. Chancellor Kohl and Chancellor Gerhard Schröder could not discount this. Meanwhile, the Japanese are very worried about the elderly population in their country, whose numbers continue to grow. How to keep them occupied? How to help them adapt to the modern world, which is entirely focused on youth? This is a legitimate issue. But to be honest, I wasn't very adroit in discussions about it. The situation with Russian pensioners is much more dramatic. Problems of pension security and social and medical care still haven't been solved. But it's clear that even taking care of pensioners doesn't reduce the acuteness of the global demographic situation. Sooner or later we Russians will have to address similar problems.

There are sometimes funny clashes during the global discussions. I remember during one of the summits I glanced over Clinton's shoulder and saw that he was getting ready to make a presentation on the same theme I had chosen: the Y2K computer problem. We were going around the table speaking in turn, and as it happened I was to speak just before Clinton. What was I to do? When I began, Clinton went white. I decided to throw away my five-minute speech—I had done serious preparation on the subject—and start an impromptu discussion so that Clinton could join in. I don't think he was offended.

One of the great advantages of the summits is the opportunity to chat casually during the recesses. This was certainly true of our 1997 Denver summit. Clinton, Chirac, Schröder, Blair, Hashimoto, Romano Prodi, Jean Chrétien, and I discussed our joint proposals and plans without tension or protocol. Any combination of leaders was possible —two of us, three, four. We would go out onto the lawn; the sun shone; it was summertime. Chirac would come up to me, and we would have a fleeting conversation about future global agreements.

Important international issues were brought up here, often in the space of two minutes. Such informal discussions are simply impossible in the framework of official state visits.

At night there was a dinner break. The simplest jokes were hailed with hurrahs. The sherpas' table was 5–6 meters away from ours. Kohl has his own particular German humor, and when he walked over to the deputies, everyone was waiting for him to say something outrageous.

"What is this?" Kohl burst out as if in a tirade. "You came here to eat? We are going to eat, but you should be working!"

Loud guffaws broke out, but some deputies grew a little pale.

The cultural program in Denver was a concert by Chuck Berry in a huge airplane hangar full of people. All the leaders had been given cowboy outfits as gifts the night before. Bill Clinton came to the concert dressed in that costume, with boots and a cowboy hat. The audience gave the leaders a warm greeting. The almost seventy-year-old rock-and-roll star evoked warm feelings of nostalgia in the other listeners, but I felt far removed from that musical culture. In my youth I sang Russian folk songs—Vizbor, Okudhavu, the songs of Fradkin and Dunaevskogo. It was the middle of the night in Moscow. I went to bed. I guess that night the Eight turned back into the Seven, though I heard that some of the other leaders also dozed off during the concert (from the heat, of course, not from the music). But Clinton was in heaven.

At one of my last summits of the Eight, I looked around and realized that I was the oldest leader there, in both age and political experience. Where had all the elder statesmen gone?

I will always remember François Mitterrand, the noble and refined president of France. It was with Mitterrand that we began the dialogue between Russia and France. To this day I cannot forget the extraordinarily fancy reception he arranged for me at the Elysée Palace when I came to Paris. I personally felt sorry for Mitterrand because he had given so many years of service to his France but then suffered through his last years with a severe, painful disease. Chirac had a completely contrasting personality; he was open, candid, and emotional.

I had also felt connected to John Major, prime minister of Great Britain, a wonderful diplomat who supported me both during the 1991 coup and the 1993 crisis. Though he seemed dry in the typical British style, Major was actually rather warm. Of course his successor, Tony Blair, a child of the 1970s, was strikingly different—lively, passionate, and direct.

Would I fit in here, among this new generation of politicians? It wasn't just that they were younger. They saw the world in a different way, and they saw me, too, in a different way.

I was particularly concerned about the departure of my friend Helmut Kohl, with whom I had met so many times. Kohl, the eldest in age and experience, had always been our unofficial leader. Kohl and I always found it easy to understand each other psychologically. We were similar in our reactions and style of communication. Our great resemblance in terms of appearance, character, and temperament made its impact, and Kohl became the closest to me among the leaders. We viewed the world from the same generational vantage point. Moreover, we wanted to melt the ice that had accumulated in the postwar era between the USSR and Germany. We wanted to warm our relations. After the fall of the Berlin wall, that seemed very important. Gerhardt Schröder, a politician of the new, liberal wave, with social democratic views, would strive for a new standard of relations with Russia, more sober and rational. I realized that from the outset.

Although I encountered a difficult psychological barrier while getting to know these new European leaders, there was a positive side to it all. It would be easier for me than anyone else to secure the succession of relations with Russia, especially because I was the senior politician there. In Kohl's absence the position of the eldest naturally fell to me. That's just how it turned out. Of course there are no "senior" members of the Eight. There is no rank. In general the summits are fully democratic, which was a most valuable feature. I think that the future depends on these meetings. The informal use of *you*, the friendly setup, the lack of protocol are all fundamentally characteristic of the next century.

At one point a very long time ago, Kohl joked: "Don't be afraid, Boris. If you lose the elections, I will find work for you in Germany. I know that you have a degree in construction."

Helmut and I built together all that we could in our lifetime. And I really hope that the building we constructed—our countries' relations—will never fall down, that it will stand solidly for centuries. I hope that my diplomacy in this regard truly helped.

· 9 ·

Meetings in Shirtsleeves

Yeltsin enjoys the camaraderie of other world leaders. He attributes his good relations with them to his own charisma, energy, and innovation, which he considers key factors in winning over skeptical Westerners and gaining Russia a place in the Group of Eight. Yeltsin believes his "meetings in shirtsleeves" are the reason for his successful foreign policy efforts. Whether he's dining in a Moscow restaurant with Jacques Chirac or fishing in the Far East with Ryutaro Hashimoto, Yeltsin demonstrates how casual, off-camera moments improve Russia's role in the world.

·   ·

DEALING WITH DOMESTIC, political, and economic crises isn't the sole duty of a national leader. Equally important is the need to establish and maintain close relationships with other countries' leaders. Fortunately, this is an area in which I've been able to be effective—as well as one that I personally enjoy.

I have already mentioned that Helmut Kohl and I always had a close personal relationship. I could go on about my informal meetings, about our fishing trips, and our excursions to Russian *banyas*. Honestly, Helmut and I often forgot about diplomacy entirely—all the more so in such settings—and kidded around like old friends.

As it happens, Kohl and I stepped down from office at about the same time. Both of our administrations were epochal: Kohl's oversaw the reunification of the two postwar Germanies; mine saw the fall of communism, the breakup of the Soviet empire, and a deep change in the political system and moral values in the former Soviet Union.

But we left our posts in different ways. Kohl, who had already been in power fifteen years, campaigned for reelection, hoping to hold on to his position as head of state. I know that many people advised him not to do this. Despite the immense respect he had gained for his handling of the reunification, Germany was already psychologically weary of him. But he didn't listen, and he lost.

Kohl's example made me realize that the ability to leave is also a component of our presidential work and a part of politics. Great politics is usually the lot of strong, willful people. Power takes hold of a person and seizes him entirely. It's not a pleasant rush to the senses or some kind of instinct; that's only how it seems from the outside. In reality, I think that after several years of rule, many of us experience a total emotional drain. The struggle with circumstances, the political logic, and the terribly stressful work require all of a person's physical and emotional strength. That's what takes hold of you. Few people are capable of enduring such self-sacrifice. Power attracts people of this kind.

Despite the received wisdom, I never clung to power and was always willing to step down on my own. Both in 1996 and in 2000, the decision whether or not to resign was not about myself and my needs but what I would leave behind me, what legacy, what testament. Several times, both before and after 1996, I initiated discussions with my closest aides about an early resignation. I told them that I was tired and that the country was tired of me. But again and again I was convinced that there still wasn't an alternative. I couldn't leave if my departure would threaten the democratic process, stop the progress of reforms, or possibly throw the country into reverse. Who among the new politicians could have been nominated as a national leader? Who was ready to take responsibility for a country with a transitional, crisis-ridden economy; a leftist parliament; and misfiring mechanisms of civil society? I couldn't throw an already unstable Russia into a new whirlpool of political passions. As God is my witness, I was absolutely sincere.

Even while I struggled with these personal decisions, I had to maintain a strong, bold stance to the outside world. It was crucial that Russia preserve its international relations, especially with the leaders of Western Europe, China, and Japan. Thankfully, I had been blessed with two great allies, Helmut Kohl and Jacques Chirac. Not only had we grown up together at the negotiating table, but we are also cut from the same mold. Kohl and Chirac are not just my colleagues, not just my counterparts; all three of us are children of the war. We are from the same generation. We are direct, outspoken, even harsh. We feel a sincere sympathy for one another.

Now, one can argue that real-life diplomacy is a lot more than personal understandings or psychological relationships. But only someone who has attended high-level diplomatic meetings knows how much depends on the atmosphere and the contact between people. Security and trust are often built by diplomacy in shirtsleeves, the diplomacy of friendship. The more casual, friendly meetings we could have, the more secure Russia's international relations would be.

I first came up with the idea of a meeting in shirtsleeves at a forum in Strasbourg in 1997, when Chirac, Kohl, and I took questions from journalists in the hallway of a building. I realized that we had many more issues to discuss and that we could all benefit from a more informal setting. The others agreed.

We decided to meet in March of 1998. I had originally wanted to invite Kohl and Chirac to Yekaterinburg, my native region. I wanted to cross the border between Europe and Asia on foot; I wanted to show them where the geographical limits of Europe in fact ended. I wanted to exalt the mighty Urals before my friends. It was a beautiful, symbolic plan. But it was difficult to coordinate the schedules of all three leaders, even for two to three days, and I didn't want to postpone the meeting. That's why we transferred it to Moscow, to the holiday resort at Bor, located within the city limits. Chirac and Kohl flew in around midnight and departed the next day. Our gathering was short but very memorable.

The Russian press was keen on the idea of the meeting. Chirac called it "a world premiere." It was evident even to the most cynical of observers that something unusual was going to take place. At the same time—and this was absolutely justified—people wrote that our "informal" diplomacy, our unofficial negotiation table, would not pose any threat to Atlantic solidarity. The special relationship shared by Germany, France, and Russia was a given for the Atlantic alliance. Besides, discipline within NATO is iron-clad. Britain and the United States were the steel backbone of NATO. And I am sure that Kohl and Chirac coordinated our three-way contacts with the Americans. The latter had a fairly mild reaction to the meeting.

The British did not react so calmly. They started sending signals to our foreign ministry, using different diplomatic channels, saying that they were also ready to participate. On the one hand, I was glad. On the other hand, I didn't want to expand the meeting, and the presence of the recently elected Tony Blair would have ruined our psychological and political comfort, which was the specific background to our coming together. Without this element of freedom, meetings could become very stuffy. But most important, Blair was from another generation and another mentality. With him present, the meeting would have become too official. And the whole point was to have a personal, friendly discussion among three old-style leaders. In short, we sent a reply to the British department of external affairs that the "casual" meeting should first be tried out in this format. We would then see what would come after that.

Later, as we were getting ready for the gathering, the Italians and other European countries displayed a cautious interest as well, but we carried on with preparations for a three-way meeting.

We proposed to Chirac and Kohl a discussion of the concept of a "Great Europe"—a "Great Europe" extending to the Urals as a space for an entirely new Pan-European policy. We did not want a policy of blocs or alliances; we hoped instead to build truly new links and personal contacts inside this area. We discussed a full range of international programs: a twenty-first-century transport plane (AN-70); a London-Paris-Berlin-Warsaw-Minsk-Moscow transport corridor, heading toward Yekaterinburg and Siberia, which would include a high-speed autobahn and railway; a rapid-reaction force to cope with technological and natural disasters; an exchange of undergraduate- and graduate-level students among the universities of Russia, France, and Germany; the creation of a common French-German-Russian university; and a provision to ensure mutual recognition of diplomas of the three countries. We agreed to hold a major Moscow-Berlin-Paris exhibit. Our historians would write a textbook entitled *The History of Twentieth-Century Europe,* a history without ideological partitions and walls.

We all understood that our troika had been called to counterbalance the disequilibrium that occurred in Europe after NATO borders came closer to Russia. To quote Kohl: "France and Germany carry a special responsibility for the policies of the European Union, and they want to do all they can so that nobody gets the impression—in the world at large or in Moscow—that the processes occurring in Europe are leading to the isolation of Russia." During our first meeting with journalists, I emphasized my idea of a "Great Europe": "There is no more terra incognita in Europe. There is only one common world on the continent, on our continent."

The very atmosphere of the meeting was infused with an important idea: Something was needed to oppose the American pressure—a will to collaborate, an independent European determination. I was inspired. It seemed to me that a fresh attitude fluttered in the European air. Kohl and Chirac's faces were not at all as they were in official summits and conferences. I saw a great understanding in their eyes.

Unfortunately, the English-speaking world didn't see it that way. They reacted to the troika summit with a certain jealousy. The British press wrote that the three-way meeting was the first step toward an "almost undisguised anti-American bloc in Europe."

And two years later it was clear that we were already approaching the very issue of the troika in different ways. Kohl and Chirac—as the guarantors of internal European stability—wanted to soften my tough attitude and statements about NATO, while I was only dreaming of creating, albeit temporarily, a purely humanitarian axis: Moscow-Berlin-Paris.

Our casual troika had a talisman, a souvenir created by our Ural craftsmen: a gold key with a globe on top. The capitals of the three states shone prominently on the globe, which held three silver ladles of friendship. At the meeting I started to unscrew the key from the globe, but it wouldn't turn. I called Yastrzhembsky for help. Everybody laughed. Finally, with great effort, I managed to unscrew the key and hand out the ladles, which looked like little boats. But then, when I wanted to present the guests with their own keys, I discovered there was only one. Where were the other two? What was I to do? Kohl always understood me well. Now, in his inimitable way, he grinned broadly, and said, "We understand, Boris. The key stays with you. The key is Russia's. But it belongs to all of us."

Thank heavens I had also prepared another gift for the leaders of the two countries. At my request a talented thirteen-year-old girl named Pegaleya sang Russian songs for the guests, dressed in a brightly colored national costume. She was the genuine, living, smiling, and charming Russia. Her voice was so light and pure, and the girl herself so spontaneous, that Kohl and Chirac were enchanted. Chirac was so moved that he even invited her to perform in Paris. To this day I am grateful to this girl for her participation in "great politics." Not every diplomat has given me such invaluable help during a major international meeting.

Although these informal meetings went rather well, international protocol has always been a kind of stumbling block for me. I quite frequently violate established rules. My "mistakes" are simply due to a feeling of inner freedom, relieved that the vestiges of Soviet diplomacy no longer weigh on me. But by violating the protocol I grew to understand its worth. Experience over the centuries shows that heads of state are obliged to comport themselves not simply as friends but also as guarantors of national interests and as envoys of their countries. How to combine my aspirations for complete sincerity and freedom given strict protocol? At times I made statements that appeared completely unjustified. It was difficult for my press secretaries, first Sergei Yastrzhembsky and then Dmitry Yakushkin, to explain their meaning. But these statements always took place within the context of concrete agreements, during very difficult negotiations with the other leaders of the Group of Eight, and they were necessary right then and there. But more often than not the press didn't understand this context and reproached me for being undiplomatic. It seems to me that I took this direct approach from the time I became president. I wasn't afraid to show myself exactly as I am. And this almost always produced results.

One particular instance in which lack of protocol helped bring about cultural and diplomatic rapprochement occurred in September 1997, when my wife and I invited Jacques Chirac to a restaurant, of all places. Usually ceremonial meals during such state visits are held in the Kremlin, but this time it was different. I wanted to show Jacques something that touches the heart of a Frenchman: a normal, private restaurant, where anybody with a good salary—a businessman or a representative of the middle class—can go to have a good time, just as in Paris. There are hundreds of such places in Moscow now; expensive ones, cheap ones. But it's one thing to know about them in theory and another to see for oneself what a regular Russian restaurant is like.

The most competent person to handle the task of choosing our dinner spot was Sergei Yastrzhembsky. He thought for a long time, mulled over the various establishments he had visited in both an official capacity and for pleasure, and said: "The best place for you to take President Chirac would be the Tsar's Desire. It's the most stylish Russian restaurant."

Sergei wasn't wrong. The restaurant turned out to be very original. It had a wood-paneled interior, with rifles, bearskins, and hunting trophies on the walls. In fact, the excursion to the restaurant was quite a treat for me, too. I couldn't remember for the life of me the last time I had been to a normal restaurant instead of an official reception or my residence. Maybe it was thirty years ago, in Sverdlovsk?* For a president, it's exotic to go to a restaurant, to sit side by side with normal people. For security precautions and other reasons, it hardly ever happens. But just like that, Chirac and I successfully broke this tradition.

---

* Now renamed Yekaterinburg as in the pre-Soviet period. Yeltsin served as Party Secretary of the Sverdlovsk region in the 1980s.—Trans.

(And at the same time, we created another one; within a year he took me to a cozy little restaurant in France.)

Besides, we didn't put ordinary people out of their way. Instead of closing the restaurant for a "private party," the security people let in all those who had made advance reservations. We were eight at the table: Jacques; his wife, Bernadette; their daughter, Claude; myself; Naina; Tanya; and two interpreters. I really liked Jacques's interpreter, a small, brunette Frenchwoman with instantaneous reactions and a superb knowledge of the Russian language. Incidentally, Chirac has a reputation of being a Russophile, intensely interested in anything Russian. In his youth he loved Pushkin's works and recited his poetry.

The table was well chosen—we sat a little off to the side—and nobody bothered us. Among the drinks, Chirac especially liked the specialty vodka called Yury Dolgoruky. We talked animatedly, laughed, and told Jacques and Bernadette about Russian traditions and Russian food. As the host, I paid for the dinner, of course. There were no reporters or photojournalists, only personal photographers, so the evening was quiet.

In fact, one cannot underestimate the significance of all these informal meetings for Russia. Within a year, Russia became a full-fledged member of what was now the Group of Eight. We became a valued participant in the international dialogue. There was meaning behind every summit; every meeting of the leaders of the eight countries was for us like a serious test. Because of this, any help, any support from my international friends was extraordinarily important. I felt Russia's position strengthen with each summit. My political experience contributed to this, along with these meetings in shirtsleeves.

But then a cold wind began to blow in our relations. Several domestic crises reversed the progress of our casual diplomacy. In August Russia's financial system crashed. Of course the Western European countries reacted with great sympathy. They telephoned constantly, offered the help of technical specialists, and made statements of support and understanding. But Russia's default and refusal to pay back its loans was still a very painful issue in international affairs. The fall brought the feverish activity surrounding Primakov's nomination as prime minister. The second meeting of the troika had to be postponed indefinitely. And then the Kosovo crisis struck.

During the course of one year, our relationship took a huge step backward. The war in Yugoslavia allowed the Americans to put North Atlantic solidarity back on the track they wanted. What the conflict cost Europe and what such "blood brotherhood"—unification through bloodshed—would lead to was another matter. But nothing is in vain. I am deeply convinced that present-day leaders will come back to the idea of a "Greater Europe" and the humanitarian construction of a new European civilization, together with Russia.

Informal meetings improved our relations with more than just the West. In early November 1997, I went fishing with Japanese prime minister Ryutaro Hashimoto in the environs of Krasnoyarsk. There was an entirely different, special subtext to this informal meeting. We didn't choose Krasnoyarsk, a city located between Moscow and Tokyo, by chance. And it was no accident that we hid far away from the eyes of observers, including journalists. It may have seemed like two leaders taking a tourist outing on the great Siberian river, but it was much more. The sensitive subject of the southern Kuril Islands had long stood between Japan and Russia, practically bringing our collaboration to a standstill. The issue had prevented us from signing a peace treaty between our countries, a treaty that the peoples of Japan and Russia had been awaiting throughout the postwar decades. Ryu and I wanted not only to catch some fish but also to find peace, a true peace, based on precise agreements.

Zubov, then the governor of Krasnoyarsk, had arranged for the presidential and prime ministerial delegations to spend a day at two wonderful, small houses called the Pines. On November 1, under damp, gray, and unpromising skies, our cutter took off from the landing. Hashimoto wore a bright yellow down jacket. He looked like a photojournalist, and like a typical Japanese, he constantly took pictures. Finally, he put away his camera and smiled, and I was sure then that our meeting would be successful. Despite the rain, the cold, and the piercing wind, the Russian landscape—thick woods, smooth river, fresh air—made a powerful impression on Hashimoto. He laughed and joked.

We were told that a fishing spot had been prepared for us several miles from our residence. The temperature was 2 degrees celsius, and a strong wind cut us to the core. On shore there was a hastily erected hut draped with skins and some tents from which wafted the aroma of fresh fish soup. I thought, "If they are already making fish soup, why should we fish?"

The backwater contained several man-made pools, enclosed by rocks. I was told that there was a bend in the river where the current was not as strong. We went to take a look. Long fishing rods were lying waiting for us. I didn't like this: Should I go ahead and cast a line? But Hashimoto went first, felt a tug on the line, and smiled broadly: He had already hooked a fish. It was, shall we say, a surprise for the guest.

I looked at Ryu in mock surprise—"You already caught one?"—and smiled to myself.

The Yenisei is a willful, mighty river, not really amenable to fishing trips. The wind rocked and whipped the water, washing away all those artificial fences. The fish fled instantly. I realized this right away, but I kept on fishing. The rain poured down, the wind whipped about, and Hashimoto and I stood in our pools and held onto our fishing rods. I didn't know what to say to him, and he didn't know what to say to me. This went on for about an hour, until we were almost stiff with cold.

Only vodka could have warmed me up, but I was forbidden to drink at that time. So it took me a long while to recover from our fishing trip. But Hashimoto smiled as he sopped up the fish soup with bread. The skins he had taken from the hut and the yellow down jacket had protected him well from the wind.

We conducted the most difficult and secret part of the negotiations in that exotic setting, on the cutter. The situation was very clear to both Hashimoto and myself: Our countries couldn't continue to build relations without a peace agreement. It simply had to come about, just as the 1975 Helsinki agreement had, greatly relieving tension on both sides.

But for the Japanese, peace was tied to the question of the northern territories. They were unable to make concessions on this matter. They are raised on the issue; it's as though they consume it with their mother's milk. But we couldn't make concessions either. The territorial integrity of Russia has its basis in the constitution. Neither the Duma nor public opinion would agree to a voluntary and one-sided revision of the postwar borders. We were at a stalemate.

But there can't and shouldn't be dead-ends in international politics. It was extremely important for Russia to reach a peace agreement with Japan. In the offing were major Japanese investments in Siberian industry, the energy sector, and railways. In essence, Russia's economic revival depended not on the West but on the East. Yet the territory of the southern Kurile Islands was home to many generations of Russians. We had a real geopolitical conundrum on our hands.

The issue of the northern territories had long been under discussion. The Japanese had proposed many different solutions: joint ownership, joint access, rental for ninety-nine years, and so on. At the root of all these proposals was one important but absolutely unacceptable element for us: The Japanese considered the islands their own. At one point in the discussions, I thought that we should cut through that proud knot with one swipe. There was one legal option that allowed the Japanese to quietly make use of the islands without encroaching on our territorial integrity. But I quickly and categorically rejected that alternative. The period of secret protocols had come to an end. Nothing good would come from a return to this practice.

But neither Hashimoto nor I wanted to leave without results. We took another route. We proposed not linking the territorial problem to economic collaboration. The Japanese named this approach the "three new principles": trust, mutual advantage, and a long-term perspective. The trust took root right there, on the banks of the Yenisei, where we began to address each other using the informal *you*: Ryu and Boris. The journalists declared that our personal relationship had risen to a "qualitatively new level." And in fact we began to get a better sense and understanding of each other. Both Hashimoto and I wanted to present our countries with at least the prospect of a peace agreement.

At the press conference we stated that a peace agreement between Russia and Japan would be signed before 2000. This was good news for the Japanese and the Russians alike. Although Hashimoto and I were unable to fulfill our promise, the tone of our relations did change for the better beginning at Krasnoyarsk. There at the Pines we concluded a few concrete resolutions on joint fishing arrangements and bank guarantees for Japanese investments.

"Moscow," the newspapers wrote, "saw in Japan a government with the vital capacity to help Russia financially and technologically. And Tokyo saw in Russia a powerful potential strategic ally with the capacity to strongly influence world policy in accordance with Japan's wishes. In addition, Japan is seriously interested in developing a broad military-strategic cooperation with Moscow. The pure economic interests of both Japan and Russia shouldn't be ignored as regards Russia's huge consumer market and the inexhaustible supply of valuable natural resources, which frankly go beyond our share of the Japanese islands."

As a farewell present, Ryu gave me an outfit for my grandson Vanka, who had just been born. I brought it back to Moscow with immense pleasure.

My visit to the Vatican in December 1991 occupies a very special place in my series of official travels. Pope John Paul II is one of the last legends of the twentieth century, an enigmatic, great personality. After the revolution, that is, throughout most of the century, there were no diplomatic relations between Russia and the Vatican. They were reestablished only in 1990, thanks to John Paul II. During his long reign of more than twenty years, the pope probably conversed with hundreds of presidents and prime ministers. But I somehow think that our discussion made a particular impression on him.

First of all, we conversed in Russian. The pope grew up in postwar Poland, and he had not forgotten the Russian language. I found it interesting to hear the way he chose his words, how he constructed his speech. From the beginning, it seemed that this stooped, wizened old man didn't consider himself to be important at all. But when he cast his clear, penetrating gaze upon me, I was astounded at the lively intelligence that shone in his eyes. Even within the rigid canon of the Roman Catholic Church and its measured life, he had managed to maintain his restlessness, his passion for reform, and his profound individuality.

I told the pope that I very much wanted him to come to Moscow. I knew that this suggestion was risky, as much depended on the position of the Russian Slavonic Church. But I couldn't help admiring the reformist strengths of the pope and his missionary activities. The previous popes in Rome had never recognized the sins of their predecessors. John Paul II was the first in history to recognize that the church had committed sins in the past, including the split in Christian unity, the religious wars, the trials of the Inquisition, and the Galileo affair.

John Paul II has also confessed the modern-day sins of the church, including its silence in the face of totalitarianism. He has always struggled against communism. This quality made him accessible and understandable to me. I liked the fact that he is a many-sided man: a philosopher, a sportsman, an actor, a poet, a playwright, and a political figure. So it was with great pleasure that I gave the pope a collection of his own poetry, translated into Russian and published in Russia. He thanked me and wished me good health. Then he asked whether he could meet the entire Russian delegation. I honestly can't recollect such an occurrence during the whole of my lengthy political service. All those who had traveled with me to Italy stood in the immense hall of the Vatican: drivers, guards, waiters, the hairdresser, all my advisers, all the interpreters. There were thirty people in all. The pope greeted each one, gave each a souvenir, and looked each person directly in the eye. It was the gesture of a holy man—not a holy man by trade but by calling, from the soul.

At one time the role of church hierarchies and members of royalty was well defined in politics. This is less true today. One of the more colorful exceptions is the Spanish king Juan Carlos II. His story represents a striking paradox in the history of the twentieth century. The dictator Francisco Franco, a person with extremely right-wing views, decided to resurrect the monarchy in his country so as to forever preserve Francoism in Spain. For this purpose, he brought the ten-year-old heir Juan Carlos (in agreement with the boy's father, the count of Barcelona) to study in Spain.

In 1969 Franco named Juan Carlos to the throne. But the young king didn't adopt the general's hatred for the republican, democratic structure of society. On the contrary, Juan Carlos became the guarantor of Spanish reform. After the death of Franco in 1976, he declared a general amnesty, rehabilitated political parties, replaced the head of government, and in 1981 prevented a military rebellion. Spain became a democratic country and remains so today, thanks to the king. It was his solid stance that proved a reliable shock absorber for diverse political crises.

It was very interesting for me to meet the king and his enchanting wife, Sofia, the daughter of the last king of Greece. We met in Madrid in 1994 and again in Moscow in 1997. They make a wonderful pair—beautiful, totally democratic, and unusually lively people. Naina chatted with Queen Sofia about art, and the king and I conversed about hunting. Like myself, he is an avid hunter.

The 1994 visit to Spain was memorable for its wonderfully positive atmosphere. Perhaps this sensation was heightened by a personal encounter I had; in Barcelona I was reunited with a surgeon who had saved my life: He had performed a difficult spinal operation on me after an airplane accident back in May 1988, saving me from total paralysis. It was a delight to see this smiling man again. No doubt I felt a special warmth toward the Spaniards because of my unofficial hospital visit.

When the king and queen showed us the Prado Museum, with its wonderful paintings, when they spoke about Goya and Velázquez, I saw in the king not just the figure of a monarch but a nice, ordinary fellow who, owing to his extraordinary fate, had become the spirit of Spain, the favorite of all Spaniards. I envied the king a bit because, after all, he could distance himself from everyday politics and the passions and scandals that are a part of public life. I recalled looking at the king and thinking, No, it's not wrong that humankind wants to cling to the tradition of monarchy. Although we are already entering the third millennium, there is something to it. For Spain, which had thrown off a totalitarian system, the king was a true savior.

In contrast to these unfettered, informal meetings, I often recall one of my most demanding state visits, at least with regard to protocol: the 1994 Moscow visit of Queen Elizabeth II of Great Britain and Northern Ireland and Prince Philip, duke of Edinburgh.

These magnificent titles were so unfamiliar to us, the royal ceremony so unusual, and the protocol so precise and detailed that looks of confusion registered on the faces of the Russian officials witnessing the affair. Not everyone was able to dress in the proper formal attire, as few people had such clothing in their wardrobes. The Foreign Ministry's stock of official formal wear quickly ran out, and when someone sought out a theatrical supply house, it soon became obvious that formal attire for the stage is completely different from what is appropriate for royal state visits.

This trip to Russia was no mere exoticism. The queen of England was visiting our country for the very first time. Over the course of several decades of rule by the House of Windsor, no British monarch had set foot on Russian soil after the revolution because the Windsors were relatives of the Romanov family, which had been executed. The queen couldn't visit a country that hadn't repented after that bloody execution and after all the horrors of the Stalinist years. But then came the years of repentance, repentance before the memory of all the innocent persons who were murdered during the revolution, the civil war, and the repression. The queen's first visit to Russia was a historic acknowledgment that our country had finally rejoined the community of civilized nations. I understood that the queen's status was so great that it was necessary to regard her visit as historically symbolic.

But of course the queen and her husband are also real, live people. I very much wanted their days in Russia to be warm and festive. We went to *Giselle* at the Bolshoi Theatre. Queen Elizabeth had seen a pro-

duction of this ballet in London forty years before, during the Bolshoi's first world tour. At that time the legendary Galina Ulanova had
performed the leading role; this time Ulanova's student, the soloist
Nadezhda Gracheva, danced the lead. I thought the queen would experience something more than a mere ballet, that this would revive a
memory from her youth, a memory of those scenes and impressions
that sometimes accompany us throughout our lives.

I remember the crown that Queen Elizabeth wore while seated in the
theatre box—the real thing, no museum piece. It gleamed as a symbol of
the British monarchy that had lost none of its strength. I remember our
visits to historic monuments and sacred places in Russia—the Kremlin,
Peter the Great's Hermitage, cathedrals, palaces, the Piskarev Memorial.
At the same time, Queen Elizabeth had the opportunity to see our life
from a completely different, nonceremonial point of view. For example,
her highness was invited to a recital by a drama club at Moscow School
Number 22, which is well known for its English traditions. *Hamlet* was
being staged in the original language. She mingled with ordinary
Moscow children, and they caught a glimpse of a real queen. I think
everyone was fortunate—the queen as well as the children.

The queen left us a wonderful gift: a simple, polished wooden box.
It reminded me of some kind of children's fairy tale. I opened it, and it
turned out there were several sliding compartments within the box.
Inside the compartments were packets of seeds. It was a complete collection of seeds from the royal garden—a truly English gift. Naina,
Lena, and Tanya spent a long time studying the seeds of these exotic
plants. They first cultivated them in a greenhouse and then planted the
seedlings. Of course in Russia not all of the plants from this royal collection, transplanted at one time from southern colonies, could grow.
To our great regret, many did not take root, but others are thriving.
They please the eye. The royal family remains forever in our memory
and in our family garden.

After many years of cool relations, China is gradually becoming one of
Russia's most important strategic partners. With its powerfully devel-

oping economy, China is now entering the multipolar world.* The time has long past when Communist China suffered complete isolation from the world and posed a potential threat to Asian security. Today, China, which has preserved ruling tradition from Maoism, is a different country, a modern, dynamic state that advocates a pluralistic approach to the resolution of difficult international problems. It is also a very important ally of Russia.

When the Russian-Chinese informal meetings began in 1997, the Chinese suggested converting one of the regular higher-level meetings into an informal dialogue. This was difficult both for us and for the Chinese. Perhaps the caricature of the Chinese politician, in a tightly buttoned semimilitary French jacket, hovered somewhere in the air. But we greeted each other, joked, laughed, and tried to have our aides act informal.

By the next meeting in China, relations had warmed. Our ambassador in China, Igor Alekseevich Rogachev, helped in this regard. He is in love with China. He lives for the country and knows it inside out. He may be the one ambassador in Beijing whom the Chinese people recognize and greet on the street.

During our last meeting in 1999, Rogachev even sat down at the piano to accompany the chairman of the People's Republic of China. I remembered our first informal summits and thought to myself, "Now this is truly a meeting in shirtsleeves!"

Beijing is an immense, cheerful, bright city. There are so many unusual sights and everything is so exotic that one can sometimes lose one's head. I remember one funny episode during one of our important state visits. On the morning of our return to Moscow, Tanya got up early to help me get ready. She threw on her bathrobe and came to my room to help pack my things. When she returned to her room, she discovered that her suitcase with her clothes was missing. It turned out

---

* Since the end of the cold war and the demise of the Soviet Union as a superpower, Russia has been searching for its own place on the international scene. In his efforts to counteract American dominance, Yeltsin has embraced the idea of a "multipolar" world, in which global influence is distributed among several world powers. Such views have found support in France, China, and other nations concerned about excessive American influence in the world. —Trans.

that Naina had already sent it to the airport together with the rest of her belongings.

There was Tanya in Beijing, an hour before takeoff, in nothing but her bathrobe. What was to be done? The women phoned around and ran about looking for something for Tanya to put on, while I guffawed wholeheartedly and couldn't stop.

"Papa, why are you laughing? How will I be able to travel in this?" my daughter said angrily.

Not until we boarded the plane did I stop laughing, when Tanya, awkwardly wearing an outfit of the wrong size, sat down in the seat beside me and began to laugh herself.

It was in China, during all of our visits abroad, where we felt ourselves to be light and free. We came away from Beijing with only the happiest emotions.

I especially remember a family dinner with Jiang Zemin and his wife. There were three of us, Naina, Tanya, and myself. The traditional Chinese paintings that adorned the dining room were striking, with fantastically beautiful colors and vivid images. I particularly recall one of a plum tree in bloom. It looked so real, as if it were holding out its branches to me, that I could hardly turn away from it. I received one of these works as a gift, a red one with a white background. It remains my favorite painting.

The women discussed a favorite subject: Chinese cooking. The cooking there is indeed delicious. I adore Chinese tea. At each of our meetings, Jiang presented me with traditional cups with thick lids for making tea and a selection of long-leaf imperial tea. But I particularly remember the yellow Chinese wine. A tiny tumbler of this viscous liquid is placed in hot water. You take a sip, and a slightly sweet, warm aroma spreads through your body.

I think that the Chinese have a special mission on the earth: They live in a country with an uninterrupted culture and history. Many thousands of years protect their traditions and their national philosophy. I felt this acutely when Jiang Zemin invited me to his residence and brought me to the Summerhouse of the Moon, an airy building on the banks of a canal. There stood two armchairs. Nothing else. It's a place designed for the contemplation of our higher origins. We sat in the armchairs and contemplated our long lives already gone by. We remembered the past, the 1950s, when he did his student apprenticeship in Moscow at ZIL automakers. We recalled those hungry, merry student days, when we both drank a sweetened condensed milk in blue cans. It was unbearably sugary, but we considered it a magical delicacy. So much time had gone by. So many political eras had flown past. So many conflicts had descended on our green globe. So many leaders had entered and left the political stage. But we still remembered our condensed milk.

When I described how my grandson Vanka loves sweets, Jiang Zemin became unexpectedly animated. He told me a story about his own grandson, who lives and studies in another city. One time he phoned his grandfather, the leader of China, with an unusual request: He needed help with an algebra problem. The Chinese leader grew agitated but didn't want to lose face in front of his favorite grandson, so he wrote down the problem and told him to call back in five minutes. His first thought was to turn to the Beijing Academy of Sciences. But then he decided to tackle the problem himself. And he solved it. Jiang probably didn't get as much satisfaction from China's international successes as he did from solving that algebra problem.

On November 23, 1998, Jiang Zemin visited me in the hospital. It was the visit of a friend. I never held international meetings in the Central Kremlin Hospital, but I made an exception. It was very important for us to meet and coordinate our positions.

At the end of 1999, I took my final trip to Beijing. I had already decided that I would soon resign, though of course nobody knew about it yet. So it was in China that I made my last international appearance as head of state. This was far from a coincidence. Trade with China is crucial to Russia's economic development. Every kind of good, from space and defense technology to simple consumer products, flows across our border. All of this creates work and a livelihood for millions of ordinary people. It is very important to promote this trade with solid governmental guarantees. But even more important, China had always supported my concept of a multipolar world. The Russian-Chinese dialogue was one of the few levers that could turn the concept into a reality.

Russia's strategic partnership with China restrains conflicts. Today, when the borders with Afghanistan or Pakistan become hot spots or when localized conflicts involving the Taliban and Islamic extremists flare up, military cooperation with China takes on an altogether new significance. It is crucial for us to use China's support to establish a system of collective security in the region. There are many ways in which the joint position of China and Russia could change the world situation for the better, as in relations between the states of South Asia (India and Pakistan) and North and South Korea.

The geopolitical situation isn't at all black-and-white. The opposing forces of the mid-1980s have shifted. The most difficult processes of the contemporary world—the globalization of the economy, the development of information technology, the intense dialogue about human rights—compel us to consider a new understanding of the structure of the world. Who will set a worldwide strategy? Who will write the rules of the game for all countries? Who will be able to solve international problems while taking into account the interests of all nations?

China and Russia have a common approach: One shouldn't just push all the buttons on the control panel of world development with only one hand. One shouldn't place all stakes in only one system of world security, the American one. One shouldn't resort to authoritarian means in order to attain democratic values imposed by the United States. But one shouldn't slip back into the bog of the cold war. An ongoing dialogue among equal partners is necessary.

In our discussions Jiang and I persistently tried to bring our positions closer and to draw up a new understanding of a multipolar, complex world without any kind of dictatorship. The deep freeze in relations between our countries has long thawed. The broad river of trust and personal contacts can flow freely. For this, I have our meetings in shirtsleeves to thank.

· 10 ·

The Collapse of the Ruble

On August 17, 1998, the Russian stock market collapses, and panicked investors and account holders make a run on the banks. Yeltsin and his team of young advisers hold all-night emergency sessions to solve the crisis, but it spins further and further out of control. A massive coal miners' strike exacerbates the situation. Although he admires Kiriyenko's rigorous work ethic, intelligence, and youthful energy, Yeltsin realizes that he must sacrifice the new prime minister in a tactical maneuver to help stabilize the economy.

· ·

IN THE SUMMER of 1998, Russia suffered a terrible financial disaster. This type of disaster had happened in other countries affected by the same global crisis, in countries with different economies, histories, and mentalities. But it was a new phenomenon for us. For many years, we had been cut off from the rest of the world by a high wall. We were utterly unprepared for such a collapse. We had joined the world economy like obedient pupils, and the "teacher" had punished us harshly for our Cs and Ds.

For ordinary people, the foreign currency crisis must have seemed like a freak snowstorm in the middle of summer. But businesspeople were perfectly aware of the fire already raging on the Tokyo stock market, the collapse of the national currencies in Southeast Asia, the mass firings in Japanese corporations, and the wave of suicides in Hong Kong. Financial panic had reigned in the world markets for a long time.

Could we have avoided this disaster? During the days leading up to the August crisis, bankers, analysts, journalists, and economists offered much valuable advice. Why did the government remain deaf to this advice? I think the reason is rooted in our Russian psychology. We had talked about the approaching economic catastrophe so frequently—about how everything would collapse and how the ruble would plummet—and we had sounded the alarms so many times that our sense of danger had become somewhat dulled. The global economy of our time, however, cannot wait for anticrisis measures. A fire at a stock exchange flares up in an hour. Within twenty-four hours it has spread to the whole world.

There was another important reason. Despite all the talk about our new market economy, we still had not become accustomed to the fact that our country was part of a greater economic civilization, a world market. We were not fully aware of our dependency on world markets and the world financial situation. It was precisely the globalization of the world economy, which had seemed like some kind of abstract postulate before the crisis, that struck such a painful blow throughout all of Russia in 1998. It struck all our cities, big and small, and all our people.

The Kiriyenko government immediately announced the creation of an anticrisis program. Under Kiriyenko's leadership, economic laws were written and precise macroeconomic blueprints were finally designed. (The work of the Kiriyenko government, by the way, has been used by all subsequent cabinets of ministries.) But here was the trouble: By focusing on the long-term prospects, the young economists entirely overlooked the current disaster. In laying the foundation, they completely forgot about installing the roof. It was an amazing paradox; the most highly educated Russian government, in the economic sense, made the most uneducated, ill-considered decision: It announced that it was refusing to pay its own domestic debts.

Outwardly, everything looked very simple. Western investors were slowly but surely beginning to withdraw their capital from the "problematic" Russian market. The interest rate on the GKOs (the Russian acronym for state short-term treasury notes) grew constantly. Already by early 1998, many specialists were saying that the market in state securities was not working for the government but seemingly for its own sake. The government wasn't using this market to back its budget; instead, the players in the market were using the government, sucking up all its financial reserves.

The Central Bank, which occupied 35 percent of the GKO market, bought new securities from the government, and the government used these rubles to pay for the old GKO issues. After receiving the rubles, the owners of the securities (mostly commercial banks, of course) took them to the foreign currency market and bought dollars. That increased the pressure on the ruble-dollar rate, but it had to be kept steady. (At the time the exchange rate was determined by the Russian government's "foreign currency corridor," a fixed ceiling and floor for the exchange rate, and had remained at the rate of 6 rubles to the dollar for a long time.) In order to keep the rate the same, the Central Bank was spending its gold foreign currency reserves. In January alone the reserves of the Central Bank were reduced by $3 billion. Only by paying such a price did we manage to keep the rate within the foreign currency corridor.

That's how the crisis of 1998 was playing out. It ground to a halt only when the fuel ran out—when the government ran out of rubles to pay for the old state treasury notes and the Central Bank ran out of foreign currency to maintain the rate.

Back in late 1997 I had told officials at a government meeting: "You always blame everything on the world financial crisis. Of course the financial hurricane did not originate in Moscow, and it has not left Russia unscathed. But what about the deplorable state of the Russian budget? Here you have no one to blame but yourselves."

It was true. Another simply repulsive situation had developed along with the crisis in the financial market: the failure of tax collection to back the budget. During January 1998 the federal budget received only 6 billion rubles in tax revenue, half of what was called for in the budget. Loans from the World Bank and any other trickles of income all quickly disappeared into the enormous hole of the budget. We would do anything to pay back the debt.

The rates on the GKO market during February didn't go below 40 percent. According to some official estimates the budget "hole" was 50 billion rubles. According to other, unofficial estimates, it was 90 billion rubles. The pressure on our financial market continued. The international financial agencies announced they were lowering Russia's credit rating. Foreign investors and our own banks grew cautious. They no longer trusted the Russian securities market.

At the end of May, we were hit by another wave of the crisis. World oil prices dropped. Major deposit auctions were disrupted (including that of Rosneft, the Russian oil company about which there had been great expectations). The railroads also suffered huge losses. Tremendous amounts of money went toward putting down the coal miners' strikes. Furthermore, the financial market in Indonesia collapsed. For investors who had purchased our securities, all of this was very bad news.

It couldn't go on this way for long. Foreigners alone possessed state treasury notes valued at about $20 billion. If those investors suddenly sold their notes and took their money out of Russia, the ruble would collapse immediately. Evidently, the Central Bank should have quit the GKO market, but it continued to cling to it, relying on the government.

Early in the year I had said that although we had skipped over the first stage of the financial crisis, it had become abundantly clear that our system of protection from these cataclysms was insufficient and dysfunctional. The Kiriyenko government had only just begun establishing relations with the Central Bank and learning to manage this difficult mechanism. It was terrified of the devaluation of the ruble. The only measure that could have saved us in the summer of 1998—a gradual devaluation of the ruble in anticipation of the crisis—had been rejected out of hand by Kiriyenko, Dubinin (chair of the Central Bank), and others. Why? The main reason was that they found it morally and politically difficult to start their term by devaluing the ruble. The major bankers, the Duma, the governors, the industrialists, and the trade unions—all the players on the financial and political scene—had rejected Kiriyenko and his technocratic clan of young upstarts (all of whom came from Nizhny Novgorod to boot). The Duma blocked their draft legislation; the coal workers' union staged a rail war and blocked the main railroad corridors of Siberia; the governors proposed tough and unpleasant resolutions in the Federation Council. Under these political circumstances, a devaluation of the ruble seemed unthinkable. It was too risky for the new government.

I remember Sergei Kiriyenko's psychological state that summer. He tried to look condescendingly calm and he tried to distance himself from the previous liberal economic team of Chubais and Gaidar. In any other situation, this tactic would probably have worked. At the beginning of his term, any new prime minister has to rid himself of his complexes and get used to the feeling of power. Yet Kiriyenko knew that a horrible financial crisis was bearing down on the country. He needed the support of the major bankers and the financial elite. But they simply didn't trust him. It was as if an accident had happened at a nuclear power station; what was needed was not great academic learning but years of experience in working the buttons. But the government couldn't figure out how to work the buttons right away.

Perhaps few people recall the famous rail wars of the summer of 1998, but I'm sure Kiriyenko shudders as much as I do when he remembers the wave of coal miners' strikes. That summer workers in the Kuzbass region faced off against the local government. The miners hadn't received their pay in several months, but they continued to go down into the mines. The bosses kept promising that they would eventually receive their accumulated pay, but they were lying. The explosion of open dissatisfaction came during the summer, when children were supposed to go away for some fresh air to improve their health but the coal miners' families had no money to pay for vacations.

The main problem was that these miners had long since ceased to be part of the government sector of the economy. Their mines had been formed into joint-stock companies in which they owned shares, and in some cases they had sold the shares and had changed their companies' owners a number of times. But the workers didn't want to engage in talks with the new bosses or the local government, which weren't capable of dealing with the situation. They continued to believe that someone far away in Moscow—a ministry, the government— was to blame for all their troubles.

Coal miners' strikes had occurred before in Russia. Reforms in the coal sector had proceeded by fits and starts, and huge efforts had to be made to close the mines that were running at a loss and weren't economically viable. There was generally neither the political will nor the funds to make these necessary changes. The coal that miners were digging out of deep veins in the earth cost so much to extract that the consumer couldn't pay the costs for the normal functioning of the mines.

The previous government had somehow managed to adjust to the seasonal rise in tensions in the mining areas. Usually the prime minister would hold a meeting in the spring with the governors, heads of sectors, and trade unions. The government gave the miners loans, wrote off their debts, and were able to stave off the latest miners' crisis. But this time Kiriyenko, just appointed and confirmed by the Duma, had overlooked the impending crisis.

Coal miners' solidarity is a unique thing. One mining district followed another in the protest. Within several days, the miners' action seized almost all the mining regions of Russia. But that wasn't all: The miners began to block the railroad lines. That was a protest of another magnitude.

The trains stopped, and connections between regions were disrupted. Businesses suffered enormous losses because they couldn't deliver their freight. People couldn't go away on vacation. Goods didn't reach consumers. Public discontent grew. In our vast Russia, so dependent on rail arteries, cutting off the railroads is the same thing as cutting off electricity. It was now considered a criminal offense. People began to call for the arrest and jailing of the miners and for special troops to be called in to put down the unrest. But we didn't want to create the severe precedent of criminal prosecution of poor, desperate people, made worse by the mass clashes with law enforcement. Therefore the young government of Kiriyenko held emergency talks with the miners.

I have to say that the miners' leaders assessed the situation rapidly and realized that with the impending economic crisis their actions would have considerable political resonance, much like the time they had held strikes in my support in 1990. Back then they had promoted the slogan "Dump Gorbachev! Yeltsin for president!" Now, almost ten years later, the miners had placed great hopes in the system of private ownership. They thought that it would help to modernize the mines and even turn a profit. I had once promised to make every effort to promote this reform.

But we hadn't taken into account one factor: The mining sector was exhausted, and it was naive to expect some kind of economic miracle. That's why the miners' protests had continued all these years.

In 1998 the miners' protest banners included more than the usual economic calls for back wages and so on. For the first time in recent years, the miners coordinated a large-scale political platform and took to shouting, "Down with the government! Dump Yeltsin!"

This troublesome resistance continued for more than three months. The miners set up a picket line in Moscow, right outside the House of Government, on Gorbaty Bridge, where they would bang their miners' helmets on the pavement, declare hunger strikes, and attract reporters. News stories attacked the government. Celebrities and members of parliament came to visit them on the Gorbaty Bridge. The heads of all the parties and political movements met with them. The scandal was growing.

I have to say that Muscovites reacted to the miners' picket line in an unusual manner. The performers and politicians used their visits to Gorbaty Bridge mainly for self-promotion. Kindhearted women brought food and drink for the miners' leaders who were stricken by the city heat and invited them into their homes. The demonstrators were so calm, I would even say passive, that clearly nobody intended to support any social revolution in Moscow. But the miners were backed by the immense power of angry coal districts in the provinces, who blockaded the railroads in their war against the government.

Vice Premier Oleg Sysuyev, responsible for social issues, raced from one coal district to another, signing agreements almost without looking at them—anything to come to terms. In one of these signed documents, I noted a point conceding that the government agreed that Yeltsin must be dismissed. Of course this agreement didn't have a legal leg to stand on. But I asked to have it saved as a historically valuable document. It stood as clear evidence that the government was nearly incapacitated.

The miners had hypnotized the young politicians. In fact, later, after Kiriyenko and Nemtsov were dismissed, they immediately went over to drink a bottle of vodka with the miners in honor of their departure. Now that the prime minister, who had been their main political target, was removed, it was obvious that the miners' rebellion would gradually evaporate. The dismissal didn't solve their problems or pacify the mining regions. But the trains in Siberia began to run again.

Meanwhile, in early summer it had seemed as if the economic situation had improved somewhat. With apprehension, the ministry of finance stopped issuing new securities and began to pay the old ones out of ordinary revenues. That is, it paid bondholders at the expense of pensioners, doctors, and teachers. The wage debt to state employees immediately began to creep upward. There was no alternative. Both the Central Bank and the government instituted tough new measures. Boris Fyodorov was appointed head of the State Tax Service, and he promised to punish tax evaders harshly.

This was the time of Kiriyenko's famous meeting with the major Russian businessmen behind closed doors at Volynskoye, the old government rest home near Stalin's old dacha. Kiriyenko was forced to back off from his vow never to deal with the oligarchs or depend on them in any way. Kiriyenko told them bluntly that he needed help. He didn't have the political backing to fix the situation.

At this meeting they agreed to form a sort of economic council attached to the government in which all the heads of the major banks and companies would participate. The businessmen made a rather harsh assessment: The government was weak. It could not hope for financial aid from the West. Who in the world would talk to the little-known Vice Premier Khristenko or to other young officials in the Kiriyenko government?

It was proposed that Anatoly Chubais be sent in temporarily to help the government. The meeting began at 4 A.M. By 8:00 A.M. they had agreed on Chubais's candidacy, and by 9:00 A.M. there was a decree waiting on my desk for me to sign. It was a real emergency situation. Chubais, who had just left the government recently, was once again in demand. He was appointed as a special representative to talk with the international financial organizations, and he was given the rank of vice premier.

This was a compromise for Kiriyenko, who had wanted to rely from the outset on his new economic team and not make contact with the economists from the Gaidar school. But Chubais managed to get a major loan from the IMF, and in July $6 billion of the promised $10 billion were delivered.

At first the interest rates on the GKOs dropped sharply. But the situation had already become so dangerous that any delays in making decisions would give our market a beating. The whole thing would finally crash. If only we had received the loan two months earlier; if only the Central Bank had floated the ruble in May; if only the international agencies had not announced our lowered financial rating. Now it's easy to talk about all the "if onlys." But back then everything was in chaos. It was already too late to save the situation. The market no longer trusted the Central Bank or the government. In a matter of weeks, the IMF loan had melted away. The banks bought up dollars so quickly that we could hold the rate of the ruble steady only by intervening in the stock market. The Central Bank sold dollars, and they disappeared immediately. All the market players sold securities.

The evidence indicates that my attitude in May and June—not to interfere, not to get involved—was a grave error. I had become accustomed to trusting those with whom I worked. But neither Dubinin nor Kiriyenko could contain the crisis. Having lost the initiative, the government feverishly looked for alternative options. It was trying to keep up with the situation, but the situation was spinning out of control. Such a crisis situation tests the administrative capacity of the government—its solidity, its reliability, its ability to bang its fist on the table and take action. Kiriyenko was ready to seek anyone's counsel and listen to anyone. Despite his strong nerves, he was shaken.

But the crisis marched on relentlessly:

August 13: The Central Bank of Russia decides to reduce the volume of sales of foreign currency to Russian banks. The deputy ministers of the Group of Seven hold a telephone conference to exchange opinions on the possible devaluation of the ruble.

August 13–15: The financial world reacts to the collapse of the Russian stock market.

August 16: I meet with Kiriyenko, who announces that the situation calls for "emergency measures."

August 17: The government announces its exit from the "foreign currency corridor" and the freezing of its obligations to pay internal debts.

August 21: In an extraordinary session of the state Duma, a resolution is passed by 248 votes calling for the president's resignation. Seleznev's comment: "Starting with the president, all the bankrupts should voluntarily step down."

The dates of the disaster and the government's response are all public knowledge. But I would like to tell you what was going on behind the scenes. In early August Chubais, Gaidar, Khristenko, and Dubinin, ashen from fatigue, went into the prime minister's office and didn't come out for two weeks. They wrote the "final and decisive" anticrisis emergency plan.

On August 16 Chubais, Kiriyenko, and Yumashev came to see me in Zavidovo. They told me immediate devaluation of the ruble and the temporary halt of payments on the GKOs were the first priority. Kiriyenko began describing the plan in detail, but I stopped him. Even without all the specifics, it was clear that the government, along with him and all of us, had become hostages to the situation. I didn't want my alarm to spread to them. Perhaps with some desperate efforts we could try to keep the ruble at an acceptable level.

"Go ahead," I said. "Take the emergency measures necessary."

The package of decisions made on August 17 was a severe economic miscalculation. Economic historians found no precedent for the Russian government's decision not to pay its own internal debts. The monetarists from the Russian White House were so mortally afraid of uncontrollable inflation that they didn't print the amount of money needed for the GKO market. But for both our domestic and foreign creditors, the double default, or freezing of debts, was far worse than speeding up the money printing. The official lowering of the ruble rate could no longer save the situation. The depositors rushed to the commercial banks, the banks rushed to the Central Bank for loans, and the Central Bank shut its doors in their faces. The ruble plunge doubled, then tripled.

After August 17 I made the decision to dismiss Dubinin, the chair of the Central Bank. I thought it was absolutely natural that the chief banker of a country should resign following the collapse of the national currency exchange rate. At my request Yumashev invited Dubinin to the Kremlin and asked him to write a letter of resignation.

That day all the major bankers who had attended the meeting in Volynskoye reconvened. Through Yumashev they conveyed their main request to me: not to dismiss Dubinin. The Central Bank was in fact taking measures to save the major banks from total bankruptcy, and Dubinin was the one putting the brakes on the falling ruble. In order not to create a total panic in the financial market, Dubinin had to remain.

After some thought, I changed my decision. If the major banks of the country were to close their doors all at once, the crisis would spill out onto the streets. But it was significant that none of the bankers asked me to defend the government.

At this time my economic adviser, Aleksandr Lifshits, offered to resign. Though he was the least to blame for this crisis, he was the only person who decided to leave at his own initiative. His job had simply become a matter of sending me one desperate memorandum on the economy after the other. In his request to resign, Lifshits asked my forgiveness for the fact that he couldn't protect the country from economic crisis.

On August 21 Valentin Yumashev met with Sergei Kiriyenko. Yumashev later told me that he had caught up with Kiriyenko at the airport, where he was returning from a trip. They sat together in the empty government lounge. They had a long, hard conversation. Kiriyenko said, "I have the feeling that I'm sinking the president. Every move I make is a fresh blow against him. I'm doing everything I can, but we're unable to control the situation."

The foreign currency corridor was overridden within two days; the banks were thinking only about how to save themselves. At this point the crisis had reached the Russian account holders. They realized they had to rescue their cash savings, and the lines at the ATMs and the tellers' windows grew longer and longer by the day. That was it. The worst thing that can happen to a country's financial system, a run on the banks, was now in full swing. While the government was quarreling with the Central Bank, no one noticed the panic of the savings account holders except for specialists, stockbrokers, and bankers. But the crisis had reached the street and touched every person.

It was horrible to watch the country in the last few days before the complete financial meltdown. Out of habit people finished their summer vacations; got tan; watched soccer; went out to their dachas. Meanwhile, the shadow of a total crisis hung over each family. After all, people pick up their pay at the bank and keep their savings there. The companies where they work cannot live without bank loans. Millions of Russians now faced this new reality for the first time in their lives. Obviously, all the subsequent gradual improvements and stabilizations would not compensate for this psychological shock—the exploding prices of consumer goods, which shot up in the fall; the firings and the cutbacks; the nonpayment of wages, even in solid organizations. In this kind of crisis in a country like Russia, nothing will work without a powerful political figure who can stabilize the situation.

Unfortunately, Kiriyenko was not that figure. I tried to figure out why he had lost support. Why were both the financial and political elites turning away from him? Kiriyenko himself realized he needed more stability and weight and tried to persuade Yury Maslyukov and

Yevgeny Primakov to become first vice premiers in his government. But once again there was no time. On the whole I bet that everything in Russia could have turned out differently if Kiriyenko's team had had even a half year more. But the crisis crushed their plans brutally and quickly.

On Saturday, August 22, I invited Kiriyenko to visit me. We both understood the reason for the meeting. And strange as it may seem, we both felt a sense of relief. He thanked me for giving him the chance to work and try to do something. Then he fell silent, unable to find the right words. It was clear that he felt a load lifting from his shoulders.

My own feelings were curiously ambiguous. I very much regretted that people were leaving, people in whom I had had such high hopes. Still, I was aware of the tremendous stress of these last few months. I had used all my moral and physical strength to protect them from public criticism. In order to support the Kiriyenko government and prevent the spread of panic, I had recently told a correspondent, "There won't be any inflation." It was difficult to admit this now. I had believed that the country could be kept from crisis. I had believed it because I had seen how hard this young team had tried and how hard they had worked. We hadn't allowed the panic to break earlier, in May and June, and the ruble had held. I had hoped that it would hold again. But it didn't. So Kiriyenko had to go.

On August 21 I took part in naval exercises of the northern fleet. I was on board the heavy nuclear missile cruiser *Peter the Great*. In order to avoid excess panic, I had refused to cancel my scheduled trips or postpone any plans. This was also a demonstration of the military strength of the state: We had to remain strong even during such dark days. The powerful ships, the sea, the planes swooping low in the sky —all of this was distracting and reassuring.

As I gazed upon the hulking ship—gray, dense, impenetrable—I thought about how all our efforts had run into the same kind of impenetrable wall. The wall was our Russian economy, with its "special" relations. That unofficial, gray sector, with its unwritten rules and laws, was several times larger than the aboveboard "white" sector. Like a steel hulk, it had resisted all the efforts and ideas of the young reformers. It seemed as if it was impossible to break through it. But even as the reforms failed, the people didn't dump the blame on Kiriyenko. There was no anger toward him, even from the businessmen who had suffered the most. They understood that when there is a tsunami, there are casualties.

· 11 ·

The Autumn Jinx

As the economic situation worsens in the fall of 1998, the Communist parliamentarians begin an impeachment procedure against Yeltsin. Meanwhile, the president and his aides search desperately for the right man to replace Prime Minister Kiriyenko. They need someone who can clean up the economic crisis and stabilize the country. They need a heavyweight—a solid, powerful candidate who will be acceptable to the hostile Duma.

· ·

IT'S AN AMAZING THING. All the most severe crisis periods in the last eight and a half years of my presidency happened during the same three months: August, September, October—the golden autumn, the velvet season.

In 1998 there was no exception to this autumn jinx. That was the autumn I had to replace Kiriyenko with a stronger, more powerful prime minister. That was the autumn I nearly disbanded the Duma. That was the autumn Russia's economy dissolved into chaos. That was the autumn that almost tore us apart.

On Monday, August 24, I went to the Kremlin to tape a televised speech:

Dear Russians!

Yesterday I made a difficult decision. I proposed to Viktor Stepanovich Chernomyrdin that he lead the government.

Five months ago, no one could have expected that the world financial crisis would deal such a painful blow to Russia and that the economic situation in our country would become so difficult. Under these conditions, the main priority is to not slip backward and to guarantee stability. Today we need people who are usually called "heavyweights." I think that the experience and weight of Chernomyrdin are needed.

There is another reason for this important decision: to guarantee the succession of power in the year 2000. Viktor Chernomyrdin's main qualities are decency, honesty, and thoroughness. I think these qualities will be decisive during the presidential elections. Chernomyrdin has not been spoiled either by his time in office or his time out of office.

I am grateful to Sergei Vladilenovich Kiriyenko for courageously trying to correct the situation.

Today I have raised Chernomyrdin's candidacy for discussion at the state Duma. I ask the deputies, the regional leaders, and all citizens of Russia to understand me and to support my decision. In the current situation, there isn't time for long discussion. The crucial thing for all of us, after all, is the fate of Russia and stability and normal living conditions for Russians.

After this statement, I held three brief meetings with leaders of the power ministers, Putin (Federal Security Service), Stepashin (Interior Ministry), and Sergeyev (Defense Ministry). I warned them that the situation in the country was serious. Then I returned to Gorki-9. I wrote decrees appointing Sergeyev and Stepashin as acting members of the new cabinet. As head of the Federal Security Service, Putin didn't need to have his status confirmed. For him, everything remained as it was. Now came the hardest part: persuading the state Duma to vote for my candidate for the new prime minister. Under the constitution, the president has the right to submit candidates for prime minister only three times to the parliament for a vote. (If the parliament rejects his proposal three times, the president has the right to disband parliament.)

During the previous week, events had moved forward rapidly. On

Speaking before the Kremlin

Greeting supporters during the 1996 election campaign

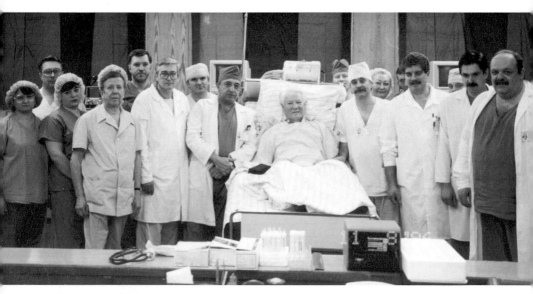

Recovering from heart surgery at the Central Kremlin Hospital
(November 8, 1996)

Naina

My growing family

With my grandson,
Gleb

With Tanya during the taping of a radio broadcast

Working with
documents

With Valentin Yumashev in my Kremlin Office

Discussing matters with
Anatoly Chubais

Members of Chubais's
1997 team, including
(from left to right)
Valentin Yumashev,
Boris Nemtsov, Sergei
Kiriyenko, and myself

With Jacques Chirac
"in shirtsleeves"
(September 1997)

A happy reunion with Helmut Kohl in Zavidovo (November 30, 1997)

On a fishing trip with
Ryutaro Hashimoto on the
banks of the Yenisei River
(November 2, 1997)

With Bill Clinton after our shared victory in the 1996 elections

Resting in the Roosevelt chairs

Bill and Boris (June 5, 2000)

Leaving the Kremlin after my surprise resignation. Acting President Vladimir Putin stand beside me. (December 31, 1999)

Enjoying the retired life

August 18 Chernomyrdin had interrupted his vacation to return to Moscow. He held constant political consultations. He met with Aleksandr Lebed and Gennady Seleznyov on August 19 and with Gennady Zyuganov and Nikolai Ryzhkov on August 20. He promised them that there wouldn't be "any Chubaises, Gaidars, or Nemtsovs in the government."

All the political elites (and the Communists were no exception) were searching for a fulcrum, a point of stability in the financial chaos. No one wanted the financial collapse to turn into a collapse of the state. I knew about Chernomyrdin's talks, and I didn't interfere with them. I took a calm, neutral position. Meanwhile, the press launched an active campaign stating that Chernomyrdin was the only candidate who could be supported by everyone, from Communists to businessmen. Among those who had a claim to the prime minister's seat, Chernomyrdin was the only one who plunged into battle. In a matter of days, he managed to negotiate preliminary agreements about everything with everyone.

On August 22, there were two important meetings at my residence outside of Moscow. I described the first one, my meeting with Kiriyenko, in the previous chapter. After Kiriyenko left, I summoned Chernomyrdin. "Kiriyenko has just left me. I have asked him to resign." Chernomyrdin listened in silence, nodding his head. It was obvious he was tense and ready for a decisive battle.

The phrase *political heavyweight* isn't very flattering, but it helps explain the reasons for Kiriyenko's dismissal fairly accurately. Kiriyenko obviously lacked that quality. I looked at the large, bulky figure of Viktor Chernomyrdin and thought, "Now here's a heavyweight." He had the stature we needed now.

On August 23, a Sunday, Valentin Yumashev asked permission to come see me at the dacha along with Igor Malashenko, head of NTV. I knew that the conversation would be about Chernomyrdin, and I could guess why Yumashev was bringing Malashenko, whom I had known since 1996, when he had been a member of our analytical group. It was clear that Valentin wanted me to listen to something besides his own arguments.

The day was warm and sunny, one of the last days of the suburban Moscow summer. We talked for a while, and then I invited my guests to have lunch. An outsider would have seen three men in short-sleeved summer shirts, eating *okroshka,* a soup. It seemed absolutely peaceful, a beautiful day with a light breeze. Patches of sunlight glimpsed through the rustling leaves. But I was pondering the most difficult political problem. And it was not only political but also personal. To return Chernomyrdin to the government would mean admitting my own moral defeat, my loss. After all, I had dismissed him only five months before. I continued to think that despite all his indisputable qualities, Viktor Stepanovich Chernomyrdin was simply the wrong person to head the Russian government and to run as the main democratic candidate for president in 2000. But the current crisis was like a spring wound so tightly that it could snap at any moment and sweep away the entire political structure. There was no time left for reflection. We would need enormous strength and experience to unwind this spring slowly and calmly. That is exactly what Chernomyrdin possessed.

I asked Valentin about his conversation with Kiriyenko in the empty airport. He said that Kiriyenko seemed to understand everything.

"Whom does he propose as a replacement?" I asked.

"Stroyev," Yumashev replied after some hesitation.

That meant that Kiriyenko couldn't overcome his jealousy of Chernomyrdin. His suggestion was not realistic. Stroyev was a person of the old type, a former member of the Politburo. He didn't suit me at all as prime minister.

"Well, what do you think, Igor Yevgenyevich?" I asked, turning to Malashenko.

Malashenko spoke in his typical manner, firmly and definitely, carefully weighing his words; "The Chernomyrdin of five months ago and the Chernomyrdin of today are two different people, Boris Nikolayevich."

"Why?"

"Because everything has changed. He was forced to rethink a lot of things and understand a lot. A politician who returns to power after a resignation is always a different person. He has gained tremendous new experience. Now he understands that he has to fight for the new position and that he has to work differently than he did before."

"What about Luzhkov?"

"No, that's not even worth discussing," Malashenko replied.

"Boris Nikolayevich," said Yumashev. "Chernomyrdin promises that he won't appoint people who are convenient and obedient but weak enforcers. He promises to create a team of young, aggressive professional economists. This is good. But there's something even more important: If he is confirmed by the Duma on the first try—and there is a very good chance of that—he can really claim the role of a national leader, a savior, the anticrisis prime minister, call it what you will. Then he will have gained a new reserve of credibility with the public."

I understood all too well what Yumashev wanted to say. After his resignation and his triumphant return to the White House, Chernomyrdin would acquire the aura of an unjustly offended person, the kind of figure so beloved by the people. "Look what a mess you have made here without me," he could exclaim. Yes, that was a very important consideration. Chernomyrdin not only had a good chance to resolve the crisis using his experience and connections, but he could also go further, to the elections in 2000, having built up a store of credibility. In that sense, my loss of morale would be a win for Chernomyrdin. Well, what of it?

Still, I continued to have my doubts. What if he was not confirmed by the Duma on the first round?

"Then we'll try to find another candidate," said Yumashev.

We didn't even discuss the Primakov option on that day. Primakov had already told everyone—my aides, the parliament, the left and the right—that he didn't want to serve as prime minister in any way, shape, or form.

It is not easy to talk about these events of the autumn crisis of 1998. It's hard because the situation changed practically every day and then every hour. Frankly, I don't remember such tension in the entire

Russian political history of the 1990s, except for the military coup attempts of 1991 and 1993. The situation in 1998 was supposedly completely different; it was peaceful and constitutional. But under the same gentle, mild sun, the political kaleidoscope was turning frantically. Some devil was twisting the cardboard tube of our fate, and the colored glass of various combinations and compromises kept coming together and then falling apart.

On August 24 the televised speech to the nation nominating Chernomyrdin aired, and I signed the corresponding decrees. At the same time Chernomyrdin held a meeting with the government in the White House as acting prime minister. With a frenzied persistence, Chernomyrdin kept driving the heads of the parliamentary opposition into a corner. He used his two trump cards: the lack of another realistic candidate and the desire of the entire elite, both political and economic, to resolve the financial crisis as rapidly as possible. The strategy worked. During the first three days of that week, the main parameters of the so-called political compact, which would define the new relations among the president, the government, and the Duma, were agreed upon. On Thursday and Friday we began drafting the actual document.

Chernomyrdin was able to achieve a great deal. First, he obtained the support of Seleznyov, speaker of the state Duma and officially the number two man in the Communist Party. He also got the support of a bloc called People Power and the agrarians, Zyuganov's junior partners. He did this with the help of the heads of Gazprom, the oil company, who had influence on the leadership of the Communist Party. The leftist opposition agreed to the following conditions: If the president guaranteed not to disband the Duma until 2000, the Duma would in turn guarantee its trust in the government. For its part, the government guaranteed that it would not initiate a parliamentary crisis through its voluntary resignation. Chernomyrdin kept calling me, trying to get agreements for additional new positions: Could there be Communists in the government? Could the Duma confirm all the vice premiers?

I deliberately accepted a limitation of my constitutional powers with this compact. I was absolutely convinced that during this autumn jinx Chernomyrdin was the only real candidate for prime minister.

Despite all his efforts, the Communists still tried to wrest the initiative from Chernomyrdin. Zyuganov and his junior partners in the leftist opposition, Ryzhkov and Kharitonov, came out with a joint statement, saying, in effect, that the candidate for prime minister had not been properly prepared. Ryzhkov was even more blunt, saying that it would be a crime in the eyes of the people to blindly introduce a new player into the government without knowing his platform or his agenda.

By exploiting the crisis situation and the fact that I had been forced to dismiss Kiriyenko and his liberal government, the Communists were trying to wrest a piece of the political territory back from me. They tried to bring their people into the government and limit my initiative. But for me, the compact was a deliberately conceived, precise move. After the Duma confirmed Chernomyrdin, there would be no reason to disband the Duma. Chernomyrdin was my prime minister. I didn't intend to dismiss him before 2000. Everything was working according to plan. Everything was coming together.

But the Communists were treating this agreement as if they were standing in front of a firing squad. They had been forced into it only through Chernomyrdin's inexhaustible energy and his constant pressure. Within one week he had cleverly managed to remove all their objections, satisfy all their conditions, and respond to all their arguments. He had left them naked before the necessity of signing the agreement. They realized that without a real candidate of their own for prime minister, it would be a bitter, unpleasant fate to take responsibility for the political crisis in the middle of a financial crisis.

On Friday I was handed the compact. I added my signature to the signatures of the leaders of the political factions, Gennady Seleznyov, Valentin Yumashev, and Viktor Chernomyrdin. Only Zyuganov's signature was missing. He had to discuss the text of the agreement at his party plenary meeting.

On Sunday, on live television, the leader of the Communists turned red, sighed deeply, and made a sensational statement: The Communists wouldn't vote for Chernomyrdin on Monday. Ryzhkov's and Kharitonov's jaws dropped. Although they were Zyuganov's partners, they said they had known nothing about this decision and that they would hold emergency consultations.

At that moment, watching television at home, I suddenly realized what was going on: The decision had been made in a matter of hours by a small circle of conspirators. That could only mean one thing: The Communists had found their own candidate for prime minister. It wasn't too hard to figure out who it was: It was undoubtedly Yury Luzhkov, mayor of Moscow.

The first alarmed calls from the Federation Council had begun even before Kiriyenko's official resignation. Both Luzhkov and Stroyev had spoken rather harshly against Chernomyrdin. "The difficulties and mistakes that we are suffering from today are the consequences of the long and neglectful work of the previous government headed by Chernomyrdin," Stroyev stated.

Luzhkov and Stroyev were evidently irritated by the enormous will for power that Chernomyrdin had displayed in the first postcrisis days. Like the Communists, Luzhkov and Stroyev, heavyweights number two and three, decided that under the circumstances the most just and rational solution would be to divide government powers. Something could be left to the president, but they had to seize something for themselves. Luzhkov realized that this might be his only chance to come to power by legal means. The situation had to be exploited.

Several days before the first round of voting, I invited both Luzhkov and Stroyev to the Kremlin. Under such extreme circumstances, when the country had to be saved, I felt it was absolutely right to speak to them directly, openly, and honestly and to tell them to get rid of their political ambitions and support Chernomyrdin. We were all in the same boat and now, at this minute, we had to be united. They gave their restrained consent. Then, in front of the television cameras, Luzhkov and Stroyev said some accommodating words about how it is the president, under the constitution, who decides whom to nominate as prime minister. They were not disputing those powers.

It seemed to me that this was, if not a victory, then a tactical win.

At least Luzhkov and Stroyev couldn't publicly oppose Chernomyrdin anymore. But as it turned out, I had underestimated Luzhkov's ambition.

Monday, August 31: There were only a little more than 100 votes in the Duma to confirm Chernomyrdin. It was a complete rout. We were into the second week since Kiriyenko's resignation. It was totally different from the first; the political content, the cast of characters, and the style all had changed. Now Luzhkov moved actively into the offensive. Just like Chernomyrdin the week before, he feverishly cobbled together a political arrangement out of anything he could find at hand.

The Russian Communist Party had long since forgiven Luzhkov for 1993, when he had not supported the parliamentary rebellion. Now they wanted to exploit Luzhkov, using him as a battering ram to destroy the Yeltsin regime.

On Monday, September 7, we held a roundtable at the Kremlin with the governors and leaders of the Duma factions to discuss how to end the political crisis and choose a prime minister. At another roundtable at the Duma, Zyuganov announced his list of candidates. Besides Yury Maslyukov, a member of the Communist Party and former head of the Soviet Union's Gosplan (State Planning Office)—a logical and understandable choice for him—he also named Yury Luzhkov, mayor of Moscow. It was one more confirmation that Luzhkov was already with them. He had unquestionably made a strong move in joining forces with the Communists.

Luzhkov had also come to terms, and rather quickly, with part of the Federation Council. Such influential democratic governors as Konstantin Titov and Dmitry Ayatskov spoke in his favor. They believed that Luzhkov, having built a market system in one single city, could teach the whole rest of the country how to do it. Some of these governors sincerely saw Luzhkov as a fresh figure. Others saw him as a new master of the country. They hastened to make deals to help their own regions.

Chernomyrdin threw himself into the fray and managed to get some support from the Federation Council. A majority of the governors voted for him. I could not subject myself to the blatant pressure of the Communists, especially now that a majority of the governors had supported Chernomyrdin by proposing Luzhkov. That would have been the second phase of a political retreat.

There was a repeat of the vote on Chernomyrdin's candidacy. This time 138 parliamentarians were in favor. All our work had given us only a miserly increase. Immediately after the second vote, the leftist part of the Duma announced that if Chernomyrdin were put to a third vote, they would vote to begin an impeachment process against the president. The situation had become extremely serious.

Now, two years later, the reasons for the Communists' obstinacy have become rather obvious. They weren't going to let go of such an opportunity. The August-September crisis was their lucky lottery ticket. Power was falling into their hands; all they had to do was stretch their arms out and grab it. They could make a direct attack on the Kremlin. They simply had to ride the wave of people's considerable dissatisfaction with the government, the collapse of the ruble, the loss of savings by the middle class, the bankruptcy of businesses, and the general panic.

Their maneuvers also fit conveniently within the bounds of the law. According to the constitution, if the Duma did not confirm Chernomyrdin on the third try, the Duma had to be disbanded and new elections had to be called. But here was the legal trap: A president who is undergoing an impeachment process does not have the right to disband the Duma. The constitution offered no guidance for this situation. The disbanding of the Duma at a moment of severe social crisis was a risky move in itself. But under these circumstances it threatened to be doubly or triply dangerous. In a country where there is no parliament or legitimate government and the president is hanging onto power by a thread because of the impeachment process, complete political chaos can ensue. The legal trap was threatening a vacuum of power and an explosion of dissatisfaction—and then, possibly, a state of emergency.

But that wasn't even the issue. If the Duma were disbanded, the Communists would definitely gain their long-awaited absolute majority in the parliament. This crisis gave them enormous political odds. The disbanding of the Duma would turn into a powerful rollback, an utter collapse of the democratic reforms, and a catastrophe for the whole country.

Now I needed to do three things simultaneously. First, I had to pressure the Duma: "I have no other candidate. This question is decided. With or without you, the prime minister will be Chernomyrdin." Second, I had to convince Chernomyrdin not to insist on his candidacy: "Viktor Stepanovich, you can't raise your candidacy a third time. In the current political situation, we simply don't have the right to dissolve the Duma." Third, through Yumashev, in a state of absolute secrecy, I had to try to persuade the only real candidate to accept the nomination: Yevgeny Maksimovich Primakov.

And that's exactly what I did. I did it because I stubbornly continued to believe that I would find a way out. Still, after the second round of votes, I called in several people from my administration in order to hear absolutely all their arguments for and against Luzhkov. I have to hand it to Luzhkov: He had the energy and the will to win. Emissaries from the mayor's office came over to the Kremlin practically every day. In fact, they almost never left. Andrei Kokoshin, secretary of the Security Council; Sergei Yastrzhembsky, deputy chief of administration; and Yevgeny Savostyanov all quickly became Luzhkov supporters.

Yumashev, Yastrzhembsky, and Kokoshin came to visit me at my dacha. I asked them to lay out both positions thoroughly. "Luzhkov was always for the president, at all stages of his career, during all the difficult situations," said Yastrzhembsky. "They say he is against you now. I think this is just slander. I spoke personally with Yury Mikhailovich and he asked me to tell you that Yeltsin is a sacred notion for him. But that's not the only point. Luzhkov is a real candidate for president. He is a strong manager, and he will quickly establish a normal vertical command of authority. He is a reliable person who will continue both the economic and democratic reforms in the country. We can't give the Communists a chance to inflame the situation by exploiting the crisis."

Kokoshin outlined approximately the same position.

I looked at Yumashev. "Your arguments, Valentin Borisovich," I said.

"The candidate for prime minister today must be a uniting, reconciling figure. But with his crude intensity, Luzhkov is striving for power, and he isn't above taking advantage of any scandal. If Luzhkov is made prime minister, will he really be able to refrain from an attempt to seize power before the 2000 elections? Of course not. This could totally destabilize the situation in the country."

"Thank you," I said. "I've listened to both opinions. Now let me think."

Several minutes later, I called Valentin Yumashev—he had already left in his car—and said just two words: "Persuade Primakov."

The situation remained critical. I made my last moves. First, I continued to pressure the Duma with all my might, using all available means. Despite the failure of the first two rounds of voting, one could still hope for a sudden breakthrough. I asked that a letter be prepared to the Duma for a third vote with the name of Chernomyrdin. For the deputies, this meant one thing: the dissolution of parliament.

Meanwhile, I decided to meet with Yuri Maslyukov, yet another candidate from the Communists. Yumashev brought him to me immediately, dragging him away from vacation. We held a meeting on September 10 at 7:30 A.M. Maslyukov said, "I'm ready to work, but only under Primakov's leadership. Talk Yevgeny Maksimovich into it. He's the best. I will only go along with him."

At 9:00 A.M. on that same day, I went to the Kremlin. Primakov was waiting for me. Then Chernomyrdin and Maslyukov came. I brought the three of them together to discuss the final decision. It was impossible to delay any longer.

My first conversation with Primakov had taken place at my dacha in early September, between the first and second rounds of voting on Chernomyrdin. "Yevgeny Maksimovich," I had said to Primakov. "You know me and I know you. Right now, you're the only candidate who will suit everybody." We had a long and substantive conversation. I sensed that Primakov really did not want to become prime minister. He didn't want to don the heavy mantle of power and take on the huge responsibilities. He had grown accustomed to his comfortable niche at the Foreign Ministry.

"Boris Nikolayevich," he said. "I will also be totally frank with you. Such a burden is not for a person of my age. You must understand me on this. I want to finish out my career normally and quietly until the end. We'll go into retirement together in 2000."

After the first vote on Chernomyrdin, Yumashev had held several more meetings with Primakov. "Yevgeny Maksimovich," Yumashev said, "What do *you* propose? What should we do?"

Primakov replied, "Let's propose Yury Maslyukov. He's a good economist."

"Boris Nikolayevich will never agree to having a Communist prime minister. You know that, Yevgeny Maksimovich. And then what will we do? Dissolve the Duma?"

Primakov replied firmly, looking Yumashev straight in the eye, "Under no circumstances should the Duma be dissolved."

And now it was September 10 and the third and last round of our negotiations in the Kremlin. Today would decide everything. But how it would be decided was still not clear. At first Primakov again categorically refused. But I asked him to wait in the outer office until Maslyukov and Chernomyrdin arrived. So as not to lose one minute before the other two candidates arrived, Yumashev kept working on Primakov, trying to talk him into accepting the post. It was in this last half hour that everything was decided. Suddenly Primakov said, "Ivanov, my deputy, is not yet ready for the role of minister. And tomorrow I'm supposed to go on a big international trip. What will I say to my partners?"

Valentin looked at him hopefully. Was he ready to accept the job?

"No, no, I can't," Primakov said, waving his arms. At that moment, Yumashev realized it was his last chance.

"You're a wise man, Yevgeny Maksimovich. You must understand this. What if something suddenly happens to the president? Who will run the country? Who will end up in power? Luzhkov? Do you want that?"

"No."

"So I can tell the president that you agree?"

Primakov was silent.

"Well, *can* I tell him?" Valentin repeated. Primakov remained silent.

Yumashev flew into my office just moments before all three candidates for prime minister entered. The text of a letter to the state Duma lay on my desk. I asked everyone to be seated and said: "I am calling on the Duma to support my candidate for the new head of state. I am asking them to support the candidacy of..."

Here I paused.

All three men sat silently, holding their breaths. Each was expecting that I would name him, even Maslyukov, who had practically no chance.

"Yevgeny Maksimovich Primakov!" I said with a sense of relief and satisfaction.

Politics is the art of the possible. But sometimes it involves a completely irrational element: the wind of fate. Mostly likely Chernomyrdin hadn't sensed that fate was against him. In this last meeting before the third round of voting in the Duma, he had ignored destiny and confidently gone forward. Now, even after I had announced my decision, Chernomyrdin argued against it. He kept citing more arguments for why Primakov and Maslyukov should be appointed vice premiers and he should be nominated for a third time for the Duma vote.

"But what if they don't confirm you?" I asked.

"Well, what can they do?!" Chernomyrdin kept insisting.

Primakov and Maslyukov kept silent.

"Yevgeny Maksimovich, does Viktor Stepanovich have any chance of getting through the Duma?" I asked after a long pause.

"Not the slightest," replied Primakov.

Maslyukov said the same thing.

Chernomyrdin hesitated for a moment. Then he suddenly leaned back in his chair and said, "Boris Nikolayevich, I have always supported Primakov's candidacy. It's a good decision. Let me congratulate you, Yevgeny Maksimovich."

On that day, September 10, Primakov was proposed to the Duma. He was confirmed by a majority of votes.

. . .

Why did all the most severe crises in the last eight and a half years of my presidency happen in autumn? Why is this time so jinxed? Why is there always some sort of surge of energy, a near explosion in the government and the political component of society at exactly this moment year after year? No one knows. I even tried to get an explanation from my aides, so that they could use some scientific method to calculate all the unfavorable factors for these months. No, they told me, everything's normal. They're just regular months.

Regular months? Indeed!

1991: The August putsch. A state of emergency was declared, and the fate of the entire country hung in the balance.

1992–1993: The peak of a string of crises: the armed clash in the center of Moscow and the storming of the White House, which fell during September and October 1993.

1994: September's "Black Tuesday," which began the ruble panic.

1995: The Duma elections that spelled the complete victory of the Communists and their allies.

1996: I underwent quintuple coronary bypass surgery in November.

1997: The bank wars and the Chubais "book scandal" in November.

1998: The financial crisis, the default, the resignation of Kiriyenko, the interim between governments, the appointment of Primakov.

1999: The September apartment explosions in Moscow and other Russian cities.

I'm simply amazed at the strange pattern. Power fell into the hands of the Bolsheviks in these months in 1917, and it was during these months that the powerful Soviet army was crushed and repelled by the fascists in 1941. It makes you wonder.*

I walked along a pathway in the park. I was surrounded by the red and yellow leaves of fall. Fire, fire . . . It was my favorite autumn air: cleansing, transparent, clear. My thoughts gradually settled into a differ-

---

* The "autumn jinx" struck early in 2000. At the time of publication, Russia has already suffered two horrors. On August 8, eleven people were killed by an explosion that ripped through a crowded underpass in central Moscow; and on August 12 an explosion sunk the Kursk submarine, killing all 118 sailors on board. Russian newspapers and the public criticized President Putin's reaction to these crises. —Trans.

ent vein. After all, a political crisis is a temporary phenomenon. It's even useful in a way. I know from my own body that the organism uses a crisis in order to overcome an illness, to renew itself, to return to its customary, healthy state. The rises and falls in human life were like waves on a cardiogram. And if so many crises happened during my period, the "Yeltsin" period in the history of Russia, it was not my fault. It was the crisis era between two stable periods. We just had to get back to stability as quickly as possible.

But this crisis was also unlike all the crises before it. It had struck the middle class, which had just barely emerged; it had hit the property owners, the businesspeople, the entrepreneurs, and the professionals. But it was for their sake—so that they would have some kind of assurance, so that their children could study in good schools, so that they could take vacations abroad, so that they could accumulate some money, so that they could begin to build a house or move to a new apartment or buy some nice furniture or a new car—it was for their sake that it had all been designed. These people were my main backers. If things went badly for them and they turned away from us, we would witness a crisis that would be far, far more profound.

I walked along the path through the trees, rustling the leaves with my feet. Fire, fire . . . Would these people understand that I had not betrayed them? I didn't know. It was a difficult autumn, and a difficult winter loomed before us. But in this cold, clear air, any ordinary person had to see the truth, just by looking closely. If we could survive, if we could overcome this autumn and this winter, everything would become clear. Once the smoke from the burning leaf piles clears, the forest and the field come into view. That was nature's philosophy. Perhaps such ideas are crude, but they made things easier for me.

· 12 ·

Primakov's Stabilization

In the aftermath of the ruble collapse and the impeachment crisis, Yeltsin must deal with the day-to-day reality of having Primakov, an old propagandist and spymaster, running the affairs of state. In his clashes with Primakov, we come to realize just how much Yeltsin, himself a former Communist Party leader, has evolved into a genuine democrat. Primakov staved off massive discontent after the 1998 autumn crisis. But can he really get Yeltsin through to the 2000 presidential election?

·   ·

THE POLITICAL CRISIS of autumn 1998 was resolved. The jinx was past for another year. And most important, the dramatic events of September, when the country had gone almost a month without a government, hadn't forced us to go beyond the bounds of the constitution.

Everyone in the government took a breather to get our bearings and answer some questions: What, in fact, had happened to us? What would be the aftermath of the autumn crisis? What should we do now? Everyone wanted to know whether Russia would continue as a presidential republic. Had real authority passed from the president to the opposition?

If you read the newspapers and the political commentary during those days, you would definitely think that Russia was no longer a presidential republic. The course of liberal reforms was over. The young reformers, whom the president had fussed with for so long, had led the country to the economic precipice. Beyond the precipice was the abyss. Now the task of dragging the country away from the precipice and enduring the mistakes of others fell to Primakov's left-of-center government. Surely Primakov would take another path. Moreover, Yuri Maslyukov, an economist from the Soviet planning school, was to play a key role in Primakov's government. Maslyukov was a stern supporter of the military-industrial complex and the state procurement system. He was an ardent opponent of Gaidar's reforms. Thus, Yeltsin's policy was crossed out with a big fat X.

Despite these alarming and at times even tragic judgments in the press, I calmly took the measure of the new government. Come what may, I knew one thing: The worst of the crisis was behind us. I tried to settle on a new political strategy. Would it be defensive or expectant? That would depend on public opinion. Truth is, there was no panic in society. There had not been a total collapse of liberal values and liberal policy. In fact, the crisis had not even touched the remote Russian provinces. People in the villages asked the city-dwellers, puzzled, what the crisis was all about. Russian peasants didn't have bank accounts and, paradoxically, that was a positive factor. To be sure, the collapsing ruble caused price hikes and hurt the standard of living, and in that way everyone felt the consequences of the crisis. But the confusion had not turned into panic. People gradually adapted. To some extent that's what saved us.

The crisis of nonpayments was over, and the banking heart of the country began beating again, even if it was on artificial life support. The banks that hadn't played on the GKO state securities market were spared destruction. Local industry, which had needed relief from the overcrowding on the market of imported goods, began to pick up. All sorts of firms, from small vegetable stands to large oil companies, were learning how to live with the new prices and the new regimen of the strict economy. Everyone was saying and writing that the crisis had helped revive Russian business and galvanize it, though it all came as a real shock.

Once again we had been on the brink, but fate protected Russia. Neither a revolution nor a social explosion as dreamed of by the Bolsheviks had occurred. What had saved us? It was what Russians grandiosely call "perestroika" or "market reforms," and what the Western press more straightforwardly terms a "democratic revolution." But in Russia the transition period didn't progress at all. The explanation for this phenomenon was both simple and complicated: Russia was tired of revolutions. It was tired of the very word, which implies either rebellion or a social cataclysm by an unseen force and means destruction and famine. We Russians got fed up with revolutions in the twentieth century. Although Russian society supported democracy at its critical stage during the political reforms, it was deeply opposed to the very idea of "class warfare" or "social struggle." In the Russian mind, revolution is associated with upheaval, destruction, and famine.

Back in the 1980s I realized quite clearly that Russia would support radical reforms but would not support a state of revolution because that's seen as something violent and dangerous. All the rallies that took place in Moscow in support of democracy in the Gorbachev era were entirely peaceful. They were a show of peaceful civic resistance to Communist revanchists. That's what united such diverse groups of people in those days. It was most similar to the Prague Spring or the Velvet Revolution. Two things became very evident to me: Russian society was expecting reforms, and Russian society was fairly civilized and imbued with a positive spirit.

Time has shown that I was correct in my assessment. The country rejected any attempts to impose reform by force. Whoever took up arms first would lose. That was the case in both 1991 and 1993. Russia's choice was evident: democratic reconstruction of the country.

But "peaceful" doesn't mean "easy." On the one hand, the spirit of bloodless reconstruction (anti-Bolshevik and anti-Communist) helped democracy to withstand opposition and prevail. But it also instilled in people an unconscious wish for some social miracle. Some people expected Russia to be accepted with open arms on the world market, so that the country would witness the economic boom we had so long and so persistently desired. Others hoped that the free market and competition would somehow arrive of their own accord, and that the bad roads, dilapidated housing, and shoddy goods would all disappear. None of this happened, nor could it.

Revolution, even peaceful revolution, is nonetheless an abrupt break with the old way of life. Such rapid changes in everything in the world—forms of property, geographical borders, the government system, the worldview, national ideology—can't help but provoke shock in society. The very foundation of the state machinery was seriously weakened as a result of our quiet revolution. With any revolution, whether quiet or loud, real power seems to hang in the air or winds up on the street.

I saw this threat of chaos. And I hastened to prevent it, forcing through the establishment of a new Russian statehood, introducing new institutions of governance and backing all this with laws and decrees. But now I see all the shortcomings of this rapid, at times hasty process. We had underestimated the profound anarchism peculiar to Russians. Russians have a distinct lack of faith in any authority. There are reasons for this: In the years of Soviet rule, we became fed up with the state and the power of the Party *nomenklatura*. As a result, today's Russian worldview is in a sense extremely simple: *We need to have fewer bosses, and the state should not poke its nose into our affairs.* The antithesis of this viewpoint is the autocratic one: *We have to instill order in the state at any cost, even at the cost of abolishing democratic reforms.*

But there is no historical truth in either the former or the latter extreme. The new Russia had passed through the stage of democratic revolution. Now it was time to return to the idea of statehood, but to a statehood that would not pressure, suffocate, or interfere with the life of the individual but create guarantees for stability and prosperity. Russia is moving in the right direction, toward an intelligent and strong state.

After the autumn crisis of 1998, neither the press, the Duma, the Federation Council, the polls, nor the people on the street were talking about altering power and property or introducing emergency measures of any kind. The situation was worrisome, and the winter would be hard in many regions, but there wasn't the fear of the first days that there would be widespread starvation or food shortages, 1,000-percent inflation, the fall of the Russian Federation, and so on. The tone of the press changed from desperate to more moderate, contemplative, and sober. There was no reason for a second political crisis, no crisis of authority in the country.

What did this mean for me? In part the political landscape had been given up to the opposition, to Primakov's coalition government. Now that the parliamentary majority had concentrated a significant portion of executive authority into its own hands, it no longer had the moral right or the opportunity to keep rocking the boat. Its political initiative was limited. Anticrisis measures don't allow for political posturing or revolutionary delirium. Even if it wanted to, the Primakov government could not go backward and use dangerous Communist experiments to tinker with the economy.

I tried to pay closer attention to the tactics and behavior of Primakov. He began to operate with extreme care and gravity, taking his time. He carefully maneuvered among the political forces, eagerly and frequently consulting with the leaders of parties and regions. He made no sudden moves. Gradually, he strengthened his position. He secured the support of the governors. Besides Maslyukov, he brought other people into the government: Kulik from the agrarian bloc; Gustov, governor of Leningrad *oblast*; and Georgy Boos, a faithful member of the Luzhkov team.

Frankly, I hadn't doubted that Primakov would adapt quickly. I thought he would be able to reinforce his own position in a matter of weeks. A career *apparatchik* who had worked for many years under Leonid Brezhnev in international affairs, then in the Gorbachev Politburo, Primakov had also been a diplomat and an intelligence chief. And the objective foundations were in place—support from the most diverse political forces, ranging from the presidential administration to the state Duma, and a high credibility rating. But what was important was the public position Primakov would now take. How would he communicate with the country? People are very sensitive to tone and inflection—all kinds of people, from the humblest laborers to the highest bureaucrats. And it seemed to me that Primakov chose exactly the right tone. He was able to reassure everyone with his rumbling voice and his somewhat sarcastic, tough manner of speaking. He had a confident ease about him that was able to quell and subdue the almost panic-stricken people in September and October, convincing everyone of the possibility of stabilizing the situation. In short, Primakov achieved the kind of stable position that no other Russian prime minister had been able to attain before.

To freeze a crisis is already a small victory. But what the new government was really doing with the economy could be judged only after the country had survived the winter. For the time being, I expected from the Primakov government not decisive action but *lack* of action. The Russian economy was like a patient who, having just survived a life-threatening fever, should not be pumped full of medicine. It needed to rest, catch its breath, and revive naturally.

The press gave the Primakov government a hard time from the outset. Soon it became clear that the reason was the absolutely closed nature of the new cabinet. A directive had been given to the *apparat:* Conceal information from the press; give a minimum of interviews; all contact with journalists must be strictly supervised. Primakov's many years in closed institutions—the Central Committee of the Communist Party, the Foreign Ministry, and the Foreign Intelligence Service—had taken their toll. But in the last several years, government operations had become transparent. Journalists had grown accustomed to discussing the various steps taken by the cabinet. They were used to the open standards of the world press. Now, suddenly, they found that Soviet-style controls had been slapped on them.

Primakov did not take his relationship with the press lightly. I understood this relationship better when Primakov came to visit me for the first time and brought his "special file." In that file he had collected virtually everything that had been written in the newspapers about his new cabinet. Every clipping was carefully underlined with colored pencils. At first I couldn't believe my eyes. All those articles had been read, then clipped, and then underlined. And why had Primakov decided to complain about the journalists to me?

"Yevgeny Maksimovich," I began. "I got used to that long ago. They write about me every day; they've been doing it for years. And you know the tone they use. But what can I do? Close down the newspapers?"

"No, you don't understand. Just read this, Boris Nikolayevich. This is a complete discrediting of our policy..."

And that's how Primakov and I would talk for hours at a time.

For a while, I couldn't understand his concern. Then I recalled how I had reacted to various articles in the press in the early years of my political career. But I had to learn to distinguish freedom of public opinion from outright paid propaganda. I had been in public politics all these years, but Primakov had not. He was unable to change his attitude to the press. He was a journalist of the old Soviet type who had worked for many years at *Pravda*. So behind every article he suspected complicated intrigues, subtexts, or threats from his political opponents. The reality of a free press was impossible to explain to him. He simply needed time to change his attitude and to overcome this sensitivity. It was sad that Primakov could not rid himself of the old Soviet stereotypes, including that severe nervous reaction at the sight of a newspaper. But for the time being, I tried to deal with all of this patiently.

Then Primakov took out something else—several pages held together with a paper clip. "Read this, please," he said.

I began reading. It was an anonymous report on a rather high-level official who was accused of embezzlement, taking bribes, unlawful financial transactions, and several other minor transgressions.

"Yevgeny Maksimovich, let's go into this a little further," I said. "What are the facts? Are you absolutely certain of them? Where did you get them?"

"This memo was prepared by the security services, Boris Nikolayevich. Of course it all has to be checked, but..." he began.

"But if this is true, then why hasn't a criminal case been opened against this man?" I asked. "Or is this all speculation? You can slander a person with anything."

Unhappy with my reaction, Primakov whisked the document away.

Such scenes became routine. Evidently there was always a pile of such reports in Primakov's desk drawer. Finally, I got fed up with it. I decided to have one of Primakov's "reports" checked out for myself.

The story concerned Mikhail Zurabov, deputy minister of health.

Primakov had an anonymous memo that declared that Zurabov was a bandit, that he had ties with a criminal gang from the Caucasus, and so on. In fact, it was later discovered that this young deputy minister had had the imprudence to step on the tail of some pharmaceutical mafia. Primakov had summoned Valentina Matvienko, the vice premier, and demanded that Zurabov be fired immediately. But first I asked Putin to check these reports. Soon Putin brought me a real report on Zurabov from the economic security database of the Federal Security Service. The difference was amazing. Everything in Primakov's anonymous report had been distorted. For example, while the anonymous tipster had said that Zurabov had connections to a Dagestan gang, the document from the FSB said that Zurabov's ties to criminal gangs of "persons of the Caucasian nationality" had not been established. In the anonymous report, Zurabov had been accused of graft. The FSB report said that no evidence of taking bribes from pharmaceutical companies had been found. These were the kinds of discrepancies between the two reports. (Zurabov was in fact an honest, decent man and a bright, intelligent specialist. I met him later, when he became the presidential adviser on social issues. Now he's working as chair of Russia's Pension Fund.)

That was how I became familiar with the technique known as *kompromat*. At that time some commercial firms had found their way to disgruntled FSB agents and other special services. They capitalized on officials who had been fired from the agencies. It was easy for them to put together a "report" on a competitor or a disliked bureaucrat. Apparently there were quite a few former officers of the FSB or officials from the prosecutor's office who brought Primakov such accusations and didn't bother to provide any proof. These compromising materials piled up on Primakov's desk. Extremely cautious in politics, reserved and thoughtful by nature, Primakov forgot his scruples when he looked for suspects and enemies. He was marked by his long career as a top official nurtured in the closed Soviet institutions. He couldn't help but believe all these accusations, never thinking that someone might pay very well for such "exposures."

In addition to feeding Primakov this type of *kompromat,* the fired FSB officers began to complain to him about Putin. As the patriarch of the special services and the more senior and seasoned colleague, Primakov continued to treat Putin, director of the FSB, as a subordinate. For his part, Putin regarded Primakov with respect. Putin adhered strictly to the bounds of seniority established by age and rank. Nevertheless, misunderstandings happened. For example, the former FSB generals dismissed by Putin somehow contrived to convince Primakov that he and his family were being followed. Of course the accusations were absurd. Who could tail the prime minister of a huge country? How could you follow a person who is accompanied everywhere by a powerful security detail and whose safety is ensured by an entire security agency, the Federal Guard Service? And why put surveillance on him if his every move is public anyway? But Primakov phoned Putin immediately and demanded that he remove the surveillance. Ordinarily cool and restrained, Putin replied rather abruptly. He said that he would order an immediate investigation. He asked that the source of the information about the tail be named and said that a criminal case would be opened if the information were true. Primakov backtracked when Putin insisted on a formal investigation, but he continued to believe the ridiculous assertion was quite real.

Then there was an episode involving the so-called FSB purge. People evidently had told Primakov that the new head of the FSB was taking revenge on the old cadres. Primakov kept telling me over and over that Putin was removing the most experienced Chekists and bringing into the leadership of the "committee," as he still called it, totally green people, inexperienced acquaintances from St. Petersburg (Putin's hometown). I finally asked Putin to get to the bottom of this story.

Putin asked me for permission to hold a meeting with the FSB collegium, the governing body of the FSB, and the prime minister's cabinet. They met. To Primakov's surprise, almost all the members of the collegium were familiar faces. Most of the deputies he had thought were fired were still in their positions. Primakov was embarrassed. After that memorable meeting, he softened his attitude toward the FSB somewhat.

Just by analyzing this and other episodes, everything became clear to me: Primakov was accusing others of what he apparently wasn't above doing himself. For so long, I hadn't been able to understand why the prime minister of an immense country—an intelligent, sophisticated politician—would behave like an old Soviet politician. If I had given Primakov his way, he would have changed our political and financial landscape with his "reports" and his subjective notions about who was an enemy and who was a friend. I kept advising him not to pay attention to the criticisms of the liberal politicians, the economists, and the newspapers and the rumors about possible intrigues by special services. "I, as the president, support you. That's what's important," I told him.

For a time, it seemed to me that he heeded my words, or at least that he was trying to understand me. Then, in the fall of 1998, some government leaders began to get the impression that the prime minister was quietly trying to take away the presidential powers. Primakov was trying to gather all the reins of state control into his own hands. He was meeting more and more frequently with the power ministers, who are subordinate only to the president. He tried to place deputies and people from his Foreign Intelligence Service as seconds everywhere. The newspapers began writing that the president's close aides were "surrendering" to Primakov. Officials from the administration supposedly made agreements with Primakov so that they would retain their posts in the future. They were calmly watching as power ebbed away from me.

I was totally calm about all these rumors. I was not afraid of any "creeping coup." The main thing for me was that Primakov and his government would maintain a political hiatus and thus give the economy time to pull itself out of the crisis. The hands of the Communists were tied because of the participation of their own people in the government; they couldn't complain about economic policy going against their wishes.

Opinions differed about Primakov's economic strategy. Some economists criticized him harshly for his lack of a coherent policy. Others, more loyal to the government, claimed that he wasn't making any mistakes and that there was even a little growth in the economy thanks to the repeated tumble of the ruble. This was true. Because the value of the dollar had practically tripled against the ruble, it had now become much easier to pay wages, back the payment of state procurements, and fill the budget. Of course the real standard of living fell because of inflation, but nevertheless the "pink" government of Primakov, with its statist rhetoric and its Soviet style of leadership, had prevented social protest, strikes, and a new rail war. The government had helped the economy by the fact that the new prime minister had by and large left it in peace. People were impressed with the slogans of the new government: "Live according to your means; make and buy domestic goods." Primakov's credibility ratings remained high and stable.

Wittingly or unwittingly, Primakov helped me achieve my main political goal: to quietly lead the country to 2000 and the presidential elections. Then, as I saw it, we would find a strong, young politician and pass the political baton to him. We would give him a place at the starting gates and help him develop his potential. Together, we would help him win the elections.

· 13 ·

On the Sick List Again

Yeltsin's bad health interferes once again at a crucial moment when he needs all his resources. Primakov seems to have his eye on the presidency and the Duma goes back on the offensive, calling for a thorough medical examination of the president. Thirsty for revenge, the Communists bring an impeachment vote before the parliament.

. .

ON OCTOBER 11, 1998, I was scheduled to visit Uzbekistan and Kazakhstan. On the eve of the trip, my temperature rose above 100 degrees. By morning it had come down, but my condition was not good. My doctors gave me a preliminary diagnosis—tracheobronchitis—and began to shoot me full of antibiotics.

Naina and Tanya begged me not to go. But once again I ignored the advice of my family and doctors. It was impossible to postpone the visit, especially the evening before. If I feel that I must do something, I will, even if I have to do it by the skin of my teeth.

From the moment my plane landed in Tashkent, I began to feel even worse. I managed to overcome my physical weakness only by sheer will. Here I must thank President Islam Karimov of Uzbekistan. I don't know how the trip would have ended if it hadn't been for his deep sympathy and understanding of the situation. At one point, everything suddenly began to swim before my eyes. It happened during a ceremonial meeting at the president's residence, right on the carpeted path in front of two lines of parade guards and numerous television viewers. Fortunately, President Karimov was nearby, and he quickly stepped up to support me. I recovered from my dizzy spell in a moment.

Doctors continued to try to bring my temperature down with strong antibiotics. Once again I had difficulty breathing. I felt a weakness and a burning in my chest. The world seemed fuzzy and weightless. Nevertheless, from Tashkent I flew to Almaty, where I was scheduled to meet President Nursultan Nazarbayev of Kazakhstan. Because of my illness, the program was cut short. Then, under the watchful eyes of my doctors, I headed back to Moscow. My new press secretary, Dmitry Yakushkin, told reporters that I would be spending the week at Gorki-9. "The doctors have recommended bed rest," he said.

On October 14, despite all the best medical recommendations, I got up from my bed to go to the Kremlin. The press, the Duma, and the Federation Council were surprised to see me. Several important meetings were on the calendar, but because I was sick, they had been postponed for the week. Within two hours my aides had gathered in the Kremlin all the people who had been scheduled to meet with me. This was a wise decision. The political significance of my every move was heightened during these days. In fact, that same day the Federation Council discussed a draft resolution titled "On the Results of the All-Russian Protest Action." The resolution contained such phrases as: "Each day that Boris Yeltsin is in the office of the president, there is a threat to the statehood of Russia." The measure asked the president to "voluntarily and irrevocably tender his resignation." The resolution failed by only eleven votes from regional leaders.

In early November the Duma deputies began reviewing a draft law called the "Medical Certification of the Health of the Russian Federation President." If passed, it could have forced me into retirement. Only five votes were lacking to pass the law in the Duma. The Communists had narrowly missed something they had long dreamed of doing.

Why were the Communists out to get me? They were deeply frustrated. When the new prime minister, Yevgeny Primakov, was confirmed in September, the leftist factions of the parliament had a field day, declaring that they had managed to create a government of popular trust. But soon the fog of their political illusions lifted. The deputies realized that once again they had failed to limit my presidential powers. Moreover, both the "red wing" in the government (Maslyukov and Kulik) and Primakov's own rather sympathetic attitude toward the Communists deprived them of room to maneuver. Now they couldn't openly criticize the government or demand that it resign. They needed some other valve to let off political steam. After the draft law on my forced medical certification foundered, they immediately began to look for another means to aggravate the situation.

On Wednesday, November 4, at a rally near the Ostankino television center, where Communists often went to protest. Albert Makashov, a Duma deputy and retired general, promised to "take a dozen Yids with him into the next world." This was the prologue to all the events that ensued. That same evening the decent deputies in the Duma demanded that Makashov be censured for anti-Semitism. They hemmed and hawed and then prepared a very mild, almost gentle resolution on the "impermissible actions and statements complicating the international relations of the Russian Federation." But they didn't even pass it. The logic of the red majority was this: If Yeltsin's economic policy was leading to a "genocide of the Russian people," then it was O.K. to call for Jewish pogroms. It was disgraceful, disgusting. Blatant anti-Semitism has long existed in the Soviet state government under the disguise of the "noble" fight against Zionism and imperialism. But such outright crudity from such a highly visible platform could not be tolerated.

Anti-Semitism, like any form of racism, is a terrible evil. But I categorically refuse to believe that anti-Semitism is deeply rooted in Russian society or in our people. If life were calmer, more stable, more prosperous, everyone would gradually forget about this problem.

The next day I made an official statement: "Any attempts to offend national feelings or to restrict the civil rights of citizens on grounds of their nationality will be stopped in accordance with the constitution and the laws of the Russian Federation."*

Our usually threatening Prosecutor General's Office seemed to have suddenly disappeared. At the request of the justice minister, the prosecutors reluctantly began to investigate Makashov's anti-Semitic outbursts to see if they violated the constitution. But they found it awkward to question such a respected personage as Makashov. The Prosecutor General's Office, headed by Yury Skuratov, found no evidence of a crime in Makashov's statements. The case was closed.

It didn't stop there. Viktor Ilyukhin, a Communist deputy, stated that there were "too many persons of the Jewish nationality" around the president, and proposed a draft resolution to that effect on the floor of the state Duma. In an entire region of Russia, Krasnodar Krai, it became fashionable to blame Russia's troubles on "the Yids" and the "Zionists." Everyone got into the act, from the right-wing parties to the governor, and Krasnodar television gave wide currency to all these statements.

Makashov had his supporters, too. Kuvayev, secretary of the Moscow City Committee of the Russian Communist Party, declared that even if what Makashov had said wasn't right, "[w]e are still in solidarity with him." At rallies, Gennady Zyuganov stood shoulder to shoulder with Makashov. And now, like some sort of windup doll, Makashov, at all his meetings and all his trips throughout the country, kept repeating over and over, "It's a Jewish conspiracy, a Jewish conspiracy." He simply couldn't stop himself. In late February in Novocherkassk, speaking to an audience of Cossacks, the general said, "Everything that is done for the good of the people is lawful. The people are always right. We will go on being anti-Semites, and we will prevail."

The public reacted sharply. Gaidar called Makashov "a beast of an anti-Semite" and declared that the Communist Party should automatically consider itself a Nazi party since it was in solidarity with him.

---

* In the Russian context, *nationality* is not necessarily citizenship but ethnicity. Jews are identified not only with a religion but with an ethnic group, known as a nationality, within the many different nationalities of the Russian Federation. — Trans.

"Today we have the right ... once again to raise the issue of the ban on the Communist Party," he said.

All the newspapers were full of articles and cartoons of Makashov. He became a laughingstock. The sick nature of his worldview was so obvious that many began to say, "Retire that retired general."

But apart from Gaidar and me, the government barely reacted. The Ministry of Justice was unable to find a legal basis to shut down the Communist Party of the Russian Federation as a party whose actions violated the constitution. Makashov's case was buried in the Prosecutor General's Office. Primakov entrusted the expression of the official view of the government to the modest Ministry of Nationalities. He himself spoke against the elimination of the Communist Party, saying: "I regard this extremely negatively."

That same autumn, on November 20, a real tragedy occurred: Parliament member Galina Vasilyevna Starovoitova was murdered in St. Petersburg.* The news came like a stab to my heart. In her many years in the political arena, Starovoitova had shown the greatest decency, humanism, and loyalty to our common ideals. She could not have gotten in anyone's way; she was a real political idealist. But who killed her? Fanatics? The outbreak of Communist hysteria in late 1998 and early 1999 made it quite reasonable to surmise that some leftist extremists were involved in the murder. The killing created a sense of general alarm, insecurity, and fear.

I kept on top of the investigation, and even now, many months after Starovoitova's murder, I continue to follow the progress of the case. I have a report on my desk from the Interior Ministry, dated July 4, 2000, in which three main hypotheses are being probed. I cannot take it upon myself to judge which of these hypotheses will lead to the real criminals, of course. I do hope that the perpetrators will be caught and punished.

Events were unfolding rapidly. And it was clear that the Communists intended to aggravate the situation even further. "If you want to

---

* Starovoitova, a longtime member of parliament associated with the liberal cause, was investigating allegations of financial impropriety by the Communist Party at the time of her murder and was also planning to run for office in St. Petersburg, where there have been numerous contract killings of politicians, bankers, and journalists. —Trans.

disband the Communist Party, go ahead! But then just wait and see who gets theirs!" was what you could clearly read in their statements in late autumn. And they weren't joking. Calls to take revenge on Yeltsin's circle resounded louder and louder. In mid-December the Duma impeachment commission held a session. The fifth item on the agenda was "genocide of the Russian people." Once again there was talk about the "Jewish conspiracy," about the betrayal of Russia's interests, and the influence of Western intelligence agencies on Yeltsin. The person giving the report at the impeachment commission was Viktor Ilyukhin. The Prosecutor General's Office refused to give a legal interpretation of Ilyukhin's statements.

In late November Yumashev had come to me and asked how I would feel if he were replaced by Nikolai Bordyuzha, who would still remain secretary of the Security Council. There was a certain logic to this request. Primakov's confirmation had been a tactical victory and had given us some room to maneuver, but in the eyes of the public it was still a major political setback for the president. The situation in October and November illustrated clearly that the opposition was prepared to embark on a further offensive, even to the point of restricting my constitutional powers, and that the governors would support this under certain conditions. The office of the president needed some force behind it, at least for show. It was easy for them to bang their fists on the Duma's rostrums, make calls to send the hated Yeltsin into retirement, and bring columns of demonstrators with red flags into the square while I was in the hospital. But it would be harder to do that if I were supported by a colonel general who simultaneously held two of the most important state posts, the head of the administration and the secretary of the Security Council.

During Chubais and Yumashev's era, the presidential administration was a purely intellectual team in the political shadows (and to this day that position seems the most correct to me). But now, at this critical moment, such a lateral move would clearly benefit my position on the political chessboard. I needed a surge of sheer power. Unfortunately, I had doubts about Bordyuzha. The young general had just been named head of the border service, replacing Andrei Nikolayev, who had been asked to head the Security Council. And now, after having worked in the Kremlin for only three months, he was to make another grandiose career jump. Wasn't he a little green?

Yumashev tried fervently to persuade me that it was necessary to "change the scenery" in the administration. Bordyuzha was a really sophisticated military man; his worldview was closer to that of the generation of young politicians than to that of the generals, and he had agreed in advance to clear decisions with Yumashev, at least for the time being.

"I won't leave, Boris Nikolayevich," Yumashev explained. "I will still be right next to you and Bordyuzha."

I would later see that Yumashev wouldn't let me down. He stayed by my side, as always, helping me. Since my retirement, we have remained friends and continue to work together (just as we tackled the writing of this book). But back then all of these backroom plans to coordinate the current and the former head of information didn't sound too persuasive. I agreed, not under the influence of Yumashev but for a completely different reason. For some time now, I had been sensing the public's need for a new quality in the state, for a steel backbone that would strengthen the whole government. We needed a person who was intellectual, democratic, and who could think anew but who was firm in the military manner. A year later such a person did appear and was greeted with enthusiasm, Vladimir Putin. But meanwhile I accepted Yumashev's resignation with enormous regret.

On December 5 Yumashev bought several decrees to Gorki-9: one on his resignation, one on the combination of the posts of secretary of the Security Council and head of administration, and one about the dismissal of several of his deputies. On December 7 I came to the Kremlin for three hours to sign these decrees. That was how Nikolai Nikolayevich Bordyuzha, former head of the Federal Guard Service, secretary of the Security Council, a career military man, and a general at the age of forty, came to take the post of chief of administration.

Still, a month after Yumashev stepped down, I summoned him and said, "Valentin, are you sure you haven't made a mistake? Somehow, I'm missing something about Bordyuzha." Yumashev was surprised.

Externally, everything was running smoothly. Bordyuzha was trying with all his might to be a team player. But from the very beginning, I saw that something was wrong. Though he was an officer who had had a wonderful career in the strict military system, he had a poor understanding of contemporary politics. He couldn't catch the subtle nuances or notice the undercurrents. The entire work of the head of the administration was, in his view, illogical, unregulated, strange. Gradually Bordyuzha began to develop a real split personality. He suffocated under an internal tension. It was that strain, I suppose, that I had noticed in him.

That's how it is in life. I know from my own experience. When a strong, powerful man, even one in great health, lands in a place where he's out of his element, he suffers from constant stress. Bordyuzha simply got sick. Near the end of his brief term in the post of chief of administration, the young border-guard general began to have heart problems.

The only person Bordyuzha was comfortable with was Yevgeny Primakov. Bordyuzha accepted Primakov's way of thinking and his secretive manner without reservation. And when my relations with the prime minister grew more strained, Bordyuzha couldn't take it any more.

The whole new political system of post-Soviet Russia had been long and hard in the making. We hammered our thumbs and splintered our boards. This was the price we had to pay for building the edifice of our society correctly. We lived through the crisis of October 1993; we withstood Ruslan Khasbulatov, the leader of the Supreme Soviet, who actively undermined the constitution; we suffered the referendum on the primacy of a presidential or parliamentary form of rule; and we struggled though the constant votes in the Duma on my resignation.* After the elections of 1996, it finally became clear to me that the role of

---

* Khasbulatov, then Speaker, led the 1993 rebellion of the parliament. For more information, see Yeltsin's *Struggle for Russia* (Times Books, 1994). —Trans.

the administration had to change. If, after 1991, my administration served mainly as a governing apparat or oversight office, then after 1996 it became an intellectual support staff. The work of the analytical group continued after the elections, but now it formulated development strategies, not campaign ideas.

Early in my first presidential term, I had invited Yury Petrov, former secretary of the Sverdlovsk Oblast Committee of the Communist Party, to work at the Kremlin as an experienced *apparatchik* who would keep a whole army of state bureaucrats under supervision. Then Sergei Filatov came to the Kremlin. In the public's opinion, he was a weighty and influential person, a committed democrat, and a member of the intelligentsia. But alas, Filatov was not a strong politician or a strong analyst. He turned the administration into a kind of academic research institute on the problems of democracy in Russia. He wrote mountains of memos, reports, and concept papers, but they had almost no relationship to real life.

The people who really designed political strategy were a group of presidential aides headed by my first aide, Viktor Ilyushin. It was he who essentially served as chief of administration and he who created a hardworking, intellectual staff in the Kremlin. It is enough to remember the names of the people who came to these offices at that time: Satarov, Baturin, Krasnov, Lifshits, and many others.

Meanwhile, with each month and each year the political role of the Federal Guard Service, and specifically my chief bodyguard, Aleksandr Korzhakov, was growing. Korzhakov fought with everyone who didn't submit to his influence and anyone he considered "alien." At times he interfered with the work of my secretariat, jumping established procedure to bring in his own documents. He fought first with Filatov, then with Ilyushin, and then tried to influence the economic policy of the country through Oleg Soskovets. After the elections of 1996, it became clear that Korzhakov's time had passed and that there should no longer be two or three "informal leaders" in the Kremlin. We could not support multiple centers of power. I take full responsibility for Korzhakov's incredible rise and logical fall. It was my mistake. I would pay for it later.

I also invited Nikolai Yegorov to work as chief of administration in 1995 from his post as governor of Krasnodar. He was supposed to be involved in establishing peace in Chechnya. But a completely different person, Lebed, took that task upon himself.

With the arrival of Anatoly Chubais in 1997, the work of the Kremlin administration took on a completely different character. On the one hand, it was a clear, tough vertical chain of command, with iron discipline in the collective. On the other, the 1997 team was a young, powerful group of intellectuals, people of an entirely different generation with diverse views on life and the processes under way in the country. They were not burdened by the old stereotypes, and they set to work designing their innovative, modern strategy with enormous enthusiasm.

From that moment, the most important, strategic laws were prepared in the administration: tax and land codes and reform of state structures. It was in the era of Chubais, Yumashev, and then Voloshin that the administration began to prepare completely differently for the president's annual speech to the Federal Assembly. Not just bureaucrats, and not just certain intellectuals, but all the best forces became involved in preparing this state document. All the ministers and agencies and entire institutes worked on this message, which defined the main direction of the country's development for the year ahead.

During the summer and fall of 1999, when it was headed by Aleksandr Voloshin, the presidential administration demonstrated its real potential. All the intellectual energy and political experience of the previous years were put into motion during this critical period. Voloshin and his team's stunning victory during the Duma elections of 1999 was absolutely unexpected by his political opponents. But behind that victory stood years of scrupulous, painstaking work analyzing the situation in the country, designing mechanisms to influence public opinion, and so on. The work that my political enemies call the influence of "the Family"—with a capital *F*—consisted of exactly this: meetings with the head of the administration, his deputies, and advisers; discussions of their proposals; my final decision; and then strict, unswerving implementation.

I used this system in all the latter years of my term in office. And although Chubais was called the "regent" and Yumashev and Voloshin were labeled "Family members," the essence of the accusations didn't change; they implied that somebody was quietly operating behind the president's back. And yes, that was true. Behind my back stood a large, strong, well-coordinated team. And anyone who prefers the term *family* can use it, knowing that the members of my "family" were Chubais, Voloshin, Yumashev, Dzhakhan Pollyyev, Sergei Yastrzhembsky, Vyacheslav Surkov, Ruslan Orekhov, Igor Shabdurasulov, Mikhail Komissar, Aleksandr Oslon, Mikhail Lesin, Yury Zapol, Kseniya Ponomaryova, Konstantin Ernst, Oleg Dobrodeyev, Sergei Zveryev (while he worked in the administration), Igor Malashenko (during the first years after the 1996 elections), Aleksei Gromov, Oleg Sysuyev, Sergei Prikhodko, Dmitry Yakushkin, Andrei Shtorkh, and many, many others. All these men and women helped draft the important decisions that would shape the future of the country. People may like it or dislike it, but I knew that these people had wonderful minds that generated brilliant ideas. They were supposed to work for the country. They were supposed to work for the president.

The summer of 1999 was approaching. I needed to find a new politician who could lead Russia on the path of democracy after the elections in 2000. Primakov's chances for the presidency were gradually increasing. The Duma Communists were the first to speak of it. And since the public opinion ratings of other likely candidates—Lebed, Yavlinsky, and Luzhkov—were significantly lower and only Zyuganov could conceivably match Primakov, the press began to take Primakov's candidacy seriously. Some wrote about the total rollback, the Communist *revanche*, the return to a Soviet model of life. Others wrote about the inevitable choice of Russian society. Any anticrisis prime minister would have a naturally large political base. The Primakov "stabilization," which was still not very visible in the economy and not very obvious in the lives of ordinary people, was nevertheless the political banner of the opposition.

Of course, I guessed that the prime minister's plans might change. He might develop presidential ambitious. I waited for Primakov to say something about this. But he preserved his utter calm. "We'll retire together in the year 2000, Boris Nikolayevich," he would say. "We'll go fishing together."

Outwardly, we kept up the same behavior—we worked together; we continued to discuss the ongoing economic issues; we looked for a presidential candidate. I considered those who were close to Primakov. Stepashin? The foreign minister, Ivanov? But Primakov didn't take any of them seriously. These were not people of the right caliber; they didn't fit. What kind of authority did they have? We needed a different type of person.

My aides pointed out the contradictions in Primakov's statements many times, noting how reluctant he was to talk about the future political situation; how he didn't want to reveal his own plans. Of course, this could have been a habit he acquired during his years of works in intelligence and in the Foreign Ministry. Regardless, in January and February people in the administration began to debate fiercely whether Primakov would run for president, and I gradually began to sense the danger of this situation. Yes, Primakov was able to attract that portion of the elite which quietly dreamed about a political *revanche* and the return of the old ways. I suppose it was not just the Communists, although it was them, too. It was also the "fifth column" of Communists in the special services, a group of governors and those we call the "strong managers." For broad segments of the Russian population, Primakov was a fairly hopeful figure. He promised order, stability, and the absence of change and reforms, which, after the autumn crisis of 1998, were perceived only as a threat.

I realized that Yevgeny Maksimovich Primakov—someone close to me, someone I personally understood, someone I knew as no other leader—objectively, almost against his own will, was becoming a serious political alternative to my course and my plan for the country's development.

The reader, especially an older reader, might wonder why I had sought to replace Primakov and, before that, Chernomyrdin, with younger leaders. Why was I so persistently placing my bets on people in their forties and sometimes (as in the case of Kiriyenko) even in their thirties? Wasn't that irresponsible?

Let me illustrate my answer with an episode from my private life. One day, my grandson Borya was trying to explain to me how a computer game worked. I listened to him for a long time, realizing it wasn't so simple. Then, as I sat before the flickering monitor, I suddenly saw that I simply had to ensure that Russia in the third millennium would be ruled by people with other types of brains, with other minds. Let the new president point out all my mistakes and failures and unsuccessful reforms. But let *him* be the creator.

I know that youth is not a panacea. There are forty-year-olds with totalitarian natures. You can work behind a computer every day but be a Neanderthal at heart. That's not the point. The person who would replace me had to enter another spiritual realm. He had to think in categories other than those of the generation of older politicians who had lived through the destruction of communism and the political crises of the new Russia. Just as in a more sophisticated computer game, he couldn't simply shoot at the enemies and get through the mazes; he would have to create a new civilization. And in order to do that, this new leader had to understand the language of world civilization—another world, in which the next generation would live, including my grandsons and great-grandsons.

· 14 ·

Prosecutor Skuratov

Yury Skuratov, Yeltsin's prosecutor general, is caught with his pants down. As Yeltsin relates the ugly story of the Skuratov sex scandal, he reveals a much wider web of corruption, bribery, and rampant crime. There seem to be shadowy forces at play in the criminal justice system—the police, the prosecutors, the politicians, the courts—who are misusing their powers to settle personal scores.

· ·

I DON'T EVEN feel like beginning this chapter. Yet the story it contains must be told. So be it.

Nobody has ever been able to force me to play by his rules. But Yury Ilyich Skuratov managed to drag me, the Federation Council, and the whole country into a petty, sordid scandal. The "quiet prosecutor" turned his own shame and disgrace inside out and tangled all of us up in it.

People say Russia hasn't been lucky with its prosecutor generals.* Stepankov, Kazannik, and Ilyushenko were Skuratov's predecessors. Stepankov left under a cloud during the White House rebellion of 1993; Kazannik released the 1991 coup plotters before the end of their

---

* In Russia, the president nominates the prosecutor general and the Federation Council has to approve his choice. The prosecutor general is the highest representative of the criminal justice system. Unlike his U.S. equivalent, he combines powers of investigation, prosecution, and oversight.—Trans.

sentences and then left, slamming the door behind him; Ilyushenko wound up in Lefortovo Prison (thanks to his successor, Skuratov). Each prosecutor departed amid scandal. And each one left behind a file cabinet of unsolved cases.

Is it only Russia that has such bad luck? I am sure there are dishonest prosecutors all over the world, fools in prosecutors' uniforms, but in our country, where the whole system of social relations has been dealt a crushing blow, prosecutors are particularly vulnerable to politicization. That's why our three previous prosecutors went down in flames.

In essence, the prosecutor general is merely a government bureaucrat. He doesn't need to hold particularly broad views or strong political opinions. In fact, in this post, such indisputable virtues can instantly turn into vices. The job of a prosecutor is simply to be the enemy of *any* lawlessness.

For a while after Skuratov was appointed, it seemed to me that we had at last found such a prosecutor. We met regularly, and Skuratov kept me informed about the progress of the investigations into the most notorious murders: those of the popular priest Father Aleksandr Men, the television host Vlad Listyev, the reporter Dmitry Kholodov, and the businessman Ivan Ivilidi. I was concerned that year in and year out these murders remained unsolved. I raised this issue with Skuratov many times. In his quiet, totally colorless voice, Skuratov would explain that the investigations were under way, that a list of suspects had been drawn up, that this or that theory was being developed. But I saw that nothing was moving forward. The endless monotone of Skuratov's excuses was beginning to annoy me.

Another feature of Skuratov, which at first instilled optimism, was his totally apolitical nature. But then the prosecutor general found himself a "spiritual mentor," the Duma deputy Viktor Ilyukhin. This was the same Ilyukhin who had once tried to open a criminal investigation against Mikhail Gorbachev for "treason against the motherland" and had tried to bring charges against me for "genocide of the Russian people." He was also the author of all the draft laws on my apparent incapacity to rule the country. According to the newspapers,

Ilyukhin had once worked in the prosecutor's system in liaison with the KGB. Now he was able to open any door at the Prosecutor's Office. This was hardly a good mentor for the once-apolitical Skuratov.

Skuratov, who possessed a number of indispensable qualities for a prosecutor—dogged thoroughness, a good memory, and stubbornness—lacked the most important qualities: a strong will, assertiveness, and belief in himself and his own powers. Thus, he turned out to be rather hollow. And this hollowness had to be filled immediately with some vivid, timely content. That's where Ilyukhin came in handy. Skuratov succumbed to the influence of those who prompted him to take the easy way out, the way of political show trials.

There were some bankers and businessmen who in one way or another took personal part in Skuratov's fate. As it turned out later, these "buddies" of Skuratov's had a fairly accurate understanding of the prosecutor general's weaknesses. Nikolai Bordyuzha was the first to learn about the pornographic videotape of Skuratov in the *banya* with some prostitutes. Bordyuzha was a military man, a border guard, who tended to be very suspicious of the slightest excesses. He was shocked when he saw the videocassette. At first Bordyuzha, who was my chief of administration at the time, decided not to tell me or anyone else about this nightmare. He met with Skuratov and tersely informed the prosecutor general that in this type of situation, one didn't have to reflect long. Skuratov obediently wrote his letter of resignation.

"Highly Respected Boris Nikolayevich!" Skuratov wrote to me in a memo dated February 1, 1999. "In connection with my great workload, the state of my health has recently deteriorated (headaches, chest pains, and so on). Taking account of this, I would ask you to put on the agenda for discussion at the Federation Council the issue of my release from my position as RF prosecutor general. I would ask you to review the question about providing me with a lighter workload. Sincerely, Yuri Skuratov."

But the next morning, Skuratov came into Bordyuzha's office and begged him not to let the videotape be shown anywhere. "Let's forget about it," he pleaded. "Forget about what you saw. I am ready to fulfill all your instructions."

Bordyuzha said, "Your resignation letter is already on the president's desk, and he has to make a decision. But if you have any common sense at all, you have to realize that if there is one copy of this tape, there must be fifty."

Skuratov begged and pleaded. A month later, however, he changed his tune and announced that the tape was forged and that he wasn't the one in it.

Not everyone could suffer such disgrace. Skuratov, most likely for real medical reasons, checked himself into the Central Kremlin Hospital. The meeting of the Federation Council, at which the senators would review his letter, was scheduled for March 17.

On the night of March 16, the tape was shown on Russian television. The next morning the senators almost unanimously voted against dismissing Skuratov. The political battle in the Federation Council reached a feverish pitch. In a television interview, Yegor Stroyev said something like "What's to discuss? The man had a misfortune!"

Before the vote on the Skuratov scandal, I had not known anything about the pornographic tape. Neither Bordyuzha nor any of my other assistants had told me. Reading Skuratov's letter of resignation, I had frankly felt a great sense of relief. The weak, colorless prosecutor was going to leave of his own accord. He didn't need to be forced out.

Then came the vote in the Federation Council, like a bolt from the clear blue sky. Suddenly I had a folder on my desk in front of me containing black-and-white stills made from the videocassette. These were the results of the preliminary investigation, materials from the session of the Federation Council at which Skuratov's dismissal had been reviewed. The attached experts' report said that an analysis of the voice and scenes on the tape had proved that the prosecutor general really was the man in the tape. I didn't look at the photographs or the tape but quickly pushed them away from me.

I summoned Skuratov, Primakov, and Putin to get to the bottom of the matter. It was in this meeting with Skuratov that I heard for the first time about a criminal investigation that Skuratov had launched into a Swiss construction firm called Mabetex. Skuratov said that he was being persecuted because he had opened an investigation into bribes that Mabetex had supposedly given to Pavel Borodin and other officials. Then Skuratov added a surprising comment to the effect that I, Boris Yeltsin, wouldn't have to worry about the Mabetex case if I left Skuratov in the post of prosecutor general. The investigation was under his control.

"What does that case have to do with anything?" I demanded. "If you have to investigate it, then do so. Do whatever is necessary. But we're talking about something else now, Yury Ilyich," I said. "After what's happened to you, I don't think that you should remain in the post of prosecutor general. I won't fight with you; I won't try to persuade you; just write your resignation letter. I will no longer work with you."

Skuratov fell silent, but not for long. He said that he thought it was harmful to the cause when such abnormal relations develop between the president and the prosecutor general. He said that he wanted to work on the president's team. Then Skuratov mentioned the Mabetex case again and said that if another prosecutor general were to come in, he wouldn't be able to deal with this complicated case. Casting about for support, he said to Primakov, "Go on, Yevgeny Maksimovich! You tell Boris Nikolayevich!"

I waited to see what Primakov would say. Primakov was quiet for a long time. Then he said, "If Boris Nikolayevich told me that he didn't want to work with me, I would leave without a second thought. You have to leave, Yury Ilyich."

Skuratov turned on Primakov. "But you've betrayed me, Yevgeny Maksimovich," he said.

I had the repulsive, horrible feeling that Skuratov was blatantly trying to make a deal over this Mabetex case. He seemed to be saying, "I'm yours. I'm ready to do anything. Just leave me in my job!"

I clearly repeated to him several times: "Yury Ilyich, I won't work with you. Write your resignation letter." I took a pen and paper and pushed them toward him.

With each passing minute I grew more convinced that we were doing the right thing by removing Skuratov from his post. Skuratov wasn't just weak and incoherent; he was extremely dangerous. Any criminal or opportunist politician could exploit these tapes for their own selfish purposes. And was it really only about the tapes? What sort of "services" — and from whom — could this slippery fellow accept?

That same day Skuratov wrote another resignation letter: "I have thought deeply about the last session of the Federation Council, and first of all I would like to thank you for your appreciation of my work. Nevertheless, taking into account the real state of affairs, the moral and psychological circumstances that have developed around me, I have decided to resign."

On that day, March 17, a fierce battle began. Skuratov stood at the center of it. It seemed obvious to me that the prosecutor general simply was not worthy of occupying such a top post. But the senators of Russia had ruled otherwise. Skuratov was a valuable tool in the fight for political influence. I have to hand it to Skuratov. He hadn't wasted a minute of his month in the hospital. Despite all the "pains in his head and heart," he had dug up all the cases that were in some way connected to politics and paraded them around. There was the case of Chubais's allegedly unlawful appointment as head of Unified Energy Systems, the electric company. There was the case of those accused of bringing about the banking collapse of August 17. There was his letter "on measures to return Russian capital from abroad." There was the case of abuses at the Central Bank.

As it later turned out, all of these notorious cases weren't worth a damn. Only one of them still has legs: the Mabetex affair, involving the renovation of the Kremlin. But Skuratov didn't hesitate to try to use these flimsy cases to bolster his own political standing. Skuratov was no longer a cringing, humiliated, lost fellow who couldn't get his story straight. Now I was dealing with a man who had clearly made a choice and had marked his place on the political stage. Doggedly, in his slinking manner, he tried to please his new allies in every way. No one else had ever managed to set the president head-to-head against the Federation Council. Skuratov did.

But the "quiet prosecutor" was only a pawn in the game of bigger people. Yury Luzhkov, the very powerful senator and mayor of Moscow, secured Skuratov the support he needed in the Federation Council. That was exactly what worried me most of all. After that memorable meeting of March 18, I could see through Skuratov completely. I simply could not tolerate his presence in the Prosecutor's Office any longer. But Luzhkov's behavior in the Federation Council, his speech in defense of Skuratov, was a new, unpleasant discovery for me—and not just in the political sense.

I knew that the ambitious Luzhkov was capable of a lot. That fall, during the effort to get Chernomyrdin confirmed, for example, Luzhkov had openly gone on the offensive against me. His attacks were related to his own fierce desire to become prime minister. But now Luzhkov was rushing to save Skuratov. Why? As a model family man and exemplary husband and father, Luzhkov couldn't help but know how repulsive the revelations about the prosecutor general would seem to the public. He would know how important it was to take a strong moral stance against such behavior. As the head of a large city, Luzhkov would know how important the integrity of the prosecutor general was and how dangerous it was when that person, who was supposed to enforce the law, had such criminal connections. As a state figure, Luzhkov was fully aware of the consequences of destroying the vertical command of the state, setting the president against the governors, and disrupting the balance of power. And as a politician, Luzhkov would realize that his protection of Skuratov would hardly endear him to the people. Still, he came to Skuratov's defense.

I can't find any other explanation or justification for Luzhkov's behavior in the Federation Council except his desire to provoke a crisis, no matter what, and to lead a group of governors to create a new center of power. It would be an illegitimate, unconstitutional center of power, crudely overriding the boundaries of the political process, but power nonetheless.

I could not allow that to happen. No one had yet managed to drive me into a corner. This tandem of prosecutor general and mayor would not succeed this time, even though the episode was discouraging and distracting, with its foul odor and sordid taint.

So why did only six senators vote for Skuratov's dismissal on March 17? Was it merely political calculation? I didn't believe that the senators would immediately fall for a story like our Russian "Commissar Katan" in the person of the unfortunate Skuratov. There were other, more primitive reasons. Most likely, some of the senators were thinking about themselves, recalling their own saunas and little "vacation getaways," which they had retained from the Soviet era. Not all of them were thinking this, of course. But a lot of them were. The traditional Russian inability to live according to the rules and the laws was depressingly evident throughout the entire Skuratov affair.

On March 27, investigators from the Prosecutor General's Office searched the Kremlin and seized documents from fourteen buildings. I must admit, this made me happy. I was confident that Skuratov's attempt at blackmail—the Mabetex case, which he had opened in the deepest secrecy—was only a minor diversion, an effort to keep up appearances. I understood that I was taking the right path. Let the investigators and the prosecutors continue their investigations within the law. The president had the same kind of obligation: to protect state interests no matter what. I had to remove an indecent prosecutor, and I would do it.

On April 2 the deputy prosecutor of Moscow opened a criminal case against Prosecutor General Skuratov on charges of abuse of office. Immediately afterward, I signed a decree to remove Skuratov from his post in connection with the ongoing investigation. The decree was drafted in strict accordance with the law on the Prosecutor General's Office and with the Russian constitution.

This criminal investigation is still ongoing. Further checking by the investigators has revealed that there had been at least seven encounters with the call girls. Each time these visits were paid for by "friends" who figured in various criminal cases. I hope that someday all the i's will be dotted and the t's crossed in this case.

Back in April most people didn't understand why I was taking such a harsh attitude toward Skuratov. The Federation Council was particularly perplexed. Governors have always been a major political force in Russia. Even in the Soviet era the first secretaries of the oblast committees—people who, it would seem, were elected and not appointed —could become "eloquently silent" in order to help turn the helm sharply to the left or right. The removal of Khrushchev took place within the context of a Party conspiracy, when the Brezhnev group managed to make a secret agreement with the majority of the first secretaries of the oblast Party committees. And the appointment of Gorbachev was accompanied by something similar. Not a single decision of this nature was made without the consent of "the firsts"—that is, the governors. In the case of Gorbachev's appointment, they managed to meet quite openly in the lobby of the Palace of Congresses, in specially reserved rooms, and at their hotels. There was no need for a secret conspiracy.

In the new constitution—which incidentally is called the "Yeltsin constitution," even though many experts, lawyers, and politicians helped draft it—the role of the regional leaders is clearly perscribed for the first time in the entire history of modern Russia. There is no longer any need to meet in the lobby. There is no need to arrange secret midnight meetings behind the leaders' backs.

Now the Federation Council ratifies every law. Its members discuss every major decision of state openly. We had quite deliberately taken that step when we perscribed the Federation Council's role in the constitution as a guarantor against political crises, shake-ups, and turmoil in the state. While the Duma is extremely politicized, especially in the tumultuous post-Communist era, the Federation Council is restrained and politically balanced. After all, each governor carries on his shoulders the enormous responsibility for his region.

Thus, any clash between the president and the governors would be extremely dangerous for the country. In order to create an atmosphere of confusion and dissension, the senators—who were also governors— hardly need a military coup, an impeachment, or a vote of no-confidence in the government. They are the 100 masters of Russia. Actually, *princes* might be a more accurate term, as such an incredibly powerful assembly could strip the tsar of his crown in ancient times.

Back in the fall, Yury Luzhkov had actively supported the Communist line in order to raise the issue of my incapacity as president. Now, on April 21, Luzhkov gave another fiery speech at the Federation Council meeting, supposedly in defense of the rule of law and in defense of Skuratov. But it was clear as day that Luzhkov was mounting his usual hobbyhorse. Once again he was placing his bets and trying to disrupt the political powers that be.

In the dispute surrounding the prosecutor general, the governors lined up behind Luzhkov for two reasons. First, they really wanted to have their own puppet prosecutor. Second and more important, they realized that they had found a weak point in our constitution that they could exploit. With the help of a simple vote on the prosecutor's dismissal, the regional leaders would obtain an instrument of authority in the country, a powerful instrument they could use to put pressure on the president. They weren't sure how to use it yet, but they wanted to try it out. Noting the weakness of the executive branch during the autumn crisis, the governors tested the government over and over again to see how it would hold up. This was their way of creating their own political configuration in the modern Russia.

I think the reform of the Federation Council under way today will help prevent such clashes between the president and the leaders of the regions in the future. It is too dangerous for the country when the governors, who are responsible for the stability of the Russian provinces, become involved in political intrigue.

I met with several governors and asked them their opinion of the Skuratov case. They generally supported my position and said that the country didn't need such a prosecutor. But behind the scenes Luzhkov was whipping the governors up into a legal protest and a constitutional rebellion, exploiting the fact that many of the weaker regions depended on the Moscow region. Eventually, out of a total of 178, 61 votes were in favor of Skuratov's dismissal and 79 against.* A number of the opposition were heads of the legislative assemblies of their regions. (Recall that the first vote had yielded entirely different numbers—only six had voted for Skuratov's resignation.)

Did many of these seventy-nine governors really believe that Sku-

---

* Some deputies abstained or were not present for the vote.—Trans.

ratov would open his magic briefcase to reveal the Swiss bank account numbers and the names of the contract killers in the most notorious cases? I don't think so. The vote was a pure political gamble. You could say that the entire staff of people who worked on supporting Skuratov and met with the senators were Luzhkov's people and Communist Party representatives. And then of course on the day of the vote they all showed up at the Federation Council—both Zyuganov and Ilyukhin and many other deputies who had a vested interested in stoking the scandal. I think that over the next year these same people gradually realized that Skuratov's legendary briefcase was as empty as its owner. It contained not a single new fact or a single new document.

Prior to the second vote at the Federation Council, my team tried to make peace with Luzhkov. Among the candidates for a new prosecutor general, I had reviewed the possibility of Gennady Ponomaryov, former head of the Moscow City Prosecutor's Office. I asked Lisov, deputy head of the administration, who had recently worked in the Prosecutor General's Office and knew Ponomaryov, to tell me about him. Lisov thought that Ponomaryov was a strong, independent prosecutor and a worthy candidate. Luzhkov backed him as well. But in exchange for supporting the Skuratov dismissal, Luzhkov demanded a letter naming Ponomaryov, already signed by me, addressed to the Federation Council. I was surprised that Luzhkov was trying to dictate conditions to me.

Throughout late April, I tried to understand how the ridiculous adventures of one prosecutor had evolved into such a huge political drama. Was the Federation Council the problem? No, it wasn't only that. A new era was emerging in Russia, the era of economic repression when economic regulations were used to intimidate and control people. It had begun gradually, unnoticed. But now it was already acquiring the status of a state ideology. Such a comparison might do violence to historical truth—it had been a long time since Russia had a Communist dictatorship; there were no longer mass arrests and black cars taking people away at night. In our country, however, it isn't considered wrong to put people into an investigation cell before trial, even if they're charged only with an economic offense. This happens even though international experience has proven that such restraints are merited only when a person is suspected of a particularly grave crime. With our imperfect tax and accounting systems, practically any citizen can be charged and sentenced. Given the existing holes in our laws, prosecutors can issue an arrest warrant for practically any banker, business owner, accountant, or economist as long as there is a political need to do so. "Economic crimes" can be freely interpreted by the Prosecutor's Office or secret police agents and can thus become the basis for blackmail, kompromat, bribes, and other abuses. It was in this muddy water that the Skuratov cassette surfaced.

The Prosecutor's Office was baiting and hooking some business-men. Meanwhile, the businessmen were hooking the Prosecutor's Office. Gradually this system of pressure on essentially normal, hon-est people went beyond individual criminal cases. By the spring of 1999, as "show" arrests, searches, and confiscations occurred in more and more banks and firms, the Russian business community was seized with a fear of people in uniform.

For me, it had all begun with the Sobchak affair, during the 1996 elections for the St. Petersburg governor.* An airplane flew over the city dropping flyers that claimed, "Anatoly Sobchak is involved in two criminal cases." It was true that Sobchak was "involved" in two crimi-nal cases, but as a witness, not a suspect. Of course not everybody in his entourage was clean. But as a deeply decent, honest man (and inci-dentally, a lawyer), he never exploited his "telephone law" in order to pressure somebody or otherwise abuse his political power as other governors and mayors did.† It was he who was exploited in this power play. But who exploited it?

Back then there were Moscow politicians like Korzhakov who were backing Yakovlev in the race for governor. The plane with the leaflets never could have taken off without their direct involvement. The power structures—the Prosecutor's Office, the Interior Ministry, the Federal Security Service—campaigned openly against Sobchak.

---

* When Sobchak held the post of the top city official of St. Petersburg, the name of the position was changed to "mayor"; it was subsequently changed back to "governor."—Trans.

† Telephone law was a term that emerged in the Soviet perestroika era to describe the pressure high Communist Party officials placed on the criminal justice system through their private phone calls to judges, thereby defying the rule of law.—Trans.

After the elections Skuratov became interested in the Sobchak Affair. "There must be an investigation," he said. "Sobchak is suspected of large-scale embezzlement."

I would always give him the same answer: "Operate strictly within the law." I had one simple principle: Everyone is equal before the law. There is no "mine" and "yours" when it comes to legal matters. Anyone who takes a different approach shouldn't be considered a politician or even an honest human being.

But my aides had their own information from St. Petersburg about the Sobchak affair. Apparently, several different investigation teams were unable to find anything incriminating. They were trying to dig up something related to Sobchak's apartment or his bank loans, but they were coming up with zero. How long could this go on? I kept repeating the same thing to the people who came to Sobchak's defense — Chubais, Yumashev, Nemtsov: "If there is any suspicion, it has to be investigated and proven whether the man is guilty or not."

Meanwhile, the Interior Ministry investigative team and the Prosecutor's Office continued to work in St. Petersburg. They were really hoping to find some big *kompromat* on Sobchak, something that would rise to the level of a serious corruption case.

Things went on this way for a long time. Yumashev met again with Skuratov in the Kremlin. Then he met with Interior Minister Kulikov. He told them that he thought the actions of the police and the Prosecutor's Office came from outside political pressure, not from a desire to find the truth. Then they came to me, asking for protection against interference by the administration. And once again I told them that an investigation within the bounds of the law must be continued, that there wasn't any interference now and that there would be none in the future.

In the fall of 1998, after another interrogation, Sobchak had a heart attack and went into the hospital. I remember vividly a conversation I had with Nemtsov in Zavidovo. Nemtsov told me that Sobchak had had a terrible heart problem and that within a few days the Prosecutor's Office had issued a warrant for his arrest. It looked like deliberate harassment. I recall I was silent for a long time during this conversation with Nemtsov, staring at a fixed point, my thoughts tortured and

heavy. I asked that Skuratov be sent a message from me: "You can't ha-
rass a sick man."

Even Putin, the head of the Federal Security Service, intervened in
the Sobchak case. Putin understood the injustice of what was happening to his former boss and political mentor better than anyone. He immediately left to spend the November holidays in St. Petersburg. There
he met with a team of doctors, including Shevchenko, who is now Minister of Health, and told him that he was going to try to get Sobchak
out of the country. Thanks to the holidays, the city was quiet. Using his
connections in Petersburg, Putin made a deal with a private airline and
brought Sobchak out to Finland. From there Sobchak made his way to
Paris. Sobchak had been ordered not to leave town, so he was being followed. But they were not watching too carefully, probably because they
didn't think anyone would help a man who was five minutes away from
finding himself behind bars in Kresty Prison—that just wouldn't happen in our pragmatic day. But they were wrong; there *was* someone
willing to help. Later, when I learned about what Putin had done, I felt
a profound sense of respect for and gratitude toward him.

Corruption in Russia is a huge and sensitive topic. I'm absolutely convinced that an ineffective economy and nonfunctioning laws are
mainly to blame.

Not once during my term in office as president of Russia did I
shield anyone from criminal prosecution. I never defended anyone before a court, the police, the Prosecutor's Office, or the FSB. Let me repeat: I believe that absolutely everyone should be equal before the law.
Nevertheless, I found that the problem of corruption could not be
solved. In any economy undergoing the privatization of property, corruption inevitably emerges. It can be fought only with common,
united efforts.

How can you force a bureaucrat not to take bribes to feed his family, when he earns only 5,000–6,000 rubles per months but is involved
in monitoring multimillion-ruble transactions? Naturally, the only way
is to raise his salary and make him more prosperous. But the Communist state Duma, other politicians, and the general public were always

sharply opposed to raising the bureaucrats' salaries. And how could you raise the salaries of the bureaucrats when other state employees, like teachers and doctors, were paid so little? So the wages of bureaucrats remained low, and the bribes and payoffs remained high. There was no consolidated public opinion on many other questions—taxes, the clash between local and federal laws, or on the freeing of Russian business from various unnecessary and even ridiculous bans and regulations. And when we interfere with business, we inevitably create a climate for corruption.

It's probably not just a question of laws. Our mentality itself forces ordinary businesspeople and ordinary government clerks to give and take bribes; ever since the Soviet era we've been taught to get around bans and regulations by paying under the table. But I am deeply convinced that Russians are prepared to live by their consciences. Everyone understands that we can't go on this way.

For this process of cleansing to go faster, only a few things are needed: a functioning economy, low taxes, and higher salaries for government employees. We must return to the law of common sense. Moreover, we should not jail or punish selected scapegoats but rather demonstrate our moral purity ourselves. We can beat corruption only with clean hands and honest people. I always had faith in my team.

I believe that all sensible law-enforcement officials understood that the story of the Skuratov cassette was but the logical culmination of the double or triple game that had been played out for years in the Prosecutor General's Office, the FSB, and the Interior Minister by former Skuratovs and other powerful men who had lost their moral bearings.

Of course there were also ordinary investigators at the Prosecutor's Office who just tilled the earth, so to speak. And there were Interior Ministry and Federal Security Service workers investigating economic crimes, who were really battling organized crime and corruption. It was hard to say how they felt about the Skuratov story. Were they embarrassed, confused, angry? What were they supposed to do? How were they supposed to act after the prosecutor general himself turned out to be so deeply involved with dubious people who had supplied him with call girls?

The Skuratov saga continued for many months. There was a third vote in the fall of 1999, and the senators once again voted against dismissing Skuratov. But by then the case was no longer attracting much interest. Its political component had been exhausted, and its legal side was boring and banal. Skuratov, suspended but not dismissed from his post, continued to make loud pronouncements and to expose people, but hardly anyone listened to him. His very figure seemed comical. He continued to ride around in a black car with a flashing light, to live in a state dacha, and to play soccer with his bodyguards. Apparently he found satisfaction in his free and easy lifestyle. But all that time—during his meetings with the Swiss prosecutor Carla del Ponte and his noisy interviews and press conferences—Skuratov didn't say anything that advanced his spring accusations by even one step. And despite his prominent international reputation as a Russian mafia fighter, Skuratov was in total oblivion in his own country.

I was repeatedly criticized for losing the round with Skuratov. People complained that we had artificially pumped Skuratov up with our actions, lending him needless political weight. It is hard to say what position the prime minister would have had on the Skuratov case if it hadn't been for my pressure. I think Primakov probably found Skuratov convenient. Although Skuratov was weak, powerless, and involved in blackmail, he didn't get in Primakov's way. But it was impossible to leave Skuratov in the Prosecutor General's Office. It was dangerous. In my opinion a person without principles like Skuratov could use his prosecutor's powers to stir up God knows what kind of trouble in the country. Russia without a prosecutor general was the lesser of two evils. I think that my decision in the Skuratov affair also cooled many of the hotheads in the Federation Council.

The lesson of the Skuratov story is that we cannot leave a compromised prosecutor, a criminal case, a highly publicized investigation, or a question of moral responsibility in a prolonged state of suspension. If the law is not kept in a democratic country, if the institutions of civil society do not work, then democracy risks turning into totalitarianism.

In May 2000 the Federation Council finally dismissed Skuratov. Thus ended the saga of the prosecutor general.

· 15 ·

Neighbors

Russia's often troublesome relationship with its neighbors mirrors its own internal struggle against communism and separatism, which led to the breakup of the USSR. Yeltsin describes Russia's altercations with various CIS countries, from the fight with Ukraine over the Black Sea fleet to the controversial Russian-Belarus agreement. It soon becomes clear that the threat of Communist "Soviet reunion" hangs over the heads of both Yeltsin and his suspicious neighbors.

·   ·

ECONOMIC TRANSITION was difficult for Russia. But it was even more difficult for those beyond Russia, in the countries of the Commonwealth of Independent States (CIS) formed after the collapse of the Soviet Union in 1991. Our common illusions—that the republics of the former USSR would find it easy to enter the world market on their own and that their lives would become more prosperous—dissolved. Other illusions crashed as well, including the belief that Russia would achieve some kind of unprecedented boom without the load of economic obligations to its younger brothers.

In the CIS countries, people's lives became significantly tougher and more impoverished. I always knew that. And though I clearly realized that it was not my fault, I felt bad. What was "at fault" was the entire history of the twentieth century, which had brutally and ruthlessly destroyed one empire after another. A simple analogy could be cited here: When a couple divorces, it's very important that the husband and wife preserve friendly, normal relations. It's important for the children and important for the rest of life. In the case of the CIS, we weren't just divvying up pots and pans but armaments. It was very important that this process of divorce be peaceful and that the nuclear capacity be kept intact and eventually, by mutual agreement, turned over to Russia.

Still, I think one would be hard-pressed to find another state organization like the CIS in the history of the world. It was not so long ago that people in our countries lived by the same rules and worked in the same economy. We shared similar everyday lives, the same system of education, and a single state. We understood each other. We could finish each other's sentences. After all, we rode in those same old-fashioned Soviet buses and trolleybuses, watched the same movies, and told the same jokes. In short, we shared the same mind-set. At the same time, each country was extraordinarily distinctive in terms of climate, geography, history, and national mentality. It is this unity in contradictions, this paradox, which is now known by the acronym CIS.

Many people in Russia and the CIS countries now wonder what will become of the CIS. Many say that the CIS is merely a smoke-screen standing in the way of true integration; that relations among countries should be strictly bilateral; that when all of our complex problems are finally resolved, the former Soviet republics will no longer have this mechanism that helps them crush decisions unfavorable to Russia.

I completely disagree with this point of view. The CIS is an objective reality. Most important, it is a single labor market. Millions of citizens of the former Soviet republics live and work in the CIS, though not in their home states, and I cannot imagine how they could otherwise feed their families. It is a common market for goods and services, integral to the budget of each CIS country. This market most likely could not exist without our open borders and our customs union. It is also a common market for energy resources, oil, gas, and electricity, which are fundamental to the economy. A natural monopoly emerged in Russia but will not translate into a Russian diktat on the energy market—it never did. But it will, just as naturally, result in Russia's full integration with other CIS countries.

The CIS also has a common cultural and news system that continues to develop, albeit not in its previous, Soviet form. Finally, it is a collective security system. The Karabakh and Abkhazia conflicts, the Chechnya problem, clashes with Islamic extremists in Central Asia— they all are our common agony. And the lesson we have learned from these tragedies is that without each other, we cannot cope with these bleeding geopolitical wounds.

More than anything, I am deeply convinced that one day we will share a common finance system, common administration of law enforcement agencies, common international priorities, and perhaps even a common parliament. These prospects may frighten some people today, but our integration is inevitable. This is precisely why we Russians must not scare off our neighbors. We must not disrupt the ties we have established.

Sometimes we have had to pay a heavy price in order to maintain those ties. The year 1997 was especially difficult for the CIS. We went through a few trials, the first of which was, oddly enough, the negotiation of the Russia-Belarus agreement. Belarusians are not just our nearest western neighbors and not just Slavs. The history of Belarus is so interwoven with the history of Russia, and the relations between the two peoples are so close, that we have always felt ourselves historically to be blood kin. With the CIS as well we have had special relations. Both of us have tried to enhance our cooperation.

Back in 1996 the heads of state set about the task of drawing up a treaty for fuller integration. The treaty was drafted by a group headed by then vice premier Valery Serov, whose specialty in the Russian government was integration issues. On the Belarusian side, the draft was approved by Foreign Minister Ivan Antonovich and Mikhail Myasnikovich, who was then head of the Belarusian presidential administration. On the Russian side it was written by Tikhonov, chair of the Duma Committee for CIS Relations. And on the Belarus side it was written by Antonovich, who had moved to Minsk and changed citizenship. Both were members of the Russian Communist Party. The fact that the foreign minister of Belarus was an active member of the Russian Communist Party should have made us cautious. But it didn't. And it's a shame.

It soon became apparent that the draft charter did not correspond to my conception of the future union. The draft would have essentially meant one thing: Russia would lose its sovereignty. A new state would appear with a new parliament and a new supreme executive authority, the so-called Supreme Soviet of the Union. The decisions of this body would be binding on the Russian president, the government, and all the executive authorities of Russia. According to the draft treaty : "The decisions of the Supreme Soviet of the Union are binding on the bodies of the Union and the bodies of the executive authority of the participating states."

The charter stated that the leadership of the Supreme Soviet of the new federation would alternate between the Belarusian president and the Russian president. First one would serve two years, then the other would serve two years. That would mean that the Russian Federation would be ruled for two years by Belarusian president Aleksandr Lukashenko.

Regarding the parliament, the draft charter stated, "The participating states create the conditions for the change of the Parliamentary Assembly into a representative and executive body of the Union, directly elected by citizens of the Union." The statute on equal representation in the federative parliament also caused indignation. It stipulated thirty-five seats for both countries, although 150 million people live in Russia and 10 million in Belarus.

It is not only the Communists who dream of restoring the Soviet Union at all costs. For Communist Party members, it was chiefly a political tool, an ideological postulate. But for other Russians the desire to revive the Soviet Union gave rise to a kind of personal cri de coeur, a reaction to the pain they felt for relatives, colleagues, friends, and others who were left behind in other countries. It was—pardon the expression—the call of blood kinship. At times the subconscious can have a powerful influence on the conscious, even among government bureaucrats.

My assistant for international issues, Dmitry Ryurikov, turned out to be a passionate supporter of this ill-conceived and dangerous unification of the two states. This charter of the federal state had the support as well not only of the Russian Duma speaker, Gennady Seleznyov, but also a huge number of government bureaucrats. The agreement had already been signed. It was on President Lukashenko's desk. A huge international scandal was brewing. In order to fix the situation, I had to set my administration to the task immediately. Working overtime, lawyers discovered in the draft charter a whole range of other egregious violations of the Russian constitution.

I wrote a letter to Aleksandr Lukashenko, requesting that he postpone signing the treaty so that there could be a nationwide debate about its content. I knew that a demarche like this from the Russian president would be a very unpleasant surprise for the Belarusian president. I entrusted this delicate mission to Ivan Rybkin, the secretary of the Security Council. I told him, "Ivan Petrovich, don't come back home until Lukashenko agrees to this." Sighing deeply, Rybkin nodded his head. He flew immediately to Minsk with my letter.

A surprise was awaiting Rybkin at the airport. Right off the bat Lukashenko told him, almost word for word, what was in my letter. (I later found out that Ryurikov, my assistant, who advocated the pro-Communist merger, had told him the letter's contents.)

To this day I am profoundly grateful to Ivan Petrovich Rybkin for his patience and persistence. He and Lukashenko spent many hours together, and (as malicious tongues often say) there were a fair number of empty bottles of hard liquor after the negotiations. That was real Slavic diplomacy.

Rybkin was very tired when he got back to Moscow. Soon thereafter, on April 10, the new text of the treaty was signed. It read more like a statement of intention for interstate unification. As I had proposed, a nationwide public discussion of this document ensued. It was exceptionally important for the peoples of the two states, and we received quite a few valuable suggestions from our citizens.

On May 21 a ceremonial signing of the new treaty between Russia and Belarus took place. During the signing, President Lukashenko looked pale but calm. We were both absolutely sure that state integration was not far off. And in 2000 the full-scale union of the two countries took place.

I always hoped that a variety of associations would exist within the CIS and that the CIS countries could join gradually. The conditions for these unions were supposed to be realistic and fulfillable. Unfortunately, there are still difficulties hindering the complete economic integration of Russia and Belarus: the lack of transparency in the Belarusian financial markets, antimarket legislation, and barriers blocking privatization. If Russia were able to bring Belarus into a common market, it would be a tremendous success. But before this can happen, the Belarusian economy has to undergo radical reform.

I also had quite a few bones to pick with Lukashenko about his leadership style, about the way he treated the press, including the arrest of journalist Pavel Sheremet.* But we had to remain friends if the Russia-Belarus union were to become the flagship for the CIS and lead us forward to our common integration. I really hope that democratic reform in Belarus will only benefit from the union process. We in Russia must use all available means to assure its success.

I cite the example of the marginally successful Russia-Belarus union of 1997 for a reason. It is absolutely inadmissible to use the often difficult relations among CIS countries as a pawn in the domestic political game. But this is exactly what the Russian Communists did in 1997, trying at all costs to push the Belarus treaty through the Duma.

A second glaring example of how major interstate problems were used to ignite internal political passions was the issue of the Black Sea fleet in Sevastopol on the Crimean peninsula. This became the biggest stumbling block in our relations with Ukraine.

---

* Pavel Sheremet, a Belarusian citizen, served as bureau chief of ORT, Russia's public television, and was arrested in 1998 and held in pretrial detention on charges of unlawful border crossing for filming the Lithuanian-Belarusian border. After Yeltsin protested Sheremet's arrest and also refused to allow Lukashenko's plane to land in Russia, the journalist and his codefendant, cameraman Dmitry Zavadsky, were released. Sheremet then moved to Moscow, and in 2000 Zavadsky disappeared and was believed to have been abducted. — Trans.

Relations between Russia and Ukraine are a special, complicated topic. To Russians, Ukrainians are the same kind of kin as Belarusians. We have an enormous affinity in everything—language, customs, and lifestyle. Most important, Kiev in Ukraine was the capital of ancient Rus, and Ukraine is the cradle of our national identity, our national history. Without Ukraine, it is impossible to imagine Russia. But the twentieth century revealed Ukraine's great yearning for independence. Its attempt to find itself and its own path of development is stamped on all the main events, all the wars and revolutions. In its democratization Ukraine felt another powerful impulse to separate from Russia.

I had met Ukrainian President Leonid Kuchma a number of times. But I had to postpone my first official visit to Kiev because of conflicts regarding the Black Sea fleet. Doubts had been growing in our relations; they had become artificially frozen. We were unable to sign a single major treaty.

The situation came to a head in May 1997. My state visit to Kiev took place after negotiations between both prime ministers. The chestnut trees were in bloom. Crowds of happy people greeted us. When I stopped the car in the center of the city and got out to talk to Kievans, many held out their hands, saying warm words of welcome. The gloomy people with anti-Russian posters were sidelined by this emotional, warmhearted crowd.

I thought to myself: "My God, how many years could this incomprehensible pause in our relations have dragged on? How much longer could we have pretended that we could live just fine without one another?"

The problems of the Black Sea fleet were serious. The fleet was in a state of decay. There had been no upgrading, no repairs. Sailors didn't know which state they were serving, didn't know who was supposed to pay them their salaries, benefits, and pensions. Of the 400,000 residents of Sevastopol, 100,000, or one-fourth, had their lives tied up in the work and fate of the fleet. These people all waited tensely for the outcome of our disagreement. The decision of how to divide the fleet was a major victory for both Ukraine and Russia.

The treaty we negotiated had the following provisions: Russia would lease the Sevastopol, Southern and Karantine Bays, where 338 Russian military ships were to be based, among them major battleships. The average yearly cost of the lease under the terms of the treaty was $98 million, which would go toward the debt Ukraine owed Russia for natural gas, which amounted to about $3 billion at the time of the signing of the treaty. We agreed on a twenty-year lease of military bases, including Sevastopol's infrastructure.

And so the period of estrangement, when the Black Sea fleet belonged to no one, came to an end. Now, instead of the old Soviet flags, new Andreyev banners, historically used by Russia's navy, appeared over Russian ships, and the yellow-and-blue Ukrainian flag hung over the Ukrainian ships.

Everyone breathed a sigh of relief. After so many years when the issue of the fleet had seemed to be at a complete impasse, it was finally resolved. At last the issue of the ownership of Sevastopol was removed from the agenda and Ukraine's territorial integrity was reinforced.

I considered the fleet treaty a win-win agreement. We could now maintain a military presence in the Black and Mediterranean Sea basins, where a large number of our merchant and cargo ships sail to this day. This was very important for restoring Russia's prestige. But the most important thing was that we signed a full-scale friendship and cooperation treaty with Ukraine, covering customs duties, joint economic projects, and the debt issue. Once Sevastopol was off the agenda, new life was breathed into all of these issues.

But not everyone in Russia and Ukraine agreed with this outcome. The division of the fleet pulled the rug out from under both the Ukrainian nationalists and our left-wingers. Even Yury Luzhkov, a prominent federal politician, joined the left. He called it abnormal for us to be in a position where we are in fact leasing Sevastopol from ourselves. Luzhkov clearly would have preferred to declare war on Ukraine or declare Sevastopol a district of Moscow.

There is another episode that illustrates the difficult yet important role of the CIS. A closed session of the council of CIS heads of state took place in Chisinau, the capital of Moldova, on October 23, 1997. First there were all the usual things—the greetings at the airport, the hugs, the reception ceremony, the press conference. I was in a regular, working mood and did not expect any surprises. But the surprises came as soon as we sat down at the negotiating table. One president after another went on the offensive, making speeches with tough anti-Russian positions. Each one had drawn up a list of complaints.

I listened attentively, jotting down the main points in my notebook. The presidents were clearly weary of unresolved problems. It was tempting for them to lay their enormous burdens on the shoulders of their big neighbor. The Georgian leader Eduard Shevardnadze said that the fratricidal Abkhaz war cast a shadow over his country. And Leonid Kuchma complained that Ukraine had its own problems, and they weren't just economic. How can democracy be reconciled with vehement and aggressive nationalism? Petru Lucinschi in Moldova, Emomali Rakhmonov in Tajikistan, and Askar Akayev in Kyrgyzstan all had their own radical nationalists. The painful conflict in Karabakh kept coming back to haunt relations between Azerbaijan and Armenia; it was unclear when relations between these two countries could be restored.

There were a lot of sharp words at the summit in Moldova about the scandal involving Russian arms deliveries to Armenia. Our military had sent weapons to Armenia under an unpublicized agreement within the power ministries. Azerbaijani president Heidar Aliev was angry about this. In response, I said that I had already fired several administrative heads in the Ministry of Defense and would remove many more. This created quite a stir in the room.

I probably could have responded to each speech in tougher terms. But I didn't want to. The Moldova summit was one of the most dramatic, as it determined the fate of the CIS.

I once visited the famed wine cellars in Chisinau. I remember the huge casks, barely visible under a dim light; the slightly acidic fragrance of old wood; the dampness of the cellar; and the wine—tart, velvety, almost viscous. This wine cellar provided an apt metaphor for the CIS. Throughout many hundreds of years, we had been maintaining our faith in one another. We were like farmers who together plow the same field, cultivate grapes, trample them, put them through the press, and pour them into the casks. We could not get this peasant work done without one another.

The story of Boris Berezovksy's appointment as CIS executive secretary shows yet again how I tried to meet my fellow presidents halfway. From summit to summit, there was growing dissatisfaction with the work of the executive committee and its leadership. Finally, all the state leaders agreed that the head of the executive committee, Vladimir Korotchenya, should be removed from his post. Then we had to find a new leader.

The foreign affairs ministries wrote to each other, and several of the candidacies got lost in the paper shuffle. I was told that there still hadn't been an agreement on who would be the new leader before the next regular meeting of the heads of state. To my complete surprise, as we were gathered in the Kremlin's Catherine the Great Hall, Kuchma proposed Boris Berezovsky for the post of CIS executive secretary. He explained that Berezovsky was exactly the kind of vivid public personality who could give a powerful impulse to important structures within the CIS. I was shocked.

But that was only the beginning. One head of state after another took to the podium and supported Berezovksy's candidacy. Finally I asked for the floor and explained to my dear colleagues that feelings toward Berezovsky were far from simple in my country, especially among the political elite. I asked them to think of another candidate.

They were surprised and skeptical. They knew Berezovsky's pluses and minuses, but how could I oppose a Russian candidate?

I asked for time to think about it, called a break, and left. I sat down in the armchair in the lounge next to the Catherine Hall. I asked Shevchenko, the head of protocol, to find Berezovsky and bring him to the Kremlin immediately.

I summoned Yumashev, head of administration, and Kiriyenko, chair of the government, and asked them what they thought about this development. Berezovsky had gone to all the state leaders, asking them for their support. Now we were dealing with the results.

Truth be told, I had never seen Yumashev so mad. He said that he was categorically against it. Moreover, he considered it out of the question that any CIS decision be imposed on the president of Russia, especially since it had all been done in secret, behind my back. Kiriyenko was agitated as well and said that the president should not take such a heavy additional political burden upon himself. Berezovsky's appointment would create an enormous scandal inside Russia.

Just then Berezovsky arrived. I asked Kiriyenko and Yumashev to wait outside.

"Boris Abramovich," I began. "I think you're already aware of what happened today. Practically all of the presidents proposed that you be appointed executive secretary of the CIS. You understand that people in our country are going to react to this with a great deal of misgivings. I'd like to hear what you think."

Berezovsky looked slightly disheveled. He had rushed to the Kremlin from somewhere outside the city. He looked at me hard and said, "Boris Nikolayevich, if you want to do something helpful for the commonwealth, then I have to be appointed. I am certain that I can be useful. If you are concerned about what people will say on the street, then don't support me. But if you do support me, I will try to justify the faith you and the other CIS presidents have in me."

I thought about it for another minute. It was, of course, a strange situation. The Russian president was against a Russian citizen.

I walked back into the hall. The presidents looked at me, worried. I said, "My dear colleagues, I agree with your suggestion. Boris Berezovsky's candidacy for the post of executive secretary of the CIS has been accepted."

Berezovsky was appointed to this post unanimously, as required by the CIS charter. A year later, he was dismissed—upon my initiative, and it was a scandal—but to this day the presidents of the commonwealth say that he was the strongest CIS executive secretary ever.

Any CIS summit usually provokes accusations from various sides. Our own politicians, both right-wing and left-wing, complained that I put

up with too much from the presidents of the independent states; that I
didn't respond to their attacks; that I give out far too many benefits
and made too many allowances on economic issues; that I forgave
debts and granted credits; and on and on. And the presidents and parliamentarians of the CIS countries likewise had their complaints: Russia wasn't engaged in real integration but was getting away with a lot
of talk; we announced new customs and tax barriers; we didn't abide
by the free trade agreement; we didn't compromise on natural gas and
electricity prices.

It was my deliberate policy to keep conflicts in check. I tried to put
the brake on them. No, we weren't getting away with a lot of talk. All
the problems inside the CIS were solvable. The leaders knew and understood each other well; the countries had good, neighborly relations; and the people were bound together as families, friends, and
colleagues. That was the kind of cooperation that we were trying to
preserve.

And I think I achieved the most important thing: Despite all the
talk about the changing winds and despite all the obvious attempts by
certain third countries to turn the international community against
Russia, our economic and political ties with CIS countries were
strengthened. They turned into a system of mutual dependence which
will be very difficult to destroy.

I really hope that someday people will remember the Belovezh Forest in completely different terms. I hope they will say that it was the
beginning of a completely new stage: We started to build a totally new
reality, following the European Union, a reality that was a single economic realm, a spiritual realm, a common home; a reality where new
states could coexist comfortably, despite their vast differences in climate, geography, national history, and mentality. This was our reality,
a new union, the Commonwealth of Independent States.

Soon after my resignation on December 31, 1999, all of the leaders of
the CIS countries gathered in Moscow. Everyone arrived a full day in
advance of the official events, and I invited them to my home at Gorki-

9. Of course it is not customary to invite official visitors, let alone an entire summit, to one's home. It had never been done before. But Naina and I decided to break with tradition. We had never had so many honored guests at once. Naina was even worried that we wouldn't have enough plates in our china set. We served the presidents our best home-cooked family dish: Siberian dumplings stuffed with pike. I think they liked it.

In his own way, each president tried to say something cordial. Each invited me to visit.

I remember how Islam Karimov, president of Uzbekistan, a wonderful person, a subtle man in the Oriental tradition, made a toast about my voluntary resignation, saying, "Boris Nikolayevich, nobody but you could do something like that."

What does Uzbekistan mean to Russia? It is the most colorful and the most exotic Central Asian republic. During the war masses of refugees were evacuated to Uzbekistan, and many hungry orphans were saved by Uzbek families. Throughout the entire century, Russians offered assistance to Uzbek culture, education, and industry. In 1966 the Tashkent earthquake sent shock waves through the entire country. With the help of the whole world, we restored the city, which had been destroyed. Such blood ties leave an imprint in people's memories.

I doubted that my good friend Nursultan Nazarbayev, the president of Kazakhstan, approved of my retirement, but he said nothing about it. As usual, he kept his thoughts to himself. Nazarbaev has kept his republic solid. I think this is because he doesn't acknowledge sharp changes, abrupt movements, or radical vacillations, whether in politics or in the economy. He combines a modern sensibility with an Oriental caution and discretion. He instills confidence. Not everyone has this gift.

It is always more difficult to know what Heidar Aliev, the patriarch of Azerbaijan, is thinking. I remember him from as far back as Gorbachev's Politburo. How much, I wondered, had this wise man lived through? How many changes had he been forced to make? With tremendous effort, Aliev managed to lead his people along the path to peace and to end a difficult and unnecessary war. People will certainly never forget this. They understand it in Russia, too. Aliev knows that. He is counting on this understanding.

The youngest president of the CIS, Lukashenko of Belarus, attracts a lot of attention in the Russian press with his sometimes excessively harsh declarations. He is regarded as aggressive, even crude. This is something I have never sensed during our personal interactions. Certainly he is a brash man, easily carried away. But we accomplished the dream we shared together: We united our two states. This is an event of great consequence, and it occurred in part thanks to the amazing persistence and energy of Lukashenko.

Eduard Shevardnadze of Georgia is also respected in Russia. He would be facing elections soon after our meeting, after Easter. Like Aliev, Shevardnadze saved his nation from the abyss of civil war. Today Georgia's problems are of a completely different nature. The economy is improving, and efforts are being made to expand to foreign markets and to stimulate industry. Georgia needs peace and stability. In this respect there will always be complete mutual understanding between us.

It was harder to relate to Leonid Kuchma. As a Ukrainian, he is kind and genial on the surface. But he is strong, stubborn, and determined. Fortunately, we no longer need to divide the Black Sea fleet or discuss customs issues; we can simply eat dumplings and enjoy life. Ukraine is slowly extricating itself from its economic crisis, and the political situation is stabilizing as well. The people are beginning to live better and more happily.

Luchinski reminisced about our summit meeting and invited me back to Moldova, a beautiful country, full of goodwill. Moldova is inherently peaceful. The people have a positive peasant mentality. But the scars from the collapse of the USSR remain, especially in the Transdniester region, home of a large Russian-speaking minority. Moldova can hardly resolve this problem without us.

Saparmurat Niyazov invited me to visit sunny Turkmenistan. Soon everything there would be in bloom. Fruits and melons would fill the tables. Turkmenistan, unlike all the other former republics of the

USSR, continued to follow the path of a state-controlled economy. Correctly and prudently, Niyazov is now trying to use the country's natural wealth in gas and cotton. And why not, as long as he is able to feed everyone without changing the customary precepts and exploiting natural resources?

It is Robert Kocharian who perhaps has the most problematic republic at the moment, though one would never know it from looking at him. Armenia, small but proud, is going through a period of political turbulence. But of all the CIS countries, it remains the republic with the greatest feeling of culture and enlightenment. The Armenian intelligentsia and its science, literature, and art will always remain at the very top. That is the best security for the future prosperity of the country .

Askar Akayev, always my faithful ally, was trying to cheer me up. He felt I was suffering too much, and he suffered along with me. I think he was worried about whether Russia's relations with Kyrgyzstan would now change. Would the understanding that we had established disappear? He had done a lot to strengthen our relations. And his concern about the future of his own country, which he could not imagine without the friendship of Russia, was a concern I had always shared.

And then there was Emomali Rakhmonov. In his country, Tajikistan, there is still periodic violence. The border is anything but calm. Although he maintains his Oriental charm and keeps smiling, I see the shadow of worry and protracted exhaustion on his face. He is also concerned about the future of relations between our two countries. I place my hand on his shoulder. I want to convey my confidence that everything will turn out all right. I am no longer president; I'm just a person. I think he knew what I meant.

That's how we sat at the table, talking in leisurely fashion. Meanwhile, there was a new person among us, Vladimir Putin, acting president of Russia. I realized that soon it would be time for him to break off a piece of this loaf. He was sizing everyone up. And everyone at the table was sizing him up as well. They realized that he was not there accidentally. I could not directly recommend him for the position of chair of the CIS. But the other presidents understood me perfectly, without words. The next day, Putin was elected head of the CIS.

I flew to Chisinau and reminisced about Belovezh Forest, the meeting in the Belarusian woods among Russia, Ukraine, and Belarus that ended the Soviet Union. What a host of accusations were launched against me at that time! People tried to pin so many labels on me. But I have never doubted that I made the right move in 1991. We were not trying to destroy a political entity at Belovezh; we were trying to save it. It would have been impossible to preserve the Soviet Union as a single, united state; it was already coming apart at the seams. We made this compromise in order to save the traditional ties and to avoid open clashes and interethnic conflicts. We were really hoping that the divorce process would be gradual and gentle, thanks to the CIS.

The only factor we underestimated was the influence of political elites within the republics themselves. The nationalist card was played with irresponsible independence in practically every republic. Anyone who wanted to keep Russian-language classes in schools, who wanted to trade with Russia or who spoke out in favor of common rules of the game was branded an imperialist. A tumultuous process of disassociation got under way. The rights of Russians in the other former Soviet republics began to be violated.

What is one supposed to do in a situation like that? What should our policy line have been within the former Soviet entity: confrontation or compromise? Deliberately and unswervingly, I chose the latter. I did this because I understood that if the new states were left to their own devices, they could cause trouble in their domestic political scene. If they weren't going to be with us, they could end up allied with countries that could try to turn this union against Russia.

Moreover, people, millions of people, would end up suffering more as a result of our harsh division. Where would the huge number of seasonal workers—Azerbaijanis or Ukrainians—find work, if not in Russia? Where would Moldova export its wines and fruits? What would happen to Tajikistan and Armenia without our military presence? What would independent Ukraine and Belarus do without our natural gas? The issues just kept multiplying.

Most important, hundreds of thousands, even millions of Russians could lose their spiritual connections, the family and cultural ties that unite all of us who emerged from the USSR. How to deal with this? I believed that Russia had to be a real leader and had to take on an additional political burden for the sake of preserving and strengthening the commonweal.

In 1991 Russia declared itself the legal heir to the USSR. This was an absolutely informed and logical juridical step, especially regarding foreign relations, as we were bound by a whole range of serious obligations as members of various international organizations, conventions, and agreements. If we had forfeited this legal obligation, we would have wound up with many issues and headaches that we weren't prepared to handle at that difficult time.

But now I wonder what would have happened if the new Russia had taken a different route and had restored the legal succession of the other Russia, the Russia destroyed by the Bolsheviks in 1917. What would it have been like to go from 1917 to 1991? Of course any number of pitfalls would have emerged had we taken that path. The idea of restoration of the old Russia always frightened public opinion greatly. Restoring the monarchy? Giving back property? Compensating the descendants of the émigrés who fled for what they lost in the revolutionary years? All of this would have been very difficult, awkward, and incomprehensible.

It was easier to break with the revolution abruptly rather than drag it out or complicate the already tortuous process of dealing with the historical past. We would reject Soviet laws, constructed on the idea of class warfare and the obligatory diktat of the socialist state, in favor of completely new laws that respected the individual. We would recreate the conditions for business, freedom of the press, and the parliament that were present in Russia in 1917 (even private property was for sale in 1917). Most important, we Russians would think of ourselves in a different way; we would feel that we were citizens of a newly acquired nation. We would be proud of this restored historical justice.

Admitting our historical mistakes and restoring historical succession would be a bold step that would command respect. Look at what we have had to do in the past years. Since 1991 we have had to destroy and build at the same time, living between two epochs. And that is much more difficult than simply adapting to modernity and modernizing the old Russian laws. The unquestionable advantages of such a step, such a turn of events, were quite possibly lost back in 1991. Not everything is as simple or smooth in real life as it is in a political diagram. Perhaps Russians will want to take this bold step some day.

· 16 ·

The Kosovo Crisis

Yeltsin is horrified by NATO's bombing of Serbia. He does not see the justification for killing thousands of innocent people. Although he holds no admiration for Milosevic, whom he blames for the Kosovo crisis, Yeltsin believes the solution lies in negotiation, not military retaliation. The war is also too close to home; it traumatizes the Russian public. Anti-Western sentiments flourish. With his country in such an unstable state, Yeltsin sees every rocket strike against Yugoslavia as an indirect strike against Russia. In the post–cold war world, will the United States override any and all checks on its powers?

· · ·

SOON, on top of the whole complex domestic political situation, another bomb went off. In late March 1999 a global crisis broke out in international politics: the war in Yugoslavia.

What was the difference between Russia's approach and the approach of the countries of Western Europe to the Kosovo crisis? The West persistently believes that the war in Yugoslavia was a specific retaliation against Milosevic, a fight for national minorities and human rights. We, in contrast, think the Kosovo crisis is a global crisis.

After the bombing of Belgrade, all the rules that had been established by the UN during the long postwar decades collapsed. Yes, the bombing stopped the conflict in Kosovo. But the problems within the territory weren't solved. No one knows what to do next. The war reinforced the Milosevic regime, at least in the short term. There is nothing more dangerous to humanity than the idea that international force should be used to retaliate against any one country, its residents, its economy, and its culture. Industry, ancient cultural monuments, sacred places, and museums were destroyed in Yugoslavia. If we accept such rules of the game, we risk creating a global crisis of democratic values. Soon the force of only one country or one group of countries will decide everything in the world. Instead of the mentality of a world peacemaker, we are seeing the psychology of a world enforcer and a dictator country.

I had understood all this for a long time, but the Yugoslav crisis forced me to make rapid decisions on all these issues. I was in constant telephone contact with the leaders of the major countries and all sides of the conflict. On March 24, on the eve of the NATO bombing, Bill Clinton called me to discuss the Kosovo situation. Milosevic was continuing his offensive, he said, bringing in additional troops, killing totally innocent people, and burning whole villages. I was aware of this. But I knew something else: We had to try to conduct political negotiations. Negotiating in any way, even unsuccessfully, is better than bombing and destroying everything in one fell swoop. By this time Prime Minister Primakov, who had been on his way to visit Clinton in the United States, had already turned his plane around over the Atlantic Ocean. I told Clinton that Primakov's reaction was only the first step. There would be many more.

Clinton kept pushing, saying that it depended on me whether we would let Milosevic destroy our relations and everything that we had worked so hard to create in the past six years. He said that for his part, he would not allow this to happen. He cited concrete statistics. There was bloodshed in Europe; 250,000 refugees had already left Kosovo. If we didn't stop this, he warned, there would be 2.5 million refugees. If we didn't take measures immediately, we'd wind up with a new Bosnia. Milosevic wanted to crush the Kosovar Albanians with the help of military might.

But I was amazed by one other argument Clinton cited. Clinton said that it was too bad, of course, that Milosevic was a Serb. For the sake of common solidarity, it would have been better if he were Irish or of some other nationality. Did Clinton really think that the problem was our national sympathy for Serbs? Didn't he understand that we were talking about America's approach to the Kosovo problem, about the fate of all of Europe, about the fate of the whole world? This was not just a question of some special "Slavic kinship" attributed to Russian-Serbian relations. We would have reacted the same way if it were a question of any other country—Poland, Spain, or Turkey. The country or nationality was irrelevant.

I told Bill: "I am confident that if we had continued to work together, we would have toppled Milosevic."

Clinton cited another, very serious argument: Milosevic, he said, is the last Communist dictator, and he would like to destroy the union between Russia and Europe and move against the democratization of the continent. But I had my own arguments. "Our people will think very little of America and NATO if this bombing proceeds. I remember how hard it was to change the attitude of ordinary people and politicians here in Russia toward the U.S. and the West. It was very hard, and yet we managed to do it. And now we're going to lose all that?"

Clinton kept citing the common opinion of the European leaders. The Europeans, Clinton said, were even more determined about what was happening in Kosovo. The first air strike had to be made, and Milosevic would immediately start negotiations. That was NATO's logic.

I said to Clinton, "We can't let hundreds or thousands of people die to control the words and actions of one man. We have to try to get other people around him, so that he can't behave the way he is behaving now. A lot can be done. We should use foreign intelligence. For the sake of our future relations and the future security of Europe, I ask you to cancel this bombing. We could meet and work out a tactic to battle Milosevic personally. We are more intelligent and bigger, and we could probably achieve this. In the grand scheme of things, we have to try this for the sake of our relations and for peace in Europe. We don't know who will come after us. We don't know who will work on reduction of strategic nuclear weapons. But it is clear what we ourselves must do to keep reducing these mountains of weapons. That's what we need to work on."

I remember how I tried to emphasize every word during this conversation. I tried to have an emotional impact on the man at the other end of the line.

In reply, Clinton said that he did not share my optimism regarding the methods that might influence Milosevic. That meant only one thing: war.

I didn't have any personal complaints against Bill Clinton. I even heard some sympathy in his voice. But as the president of the United States, he was letting me know in no uncertain terms that negotiations with Milosevic were pointless. This was a mistake, a very big mistake. The bombing didn't stop Milosevic either in March or in April or in May. Only the joint diplomatic efforts of Russia, Finland, and the United States would eventually stop him.

I recently saw the film *Wag the Dog*. It was a very interesting movie, made even before the Kosovo crisis. With incredible prescience, the directors predicted everything—the flashpoint where the trouble began (the Balkans), the domestic political background in the United States, and the way wars break out to compensate for or distract from other problems that have nothing to do with human rights.

But war isn't virtual. It is real, and it is bloody. It corrupts the people who wage it because it teaches them the diktat of force. It teaches them to ignore the real reasons behind the violence.

And what was happening, in my view, was this: The Americans found it necessary to stimulate North Atlantic solidarity by any means. They also felt threatened by the crisis in postwar values. They were afraid of the growing strength of European independence—economic, political, and moral. For these reasons, they resorted to war. That's my personal version of events. I don't impose it on anybody. I just propose that some thought be given to this side of the Kosovo crisis.

But I must return to the Kosovo events. As I said in a statement published on March 25, 1999, immediately after the bombing started: "This is essentially an attempt by NATO to enter the twenty-first century in the uniform of the world policeman. Russia will never agree to this." Of course I didn't limit myself to a political statement. I realized that this war could be stopped only if Russia pressured both fronts, NATO and Yugoslavia, simultaneously. If the war lasted more than a month or two, Russia would inevitably be drawn into the conflict. A new cold war would begin.

Once the bombs started falling, the internal political stability in our country would depend on the situation in the Balkans. Already the Communists and the nationalists were trying to play the Balkans card in order to destroy the balance of political forces in our society. "Now we know the real value of the West!" the hysterical voices cried. "We always told you so. We warned you about NATO and what these damned Americans could cook up! Today Yugoslavia, tomorrow Russia!"

What would be next? What would happen if we could not stop this aggressive anti-Americanism and anti-Westernism? The crisis in Russia would be not only a government crisis but a crisis of faith in the leaders. It would further exacerbate the crisis in the world. I could not rule out mass disorder and unconstitutional actions. In the final analysis, wars have always provoked revolutions. That was what irritated me most. Did the NATO leaders really not understand? I had met with these leaders dozens of times! Some of them called me their friend. Wasn't it obvious to them that each missile strike against Yugoslavia was an indirect strike against Russia?

We really had some alarming days in Moscow. A crowd staged demonstrations near the U.S. embassy. People threw bottles and stones at the windows and wrote obscene graffiti on the walls. The embassy building on Sadovoye Ring Road is only a few steps from the street. The guard's zone is only a yard of asphalt. Any extremist act would lead to unpredictable consequences. At one point the police detained a group of extremists who had driven past the U.S. embassy with a grenade launcher ready to be fired. It's hard to imagine what could have happened.

The Duma passed resolution after resolution. The Communists held active negotiations with Milosevic on creating a military-strategic union of our two states. Volunteers were recruited to fight on the side of the Serbs. Politicians of all stripes tried to win points with the

Kosovo conflict. For example, Mayor Luzhkov openly supported the demonstrators in front of the U.S. embassy. The police were guarding the demonstrators more than the embassy.

Although not everyone in the society shared the fierce anti-NATO position of the red deputies in the Duma, Russians were alarmed and tense. People took the Yugoslav tragedy to heart. They were worried about more than the fate of the Serbs in Serbia: In each Russian family there were people who had fought on the front and children of the war, that is, children who were left without fathers. World War II is still very fresh in our minds; we do not perceive it as ancient history. Therefore we sense any aggravation in Europe as an alarming signal. NATO's aggression, no matter how noble its motivations, came as a real psychological shock for Russians. Our artists gave benefit performances in Belgrade, and our newspapers and magazines were filled with anti-American statements.

In the years since 1991, our society had truly changed. New attitudes, new values—democratic and at times naively and irresponsibly Western—had crept unnoticed into the everyday life of every Russian. Not everyone accepted this right away. Not everyone was happy with the intermixing of cultures, ideologies, economies, and political and spiritual systems. But gradually, through great effort, our people had begun to value and understand this completely new and unfamiliar world. This was a change for the better. And now, with the Yugoslav war, all of this could be finally and irrevocably destroyed within a few weeks. I could not accept this.

As I noted, I was operating in two directions, putting pressure on NATO and on Milosevic. We had to stop this war no matter what. Meanwhile, NATO's strategists and politicians had clearly miscalculated. The Yugoslav people united in the face of an external enemy. The Yugoslav army, without air cover but quite capable of ground fighting, was prepared for an invasion of ground forces and could put up a strong resistance on its own territory.

Russia actively sought a peaceful settlement to the crisis. On April 14, I appointed Viktor Chernomyrdin as my representative in Yugoslavia. He spent dozens of hours with Milosevic, both alone and together with Finnish president Martti Ahtisaari. I chose Chernomyrdin because the Foreign Ministry believed that a diplomat with experience and high rank, perhaps a deputy minister of foreign affairs, was necessary for these types of negotiations. Others said the opposite—that because of the bad state of relations with the West a highly respected politician should head the Russian mission to Yugoslavia. For example, I was actively advised to appoint Gaidar, a correspondent for *Pravda,* who had lived in Yugoslavia for many years with his father. After thinking about it for a long time, I settled on Chernomyrdin.

I suppose I couldn't have trusted any other politician at that moment. Chernomyrdin had enormous weight and authority in Yugoslavia, in the West, and in the eyes of the American political elite. This unique combination allowed him to establish a negotiating line oriented toward a single goal: the rapid halt of military action. And it was here that Chernomyrdin displayed his best qualities, the qualities of an old political fighter—patience, flexibility, and a firm will for intelligent compromise.

On April 22 British prime minister Tony Blair called me. It wasn't our first conversation about Kosovo; we had spoken three or four times since the onset of the crisis. But that conversation reflected the tension of those days, as excerpts from the phone transcript show:

"I am convinced, Tony, that NATO is making a big mistake in continuing to bomb Yugoslav territories. The consequences were not properly calculated. Instead of pressuring Milosevic, you are strengthening his position. Instead of resolving the humanitarian problem, we are now dealing with a real humanitarian catastrophe. Instead of a negotiation process, which London helped quite a bit to put into motion, we are backsliding into military confrontation. We are alarmed at reports about the plan to conduct a ground operation by the alliance in Kosovo. I will tell you frankly, this is the path to the abyss."

"Tony," I urged. "Find the strength to stop this madness. This could lead to a European and perhaps a worldwide war. Milosevic will not capitulate. If the bombing stops, a path for the restoration of the negotiation process will open between the Serbs and the Albanians, Yugoslavia and NATO, the U.S. and Great Britain. Come to your senses now, because tomorrow will be too late. Whoever unleashed this war without the consent of the UN Security Council will be responsible for everything that happens."

I include this long quotation for a reason. After I had spoken with Clinton, the situation got much worse. It became clear that the bombs would result in nothing. But the NATO position didn't allow for any changes. Blair repeated everything that Clinton had said a month before, word for word: NATO had exerted the maximum effort at the negotiations in Rambouillet* in order to find a peaceful political resolution to this problem. But the alliance could not morally permit what Milosevic had done to the refugees nor the actions taken by the Serb military police with his knowledge.

I asked: "But what about the bombing of the columns of refugees, in which there were both Albanians and Serbs? Was that morally justified?"

Blair evaded my question. At the end of the conversation, he wished me success with the talks between Chernomyrdin and Milosevic.

Meanwhile, the negotiations had bogged down. The bombing continued. Yugoslavia was gradually being turned into ruins, into a country without electrical power stations, bridges, industry, administrative buildings, roads, fuel, and food. Each day NATO pilots were making more than 1,000 overflights. They had one specific goal: to destroy the economy of a country.

On May 13 French president Jacques Chirac made an emergency visit to Moscow to see me.

I appealed to Chirac: "You're continuing the ruthless bombing of Yugoslavia, and you're handing Russia a role as NATO's special courier to Belgrade to impose your ultimatums. Can't you see that you are bombing more than Yugoslavia?" I said: "I want to tell you openly, as a friend, that we can't play these games, and we aren't going to play them. We demand that if you can't stop the bombing, you at least halt it for a time."

---

* Rambouillet, France, was the location of talks involving Milosevic, the Kosovo Liberation Army (KLA), and French and U.S. mediators. —Trans.

Chirac said that he had come to Moscow not only to speak about Kosovo. He reminded me that I was moving Russia toward the future and returning it to the community of nations. But Milosevic was a man from the past, the bad past.

I listened attentively to Chirac. The conversation was taking an unexpected turn. Chirac gave me to understand that among the NATO allies, there was an American worldview and a French worldview. The U.S. vision was simple—world leadership by the United States—but France didn't agree with that. The French didn't want a one-dimensional conception of a unipolar world to prevail, but the fact was that the Americans had the means to conduct such policy.

Chirac went on to outline briefly how the situation in Europe had changed over the past year because of the change in governments. Everything had begun in Spain; then Blair had appeared; then Schröder. All of them unexpectedly supported the tough American line, perhaps for internal domestic political considerations. But France advocated another route: the idea of a multipolar world. Even the French battalion in Kosovo had been given an exclusively humanitarian mission, Chirac explained. At least, so I understood him.

As our conversation ended, Chirac unexpectedly announced that I had to make up my mind whether I was for or against Milosevic. Russia had only two paths, Chirac more or less told me: to remain on the sidelines and become marginal or to enter the modern world under my leadership. Russia had to affirm universal democratic principles.

I agreed with that. But how could I affirm these democratic principles as bombs exploded over Kosovo?

"That's what I'm asking you to do. I'm asking you not to jeopardize democracy in Russia," I said to Chirac.

Chernomyrdin met with Milosevic a total of five times, four of them alone, in tête-à-têtes. Sometimes the conversations would last nine hours without any break. Chernomyrdin told me that at the most frustrating moments of the negotiations, he would ask Milosevic bluntly: "Do you really think you can win this war?"

Milosevic would answer No, but that he wouldn't lose it either. No one had been able to vanquish the Yugoslavs for 400 years. "Let them just try now," he said. "Let them just try to stick their noses in here! A ground operation will definitely fail."

Milosevic had his own reasons for being so sure that NATO's ground operation would fail. He believed that the Yugoslav army was prepared to fight, and that the Yugoslav people were prepared to unite around Milosevic. At times Milosevic even asked Chernomyrdin to conduct the negotiations in such a way that the ground operation would start faster.

But within about a month Milosevic's position changed. He no longer wanted an escalation of the conflict. He asked to stop the war. "But nevertheless I cannot be defeated!" he said to Chernomyrdin.

Russia could not look on indifferently as people were killed and as the civilian population suffered. Chernomyrdin pushed Milosevic toward negotiations, even though Milosevic was advancing unacceptable conditions. For example, Milosevic demanded that the troops of Russia, Ukraine, India, and other countries rather than NATO troops be brought into Kosovo.

A draft proposal to have Yugoslavia enter into the union of Russia and Belarus also played a role here. Our Duma was actively discussing the idea, although it was absolutely politicized, aggressive, and unrealistic. Nevertheless, I allowed this notion of Yugoslav's entry into our union to be used during the negotiations, in order to distract Milosevic.

In fact, Chernomyrdin's main purpose was to try to press Milosevic to conduct peace talks with the West. Chernomyrdin pushed hard, letting Milosevic know that he could expect no military support and that his political support was already exhausted.

Meanwhile, Chernomyrdin managed to get an agreement from the Americans to transfer the political mechanism for the settlement of the crisis into the hands of the UN. This took NATO out of the political aspect of the talks. Milosevic could not capitulate either to Russia or to NATO. Chernomyrdin flew to the United States twice and held talks with Clinton for two hours and with Vice President Al Gore for four hours. The eight points which Chernomyrdin had worked out with Milosevic ended up in the UN resolution, although in altered form. Formulated as a resolution of the UN Security Council, the surrender ceased to be humiliating.

Milosevic asked for time to coordinate the document with the Veche (the Yugoslav parliament) and the military. As a result, the agreement was ratified without a single amendment.

Chernomyrdin did everything he could. The war was stopped. And all of this happened even though Milosevic behaved utterly without principle. In his relations with Russia, he had wagered on an explosion of popular dissatisfaction with my foreign policy. He anticipated a split in Russian society and hoped to push Russia into a political and military confrontation with the West. These things never happened.

On May 28, while he was visiting Belgrade, the Yugoslavs told Chernomyrdin that they accepted the general principles of a Kosovo settlement proposed by the Group of Eight.

On June 1–2 Chernomyrdin, Ahtisaari, and Strobe Talbott met in Bonn and agreed that there would be two international presences in Kosovo: Russia and NATO.

On June 2–3 Chernomyrdin and Ahtisaari held negotiations with Milosevic in Belgrade. The Yugoslav authorities accepted the plan for a peace settlement passed in Bonn. The Chernomyrdin-Ahtisaari plan consisted of ten points. The most important were those which NATO had demanded before the bombing: the return of all refugees, the deployment of international deterrent forces, the withdrawal of Serb army and police units, and the settlement of Kosovo's status on the basis of the Rambouillet agreement.

Essentially, Milosevic was forced to return to square one. He got less than what he had been offered during the Rambouillet talks. With the help of the war, he had achieved only one goal: At the price of destruction and complete international isolation, he had removed all his domestic opponents and enemies from the political stage. I think he is one of the most cynical politicians I have ever dealt with.

The Kosovo conflict demonstrated the worst political tendencies and double standards of modern Europe. It was claimed, for example, that human rights were more important than the rights of a single state. But when you violate the rights of a state, you automatically and

egregiously violate the rights of its citizens, including their right to security. Thousands of Yugoslav citizens suffered in the war. Can you
weigh the rights of the Kosovo Serbs against the rights of the Kosovo
Albanians? Yes, the Albanians suffered brutal repression under Milosevic and were forced to flee the territory. Now the same thing is happening with the Serbs. The difference is only that in the first instance it
was the Yugoslav army doing the repressing and now it is the KLA.
That gives you some idea of how effective the military operation was.

One more thing: On the night of June 4, I had to decide whether to
let the Russian military land its paratroopers at the Pristina Airport in
Kosovo. All the documents had already been signed. An agreement
stipulated that the peacekeeping forces would simultaneously take up
their assigned positions. Was it necessary?*

I hesitated for a long time. It seemed too dangerous to send our
men in early. Furthermore, why were we demonstrating military bold-
ness and waving our fists after the fight was over? Still, I decided that
Russia must make a crowning gesture, even if it had no military significance. It was not a question of specific diplomatic victories or defeats;
it was a question of whether we had won the main point. Russia had
not permitted itself to be defeated in the moral sense. It had not let itself be split. It had not been dragged into the war. This last gesture was
a sign of our moral victory in the face of the enormous NATO military, all of Europe, and the whole world. I gave the order: GO.

---

* Russian troops arrived unexpectedly ahead of NATO forces and took over the Pristina airport,
  which NATO troops had planned to use as their initiative headquarters. —Trans.

· 17 ·

Primakov's Resignation

❯

Once a consensus figure and stabilizer, Primakov now challenges
Yeltsin by tacitly allying himself with various members of the
Communist Duma. In retaliation, Yeltsin hires a new chief of administration, the smart and even-keeled Aleksandr Voloshin.
Then, as the impeachment machine cranks up again—this time
with five fierce charges against the president—Yeltsin plots to
replace Primakov. As before, he masterminds an aggressive, unexpected move, one that will throw the Duma into turmoil and
swing the balance of power back to his own side.

.   .

SOME TIME around January 1999, the Fund for Public Opinion conducted an interesting sociological survey. They asked individuals
which Russian leader of the twentieth century they thought had the
most influence on the country's destiny. The results of the survey
were completely discouraging. Brezhnev was in first place, Stalin was
in second place, and Lenin was third.

I tried to understand the logic of the respondents. It couldn't be
that in a few years people's views had taken a giant step backward toward Communist ideology. It had to be something else. All this time,
especially in the last year, after the autumn crisis of 1998, the public
had been yearning for stability and actively rejecting any change. In
contrast to the president, who was trying to accelerate reforms and
heat up the political process, the prime minister seemed to focus on
stability and calm. He reflected the main social attitude of the masses
at this time, which was "Leave us alone!"

But could I really stay uninvolved? Could I allow Primakov to seize the political initiative slowly but surely and lead the country back to the socialism of yesteryear? No, I could not. I did not have the moral, political, or human right. We had worked so hard to drag the country and its people out of socialism, away from the lines and the shortages, and far from the fear of the Party Committee. To return everything to the past would be a real crime; it was not good for Russia.

My first unpleasant conversation with Primakov took place in January. Primakov proposed that the Duma discuss a plan for political settlement in the next year, before the July elections. What did this involve? If the president vowed not to dissolve the Duma or dismiss the government, the Duma would cease its impeachment procedure and refrain from expressing lack of confidence in the government. The government itself did not have the right to raise the question of the Duma's lack of confidence in it. The constitutional procedure relates only to the Duma's lack of confidence.

I was quite familiar with the text of this agreement and its key points. They had all been included in the famous agreement of the fall, when we were trying to confirm Chernomyrdin. The Duma bounced Chernomyrdin and the fall agreement fell apart in September.

Why Primakov decided to revive it was a complete mystery to me. Everything seemed to be running smoothly. In the fall the Duma's impeachment procedure and my illness indicated the need to put some brakes on the political process. But power is not arithmetic. It's not like a child's erector set. It is a living organism, which changes weekly and sometimes even daily. If back in the autumn, when we were trying to confirm Chernomyrdin, this "nonaggression pact," as the newspapers called it, had seemed like a concession, now, in late January, the same pact would seem like a total capitulation by the president.

Primakov also discussed with Gennady Seleznyov, speaker of the state Duma, a draft law on benefits for the president after the end of his term in office. This made it look as if I were asking for guarantees. My position was always this: If you want to pass a law on presidential guarantees, pass it. But why the limitation of powers? In this combination the law seemed not only damaging but also a direct undermining of me, the president in office.

Primakov came to visit me in the hospital with this document.

"Yevgeny Maksimovich," I said, "how can you draft a document that significantly reduces presidential powers and talk about it with the Duma and the Federation Council without even informing me or discussing it with me? How am I to understand this?"

Primakov was embarrassed. He sat there with his leather pouch on his lap. I remember those leather cases very well. They were used by top Soviet officials, including Central Committee members, to carry their most important documents. The officials considered it beneath their status to drag a briefcase around with them, so they used these pouches instead. Evidently Primakov wanted to open the pouch and talk about the text of the political compact, but I didn't give him that opportunity. He ended up sitting through the entire conversation with his pouch on his lap. I even felt a little sorry for him.

Primakov began justifying his action: "But Boris Nikolayevich, I was only acting in your interest, in the interest of society, and in the state's interest. I'm sorry that I didn't coordinate it with you. I will immediately withdraw the document."

The conversation was unpleasant but necessary. As he left, Primakov made an offhand remark to my aides to the effect that I apparently hadn't understood him correctly.

I could have ignored all of this, and it's quite possible that Primakov's intentions were sincere. But the incident made me think about how easily the foundations of the constitution could be undermined and how quietly the government could be transformed from a presidential republic to a parliamentary republic.

I continued to view Primakov as "my" prime minister, and I remembered all too well the cost of our incredible efforts to twist his arm into taking the position. Primakov had been exceptionally loyal to me in all his posts. He was polite, attentive, and personally close to me. Among the cohort of young politicians who came to power after 1991, he and I were the real dinosaurs who had got our start in the Soviet era. And he always reminded me of this, not in an imposing way but with his particular understanding of our generation. He was not looking for a fight. He distanced himself from all the Kremlin wars and behind-the-scenes intrigues. He sat out in Yasenevo, a suburb of Moscow where the Foreign Intelligence Service was located, then at Smolensky Square where the Foreign Ministry is located, working quietly, concerned above all about his reputation as a real professional. And he knew that I valued that reputation highly. All of these qualities —and his experience and knowledge—were precisely why I had appointed him prime minister.

Why am I going into all this in such detail? I want the reader to understand the ambiguous subtext to our relations. After all, it had never occurred to me when I appointed Primakov that an impenetrable wall of misunderstanding would spring up between us within a few months. Strange as it may seem, the "reconciling" and "uniting" Primakov was irritating the middle class, the businesspeople, the media, the politicians, and entire factions in the Duma. Unwittingly or not, Primakov had rallied the antimarket, antiliberal forces around him and was trampling on the freedom of the press. That deeply worried the journalists.

I recall the dressing-down that Primakov gave Russian television in particular. He brought together all the producers and journalists and lectured them for almost an hour on their improper tone, on the mistakes they had made, and on what could and couldn't be said about the government. Another time, during one of our meetings, he kept cursing journalists. Finally I said to him, "Yevgeny Maksimovich, don't pay any attention to them. No one is trying to make us quarrel. Just as we agreed, we will work together."

"Until the year 2000?" he asked.

"Yes!"

Primakov thought for a minute. Then he suddenly said, "Boris Nikolayevich, let's call in the television crew right now and you can repeat your words so that they all can hear them."

The television crew came into the office, and I said, emphasizing every word, "My position is that I am working until the elections in

2000. And the prime minister's position is that he is working until the election of a new president."

I kept reaching my hand out to Primakov over and over again, demonstrating to him that we were bound together, that we were working for the same cause. I kept saying this, but Primakov didn't listen to me. I don't know whether he couldn't listen or whether he simply didn't want to. Sometimes I felt the urge to say, "Yevgeny Maksimovich, come to your senses! It's another era! There's another country out there!" But I didn't want to offend or insult him. Maybe that was my mistake.

During the spring of 1999 yet another very famous episode occurred. At a government session, Justice Minister Pavel Krasheninnikov reported on the issue of the traditional amnesty, scheduled to take place in May. As usual, the prisoners who weren't convicted of grave crimes would be released. About 94,000 people would be freed.

Primakov suddenly interrupted the justice minister. As a display of humanism, that was all fine, he said. But the amnesty was also necessary in order to free up jail space for those who had committed economic crimes.

I'm sure that many people still recall this comment. That spring Russian citizens began to pack their suitcases en masse. It had become abundantly clear that the popular prime minister who claimed the role of a national leader was hostage to Soviet stereotypes. I was sad about this. It wasn't Primakov's fault, but his tragedy. Primakov drove himself and all of us into a corner.

As I've indicated, some rather alarming processes were under way in the country. Incomprehensible criminal cases were opened, and innocent people were arrested. Some of the security service agents didn't conceal the fact that during interrogations and searches of businessmen, they were seeking revenge for past years. Virtually the entire Russian business community was driven to despair about their own futures. The situation threatened to cause a real split in the country over the central issue of economic reforms.

Meanwhile, the Kosovo crisis increased the anti-Western sentiment in society. Primakov was quite capable of uniting the politicians who dreamed of a new isolationist Russia and a new cold war. If he continued in power, Primakov would polarize society, dividing it into two actively warring camps. If I let this process go on, the slow slide toward the former Soviet methods of rule could turn Primakov's ultimate dismissal into a real civil conflict. It became clear that waiting until the fall, much less 2000, was simply impossible.

In March I changed my chief of administration again. I appointed Aleksandr Voloshin to replace Nikolai Bordyuzha. I had decided to put Voloshin in this position more than a month before. Voloshin had worked in the administration for a long time, and for the past six months he had been deputy chief of administration for economic issues. I had not known him very well before, but I was reading more and more of his economic reports. In recent months he and I had been in contact almost every day.

Voloshin had been responsible for drafting the economic section of the president's address to the Federal Assembly. During the course of this complicated job, a lot of questions would crop up, both from the president to the drafters and from the drafters to the president. When I met with Voloshin, we would discuss what aspects of the address should be accentuated and which problems needed more detail. I liked his calm, almost dry manner of laying out his thoughts, and I liked the way he argued his position and disputed things evenly, without excess emotion.

Voloshin was of the generation of forty-something politicians who had come to power not for the sake of power alone or to make a career. They didn't need that. Any of them (Voloshin perhaps more than any of the others) was prepared at any moment to return to his previous, quiet, private life. Rather, these men had come into the government in order to try to make it stronger and more effective. They had come in order to prove to everyone, including themselves, that Russia could become a civilized, democratic country. Outwardly, Voloshin was a typical, bookish academic. He had the impassive face of a seemingly withdrawn individual, and he spoke very softly. But when you got to know him better, Aleksandr Stalyevich was a lively, witty person.

During the time we were working on this speech, I would usually rise about 5:00 or 6:00 in the morning. After a cup of tea, I would go up to my office on the second floor, where the urgent papers waited on my desk. The text of the address would be there. I would read it until I got to a place I didn't like, when I would pick up the special secure line and dial Voloshin. In a few seconds the operator's voice would come on and say, "Voloshin's on the telephone. It's an open line," which meant that it wasn't coded and secure. The problem was that Voloshin lived in an ordinary apartment in a residential area on Leninsky Avenue. Naturally, the special Kremlin communications lines hadn't been hooked up there, so we would talk to each other on the regular city line. (Since I had to have some confidential discussions with Voloshin, I eventually solved this problem. Specialists from FAPSI, the state communications agency, put a special scrambling device in Voloshin's apartment. Voloshin wasn't very happy about this arrangement, as the box took up half of a room in his apartment.)

Gradually, during these and other conversations, Voloshin and I developed a special personal rapport. So when I realized it was time for me to change the head of the administration, I didn't have any candidates besides Voloshin. Of course, before I signed the decree, I summoned Chubais and Yumashev, my two previous chiefs of administration. They know this work very well, and they have a sense of what qualities a person must have for this position. I asked them what they thought of Voloshin, and they both supported my choice heartily.

But when Primakov learned about this decision, he was very upset, even offended. Finally, he couldn't hold himself back anymore and said, "Boris Nikolayevich, why did you fire Bordyuzha?"

"He couldn't cope," I replied.

In fact, I had asked Voloshin himself to inform Primakov of Bordyuzha's removal and of his own appointment as the new head of administration. Voloshin called Primakov and said, "Yevgeny Maksimovich, this is Voloshin. Starting today, the president has appointed me chief of administration."

This change upset Primakov very much. And from the outset he and Voloshin didn't get along.

Russia is a country of moods and emotions. That's just the way we're constructed; nothing can be done about it. In politics these emotions and moods sometimes intertwine in the most outlandish way. Suppose there is a person in power in Russia who always provokes the harshest criticism and sometimes even anger. It is precisely this leader who will automatically become a powerful political center and consolidate the most diverse forces. Such was the case with Primakov. In the half year he was prime minister, Primakov probably sensed this tendency. He sensed his political prospects as a prime minister who could run for election in 2000 at the head of a new social movement.

But this tendency didn't suit me one bit. Despite all his honesty, decency, and loyalty to the president, Primakov would not be right for the presidency in 2000. In my analysis, Russia needed a person of a completely different mind-set, another generation, a new mentality. Primakov had too much red in his political palette.

Only those who jealously tried to guard Primakov and erect political bastions around him are to blame for the abruptness of his resignation. Back on March 19, Zyuganov had called for the defense of the government with the help of strike committees and mass actions. (In fact, Primakov began to consult constantly with the leadership of the Communist Party. I didn't interfere, preferring not to ask Primakov about anything.) The Communists were planning another round of political warfare in May: a decisive vote in the Duma on the impeachment. The impeachment commission had been working full tilt for more than a year. There were five allegations: the "genocide of the Russian people," as I have noted; the collapse of the army; 1993; the Belovezh agreements and the formation of the CIS; and the war in Chechnya.*

The Communists had timed their vote for May. Maybe they thought that the president, undergoing an impeachment procedure and hanging onto office by a thread, would not dare to force the prime minister to resign. Maybe they wanted to start an open conflict be-

---

* The reference to 1993 concerns the White House, or parliamentary, rebellion, which Yeltsin ordered put down by force. —Trans.

tween the president and the government, provoke a new attack on me in the Federation Council, or stir up mass unrest. One way or another, it was the Duma impeachment that had accelerated the entire process of dismissing Primakov. Now the problem was formulated extremely simply: Should I fire Primakov before or after the vote?*

A substantial number of people in the administration were against dismissing Primakov before the vote. If that happened, they argued, impeachment would be inevitable. The president would be walking right into it, because the leftists in the Duma would want compensation for their political defeat no matter what.

I didn't agree. A sharp, unexpected, aggressive move always throws your opponent off balance and disarms him, especially if it is unpredictable and seems absolutely illogical. I have become convinced of this many times over the course of my whole presidential career. To take a wait-and-see attitude would be dangerous. If the vote in the Duma took place and the procedure for my removal from office began, it would be far more difficult for me, in that hamstrung position, to remove Primakov. The Duma members knew this as well as I did. Just a few days after the vote, on March 17, there was to be a session of the Federation Council at which a special resolution in support of the government was to be passed. According to my calculations, an overwhelming majority of the senators were prepared to support Primakov, about 120–130 of the total of 180. The combination of the vote on the impeachment and the support of the Federation Council would very much strengthen Primakov's position. And finally, the fact that Primakov was such a serious figure on the political scene would have a powerful psychological impact on the deputies, who would also be influenced indirectly by various contacts and deals.

No matter how much I liked Primakov, I simply didn't have the right to risk the future of the country. By mid-April, I had already made up my mind to dismiss him. The first step in this direction was the appointment of Interior Minister Sergei Stepashin as vice premier.

---

* Under the Russian constitution, when the president steps down, the prime minister, who is also called the chair of the government, may become acting president and presidential elections must be called within three months. — Trans.

Under the constitution only a person who is already serving as vice premier can be appointed acting prime minister. None of Primakov's deputies suited me for this purpose. But Primakov was fine with Stepashin. Stepashin was the only person in the government whom Primakov addressed with the familiar form of *you*. He didn't think Stepashin was dangerous. And he gave his consent to the appointment. From that moment debates began to appear in the press about whom the president saw as a successor to Primakov—the economic planner Aksyonenko or the power minister Stepashin?

Expectation hung in the air. Everyone was waiting for the other shoe to drop. At a session of the Committee on the Celebration of the Third Millennium in the Kremlin, I decided to play upon this atmosphere and whip up the sense of expectation even further. In the middle of my speech, I paused and asked Stepashin to come and sit at my right hand. The procedure of moving Stepashin to a chair closer to me took place before television viewers. It was probably incomprehensible to many, but it was an important gesture for that moment.

But then I began to get annoyed at the mounting sense of uncertainty. I felt annoyed for the simple reason that I couldn't announce the decision until the last moment. And there was virtually no one with whom I could discuss the matter. The decision had to be made suddenly, and it had to be absolutely correct. I had already made my choice: The new prime minister would be Vladimir Putin, director of the Federal Security Service. But I could not put Putin into the post of prime minister now. It was simply too early.

On May 12, a beautiful sunny day, I got ready for work at the Kremlin. I had breakfast with my family as usual. I thought, "Today, my wife will turn on the TV and find out about the resignation of Primakov, whom she still regards with great respect." Looking her right in the eye at the doorstep, I surprised myself by saying, "Just don't worry; don't you get upset. Everything will be fine."

My parting with Primakov was extremely brief. I informed him about his dismissal and told him I was grateful for his work. Primakov hesitated. "I accept your decision," he said. "You have this right under the constitution. But I consider it a mistake."

I looked at Yevgeny Maksimovich once again. It was too bad, really just too bad. Primakov's resignation was the most dignified and courageous of all those I saw. In the political sense, he was a very strong prime minister. He stood as a major, towering figure. Time has passed, but my opinion of Primakov has not changed. Despite various difficult moments in our relations, I continue to have the highest regard for him. I am very glad that each of us can now stop paying attention to which side of the political barricades the other is on. Now we can take joy in the new president, Putin, and watch and worry together as he takes his first steps. And if we like, we can even go fishing together.

Back on May 12, all that was very hard to imagine. On that day Primakov walked out the door, his step heavy, his eyes downcast. And I invited Stepashin into my office.

· 18 ·

Premier Poker

Russia needs a prime minister of action and iron will who can lead the country while under enormous pressure. But the Communist Duma will do anything to stand in the way of Yeltsin's candidate. Yeltsin engineers a crafty plan to outmaneuver the Duma, catch the parliamentarians off balance, and slip his new prime minister into place.

·   ·

VOTE COUNTING has haunted my entire political career. I remember vividly how the heads were counted in the packed hall of the Palace of Congresses. A professor of mathematics went down the rows with a paper and pencil. That was when I was elected a member of the Supreme Soviet at Gorbachev's first Congress of People's Deputies in 1989. The Politburo really didn't want me to take the seat. The new Russian Supreme Soviet was chaired by Ruslan Khasbulatov. Passions ran high. In the spring of 1993, my opponents tried to declare a lack of confidence and send me into retirement. I remember all the shouts in the hall and the frenzied expressions of the deputies, with their slogans about "beggaring the people" and "stealing Russia blind." It has been more of the same for so many years.

And here, at the very end of my political career, came the impeachment. How long had the Communists been trying to do this? Almost eight years. Or was it six? I don't know when to start counting. I recall attempts to remove me and cancel me out much earlier than 1991. It's strange. They know and I know that this doesn't decide anything anymore. This is a spectacle.

But in Russia everyone thinks in terms of symbols. For the Communists, impeachment is a symbol of the long-awaited end of the Yeltsin era. It means the forced end, the premature end, even if only by a month. They are willing to work very, very hard for the sake of the symbol, for the sake of political show.

The impeachment process is a legal procedure. Essentially, it's a court. The people trying me had never made any major political decisions and were unfamiliar with the mechanisms for making them. Nevertheless, the fate of the president of Russia was in their hands. Although the vote was by open ballot, it was a faceless decision, as hundreds of deputies hid behind each other's backs. There were no live faces, eyes, or voices behind the numbers flickering on the blue screen of the vote counter. The machinery of political intrigue, almost as constant as life itself, could win over the hesitant and wobbly people.

I had been bearing the burden of responsibility for everything and everyone for so many years that this vote could not and should not change the final summation of my entire career. Fighting with parliament and the legislators has been my burden—no, not just mine, but the whole country's. Therefore, the results of the parliamentary elections of 1999 were no less important than those of the elections for president. The parliament must represent the real interests of society. Everyone realized that these Communists were not the real masters of the country. They did not have real support in society, they had no political will, and they had no intellectual capacity. Still, they managed to bring together the portion of the population that could not find its way in the new life and was in a depressed, unsettled state. Thanks to this consolidation of the negative—the gathering of weak, helpless people insecure about themselves and their lives—the Communists gained a stable majority in parliament in 1999. The other healthy and more or less active part of society was splintered and beaten. It could not find its leaders.

Chubais, Nemtsov, Kiriyenko, and Irina Khakamada never became real leaders. They are technologists, managers, specialists. The young generation of politicians doesn't have a national figure capable of consolidating whole segments of society. Perhaps one of them will become a symbol of the new generation, a leader of students, youth, the computer whizzes, the citizens of the twenty-first century. But a lot of work is still needed before that can happen, and their movement has to be developed. Without a doubt, these will be my political crusaders.

For a long time, Yavlinsky seemed to me a good, strong figure, and I thought that the moment had come when he could gather a powerful democratic movement around himself. But instead Yavlinsky was becoming more and more sectarian. For the circles of dissidents and alternative thinkers who operated under the old banner of the Soviet era, everything that came from the government was evil. All compromises were evil. Any deals had to be made on their own terms. Everything else had to be condemned. They always voted No. Such an approach was not possible in contemporary politics.

Yavlinsky's position and the position of his faction in the Duma was that the Chechnya item in the impeachment vote was to be unrestricted for his party members. That is, Yavlinsky would vote against me on that count, but the members of his factions were free to vote as they pleased. I didn't see the point of this political hodgepodge. Were they trying to put on the pressure? Or was it just for show?

I think Yavlinsky became entangled in his own strategy. Heading a protesting democratic electorate (as I know from my own experience with the democrats of the late 1980s) means being in the center of an incredibly strong energy field and having the advantage in terms of initiative and ideas. That was where Yavlinsky was really missing a lot. Young people and the intelligentsia wanted a positive program from Yavlinsky. He didn't have one. The "lesson of democracy" that Yavlinsky now wants to teach everyone may come at too high a price for those who want to live in a normal, democratic Russia.

Just who were these parliamentarians who had accumulated so

many charges against me, from the "genocide of the Russian people" to the Chechen tragedy? Essentially, there were no real leaders among them except for Zyuganov, Yavlinsky, and Zhirinovsky, who worked hard for their electorate. These three were a special kind of leader, one might say. But what about the rest? A fair number of people got into the Russian parliament around 1995 by accident. Today our political spectrum is still very narrow: We don't have real parties, there are no permanent democratic traditions, and there is no code of conduct for political conflicts. That's why there are so few professionals in the parliament and a fair number of primitive lobbyists. But I believe all this is fixable. We currently have rather shaky parties and shaky ideologies, but some day we will have a true working parliament. Meanwhile, we have to make do with what we have.

I didn't believe the deputies would vote for impeachment. Their babbling about principles for the nth time got them free publicity on the news, but I knew that they had no chance of opposing my political will. Gennady Seleznyov, the speaker of the Duma, made a tough statement after Primakov's resignation: "Now impeachment is really inevitable." But I was already convinced of the opposite. I knew that after Primakov's resignation a negative vote wouldn't happen. With my tough resolve I had disarmed those deputies who were still uncertain.

During the heat of the battle, I went outside to take a breather in my garden. I looked up at the May sky. I knew they wouldn't have enough votes this time either.

The public's attention immediately shifted to the impeachment, which overshadowed the news of Primakov's resignation. Russians categorically refused to have any more political upheavals. They didn't want anything that was too disruptive. My calculation was correct. Now everything depended on the results of the May vote. Primakov himself kept silent and waited. I have to give him credit. As an experienced and wise politician, he didn't want to get mixed up in a dangerous game. He had a completely different agenda. The explosive situation around impeachment could easily drag him in, even with all of his care and restraint. People were trying to use him and involve him in the political fight.

Much depended on the person who would be appointed prime minister after the impeachment vote. The 2000 presidential race would kick off at that moment. I had several options, and I had to weigh them very carefully.

There were only three serious candidates. I had to reject a potential fourth, the Foreign Minister Igor Ivanov, because of his iron alliance to Primakov. My administration had looked long and hard at Ivanov, knowing that he had worked for so long with the prime minister. We held a number of preliminary conversations. "I'll enter the presidential and parliamentary elections only in tandem with Primakov," Ivanov had said. "Let Primakov serve as the head of a progovernment party in the Duma elections. That would make it much easier for me to work as prime minister."

Ivanov was displaying the normal, professional solidarity of a diplomat. But the political battle that summer promised to be so hot that solidarity would melt away. We removed Ivanov from the list of prospective prime ministers. It was too bad. It would have been good to have such a young, strong figure in reserve.

So who was left on my list? One candidate was Nikolai Aksyonenko, minister of transportation was a good reserve player. He seemed suitable by all criteria. Decisive, firm, and charming, he knew how to talk to people, and he had had a long career, working his way up from the very bottom of the ladder. He was a strong manager. Of course, the Duma would not approve. They would greet him with bayonets and treat him badly from the outset. Actually, he would be a perfect foil. I could use him to bait the Duma and throw the delegates into disarray. I'd get them ready for a confrontation and then toss them a completely different candidate.*

But who could that be—Stepashin or Putin? Putin or Stepashin? The minister of the interior Stepashin or the director of the Federal Security Service Putin? Both had begun their careers in St. Petersburg;

---

* As Yeltsin explained previously, the Duma must approve the president's candidate for prime minister. If it refuses the president's candidate three times, the president has the right to disband parliament and call new elections. —Trans.

both had worked with Sobchak. Both were intellectual power ministers. They were of the new generation—young, energetic, and smart.
But what a difference in nature! Stepashin was soft, and he liked to
pose a bit. He loved theatrical gestures. I wasn't certain he could hold
out to the end or display that tremendous will and resolve needed in a
fierce political battle. I couldn't imagine a president of Russia without
these tough character traits.

Putin, on the contrary, had the will and the resolve. I knew he did.
But intuition told me that it would be premature to bring Putin into
the political ring at that moment. He had to appear later. When there's
not enough time to take a political running jump, it can be bad. When
there's too much time, it can be even worse. I didn't want the public to
get too used to Putin in those lazy summer months. We mustn't let his
mystery disappear; the surprise factor needed to remain intact.

It was a very difficult situation. It was too early to put Putin in.
Someone else had to fill the gap. I needed someone to serve as a decoy.

There was no alternative: This role had to be entrusted to the nice,
decent Sergei Vadimovich Stepashin. Of course I would try to explain
to him that the question of the future, of the presidential elections,
was still open. And he, too, would have a chance to show himself.

Virtually no one knew of this option, including Putin himself. That
was the strength of this plan; it had the power of the unexpected. As I
have noted, such political moves have always helped me win the whole
round, sometimes even when it seemed hopeless. After the impeachment vote, the Duma and the Federation Council's reaction to the
name of Putin was unpredictable. They didn't know him very well.
They didn't understand what kind of figure he was.

But the main danger lay elsewhere. Putin and Primakov were two
former intelligence officers, two representatives of the security services, and they occupied the same niche in the public mind. They
seemed to cancel each other out. Putin was irritating to Primakov, and
Primakov's reaction could be sharp. It was possible that he would totally reject Putin or even launch a counterattack against him. After the
chaos of the resignation and the impeachment vote, we needed stability. I needed to create a breather.

Only Stepashin could be that breather. Primakov was kindly disposed to Stepashin. (Later that summer, when Primakov began seriously to consider the presidency, he even thought about seeking to amend the constitution and reinstating the post of vice president in order to run *with* Stepashin in the elections.) Nevertheless, this tactical move to install a temporary prime minister was dangerous. In the few months that he would be prime minister, Stepashin, and of course many other people, would assume that *he* was the government's main candidate for the 2000 presidential elections. Was I needlessly complicating the situation? Was I planting a time bomb? Was it worthwhile waiting for Putin?

Looking back at these May events nearly a year later, I have to admit that I was rather worried at the time. The government crisis had gone on for almost a year and a half. That was far too long. The same sort of thing had happened in other parts of the world. Developed countries like Italy, Japan, and France had gone through this. But even in the Italy of the 1970s, where the post of prime minister changed hands several times a year, the economic situation was far more stable.

In Russia each new prime minister engendered a specific problem. For example, in August 1998 I could have left the young reformers in power only by declaring a state of emergency. It required nothing less. The managerial, technocratic government of Kiriyenko had no political backing—no credibility and no influence over the public. It could not come to an agreement with the Duma, the trade unions staging the rail war, or the business elite. Yet in order to implement our tough line, Kiriyenko needed the total support of the public. Or at least their unswerving obedience. But I simply could not declare a state of emergency. This was not the time or the era for a state of emergency. Russia is not Chile or Argentina.

Primakov, in contrast, had tremendous political reserves. But his rule threatened to roll back reforms, collapse the embryonic economic freedoms, and trample the democratic liberties that we had managed to nurture and preserve in these past few years, not to mention freedom of speech and the preservation of a system of normal political competition.

Though the prolonged government crisis hung over me like the sword of Damocles, I decided in May, 1999, to draw it out for a few more months. I proposed Stepashin as the candidate to the Duma knowing that I would almost certainly be saying good-bye to him soon. To embark on a third round of political aggravation (after Primakov's resignation and the impeachment vote) was too risky. Stepashin was 100 percent acceptable to the Duma, largely thanks to his loyalty to Primakov.

Yes, even as I proposed Stepashin's candidacy, I knew that I would soon be removing him. And that knowledge weighed terribly on me. After all, people perceive events in the present, today, now. They respond with happiness and excitement or anger and despair. I knew that the situation would change within two or three months, and I knew how it would change. But there was no joy in this knowledge. Instead, I felt heaviness. I was again taking responsibility for the fate of others. I would have to answer for the unpredictable consequences of my actions. In the middle of a conversation or an ordinary meeting, I would feel a black shadow suddenly pass through the room. The preordained nature of my act constantly made itself felt. But I had to bear up under this burden and not let my thoughts show.

Putin had to come onto the scene gradually. When our political opponents finally showed their hand and the election campaign was at its height, that's when Putin's decisive nature and toughness would come in very handy. But I could not even inform Putin of my plan. I needed to preserve the key element of surprise. Besides, Putin was serving as head of the Security Council and the Federal Security Service, and he couldn't be asked to keep such a secret. Not that I felt sorry for him. I wasn't just offering him a promotion, after all. I wanted to hand him the crown of Monomakh.* I wanted to give him the most important, the dearest thing I had: my political legacy. And I wanted to do this through victory in the elections—the sort of public politics he disliked —to safeguard the democratic freedoms of the country and to main-

---

* The fur and gem-studded crown of Grand Prince Vladimir Monomakh is a symbol of the leader of Russia and is kept on display in the Kremlin Museum. —Trans.

tain a normal market economy. Carrying this burden until 2000 was going to be very, very hard, even for someone as strong as I.

So it was decided. I was nominating Stepashin. But first I would announce Aksyonenko, just to shake things up. I liked the way I had sparked intrigue around Aksyonenko. The Duma delegates were expecting him and had geared up for battle. At just the right movement, I would switch candidates.

I summoned Aleksandr Voloshin, chief of administration, and asked him to write the introduction. Then I pushed the button for the line to Gennady Seleznev, speaker of the Duma. After much hemming and hawing, I said, "It's Aksyonenko." I put the receiver down and thought, "Boy, will they be surprised when they read it's Stepashin. But that's O.K.; it's good for them."

The Stepashin candidacy passed easily in the first round, no sweat. The newspapers wrote that the Kremlin had played a clever trick. Everyone was expecting Aksyonenko, whom they didn't like, and were relieved to vote for Stepashin, whom they did like. Little did they know that I had more tricks up my sleeve.

· 19 ·

The Mayor Goes on the Attack

As soon as he steps down from office, Primakov teams up with the powerful and popular mayor of Moscow, Yury Luzhkov, to form a new political party, Fatherland. Luzhkov mounts a brutal attack on the president. Meanwhile a smear campaign against Yeltsin and "the Family" is broadcast on the nightly news. As Fatherland's popularity grows, Yeltsin wonders how to tackle this new political opposition, which for the first time does not emanate from the Communist bloc.

. .

EARLY SUMMER in Moscow is usually dead. The streets empty out, and even the newscasters' voices grow tired and dull. The Duma is out on recess. A lot of people take their children out of the city and live mostly at their dachas, enjoying the rare, sunny days. The Russian elite also leaves for the quiet garden and dacha life, trying to get out of the stifling capital as quickly as possible. It is just a mood, but a mood can determine a lot in a society.

Early summer 1999 was no exception. It was clear that people were fed up with politics. The crisis that had been dragging on since September was thoroughly exhausting for all classes of people. They had no energy left to protest about Primakov or march in Communist columns or even discuss the new prime minister.

In fact, everybody liked the new premier. Sure, Stepashin had his run-ins with the government, but the public at large wasn't interested in those squabbles. And Stepashin fairly blossomed in front of the TV

cameras. He traveled a lot and met with the governors. He took a vigorous satisfaction in holding government sessions and made a great
impression on Western leaders. But most important, with his slightly
naive optimism, he created the very atmosphere that everyone
yearned for. He gave the public a little breather.

Despite the summer lull, the main political protagonists hardly
went on hiatus for the holidays. Indeed, a new movement began to
rumble around Yevgeny Primakov. After Primakov's departure—the
reasons for which really weren't evident to broad sectors of the public
and understandably couldn't be explained—Primakov's approval rating rose from 20 percent in May to 30 percent in July. Analysts began to
talk about how the former prime minister could definitely run in the
Duma elections as the head of a new movement. Then, if he won,
Primakov could run for president.

The movement that summoned Primakov was growing rapidly. Its
formal and informal head was the mayor of Moscow, Yury Mikhailovich Luzhkov. The party was called Fatherland, and Luzhkov spent a
great deal of his resources on it. Luzhkov traveled around the country,
meeting personally with regional leaders. Concerned about the absence of a strong prime minister and a future center of power to fill
the vacuum that had formed after Primakov's resignation, governors
quickly came under the banner of the mayor of Moscow. One region,
then a second, a third, a tenth, and a twentieth, enthusiastically
greeted the new Fatherland movement. Its ideological and political
mouthpiece was the "third channel," the new TV network, also
funded by Luzhkov.

The ideology of Fatherland was centrism. Its adherents were cen-
trists. What was so bad about that? Compared with the fractured democratic forces that had lost the parliamentary elections to the
Communists again and again, one could only welcome both this party
and its ideology. Right?

Wrong. I understand that it is perfectly fair, even important, to criticize a political opponent, especially during the campaign period. Attacking one's opponent is almost an obligatory political practice for
any civilized society. But when politicians don't criticize a person but

instead deliberately create a national enemy, they are not adhering to normal campaign procedures. Instead, they are practicing Soviet propaganda. And it was exactly these Soviet-style methods of attacking a political rival that the pro-mayor media used.

"The Yeltsin regime has sold the motherland to foreign capital," the Luzhkov media would blare. "He's to blame for the billions of dollars drained annually from the country. He created the system of corruption. He arranged for the 'genocide of the Russian people.' And he is to blame for the fall in the birthrate, the catastrophic state of science and education, medicine and culture. A mafialike family, a real gangster clan has formed around the president."

Every day the political programs on TV's Channel 3 instilled this crude bunch of ideas into people's minds. They used a daily diet of clichés on the news and broadcasted TV specials on "sensational" revelations—here a factory was stolen, there an entire oil industry was put into someone's pocket. The number one topic, of course, was the close tie between the Kremlin and Boris Berezovsky, this political "monster" of modern Russia, who apparently manipulated everything behind my back. Naturally, they also accused me of instigating the financial crisis (almost a world crisis) and of nearly destroying the "honest" prosecutor, Skuratov.

I tried to understand whether those who started all this really thought that this kind of crude hatchet job would bring Luzhkov success in the elections and win the trust of the public. And what had happened to my relations with Yury Luzhkov anyway? After all, we had been friends at one time. I had enormous respect (and still do) for his indefatigable energy and his efforts to reconstruct the city of Moscow. The mayor always supported the political line of reform and free enterprise because it was this line that gave him the opportunity to turn Moscow into a contemporary, flourishing city with clean streets, gleaming storefronts, and a modern infrastructure—a city pleasant to live in.

But after the incredibly pompous and overblown 850th anniversary of Moscow in 1997, the mayor evidently became dizzy with success. He began to interfere with national political matters more and more.

He shouldn't have. There were problems with his methods of making money and running Moscow. Moscow's treasury had managed to collect a large amount of money from banks and companies that, for understandable reasons, were forced to pay the city of Moscow, not the country. It was so much money that the mayor had enough for the excessive anniversary festivities, the incredible architecture, and his own political ambitions. Moreover, Luzhkov fiercely denied all accusations about tax diversions, his officials' failure to collect federal taxes, and the helplessness of the Moscow police. Not only did he deny them, but he would sue any journalist who wrote such stories. The judges carefully awarded the damages in these suits to Luzhkov. After all, judges in Moscow have their wages supplemented by the Moscow government and are dependent on the mayor's office.

Out of love for our city, I didn't speak out about any of this until it was the right time. The economic reforms in Moscow were more important to me than any political squabbles or the administrative shortcomings of the tireless city father.

When I finally saw Luzhkov in 1998 after almost a yearlong break in contact, I saw changes in his personality. Or rather, I noticed features that I had overlooked in the past. I cannot call it outright hypocrisy, but Luzhkov had learned how to control his emotions in sensitive situations that affected him personally. Outwardly, he acted with devotion to principle and sincerity, but inwardly he used tough, cold calculation.

During the autumn crisis of 1998, for example, Luzhkov publicly, in front of television cameras, promised not to intervene in Chernomyrdin's candidacy when he was confirmed in the Duma but then did not keep his word. Luzhkov thus contrived not to notice the obvious in Skuratov's case and did everything in his power to block the prosecutor general's dismissal. And so he began openly to attack the president.

That summer the campaign to discredit my family and me began in earnest. There was a series of slanderous paid-for stories, first in our Russian press and then the foreign press. These stories appeared in the same publications that the KGB had used to leak information. And Luzhkov even made a public statement demanding to see proof of my innocence. Luzhkov's demand particularly amazed me. What about the presumption of innocence?

I had grown accustomed to being insulted both in the yellow press and by deputies in the parliament who weren't too particular about the means they used. But no politician at the federal level had ever violated my rights so crudely and flagrantly. It was obvious that Luzhkov knew about the deliberate lies, unproven and unconfirmed, being written about me. But apparently the gambling spirit of a political player compelled him to ignore their dishonesty.

All of this would have been funny under different circumstances. Luzhkov is not a politician by nature. All of his "emergency" speeches —now "in defense of the Russian manufacturer"; now about Sevastopol; now about the reversal of privatization—alarmed serious people.* Ordinary Muscovites appreciated their mayor and forgave him all of his political weaknesses simply because Muscovites, like all normal people, like it when people pay attention to them.

The mayor could have continued his favorite activities in his favorite city, and I would have happily supported him. I probably would have criticized him, but I would have supported him. But Moscow was no longer big enough for Luzhkov. He wanted much more.

By the summer of 1999, the slow rapprochement of Primakov and Luzhkov had begun. Primakov, as always, kept his own counsel. Luzhkov, on a fishing expedition, tried to calculate the options: Which of them, given a certain array of forces, could become president, and which could be prime minister or the leader of the largest faction in parliament? In fact, Luzhkov had no intention of yielding to the retired prime minister. Rather, the mayor was wagering that heavyweight Primakov, with his high ratings in the polls, would pave the way to the Duma for the Fatherland Party. Luzhkov would then consolidate an absolute majority of deputies in the Duma, become prime minister, and automatically take over as president in 2000. Together, he and Primakov could obtain an overwhelming advantage in the Duma elec-

---

* Sevastopol, on Ukrainian territory, is the Crimean town where the Russian Black Sea fleet is located. —Trans.

tions, especially because Primakov knew how to make a good deal with the Communists. That would mean that the next elections—the presidential elections—would simply be for show.

In fact, there might not even be any presidential elections. If my forecasts were correct and the red and the rose (the Communists and Fatherland Party) took a clear constitutional majority in the Duma elections, they would not only immediately gain a considerable political advantage but would also have a legitimate chance to get the two-thirds majority needed to make changes to the constitution. They could then abolish the institution of the presidency in Russia. They would have the fate of the government in their hands along with draft laws and the criminal, civic, and tax codes. They would have so much room to maneuver that any further struggle with them would simply be impossible.

But how to stop them? Everything would be decided not by the summer of 2000 but by the fall of 1999. Only a matter of weeks was left.

In July, I repeatedly talked to Sergei Stepashin about this situation. I asked what he thought and why the governors were joining Luzhkov, whom they'd previously disliked, as the provinces usually distrust the capital.

"You see what you have to do, Sergei Vadimovich?" I said to Stepashin. "You have to create a firm center of power, to gather the political elite of the country, to display some resolve and try to seize the initiative from them."

At some point I realized our dialogue wasn't working. Stepashin kept insisting that he was the most faithful and dedicated member of the presidential team. He would come to see me at the dacha and talk animatedly about his plans. But as soon as the conversation came around to the main political problem, he would immediately grow somber. "I assure you that everything will work out in the fall, Boris Nikolayevich," he would say.

But *what* would work out? It was clear to me that the final round of a pitched political battle was approaching. This would be the last battle for political choice in the country. Stepashin was able to reconcile some people for a time, but he wasn't going to become a political leader, a fighter, or a real ideological opponent to Luzhkov and Primakov in the Duma elections. A new political party had to be created, and the prime minister had to be changed. I was prepared for battle.

But I wasn't prepared for what happened next: a stab in the back from people I had thought were of my mind. The blow came from the smart, sophisticated television channel NTV. Yevgeny Kisilyov, the news commentator on the program *Itogi*, aired a "diagram of the president's family."* The photographs shown on TV reminded me of wanted posters I used to see at factories, bus stations, or movie theaters in Sverdlovsk. The posters usually depicted the faces of drunks, thieves, murderers, and rapists. Now the "police," in the person of NTV, was talking about my so-called Family—myself, Tanya, Voloshin, and Yumashev. All of these people were accused of everything under the sun —bribery, corruption, the hoarding of wealth in Swiss bank accounts, and the purchase of villas and castles in Italy and France.

The NTV show put me into a state of shock. The monotonous stream of televised demagoguery on Channel 3, the mayor's mouthpiece, was unpleasant but harmless. Anyone could tell a mile away that it was cobbled-together, paid-for propaganda. But the people on NTV were masters of their craft; they knew how to conceal a lie behind a mass of "factual" details. This was a genuine provocation and real harassment.

I was interested not so much in the provenance of all these lies as in something else: How could NTV executives Malashenko and Gusinsky, people who knew Tanya's character rather well and were in fairly close contact with her, pour this stream of filth onto the television screens? They knew better than anyone else that these were all lies.

In the middle of the summer, Valentin Yumashev, who as always was trying to find some way out of this conflict, met with Gusinsky and Malashenko. When Yumashev asked them directly what was going on, he got a no-less-direct demand for an answer: "Get rid of Voloshin."

---

* *Itogi* (literally, "summing up") is a prime-time news show. — Trans.

They wanted us to remove Voloshin because Voloshin was trying
to stop the system whereby Media-Most, Gusinsky's holding company,
received government loans that were extended year after year rather
than being repaid. Voloshin was now demanding that the loan Gusinsky had received from Vneshekonombank (the state foreign-trade
bank) be returned. They struck back with the slanderous TV program.

"But what does Boris Nikolayevich have to do with all this?" asked
Yumashev. "What does Tanya have to do with it? You know very well
that there are no Swiss bank accounts or castles. You're deliberately
lying."

"Get rid of Voloshin, and the pressure will stop," they repeated.

Yumashev tried to explain that blackmail and crude attacks would
never work. That's how gangsters operate in crime novels. But Gusinsky
and Malashenko were deaf to such arguments. And to everything else.

Yumashev relayed this conversation with Gusinsky and Malashenko to me, selecting his words with care. I was even more baffled
and pained then when I had seen the "wanted" show. When would this
war of *kompromat* end? How much longer could it go on?

Yet there was nothing truly surprising here. I had always been ha-
rassed for various reasons: under Gorbachev for my dissent, in
1991–1993 for my unpopular economic shock therapy, in 1996 for my ill-
nesses. People beat me with everything that came to hand. I always
had to live with it. And I would endure it now.

Truth always wins. The lie sooner or later evaporates and the truth
remains. What will they do after the elections, when they find out that
neither I nor my family have any of these things, that there are no villas, no castles, no diamond or gold mines, no foreign bank accounts
with many millions of dollars? Will they once again lie and try to get
away with it?

But for now, I had to think about something else. The main challenge was the parliamentary elections. We would reply to their political pressure with our own political pressure. We would have our own
countercampaign to react to their news war, and it would be no less
harsh. Now I had to take the matter into my own hands. There was so
little time left before December and the elections.

On the whole, this political conflict was rather unusual for the citizens of Russia because it didn't involve the Communists. Some people were confused. If there were a battle between two parties or groups oriented toward reform and the market economy, the Communists always won in the end. At least that's what many people thought then. But this time, in order for the totalitarian past not to prevail, we had to oppose Luzhkov's Fatherland.

You see, at that moment two notions of the new Russia, two forces with different perceptions of Russia's future path, were clashing with each other. The Luzhkov model of capitalism didn't presuppose freedom of speech, freedom of thought, or freedom of political competition. It relied upon an official class, a brutal, bureaucratic, "crony" capitalism. But the other model, advocated by both the business elite of Russia and the president's team, was the model of a democratic market, where there was no *diktat* by officials or by the state. The country was facing a choice between these two models.

Though the political battle diagram had changed, the same patterns remained. There were two such patterns in 1999. First, the harassment of the president was the first really strong information virus to infect Russian society. Today, no society is immune to such a virus passed to the public by the mass media, causing phobias, intimidation campaigns, and hunts for the enemy in the news. Thus the power of mass communication can overwhelm the entire machinery of state. Any "independent" prosecutor, private person, or financial group can release such a virus. Its influence on politics is enormous both in the West and Russia. I don't know how we can protect ourselves or how we can reliably distinguish such viruses from normal public opinion. A person who enters into politics must know the rules of the game and must be prepared for the stream of lies. Still, I wish the game were more honest.

And then there was the second pattern: the yearning for an old-fashioned party, which Luzhkov seemed to embody with Fatherland. Suddenly, there were people marching around Moscow in unison, wearing identical blue jackets and brown caps, stepping along in neat columns, and being bused free of charge to well-organized rallies. Apparently, the bureaucrats at the Moscow mayor's office had created a "new" party for us. What was all this? A phantom of "Soviet democracy," when the Party, the Komsomol, and the trade unions would arrange people in rows "for the free expression of their will"? Or was it a genuine popular longing for something well organized, manageable, and voiceless? I don't know. But the crowds made a big impression on me.

Well, what of it? At least each one got a free blue jacket out of it. And a free brown cap.

· 20 ·

Personal Matters

We step into Yeltsin's home and meet his extended family, hearing about their happy and hard times, their celebrations and squabbles, their habits and hang-ups. We follow Yeltsin as he tries to shake off the pressures of the presidential office by hunting wood grouse, zipping around in his golf cart, drinking vodka, and eating Naina's homemade meatballs.

.   .   .

I WROTE the title of this chapter and paused to think. What was "personal" in my life? Is anything private in a president's life? Does he have even a little corner to himself? It's a tough question.

I want to describe an episode that would be hard to call completely "personal." From the outside, it probably just seems like part of my work. But for me, it was personal because it was so deeply felt.

On July 17, 1998, a month before the start of the banking crisis, I flew to St. Petersburg to take part in a ceremony to bury the remains of the tsar's family. The story of the burial is dramatic and rather sad. In 1917, Nicholas II, his wife, Aleksandra Fyodorovna, and all their children and household members had been shot to death in the so-called Ipatyev House in Ekaterinburg. About a year before the eightieth anniversary of those terrible, infamous executions, an official state commission was formed by Boris Nemtsov to identify the remains, which had apparently been discovered in an abandoned mine shaft in the

Urals on the outskirts of the city. Of course, it was extremely difficult to determine the authenticity of the remains after so many years. Our forensic scientists applied all the latest technology, including DNA analysis. They conducted dozens of tests and sent samples of the remains to London for spectral analysis at a special laboratory. On January 30 the commission issued its final verdict: The remains were authentic. On March 2, I confirmed the decision to inter the remains at the Saints Peter and Paul Cathedral.

Then a strange thing happened. A huge debate flared up about the funeral. First, the regional leaders got involved. Eduard Rossel, governor of the Ural region, and Moscow mayor Yury Luzhkov led the charge. They insisted on having the tsar and his family buried either in St. Petersburg, where the tragedy had occurred, or in Moscow, at the Cathedral of Christ the Savior, the symbol of the new Russian renaissance. But the Romanovs' family burial vault was located in St. Petersburg, inside the Saints Peter and Paul Cathedral within the Peter and Paul Fortress. Graves of ancestors are sacred for any family. The family had to be buried there.

Then the Russian Orthodox Church poured more fat onto the fire. They stubbornly denied the authenticity of the remains. They refused to acknowledge the DNA method of identification. When I met with Patriarch Aleksy, he asked me not to take part in the burial. He insisted that DNA analysis was too new a technique; it had not been tested sufficiently in the world of science and was far from recognized by law. But this was not strictly a church affair. It concerned all citizens of Russia. Russia had to pay its respects to Nicholas II, Aleksandra Fyodorovna, and their unfortunate children. Our memory and our conscience demanded it of us. This was a matter of Russia's international prestige. And from a common, human perspective, people must finally put their ancestors to rest in their graves. How long could this go on?

The Holy Synod proposed burying the remains in a temporary crypt until a decision could be made. And the synod insisted that when the funeral mass was held, the names of those murdered would not be mentioned. On May 12 and again on June 5, I met with Aleksy and tried to understand his position. The patriarch persisted in his view.

Mayor Luzhkov intervened, suddenly changing his position to support the patriarch.

As I later learned, another set of remains existed that had been brought out of Russia by the White Guards right after the civil war. At that time, those remains were buried as members of the tsar's family. To this day, the church cannot resolve this complicated matter. There is already too much friction between the Russian Orthodox Church inside Russia and the Russian Orthodox Church Abroad*.

Meanwhile, the preparations for the burial continued apace. What was to be done? It was an unusual problem for a head of a state. Something told me not to get involved in these delicate church affairs. The press kept drumming the message that the funeral was still in question. Everything seemed to rest on my decision about whether or not to go to St. Petersburg.

The burial of the remains of the tsar, his wife, children, and household members was not just a political issue for me as president but also a personal matter. More than twenty years before, when I was still first secretary of the Communist Party in Sverdlovsk, I had received orders from the Politburo to bulldoze Ipatyev House. The authorities were afraid that a large number of émigrés, dissidents, and foreign correspondents would come to Sverdlovsk for the eightieth anniversary of Nicholas II's coronation. In its inimitable way, Soviet power decided to prevent this from happening. At my request the archivists recently unearthed the bulldozing order. It is hard to believe that the whole country was engulfed in this style of decision-making not so long ago. Here is a taste of it:

SECRET
To the Central Committee of the Communist Party of the Soviet Union
    On the razing of the Ipatyev House in the city of Sverdlovsk

---

* The Russian Orthodox Church Abroad acknowledged and condemned the regicide; the persecuted Russian Orthodox Church within the Soviet Union was forced into silence for many years. The Church Abroad has canonized the tsar and family as martyrs; the church within Russia has not. —Trans.

Anti-Soviet circles in the West have periodically instigated various propagandistic campaigns around the tsarist family of the Romanovs, and in that connection frequently mention the former home of the merchant Ipatyev in the city of Sverdlovsk.

The Ipatyev House continues to stand in the center of town. A training facility for the regional Directorate of Culture is located there. The building has no architectural or other value, and only an insignificant number of citizens and tourists pay any attention to it.

Recently foreign specialists have begun to visit Sverdlovsk. In the future the number of foreigners could significantly increase, and the Ipatyev House will become an object of serious scrutiny.

In this connection, it is seen as expedient to assign to the Sverdlovsk Regional Committee of the CPSU to resolve the issue of the razing of the building in the process of planned reconstruction of the city.

Yury Andropov
Chair of the Committee for State Security of the USSR
Council of Ministers
July 26, 1975

Back then everything was done by the book. In accordance with memorandum 2004-A of the KGB of the USSR Council of Ministers, dated July 26, 1975, the Politburo of the Central Committee of the CPSU passed a decision on August 4, 1975, "On the razing of the Ipatyev House in the city of Sverdlovsk," in which it approved the proposal of the KGB and assigned "the Sverdlovsk Regional Committee of the CPSU to resolve the issue of the razing of the Ipatyev House in the process of planned reconstruction of the city."

When I read these strict lines now, I can hardly believe my eyes. Everything was completely cynical. There wasn't even an attempt to think up a credible explanation, but just those primitive formulations —"in the process of planned reconstruction" and "a building of no architectural or other value." How ridiculous.

But my emotions and questions come from hindsight. At that time, in the mid-1970s, I took this decision rather calmly. I viewed it in my role as the top city official. Why question it?—I didn't need any extra headaches. Moreover, I couldn't prevent this decision myself—it was an official resolution of the highest body of the country, signed and formulated in the proper manner. And what about disobeying the Politburo's resolution? As first secretary of the regional Party Committee, I couldn't even imagine doing that. If I had ignored the directive, I would have been fired, not to mention the other unpleasant consequences. And the new person in my place would have carried out the order anyway. But to this day the splinter remains. Any mention of the execution is like a stab in my heart.

Thus I perceived the proper burial of the tsar's family not only as my civic and political duty but as my own personal duty to memory. I called the Academician Dmitry Sergeyevich Likhachev just before I left for St. Petersburg. Likhachev is an absolutely unique figure in our culture.* His position on the issue was very important. His words were simple: "Boris Nikolayevich, you definitely must be in St. Petersburg."

On July 17, at 11:15 A.M., my plane landed at Pulkovo Airport. Governor Yakovlev got into the car with me, and we headed toward town. It was quite hot, but people stood baking in the sun all along the Kronwerk harbor front, which rings the Peter and Paul Fortress. There were crowds near the eastern gates of the fortress, on the side of Trinity Square. People had even taken spots on the Trinity Bridge across the Neva River. Traffic had been stopped.

I appeared in the cathedral at exactly the moment when the bell to Peter and Paul Fortress chimed twelve noon.

My sudden decision to go to St. Petersburg may have surprised the Moscow political *beau monde*, but I spotted many familiar faces at the memorial service—Yavlinsky, Nemtsov, Lebed. I also met a member of the British royal family, Prince Michael of Kent, the grandson of Grand Prince Vladimir Aleksandrovich, uncle of Nicholas II. And I

---

* Likhachev is widely recognized for his moral authority. He is a victim of the Soviet regime, a former political prisoner, and a prominent scholar.—Trans.

was astonished to see how many people had those familiar Romanov features. Fifty-two members of the imperial family had gathered together for the first time in a very long while.

Lebed, who was running for the office of governor at that time, suddenly went and stood among the Romanovs. Even there, in a cathedral, at such a moment, people continue to play politics.

I cite only a brief excerpt from my speech of July 17:

> For many long years, we remained silent about this monstrous crime, but we must speak the truth: The vengeance in Ekaterinburg was one of the most shameful pages of our history. In giving back to the earth the remains of these murdered innocents, we would like to expiate the sins of our ancestors. Those who committed this evil deed are guilty, as well as those who justified it for decades. . . . I bow my head before the victims of this ruthless murder. Any attempts to change life through violence are doomed.

The church was bright and sunny. It was a brief, solemn ritual. It was a family funeral, not a state funeral. The priests wore white vestments and did not pronounce the name of the deceased, but those names were known by everyone present. They were in our hearts. I stood next to Likhachev the whole time and lit my candle from his candle. Naina was nearby.

The descendants of the Romanovs threw handfuls of earth onto the coffins. They made a hollow thud. With the sun and the crowds of people, it was a heartbreaking scene. I stood for a little while at the entrance to the burial ground. There was that particular St. Petersburg air. It seemed to me that harmony and reconciliation would really begin here someday.

How sad, really, that we have lost the previous historical relics of the monarchy, that we have lost the sense of the wholeness and continuity of our history. How desirable it would be to have all of this restored in our country.

All of Russia watched this solemn ritual on television. It was an event that resounded through the whole country. The burial ceremony in St. Petersburg was not just a public but also a personal act. I have grown so accustomed to the political fray that I have learned to hide whatever is my own, private and vulnerable. I hide it very deep within. But now the time has come to open the floodgates. And suddenly I find it is very hard to talk about the most simple, human things.

Every person has his home, that very personal space where he is only himself, surrounded by his loved ones. But for a long time it was as if I didn't have that kind of home. My family and I live mostly in government *dachas*—now in Gorki-9—with government-issue furniture. Since 1985 I've always had guards with me. Since 1991 I have had two officers carrying the nuclear suitcase. When I'm hunting or fishing or in the hospital or on a walk, they are always with me, in the next boat, the next hut, or a nearby car or room.

My home has always been filled with people—the guards, the doctors, the service personnel. I can't hide from them, and I can't get away. By some unwritten instruction, even the doors in my home are never closed. Can you lock yourself in the bathroom? No, but sometimes you wish you could.

It's a constant stress. There's no opportunity to relax. But I gradually got used to these strangers around me. Now it's become a habit. But only a habit. And lately my home has started to fill with sons-in-law, grandchildren, and even a great-grandchild.

Our extended family has certain sacred, unwritten traditions—birthdays, for example. Every birthday celebrant knows that he or she will be awakened at 6:00 A.M. We all gather together, come into the room, and wish the family member a happy birthday. The flowers and gifts are already waiting on the nightstand. At first the sons-in-law grumbled—why get up so early? Then they got used to it.

And every New Year I play the traditional role of Father Frost. Our whole family gets together: Naina; Lena and her husband, Valera; Tanya and her husband, Lyosha; Lena's children, Katya (now twenty years old), Masha (sixteen), and little Vanka (two); Tanya's children, Borya (nineteen) and Gleb (four). I have a total of five grandchildren and one great-grandchild, Katya's son, Sanechka.*

Although this all sounds very happy, apparently I was a strict papa when my daughters were young. If they came to show me their school notebooks, I would always ask one thing: "Are there all As?" If there weren't all As, I wouldn't even take the notebooks in my hand.

In truth, I think we have quite a patriarchal Urals family, the same kind I grew up in. There is a certain court of last resort, and that's me, the grandfather. My opinion is authoritative. That makes it easier to resolve the kind of problems that quite often spring up between children and parents. If you have a conflict, you simply take it to Grandpa. Of course they all know it is better to solve the problem among themselves. They come to me only in extreme cases. For example, if Tanya has some kind of conflict with Borya, Borya might stubbornly pressure his mama, saying, "What if I go to Grandpa, and he lets me?" After some consideration, Tanya might say, "All right, go on." But she always manages to get to me first so we can coordinate our positions. And Borya has never done anything behind my back after we've agreed on something. My word is law for him.

My two daughters, Lena and Tanya, are very different. Let me start with Tanya, who helps me with all my work. On the whole, Tanya is an extremely goal-oriented person. She's like me. If she decides she wants something, she will definitely get it. But she's also a dreamer. When she was young, she first wanted to be captain of the long-distance swim team. Then she learned how to semaphore at a yacht club. Then she fell in love with volleyball and became a serious player on the Locomotive team from the Urals. Finally, you could say that she ran away from home to study in Moscow. We didn't know anybody in

---

* Yeltsin uses the Russian diminutives for his family. Nicknames correspond to full names as follows: Tanya (Tatyana); Lena (Yelena); Katya (Yekaterina); Borya (Boris); Masha (Maria); Lyosha (Aleksei); Shura (Aleksandr); Valera (Valery); Vanka (Ivan); and Sanechka (Aleksandr). — Trans.

Moscow except one of our old classmates who lived in a communal apartment. So Tanya had to live in a dormitory. Naina was categorically opposed to Tanya's leaving. But I said, "If she's decided it, let her go."

Lately Tanya has insisted on planting a lawn at every dacha. Evidently she wants to beautify our government residences. She tortures herself with our these lawns, which have to be planted according to specific instructions. She has forced all the younger men in the house to dig and plant and so on. One day I decided to go out to drink some tea on our new green meadow. I brought out a little table, placed the samovar on it, and dragged a chair outdoors. Suddenly, the furniture sank more than a foot into the ground. They had forgotten to lay down the base. Tanya came out and began laughing: I was almost flat on my back with my legs stretched out on the lawn.

In order to travel to our *fazenda,** Tanya bought a Niva car with a trailer. She had to pass her driving test to get her license. Unfortunately, she had a very unpleasant driving instructor. Not only did he try to put his paws on her thigh during the driving lessons, but after being rebuffed, he turned to politics and started cursing me as well, not knowing who Tanya was. Tanya listened and listened and then finally burst out, "Stop spouting nonsense. None of it was like that."

"And how do you know?" the instructor asked indignantly.

"Because he's my father," Tanya answered.

The instructor came to a screeching halt. He was totally blown away. "You're kidding!" he exclaimed.

"No, I'm not kidding at all."

From that time on, the driving was more quiet and refined. And that was how I was able to protect my daughter from "sexual harassment," as they now call it in America.

Lena is not at all like Tanya. She was always at the center of a big crowd from school. They would spend their weekends hiking through

---

* A *fazenda* is a Brazilian plantation. Perhaps influenced by Latin American soap operas dubbed into Russian, Russians have begun using terms for land such as *fazenda* and *hacienda*. Yeltsin is echoing a certain self-conscious pride of ownership many Russians now experience in the new Russia. —Trans.

the Ural forests. Naina would worry, but there was no need because
Lena's friends were great kids. To this day Lena writes to her old
friends and gets together with them. She's like Naina and me in that regard. We haven't lost our ties with the past either.

Lena went to the same institute that Naina and I went to, the Ural
Polytechnical Institute. She even studied at the same faculty, construction. We are kindred spirits. Lena was an excellent student, loved
books, and went to music school. She is well rounded. She has my nature. But when she moved to Moscow, Lena had to quit her job and de-
vote herself to her family and her home. To be honest, I suffered a
little over this. Lena suffered as well. She had wonderful abilities. But
she decided to stay at home with little Katya and then Masha. She became a homemaker and is now deeply involved in that side of life. For
example, she is an amazing knitter. She knits only by hand. She can
read, watch television, or talk while knitting. I think she can knit just
about anything in a day. I wear her pullovers, sweaters, and scarves.
They're special for me, like Naina's pierogi or Masha's poems. These
are my life's talismans. They protect me from fears and worries.

Lena likes order, harmony, and beauty in all things. She has taken
up gardening and now has exotic hillocks with flowers and rocks. Her
garden is like a piece of the alpine meadows transplanted to the outskirts of Moscow. And Lena never misses a single major art exhibit.
She loves the Impressionists and is interested in ancient architecture
and historical monuments. She's the one in our family responsible for
aesthetics.

When my campaign began in 1996, Lena also threw herself into
politics. She helped organize Naina's trips around the country, prepared her speeches, read and helped correct her interviews. She did a
lot of work in the campaign headquarters. And she didn't once complain or try to distance herself.

Lena was already nearly forty years old when she risked having a
third child. How much anxiety and fear and suffering accompanied little Vanka's appearance in the world! How Naina and I worried! In my
view Lena performed a heroic act. Then again, heroism was nothing
new to her. It had come to her long ago, when she married Valera

Okulov, a civilian airline pilot. Pilots' wives don't accompany their husbands on their trips. They must say good-bye every day. They get a few hours with their husbands at home and then the men fly off into the sky again. Lena began to learn the different models of planes and their technical characteristics. She could even tell planes apart from the way they sounded. And we all understood why. Lena was worried about her husband, who flew all over the country and then all over the world.

Valera loved a unique sport: racing down mountain rivers. It was hard waiting for him to come home from these expeditions. Lena and Valera hiked all over Kamchatka together, and they sailed almost all of Karelia by catamaran. But Valera would not take Lena on his more challenging athletic expeditions. He went with his friends. Once Valera's boat capsized. A friend on the ride went missing for several days. He finally reappeared. By some miracle he was still alive.

Lena is selflessly devoted to her home, her family, her children, and her relatives. For her, there are no trivialities; nothing is done merely in passing. She is the height of taste and persistence. It has always been important for her to live at home, to cultivate her own garden. Now, with Vanka and her grandson, Sanechka (my great-grandson), I sometimes sense that she is holding her home up on her shoulders. She takes responsibility for her family's feelings and relationships and the education and raising of the children. This is an enormous amount of work. Lena has put her builder's heart and soul into it. Now that Katya and Masha are finally growing up, I suddenly see with my own eyes how much of Lena's love and warmth has been showered upon them.

Lena does everything ideally, at 100 percent, nothing halfway. It sometimes amazes me. Once I saw Lena reading Pushkin's fairy tales to Vanka, who was only six months old at the time. "Lena, what are you doing?" I asked. "He doesn't understand anything."

"Don't you see, Papa?" she said. "I want him to hear the music of the words even now." Our Vanka still falls asleep only to classical music.

Lena's husband, Valera Okulov, has stopped flying and now runs Aeroflot, Russian largest airline. Being the wife of a top executive is very difficult. When Valera was promoted to this position, he came to seek my advice. Would his job interfere in any way with my political position? Would it create any awkward situations? I said he had to decide such things for himself. I couldn't get in the way of his career. But I have to give Valera credit: He never brings home conversations about work or his problems. Sometimes he answers my questions about his prospects and how things are going. But no more than that. I am grateful to him for this understanding and tact. This is what a real man's character is all about.

I have one unquenchable, burning passion: automobiles. At one time, as a very young man, I drove a truck. I have never really had the chance to get behind the wheel since. A car has become my workplace. The back seat where I ride is outfitted with a special communications channel, and the phone rings fairly often. Sometimes it's a president from another country or the prime minister or the secretary of the Security Council or some other minister. Sometimes I call someone myself. So for me a car is an office on wheels.

But when I get to the end of the usual road from the Kremlin to the *dacha* and the presidential limousine slowly, slowly approaches the house, my grandchildren run out to greet me. Before, it was Masha and Borya; now it's Gleb and little Vanka. "Grandpa, take us for a ride!" they cry. We all get into the car together and circle around the garden drive. The black, armored car glides quietly past the tulips and the ivy. I really feel great at these times.

After we moved to Moscow and I fell out of favor, I bought my first real car, a silver Moskvich. That was when I worked at Gosstroy, the state construction office. I decided that I would drive myself to work.

I remember my first ride vividly. To my right was a bodyguard. My family sat on the backseat. Tverskaya Street was very busy. I kept turning my head to see what was happening behind me (I don't see very well in rearview mirrors). Tanya cried, "Papa, look ahead! I beg you!" I was driving pretty fast. My pale bodyguard kept his hand poised over the hand brake in order to grab it if he had to. Thank God we arrived without incident.

Since that time, Naina has stood her ground and won't let me get behind the wheel. "Borya, you have a lot of drivers in the family: your sons-in-laws, your daughters, and your grandchildren. Everyone will be happy to drive you where you want to go." Nevertheless, I recently took a drive through the grounds of the *dacha* in my presidential limousine. Now that I'm a pensioner, they let me do everything. Most of the time I satisfy my passion for driving by tooling around in a golf cart. In this vehicle, I can race as much as I like. I like to zoom downhill and aim straight for a tree, then turn at the last moment. That's how I relax. Recently my bodyguard came with me. He jumped out of the cart at the last minute, just before I swerved to miss a tree. I had to apologize to him later.

I tried to pass my unfulfilled love for driving on to my granddaughter Katya. When Katya was eighteen, I wanted to give her a car. Lena and Tanya tried to talk me out of it, saying that the present was too expensive and that Katya didn't have her license. But I insisted. I gave her a fancy red car, a Scoda. It was one instance when I did the wrong thing with a present. The car was parked outside for about two years. Katya never got behind the wheel. But now Katya's husband, Shura, has begun driving the Scoda. So even though it took two years, my present has finally got some use.

Katya and Borya are my two oldest grandchildren. They were born a year apart. Katya, Lena's daughter, recently turned twenty and has taken leave from her studies to stay home with her young child. Borya is studying abroad. His last name is also Yeltsin, although he's Boris Jr. He's a fellow with a stubborn and sometimes difficult nature. But maybe that's what a man needs.

Tanya had many qualms when she first decided to send Borya abroad to study. She spent a long time selecting the school. The main criteria she considered were strong discipline and a heavy academic workload. That was how she settled on a school for boys in Winchester, England. When she told me about the living conditions there, I didn't believe her at first. Borya lived in a dormitory, six to a room. He slept on a bunk bed. If he sat on the edge of his bed, his legs would bump his roommate below. He had a table, a small bureau for clothing, and a computer, but no luxuries. Every morning there was an early wake-up call for the students to put themselves in order. Their shoes had to be shined, and their shirts had to be clean and pressed. That's how life was for Borya for three years.

It doesn't take a genius to figure out that with that kind of lifestyle, all Borya's heartstrings were tugging him back to comfortable and affectionate Moscow. He and I correspond on the Internet, sending humorous messages back and forth.

Once, in a telephone conversation with Tony Blair, I let something slip. "Tony," I said. "You know that my grandson is studying in England? He's kind of lonely there. Perhaps you could pen him a few lines?"

Imagine our surprise when Borya told us that an official letter with the coat of arms of the prime minister of Great Britain had arrived, causing a stir at his school. Blair had wished my grandson success in his studies and invited him to visit. Borya was able to figure out the linguistic subtleties in the note and understood that the invitation was strictly formal, that he didn't have to jump into a taxi and rush over to Downing Street.

Now, my younger granddaughter, Masha, would never be allowed to go abroad by her parents, Lena and Valera. Under no condition. At seventeen, Masha is a beautiful and charming girl with a poetic nature. (For my birthday, she would often give me poems she had written.) How could you let a girl like that out of your sight?

When Lena and Valera went abroad for a few weeks on holiday, Masha came to live with us at Gorki-9. One evening she came up to me and said, "Grandpa, please talk to Mama. Tell her to let me go to the disco!" It turned out that Mama was keeping a strict eye on Masha from abroad. In as authoritative a voice as I could muster, I said, "Masha, you can go to the disco. I'll take responsibility."

Katya has an independent spirit as well. She has always been a willful girl, with my character. When she went to study at the history department of Moscow State University and had been in school for several weeks, she and I had a disagreement. She came crying to me, saying "Grandpa, please tell them to take the security away!" While I was serving as president, all the members of my family had "attachments," that is, security guards. That was an unwritten Kremlin tradition, which had been in effect for many decades.

But Katya broke this tradition. She found it quite awkward to have the guards there in front of her classmates. "Grandpa, don't you see? It's just funny," she said. "I come out of the auditorium and the poor things are standing there. Please, I beg you!" So I had to grant her wish. I remember I wrote some kind of release form to the head of security. They removed the security from my granddaughter, making it my responsibility. Another kind of girl might have been proud to have such bodyguards and would have had her nose in the air.

Katya displayed her independence with her early marriage. This 1999 New Year's Eve she and her husband, Shura, were the first to arrive. I took a close look at him again. He's an excellent fellow. Shura is also at Moscow State University, studying psychology. They met, by the way, when they were in grade school. And they say there are no romantics anymore! Shura's mother teaches Russian language and literature in the same school that Katya and Shura attended, so their entire romance bloomed before her eyes. Not every mother would display such restraint and understanding. After all, they're children!

To my enormous regret, I was unable to attend their wedding, as I was in the hospital with pneumonia. But Katya and Shura came to visit me there, and I congratulated them and wished them happiness. I was told that the wedding was a lot of fun, without the usual formality and pomp, and I heard of one especially amusing incident: My grandson Borya was running a bit late to the wedding, and he wasn't completely up on everything because he had rushed over from England. He saw Shura, whom he knew from Katya's school crowd, and asked in surprise, "Shura, what are you doing here?" And Shura replied, "What do you mean? I'm the groom!"

I try to protect my family from the constant, aggressive attention of journalists. After 1996 a wave of sleazy, false stories about them began appearing in the yellow press. The stories went that Tanya had a stormy romance with Chubais or that Katya had used her connections to get into college. They said Borya had fallen in love with some Russian model in London and that Masha had become a model herself, run away from home, and was now advertising clothing for Gucci (or was it Versace?)—all sorts of other nonsense.

The stories were unfair to the adults—Tanya, Lena, my sons-in-law, Valera and Lyosha—but they've become hardened over the years and aren't surprised by anything anymore. But when my grandchildren are hurt by these lies, I have trouble restraining myself. For example, I remember when the first story appeared about Borya's supposed London romance. A girl he had been seeing in Moscow almost broke up with him. Adolescents are so easily hurt. My daughters shed many tears and suffered a great deal of anxiety because of these articles. It is hard for a mother to understand that she shouldn't pay the slightest attention to these things. I really don't want my name to cast such a long shadow over my daughters and grandchildren. I hope that will gradually pass.

Many people would probably be interested to know whether what the newspapers write about my astronomical income is true. In other words, am I a rich man? To be honest, I don't know. It depends on how you measure it. Let's look at what I have—and what I don't have.

To begin, how much money do I have? Everything has to be exact, down to the kopeck. For that, I have to take my last income tax return. As of January 1, 1999, I had a total of 8.436 million rubles in the accounts at the Russian Savings Bank. My income for 1998 was 183,837 rubles*. Aside from my government residence, I own some real estate jointly with my wife: an apartment on Osennaya Street in Moscow

---

* On January 1, 1999, there were approximately 22 rubles to the dollar. —Trans.

and a 452-square-meter *dacha* on 4 hectares in Odintsovo District in the
Moscow region.

Here is what else I own:

I have a BMW that I purchased in 1995.
There are refrigerators at the *dacha* and a refrigerator at home.
We have several television sets.
The furniture consists of sofas, armchairs, tables, beds, bureaus,
and so on.
We have clothing, of course.
My wife and daughters have costume jewelry.
We have tennis rackets.
We have table clocks.
I own hunting rifles.
We have books.
We own a stereo system and a tape recorder.

Now I'll tell you a bit about what I *don't* have.

I don't have any securities, stocks, or promissory notes.
I don't have any real estate abroad (no villas, castles, palaces,
ranches, farms, *fazendas,* or *haciendas*).
I don't have any accounts in foreign banks.
We have no valuable gems.
I own no gold mines, oil derricks, diamond mines, or real estate
abroad.
My family has no yachts, planes, or helicopters abroad.
My wife and my daughters, Lena and Tanya, have not opened
bank accounts in any Swiss or British or any other foreign
banks.
They have no castles or villas. They have no property abroad or
shares in foreign companies, factories, or mines. They never
had any such things.

I'm certainly not a poor man. But the Russian president's money is in a Russian bank, as it should be. My books have been published and continue to be published around the world. Neither I nor members of my family have ever received any income from privatization or from any deals related to my office or my "influence." All of our income is absolutely open and transparent. I think I deserve to travel and go on vacation anywhere in the world with my family.

One necessary addition: All this information is taken from the declaration submitted to the Ministry for Tax and Revenue on March 31, 1999. It is my last income tax statement as president. I hope that's enough on this subject.

Hunting and fishing are something special to me. I began hunting in Sverdlovsk* and fell in love with it. We even had a specially equipped jeep with two heaters so we could keep warm in the winter. We would hunt for moose, arranging ourselves in a line, standing in numbered spots. If a moose wandered into someone's numbered area, that lucky person would get to shoot. I also learned how to hunt wood grouse in Sverdlovsk. But when I came to Moscow, with all its political passions, I simply forgot about hunting. In Moscow I developed a new pastime to help me relax, tennis.

It was in 1991 that I first went hunting in Zavidovo with Tanya's husband, Lyosha, who also turned out to be a passionate hunter. That's when I saw what a unique and marvelous place Zavidovo was. It is stocked with stag, Siberian deer, and wild boar, and there are lakes and swamps for duck and goose hunting. There is also wood grouse hunting, which requires some effort. In the spring, when the wood grouse gives its mating call, you have to pick a place where the bird will start singing with the sun's first rays and then wait in the forest until dawn. As the wood grouse gets going with his mating call, he is overcome with love and stops hearing the rest of the world. That's when you can spot his silhouette in the dim light. This is a very rare, very mysterious, and very exciting form of hunting.

Duck hunting using a gun sight is the most fun. You try to hit a bird in flight with an exact shot from your boat. It's a real sport. I get so caught up in it that sometimes I come home with a huge, palm-sized bruise on my shoulder from the gun's recoiling.

I have been given numerous rifles as presents over the years; I now have a whole collection. But none of these new guns is as comfortable and easy to hunt with as my first carbine, a Cheski-Zbroyev, known as CheZet to hunters, with a 30-0.6 gauge. I've been hunting with it for nearly twenty years. I've got so used to it and I've shot so much with it that even when the stock cracked, I had it taped up and continued to shoot with the rifle. Of course I ordered a new CheZet, which was shipped to me, but the new model just doesn't feel right, so I'm still using the old one. Old habits are hard to break.

Hunting is a collective affair, but I don't like going out in large parties of men. Sometimes I go to Zavidovo just with Naina. I hunt with the local gamesmen, Lyosha, or other guests. There is also something soothing about hunting alone. It's a kind of compensation. I need to be alone.

Eating *ukha* (fish soup), shish kebabs, and blini outdoors is my favorite pastime. Sometimes I would go over to one of the islands in the lakes of Zavidovo and forget about everything. I would take a nap, and the stress would melt away. I especially love the Zavidovo *ukha,* made from a special hunter's recipe. You take a big pot and boil a dozen different types of fish together. Then, after you've added some huge tomatoes and other ingredients, you drop in a sizzling piece of wood from the fire. It gives the soup the flavor of wood smoke and gets rid of that fish-fat taste.

I'll never forget one time when I was sailing around the lake with a foreign guest. He kept glancing at my black briefcase on the bottom of the boat. He thought it was the nuclear briefcase, and he tried to stay as far away from it as possible, squeezing to the edge of the boat. When we got to the island, the briefcase was opened, and two bottles of vodka and some pickled cucumbers were taken out. The guest laughed for a long time. The nuclear suitcase was in the next boat, under the guard of officers.

In my day, like the majority of people, I considered it quite acceptable to raise a shot glass or two to someone's health on a special occasion. But what a wave of rumors, gossip, and political turmoil has been kicked up in public and in the newspapers over this issue! It's hard to believe now.

The traditional Russian lifestyle dictates that it's impossible not to drink at a birthday; it's impossible not to drink at a friend's wedding; it's impossible not to drink with your coworkers. I always regarded this as a tiresome obligation, and I couldn't bear to put up with drunks, but fairly early on I concluded that alcohol was the only means quickly to get rid of stress. I recall one incident from 1994, during a trip to Berlin, when all the world's television companies broadcast footage of an inebriated Yeltsin conducting a military orchestra.

Those were difficult days for me. From the outside, such behavior might seem wild and awkward. But I knew what neither my aides, nor reporters, nor my critics knew. The stress I underwent in late 1993, during the White House rebellion and thereafter, was so great that to this day I don't understand how I managed to survive it. The tension and exhaustion required some outlet. There, in Berlin, when all of Europe was celebrating the withdrawal of our last forces, I suddenly felt that I couldn't take it anymore. The responsibility and the whole atmosphere of the event, tense with the expectation of a historical step, weighed upon me. I snapped.

How do I feel now, when that all-too-familiar footage of me conducting that ill-fated orchestra is shown? I don't feel shame or indifference or irritation. But I can begin to feel my skin crawl as I think of that alarm, tension, and immeasurable weight of stress that pressed down upon me in those days, pushing me to the ground. I remember that the weight would lift after a few shot glasses. And in that state of lightness I felt as if I could conduct an orchestra.

After that incident a group of my aides wrote me a letter saying that my behavior and my impromptu remarks were harming me and all our mutual work. I didn't apologize to my aides. None of them was able to help me. The distance between us was too great. I walked along the beach in Sochi and realized that I had to go on living. I had to regain my strength. Gradually, I came to myself.

Ever since then, whatever provoked a change in my usual behavior —insomnia, a cold, or ordinary tiredness—would be ascribed to the influence of alcohol. I knew about these rumors, but I considered it beneath my dignity to respond to them. So what could I do? Did I have to prove to everyone that my heart and my blood pressure (which influenced my speech and my gait), the constant stress, the insomnia, and the medicines I had to take shouldn't be confused with alcoholism? Should I have beaten myself on the chest?

All of that was humiliating and unpleasant. And at a certain point I realized that no matter what I said, people wouldn't believe me. They thought it was my weakness. Besides, I knew that my very figure, my stubborn will, and my tough nature provoked hatred, hysteria, and slander. If it weren't the infamous alcohol, they would attack me over something else. They would find some other vulnerability. But they would beat me up, that's for sure. So wasn't it better to ignore it?

And I really ceased to notice the rumors and speculations. Then came the terribly difficult year of 1995, with my heart attack. After the operation, my doctors said that the maximum amount of alcohol that I could allow myself was one glass of wine a day. Ever since then, I have followed this recommendation.

There have been a few slipups with gifts and good wishes over the years. In about 1981 I gave Tanya a very fancy present: a set of Elan designer skis and boots. There was a terrible shortage in those years, and I knew that Tanya dreamed of a real set of skis. Tanya went to the ski resort at Dombai for the winter holidays. Unfortunately, I had given her skis and boots that were almost my own size. The skis were too long, and the boots were loose on her feet. Each run down the mountain was real torture. Later, when Tanya bought herself skis in her usual size, she didn't just glide but flew down the mountain.

While I worked and hunted, Naina raised the children and the grand-children. The role of grandmother and then great-grandmother came entirely naturally to Naina. I can't remember all the birthdays of all our family members, but Naina never misses a one.

Naina's prepared to spend as much time as necessary on her family. Lena and Tanya try to convince her not to make homemade meatballs for the children for lunch. "Mama," they say. "When guests come, you have to stand over the stove for three hours! Try to rest on regular days! These kids don't care what they eat. For them, it still doesn't mat-ter if they eat your homemade dish or what the cook makes—meat-balls or just a piece of meat."

But Babushka thinks her meatballs are much better than what the cook can make, and it's practically impossible to convince her to cook less. All our guests remember Naina's cakes, with their numerous lay-ers. There's something touching and homey about making something from scratch for your guests. It's as if Naina is trying to preserve and protect us all. There's also a more prosaic explanation: Naina just likes to cook. Besides, you would get sick of eating the same thing over and over again for ten straight years, the same "correct" dishes prepared by the cook using recipes from the ninth directorate.*

There is a remarkable contraption at our *dacha*, an old-fashioned Russian oven under an overhang outdoors. Sometimes we spend New Year's Eve at the *dacha*, and Naina bakes the traditional blini. We eat them right there at the stove, washing them down with champagne. The table gets covered with drifts of snow, and sometimes the blini do as well.

Naina and I have been together for almost forty years. We've never been apart. We've never taken separate vacations. We never separated our lives into two parts. I remember when Naina was an eighteen-year-old student. I remember that when she worked in the largest drafting institute in Sverdlovsk, she managed not only to take care of

---

* Yeltsin is referring to the KGB's ninth directorate. The Soviet leaders often had cooks with security clearances who were employed within the KGB.—Trans.

the girls and fix dinner but always pressed my suit, which took half the night, until it was perfect. (I was first secretary and I had to look the part.)

Naina has given me so much spiritual and physical strength that I simply have no words to describe it. Without her, I never could have withstood the political storms. I never could have survived 1987 or 1991 or later. And even now, when Naina is already a happy grandmother and can quietly take care of her grandchildren, she still has to put so much energy into me.

Naina is a wonderfully sincere and direct person. She has her own unique way of suffering through our political dramas. She would often turn to me and say, "Borya, maybe you should have a talk with Luzhkov? Perhaps he's simply mistaken? He should wake up!" I would smile, of course, and promise to meet Luzhkov and have a talk. If politics were made by people like Naina, we'd have a different kind of world.

And that reminds me of a funny story connected to Luzhkov. For a long time, Luzhkov, who lives nearby, would send us milk from the cow on his farm. Then one day he stopped. It was right in the summer of 1998, when he was heading up his own party. An intermediary informed us that unfortunately Luzhkov's cow was sick. It was quite a coincidence. To this day, Naina expresses surprise that the cow fell so ill for so long.

People write many letters to Naina, which continue to come to us either through the post office on Osennaya Street or from the main post office. Naina's mail is completely different from what I got as president. I got thousands of appeals, complaints, requests for help with everyday problems, projects to reform our state, various inventions—everything but the kitchen sink. But my wife's mail is personal, warm, sincere, and understanding. People have a sense of Naina's nature and her profound decency, so there is hardly ever anger or criticism in these letters. When I announced my operation to the country, Naina even got messages with medical advice from people who had suffered heart attacks. They advised her on my recovery and the medication I should take. Above all, I am amazed at the kindness in these letters. Many of the writers have every right to be angry at life. The kind of people who take pen in hand are often the poor, the lonely, or the sick.

One letter made a particular impression on Naina with its sincere tone and modesty. A woman from St. Petersburg wrote about her disabled little girl. Upon learning that I was headed to St. Petersburg and taking Tanya with me, Naina asked me to deliver a television with a video recorder as a present to this woman.

When we reached St.Petersburg, Tanya called the woman throughout the day, but no one answered. Finally, she went to the address indicated on the envelope, thinking that she could at least leave the present with neighbors. But when she rang the bell, the door was opened by a little girl. The girl didn't understand what was going on and couldn't believe that someone was bringing a present from Naina. Unfortunately, her mother was at work at the time. According to Tanya, they lived very poorly indeed. They really didn't have a television set.

Soon Naina got a letter from St. Petersburg. The gift had been a success. Thanks to the TV, the girl, who was practically unable to go outside, at least had some contact with the outside world.

When Naina goes to an orphanage, or a children's hospital, or to visit a an ailing celebrity, she never tells anyone about it. She sincerely believes that charity and good works are her private affair. On the one hand, this is an absolutely correct position. I would do the same thing. On the other hand, Naina has done a lot for children who have incurable diseases that lead to almost complete disability. If the country knew about her work, I think others would follow her example. But Naina has always avoided publicity. She gives very brief interviews on television and rarely appears in public. Still, the most prominent features of her nature—modesty, tact, humanity—can be felt on these occasions. People sense these qualities and are drawn to her.

I have always been impressed by Naina's connections to a small circle of Moscow actresses—Galina Volchek, Sofya Pilyavskaya, Marina Ladynina, Mariya Mironova, Vera Vasilyeva, and others. They are friendly relationships, without any trace of superficiality or self-aggrandizing.

Sometimes, in the middle of a family celebration, in the middle of the noise, the laughter, and the holiday bustle, there is a sudden silence. Then one of my daughters will say, "Papa, are you here?" That means that I've broken off in midsentence and fallen into thought.

I'm dismayed by these sudden pauses in front of my family. I try to control myself with all my might, but nothing comes of it. One moment I am entirely involved in home life and these happy, tranquil moments with the family, and the next a thought surfaces from somewhere in the depths of my subconscious about something that happened the day before or something that will come tomorrow. Even when I am peacefully strolling with my family along a park walkway, these thoughts break in and bring me to a stop. They are things I can no longer fix or things that await my decision, things that have to be done now or in a month. The country awaits my next political decision. And I freeze in place, fall silent, and retreat into myself.

And yet, as I've shown, the president does in fact have a private life. It is in those uninterrupted moments with the people close to him. It is while hunting or driving around in a golf cart. It is in the sacred traditions of the family. It is from the joy of being with children and grandchildren. They are my real family, not the made-up "family" they show on television.

Sometimes when I watch little Gleb and Vanka playing nearby, I try to peer into their future, to see their destinies. They will inherit a different Russia, a completely different world, a different millennium. But what kind of Russia will it be? Will they be proud of having been raised in our country, in our city, in our home? I am sure they will. There can be no doubt about it.

· 21 ·

"Yeltsin Has Gone Mad"

Yeltsin explores in dramatic detail the tense days of August 1998, when he definitively decides to replace Prime Minister Stepashin with the relatively unknown Vladimir Putin. This is Putin's first real step down the corridors of power. How could Yeltsin be so sure that the cool, tight-lipped KGB bureaucrat had the stuff of a leader?

.   .

THERE IS A term I hate in Russian politics: *access to the body.* It refers to the frequency and candor of meetings with the first person. (In America, those around the president use the term "face time.") Of course, it's unpleasant to see oneself as just "a body." But although the term is extremely cynical, it acknowledges a real problem for any person in power. It can be difficult for journalists, cultural figures, businessmen, representatives of various social groups, and even aides to establish contact with the president: *"access to the body."* But that access determines the level of effectiveness and democracy within the bureaucracy. Not all effective bureaucracies are democratic, and vice versa. There is a fine line between the two.

When Sergei Filatov was chief of administration and Viktor Ilyushin was my first aide (these two posts were combined at the time), there were regular meetings with Baturin, Lifshits, Satarov, Pikhoya, Krasnov, and other aides. Ilyushin initiated these meetings, which took place once a month or every other month. Sometimes there would be long intervals between meetings. Korzhakov, who was jealous of these "rotten intellectuals," tried to vigilantly block their "access to the body." This continued until the 1996 presidential elections.

During my second term, Chubais, Yumashev, and Voloshin made meetings with deputies of the head of administration routine. They became an obligatory weekly ritual. I was impressed when I heard new young fellows report to me regularly on their affairs. If they only knew what kind of battles and passions had once raged at meetings in this office. This new, open style of work made me acutely aware of the Soviet mentality that had reigned over my previous apparat, or "close circle."

I had noticed Vladimir Putin when he headed the chief control directorate of the administration and then became first deputy to Yumashev, who was responsible for work with the regions. Putin appeared in the Kremlin in March 1997. Sometimes he was left in charge, and I would have the opportunity to deal with him more frequently. Putin's reports were a model of clarity. Unlike other deputies, who were always trying to lay out their visions of Russia and the world, Putin did not try to strike up conversations with me. Rather, it seemed that Putin tried to remove any sort of personal element from our contact. And precisely because of that, I wanted to talk to him more.

I was also shocked by his lightning reactions. Sometimes even my most innocuous comments threw people off. They would turn red and search tortuously for the right answer. But Putin replied calmly and naturally. It made me feel that this young man was ready for absolutely anything in life, that he would respond to any challenge with clarity and precision. At first Putin's coolness even made me cautious, but then I understood that it was ingrained in his nature.

I was already growing dissatisfied with the leadership at the top of the FSB. In the summer of 1998, we were caught practically unawares by the "rail wave": Striking coal workers blocked the railroad tracks, cutting Siberia and the south of Russia off from Moscow. It was a catastrophe. Every day cost many millions in losses, which hit the most vulnerable people, pensioners and state employees, the hardest. Most important, the strikes created a real threat of massive political disorder on a national scale throughout Russia. I met with Nikolai Kovalev, then director of the FSB. He was almost panicking. I understood from our conversation that this situation was new for him and that he didn't know how to handle it. I sympathized—strikes were not technically part of his agency's mandate—but a threat to the country's security was real. A political battle was one thing, but blocking the national arteries of transportation was another thing entirely.

Kovalev, a career Chekist and a pretty responsible professional, had an enormous personal antipathy to business and to all its representatives. He couldn't help himself. He simply despised people with large amounts of money. As a result, his agency gradually began searching for these new "enemies of the people." They focused on gathering compromising materials on commercial banks and individual businessmen. I had not forgotten how in 1996 the FSB investigators had actually become involved in the fabricated Sobchak affair. This was all part of the same political line.

Around that time, in the summer of 1998, I began to think about whom I could appoint to replace Kovalev as the director of the FSB. The answer was instantly clear: Putin. For one thing, Putin had spent quite a few years working in the security agencies. Second, he had gone through a school of management. But above all, the more I knew Putin, the more convinced I was that he combined both an enormous dedication to democracy and market reforms and an unwavering patriotism.

Putin was informed of his appointment the moment the decree was handed down. I was on vacation in Shuyskaya Chupa. Kiriyenko flew down to see me, bringing a draft of the decree on Putin's appointment. I signed it without hesitation. On July 25, 1998, Putin was made director of the FSB.

When I returned from vacation, I sat down for a serious conversation with Putin. I proposed that he return to military service and obtain the rank of general.

"What for?" Putin asked. "I resigned from the agencies on August 20, 1991.* I don't want to return to full-time service. I am a civilian. It's important that such a power ministry be headed by a civilian. If you allow it, I will remain a colonel in the reserves."

We discussed the personnel problems at the FSB at some length. It was a difficult situation. Many skilled professionals had gone into the private sector, and many were ready to retire into the reserves. We had to restore the Lubyanka's authority, which had been so greatly undermined after 1991.† We had to preserve the traditions of the remaining professionals, but we also had to make the service less politicized.

Putin went about reorganizing the FSB very intelligently. He dealt with Nikolai Kovalev, the man he replaced as head of the FSB, in a humane way allowing Kovalev to resolve certain personal problems quietly. (It may seem trivial, but in the military service that sort of thing is very important.) Then he drew up a revised staff list. The new FSB collegium included, besides the deputies, the heads of the Moscow and Leningrad FSB directorates. Although the reorganization meant that a number of officers had to be retired, it proceeded calmly and, I would say, cleanly. Putin's structure would prove to be quite workable.

Putin came to the job at the FSB at a very difficult time. He was sitting on a powder keg. That fall, when it seemed that the wave of anti-Semitism raised by General Makashov in the Duma might spill over into the streets any minute, Putin made some very tough remarks condemning political extremism. He delivered his statement with Lubyanka in the background, and I think his cold expression and the almost military precision of his formulations discouraged many people from causing trouble. And Putin did not leave a single radical group in Moscow in peace. All of them began to complain in the press that the era of the police state had come to the capital.

But the most significant thing is that Putin took a very firm political position. As I have noted, the constant clashes with the prime minister, who wanted to put the FSB under his own sphere of influence, did not

---

* August 20, 1991, was the day after hard-liners attempted a coup against Gorbachev, leading to the breakup of the Soviet Union. —Trans.

† The KGB, and later the FSB, are located on Lubyanka Square in Moscow. —Trans.

faze Putin. He did not allow himself to be manipulated in political games. Even I was amazed by his solid moral code. In the insidious rumor mill of the government at that time, it was wise for even a seasoned person to avoid entanglements. But for Putin, the single criterion was the morality of a given action or the decency of a given person. He would not do anything that conflicted with his understanding of honor. He was always prepared to part with his high post if his sense of integrity would require it.

Putin did not hasten into big politics, but he sensed danger more quickly and acutely than others and always tried to warn me of trouble. When I learned that Putin had helped send Sobchak abroad, I had mixed feelings. Putin had taken a great risk. Yet I profoundly admired his actions.

In 1998, when I realized the need for Primakov's dismissal, I tortured myself with worries. Who would support me? Who was really backing me? And at some point I understood that it was Putin. But he could not be brought in just yet, and so Stepashin was inserted temporarily. On August 4, a Wednesday morning, I met with Voloshin. I wanted to ask him when we would finally resolve the issue of appointing a new prime minister to replace Stepashin. Would it be in September, October, or right away, in August?

A resignation now would look entirely illogical. But we could probably find reasons for a dismissal/resignation in the fall, reasons everyone would understand. Or was it better to let the situation ripen on its own? There was one essential issue: Stepashin could not be a political leader in the parliamentary and presidential elections. And why not cite the real reason for the dismissal, Putin? Putin was the man of my hopes. He was the man I trusted, to whom I could entrust the country.

August is the height of the vacation season in Russia. Putin's appointment would be like a bolt from the blue. Everything would heat up instantly. But we did have a few buffer weeks, weeks when people didn't really want to get involved in politics or spoil their holiday cheer. Putin would have time to take a running jump.

I summoned my secretary and told him there would be three meetings the next day. I asked Voloshin to begin preparing the documents.

Early the next morning, I met with Putin. I explained the state of affairs. A fierce battle loomed ahead. First, there was the election campaign. It would not be easy to keep the entire country under control. The northern Caucasus was very troubled. Some political provocations were possible in Moscow. It was hard to tell whether the current government would be able to keep inflation down. Everything, including the future of the country, depended on the behavior of the new prime minister over the next weeks and months.

"I've made a decision, Vladimir Vladimirovich, and I would like to offer you the post of prime minister," I told Putin.

Putin looked at me attentively. He was silent.

"But that's not all," I continued. "You must have some notion of why I was forced to dismiss your predecessor. I know that Stepashin is your friend—he's also from St. Petersburg—but now there are other considerations. Your stance must be extremely polite and restrained but firm. Only thus will you achieve authority and win the parliamentary elections."

"Whom will we rely upon in the elections?" asked Putin.

"I don't know," I replied frankly. "We'll create a new party. As a person who has endured more from parliament than anyone in history, I know how important solid support in the Duma is. But the main thing is your own political resource: your image. You don't have to create it artificially. But you must never lose sight of its importance."

Putin reflected for awhile. "I don't like election campaigns," he admitted. "I really don't. I don't know how to run them, and I don't like them."

"But you won't have to run the campaign. The main thing is your will, your confidence, and your actions. Everything will depend on that. Political authority either comes or it doesn't. Are you ready?"

"I will work wherever you assign me," Putin replied with military terseness.

"And in the very highest post?"

Putin hesitated. I sensed that for the first time he truly realized what the conversation was about.

"I had not thought about that. I don't know if I am prepared for that," said Putin.

"Think about it. I have faith in you," I said.

A tense silence hung in the air of my office. The tick of the clock reverberated distinctly. Putin has very interesting eyes. They seem to speak more than his words. I knew he would think seriously about my offer.

After Putin left, I summoned Stepashin and Voloshin.

"Sergei Vadimovich," I said to Stepashin, "I have made a decision today to dismiss you. I will be proposing Vladimir Vladimirovich Putin to the Duma as prime minister. In the meantime I would ask you to approve the decree about appointing Putin as first vice premier."

Stepashin became greatly agitated and turned red. "Boris Niko-layevich," he managed to stammer. "This decision ... is premature. I believe it is a mistake."

"But the president has already made this decision," Voloshin said.

"Boris Nikolayevich, I really beg you. Speak to me in private."

I nodded, and Stepashin and I were left alone in the room.

Stepashin spoke for a long time. His leitmotif amounted to this: "I have always stuck with you and have never betrayed you." Stepashin recalled the events of 1991 and 1993 and the events in Budyonnovsk and Krasnoarmeysk. He promised to correct all his mistakes and immedi-ately create a new party.

Although I knew this conversation was totally senseless, I couldn't interrupt Stepashin. He was right: He *had* been faithful and true. He had never betrayed me. And there were no reasons to dismiss him—ex-cept one, the most important: He was not the right man for the cur-rent struggle. But how could I explain this to him?

Then I sensed I was losing my patience. "All right, go on now. I'll think about it," I said as calmly as possible.

Stepashin left. In the doorway he whispered to Voloshin: "What have you been saying about me behind my back? Have you gone mad? And at a time like this!"

I was in a terrible mood. I summoned Voloshin and said angrily,

"What are you waiting for? Bring those decrees! You know my decision already!"

He brought the decrees for my signature.

"You tell Stepashin yourself that he is dismissed. I do not want to meet with him again," I said.

Voloshin didn't argue with me, but he encouraged me to think about my decision over the weekend. "You know better than I that only the president can tell the prime minister he is dismissed," Voloshin said.

Of course Voloshin was right. I decided that I would inform Stepashin of my final decision on Monday morning.

That same day Chubais phoned me and insisted on a meeting. I immediately understood what was going on. It only confirmed my decision to fire Stepashin. I made an appointment with Chubais for 9:15 A.M. on Monday morning. I was meeting with Stepashin at 8:00.

It was only later that I learned that Chubais had attacked the administration and especially Putin. Apparently, he believed that I was making a decision that would lead to disastrous consequences.

First Chubais met with Putin and warned him that terrible blows were awaiting him in public politics. He argued that Putin had never been in the public eye and had no idea what it meant. It would be better for Putin to refuse this offer now rather than later, under the influence of circumstances.

Putin told Chubais that he was sorry but that this was the president's decision. He was obliged to obey. Chubais would do the same thing in his place.

Chubais then decided to go through the administration. On Sunday, while there was an unexpected break—no wonder I always avoid these pauses when making an important decision—he proposed that the inner circle meet with him: Voloshin, Yumashev, and Tanya.

Chubais gave them the following argument: After Primakov's dismissal, which had been rather painful for the public, the unmotivated dismissal of Stepashin would be perceived as the complete disintegration of the Kremlin, as the political death throes of the administration. Everyone would conclude that the president had gone mad. It would be a signal for attack from all sides, from the Duma and the Federation Council. Finally, a mass demonstration of workers would kick in.

"Remember the railway war?" asked Chubais. "This is something you want to face only once. And an angry Luzhkov can bring out tens of thousands of people to Red Square. Don't you sense the danger? Yes, I agree that Putin is better and that the president's choice is correct. But still, Yeltsin has no political or moral resources left to be able to remove Stepashin and put in Putin."

Voloshin then proposed a completely unexpected idea to Chubais: "If Stepashin is left in, then only you, Anatoly Borisovich, should head the administration. I don't doubt Stepashin has high human qualities. But if you are convinced of his victory, then be the engine of the entire team. We'll help you."

This proposal must have come as a total shock for Chubais. At that time, he was working at Unified Energy Systems, a key state monopoly. And this status—he was officially on the sidelines but still managed the political situation—suited him completely. He didn't want to return to the administration. But now there was no other choice. Chubais let it be known that he was prepared.

Voloshin told me about this episode later.

I have always trusted Chubais's political instincts. At critical moments he has persuaded me of something on more than one occasion. But at that moment, frankly speaking, Chubais had no chance of changing my decision. Obviously, I, too, sensed that it was incredibly risky to appoint an "emergency" prime minister. But unlike Chubais, who analyzed the situation only by logic, I intuitively sensed the power and strength of Putin, the future prospects of this move, and the atmosphere in society. The public was ready to accept a new figure, a figure who was fairly tough and willful. Despite the complete shake-up in the political establishment, people were ready to trust Putin.

Over the past years, I had managed to create a stability factor that made it impossible for anyone to go beyond the bounds of the constitution. And that factor was in our favor; despite the continuing crisis in the government, no one could attack the new prime minister. This was especially true in the case of Putin, who had recently been head of the FSB.

I think Chubais finally sensed my resolve on this matter.

The meeting took place at 8 A.M. on August 8 in Gorki-9. Putin, Aksyonenko, Stepashin, and Voloshin were present. We all greeted Stepashin, but he would shake hands only with me. I didn't mince words. "Sergei Vadimovich," I said to Stepashin. "I have signed the decrees on your dismissal and on the appointment of Putin as first vice premier."

Stepashin became flustered. "I will not authorize that decree," he said.

Aksyonenko intervened: "Stop it, Sergei Vadimovich!"

Putin stopped Aksyonenko. "Nikolai Yemelyanovich," he said to Aksyonenko. "It's hard enough for Stepashin. Let's not make it worse."

"All right," Stepashin finally said. "I'll sign the decree. Out of respect for you, Boris Nikolayevich."

On August 9, I made a television address to the nation in which I named Vladimir Putin as my successor and as a worthy candidate for the presidential elections in 2000.

The Second Chechen War

Yeltsin lays out the Russian argument for pursuing the war in Chechnya. Like many Russians, Yeltsin and Putin truly believe that the separatist movements in Chechnya would lead to the collapse of Russia, a raging ethnic conflict throughout the entire federation, and another Yugoslavia. That's why the conflict had to be stopped ruthlessly in its tracks, while it still remained local.

. .

ON SEPTEMBER 8, 1999, in a reply to journalists questioning our policy in Chechnya, Vladimir Putin said, "Russia is defending itself. We have been attacked. And therefore we must throw off all syndromes, including the guilt syndrome."

A lot of water has flowed under the bridge since Putin said these words. A lot has changed both in and around Chechnya. But the guilt syndrome persists. There is a great deal of misunderstanding about Chechnya, even in Russia itself. But more often it's the West trying to instill this feeling of guilt in us. I would like to express my own viewpoint on this painful issue.

That Chechnya was on the verge of disaster was clear to everyone. On March 5, 1999, in Grozny, Russia's deputy interior minister, Major-General Gennady Shpigun, was brazenly dragged off a plane that was about to take off for Moscow.* Chechen president Aslan Maskhadov,

---

* General Shpigun was kidnapped by Chechen rebels and was missing for more than a year. His corpse was found in the Chechen woods in June 2000. —Trans.

who right up until this incident had maintained that his law enforcement agencies were cooperating with Russia's effort to free hostages, had clearly lost control of the situation. He no longer had any authority in the Chechen republic. We realized that the region could enter a terrible new phase of open conflict.

Vladimir Putin's appointment as acting chair of the government took place against the backdrop of the invasion of Dagestan by Chechen fighters, which had been planned early in the summer.* It occurred two days after my decree appointing Putin. As Putin later admitted to me, he wasn't thinking of his political career or his future presidency at that moment. As the new prime minister, he knew that he had at least two to three months in office. He resolved to settle just one task: saving the federation, saving the country.

The breakup of the USSR had inevitably led to a weakening of the state machinery, the security services, and the army. The attack on Dagestan threatened a second metastasis in the body of the new Russia. Putin was one of the first to sense this terrible danger. He realized that the situation in Chechnya threatened to spill over into the entire north Caucasus. Then, with help from abroad, the Muslim separatists would begin breaking other territories off from Russia.

Such a powerful explosion of separatism threatened to dissolve the country into several parts, to spread religious and ethnic conflict throughout the whole territory, and to create a humanitarian disaster on a far larger scale than that of Yugoslavia. This scenario was easy to foresee. It was much harder to find the courage and will to prevent it from happening.

Putin turned to me and requested absolute power to conduct the needed military operation and coordinate all power structures. I supported him without hesitation. Within a matter of weeks, he had transformed the situation within our power ministries. Each day he would bring together the heads of each ministry or agency into his office. He forced them to gather all their resources into one united fist.

---

* Chechen warlord Shamil Basayev staged several incursions into neighboring Dagestan from Chechnya in the hopes of establishing an Islamic republic.—Trans.

Meanwhile, I deliberately and purposefully began to get the public used to the idea that Putin would be the future president. The newspaper commentators were confused and alarmed; I was entrusting Putin with assignments I had not given anyone else. Every Saturday Putin held additional meetings with the power ministers on the situation in Chechnya. He chaired the expanded sessions of the Security Council. He represented Russia's interests at the international summit in Oslo. He handed out awards, received ambassadors from foreign countries, and made official political statements. I wanted people to start getting used to Putin and to perceive him as the head of state. I was sure that everything would work out.

The situation in Dagestan gradually settled down. It was under our control. Then suddenly terrible explosions began occurring in Moscow. First a multistory residential building on Guryanova Street was hit on September 9. A week later a building on Varshavskoye Avenue blew up. Then a building exploded in the small provincial town of Volgodonsk. Rescuers pulled the few survivors out of the rubble and removed the dead bodies. Television stations broadcast the horrific reports throughout the whole country, night and day.

An awful fear hung over Russia. People couldn't sleep. At night they kept watch in front of the entryways of their buildings. Many moved to their dacha plots, escaped to the villages, stayed with relatives and friends, or even fled to other republics of the CIS.

The terrorists' calculation was exact. They had already used this tactic once before in 1995 in Budyonnovsk.* But now their intent was even more diabolical. They didn't just want to take a district hospital hostage, as they had in Budyonnovsk. They wanted to take the whole country hostage. They hoped that the state, tired of fear and waiting and horror, would leave the bandits in peace and timidly hand Dagestan over to them.

Fortunately, this didn't happen. A man was found who stopped the fear. And that man was Vladimir Putin. His tough statements, rein-

---

* Chechen rebel Basayev took a hospital and its patients hostage, killing hundreds before some patients were rescued by interior troops. —Trans.

forced with the start of a military operation on Chechen territory, became the main political event in the fall of 1999. The bandits would be
found and destroyed no matter where they were hiding.

Putin was reproached for expressing himself crudely and abruptly
and for using slang. Can the prime minister of a great country use expressions like "wipe them out in their crappers"?* Such an expression
would have been inappropriate in any other situation. But at the time
Putin wasn't worrying about his reputation or his image. He didn't expect his political career to last beyond the Chechen events, and he
thought he used the only appropriate tone and words for the situation.
His expression didn't demonstrate hatred toward the terrorists but
contempt; not alarm or worry but the cold calculation of a real protector, a real man.

These statements, at times far from diplomatic, made Putin enor-
mously popular in Russia within a short time. Putin was not trying to
demonize the Chechens or kindle base chauvinistic instincts in Russians. I am convinced that the reason for Putin's popularity was that he
instilled hope, faith, and a sense of protection and calm. He didn't talk
big, but he reacted to situations the way tens of millions of Russians
reacted to them, with honesty and toughness. Putin gave people a
guarantee of personal security backed by the state. People believed
that he, personally, could protect them. That's what explains his surge
in popularity. The country, hypnotized by the government crises, had
not heard such a positive ideology in a long time. And the fact that this
ideology was promulgated by a young politician who had just come to
power made a very big impression on everyone. Putin got rid of Russia's fear. And Russia repaid him with profound gratitude.

Even so, we must not forget about the grave consequences of war.
There are reams of evidence proving that civilians have suffered in
what is called the second Chechen war. People have lost their homes
and their property. Many civilians have lost their lives or their health.

---

* Translators have tried dozens of ways to render Putin's infamous *mochit' v sortire*. *Mochit'*, the
verb "to soak" in Russian, is based on underworld slang meaning "to make wet or bloody," that
is, to kill. And *sortire*, which comes from the French for "going out" is a crude Russian
expression for "toilet." —Trans.

But should the Russian army bear responsibility for these woes? Could anyone have imagined a situation in which Russian soldiers would hide in the homes of civilians and shoot at an armed enemy, putting women and old people in the line of fire? I think no one could.

War always looks different from afar. Here in Russia practically everyone understands what Russian soldiers are fighting for and why they are in Chechnya. Nevertheless, the footage the world's television stations have been broadcasting day after day for many months has convinced international public opinion that there is aggression against civilians. I will repeat what Russian representatives have explained to their Western partners thousands of times: Russia is fighting an aggressor, the terrorist bands created in the territory of Chechnya, which include numerous mercenaries from the Arab world, Afghanistan, and even Southeast Asia. This is a well-equipped (sometimes with the latest technology), well-trained army of killers. It is an army of extremists who have no true religious values.

I have before me the list of awards presented to three of those who fought against the extremists on the territory of Chechnya and Dagestan: Sergeant Dmitry Nikolayevich Nikishin, an intelligence officer, risked his life when his commander was wounded in a fierce battle on the outskirts of the village of Tasuta in Dagestan. Nikishin carried his commander off the battlefield and was awarded the title "Hero of Russia."

Lieutenant Colonel Aleksandr Linovich Sterzhantov commanded a group of intelligence officers who, along with their unit, seized an overlook on Chaban mountain in Dagestan. A rebel group supported by missile launchers, grenade launchers, and snipers attacked Sterzhantov and his men for four hours, wounding forty-one soldiers and killing three. Sterzhantov led his men out of the rebel encirclement, taking with them the bodies of those killed and eventually evacuating all the wounded. Sterzhantov deliberately attracted artillery fire, covering the exit of his subunit until the last soldier escaped to safety. He was the last one to leave the battlefield. Sterzhantov was awarded the title "Hero of Russia."

Major Oleg Vasilyevich Kryukov, commander of an engineering

and bomb detonation unit, discovered a truck containing 1.5 tons of explosives near the hospital of the Russian military compound. Kryukov searched the vehicle and disabled a timing mechanism attached to explosives fifteen minutes before it was supposed to go off. He was awarded the title "Hero of Russia."

I personally handed the awards to these people and others in the Kremlin. One very young sergeant got so worked up that he couldn't utter a single word. I shook his hand and looked into his face. He had tears in his eyes. Those eyes had seen death up close.

There were hundreds and thousands of battle episodes in Chechnya and Dagestan. These were military struggles against terrorists, not a war against a people. I think it is high time that everyone in the world understood that. International public opinion would like to nail Russia to the wall of shame for its "war crimes." But the international community does not know and does not want to know the main reason for the death of civilians. We have never committed mass executions of unarmed people in Chechnya. There have been no ethnic cleansings or concentration camps. The main reason for the missile strikes and bombs that have brought pain and grief to ordinary citizens is the war unleashed by the terrorists against the Russian people. The terrorists hide behind the backs of the civilian population.

When I hear about the "war crimes" of the Russian army, I would like to ask about other "war crimes." Isn't it a "war crime" that the bandits' main source of subsistence is the income from ransoms and the sale of people into slavery? In Chechnya there are at least 2,000 slave hostages. The number is constantly growing, and not just because of the increase in Russian military personnel (though some would very much like to represent the matter in this way). Foreigners have also been taken hostage. For example, two British citizens from a humanitarian mission, a man and a woman, were subjected to torture and rape for several months until a ransom was received for them. The hostage takers also demanded ransom from the British telecommunications company that was installing satellite connections for Maskhadov and other rebel leaders. But their hostages were kidnapped by other bandits, who cut off the hostages' heads. The whole world saw these horrific photographs. But evidently, the whole world didn't understand what was going on.

Even tiny children have been abducted into Chechnya. An Israeli boy, Adi Sharon, was kidnapped in the center of Moscow, right around the time of the two apartment explosions. The kidnappers, among them several Chechens and Russians, took Adi to Penza, a city southeast of Moscow. They demanded ransom. They tortured him and cut off his fingers. What did they have against this young Israeli? He was eventually rescued, but many hostages are never saved. Some are young women, Azerbaijani peasants, Siberian and Muscovite businessmen, and ordinary workers. These hostages have been mistreated, tortured, and raped. Meanwhile, Ingush, Dagestani, and Russian gangs have been drawn into the slave trade. This mind-boggling terrorism has become a mass phenomenon.

The rebels challenge not only Russia but all of humankind. Or at least all of Europe. And no one should be distracted by the green Islamic flags of the terrorists or their quotations from the Qur'an or the white garments of the Wahhabi teaching. They have no teaching, no flag, no right to quote from sacred books. They are monsters. They have thrown civilization back at least several hundred years. Even people in the farthest corners of Russia fear being kidnapped. The brutal Chechen slave trade has entered mass consciousness as a real threat.

This facet of the Chechen tragedy concerns every person here in Russia. But as the president, I was concerned with another aspect: the geopolitical ramifications of the bandits' separatism. Their new brand of separatism threatened to destroy the country from within.

From the outset Putin warned that there would be casualties among our soldiers but that the military operation had to be completed. It had to be brought to its logical end so that there wouldn't be more horrible casualties in the future. This simple conclusion, familiar to any country and to any people that has encountered mass terror (such as the British, the French, and the Israelis), was clearly and comprehensibly articulated after several years of coexistence with the bandits as they hid behind the screen of statehood in Chechnya. And to this day, in cities and villages all over Russia, people mourn those who died defending the motherland. These victims undoubtedly place a heavy burden of political and moral responsibility on the government.

But there is another subtext to our grievous losses: The Russian soldier, the person defending the country and defending order on its territory, is being cleansed of the filth of political opportunism that was flung upon him. With each day the soldier becomes a more powerful, unifying national symbol. Russia cannot forget and betray these young men.

There are opponents to any war. And there should be. It's in people's natures. In the final analysis, I'm against war. And Vladimir Putin is against war. This military operation was necessary not only to preserve the integrity of Russia but also to protect our citizens and demonstrate our political will and the power of the state. But above all it was needed to establish a lasting peace and a return to normal life.

I know our claim that we are searching for a lasting peace and a normal life sounds like Russian propaganda. But here are some concrete facts and concrete individual fates: Russia is restoring everything that can be rebuilt or repaired in Chechnya, including forty hospitals, eleven clinics, two blood transfusion stations, two dispensaries, and one maternity home. Ambulances are now beginning to run in the regions. Soon Chechen children, who have been deprived of education for some time, will be able to go to school again. Electricity and gas are returning to Chechnya. There will be normal sanitation services and running water. Drinking water will be restored. People will no longer die of typhoid and dysentery. In each liberated region of Chechnya, satellite communications as well as regular telephone lines are being installed, and buses have started to run on schedule.

Russia is sending teachers and doctors to Chechnya. Builders are restoring mosques and railroads. I know that the Western press persistently spreads the rumor that Grozny, the capital of Chechnya, has been utterly destroyed, wiped from the face of the earth. This isn't true. Despite the enormous obstacles, Grozny has become a habitable city. It will be rebuilt. The refugees are aware of all this, and many are returning to Grozny. Each day more and more people come back to the territory of Chechnya.

Dr. Lyubov Doroshenko sees more than a hundred patients in Grozny every day, and thanks to her more than 1,500 residents of the city have received accurate diagnoses and been sent for treatment. Dr. Irina Nazarova, an emergency room physician and anesthesiologist, has repeatedly donated her own blood during operations to save the lives of the civilians of Chechnya. There are hundreds and thousands of such Russians helping in Chechnya now. We can only bow before them. Their victory is not visible against the general backdrop of military operations. But it is these builders, engineers, and doctors who have convinced the civilian population of Chechnya that, together with Russia, medicine, and culture, are returning to Chechnya and homes and towns and being rebuilt. Peace is returning as well.

In this continuing debate about Chechnya, I can accept any position and any arguments except outright lies. And today, unfortunately, both in our own country and in the world, there are people who unfairly juggle the truth. They say that it's not the Chechen terrorists who are committing aggression against Russia, but the Russian army that is committing aggression against "free Chechnya." It's not terrorists who blew up the buildings in Moscow but the Russian security services, in order to justify their own aggression. I could understand if this version of events were designed and disseminated by the Chechen separatists with their own money. To my great regret, that is not the case.

It is a professional and moral crime to spread such blasphemous theories about how the second Chechen war began, especially in view of material evidence collected in an investigation of the Moscow apartment-house explosions: Mechanical devices and explosives similar to those used in the Moscow bombings were found in rebel bases in Chechnya. The names of the criminals, who went through training at terrorist bases in Chechnya, have been established; their immediate associates have been detained. I am convinced that this case will soon come to trial. Nevertheless, the falsehoods continue. Some find it very profitable to maintain the lies.

The opposition political analysts also claim that Chechnya has been a kind of political arsenal for Putin. But in fact Putin's sudden popularity in the face of the Chechen war was not remotely predictable. Furthermore, Putin behaved like a political kamikaze, throwing his entire stock of political capital into the war, burning it to the ground. Whoever claims the opposite today is simply lying. Besides, Putin never wanted to be president. He did not grapple for power, and he hesitated for a long time before accepting my offer.

Our world is susceptible to all kinds of provocations and threats, which can come from anywhere. The most important thing is how people conduct themselves and how they face danger. To this day I can see the pieces of bodies the rescuers pulled out of the damp autumn earth and the twisted rubble of the blown-up Moscow homes. I will never forget that scene.

· 23 ·

The Last Summit

Yeltsin's final summit takes place in Istanbul in November 1999. It's a prickly situation: The war in Chechnya threatens to isolate Russia from the West. But Yeltsin will not tolerate any criticism on the Chechnya issue. He battles with his speechwriters, who warn him against using harsh language at this, his last grand international appearance.

.   .

ON JUNE 20, 1999, the long-awaited summit of the Group of Eight was held in Cologne, Germany. Once again Russia took part. The war in Yugoslavia had just ended, and the situation was extremely tense. I spent only seven hours in Germany. Essentially, I needed to say just one sentence: "We have to make up after the fight."

Newspapers and television stations all over the world carried my statement, for it marked a sharp change in Moscow's international position. Just prior to this meeting, our diplomats had made some tough decisions because of the events in Yugoslavia, as if they were preparing both Russia and the West for a prolonged confrontation. But we had to return to the international diplomatic arena. In Cologne we took the first step toward rapprochement.

At the final press conference, Tony Blair said, "We have different approaches to the Kosovo settlement. But it's wonderful that we're back together again. We are united by our effort to make the Balkans free of ethnic conflicts."

Russia had reaffirmed its status as an equal political partner, without whom it was unthinkable to resolve world conflicts and decide important issues, especially when it came to European concerns. In their statements the international leaders tried to emphasize that there were not seven but eight full-fledged members in their club.

The reason for this sincere shared satisfaction was that Russia had given NATO the opportunity to exit the conflict with dignity. Russia had decisively rejected a renewal of the cold war. The most serious crisis in relations between Russia and the West in nearly twenty years—it had even been compared to the Cuban missile crisis—was over much to universal relief. It was this sigh of relief that could finally be heard in Cologne.

But despite this tremendous relief and the satisfaction of knowing that I had fulfilled my duty, I was worried. It was easy to embark on the path of confrontation but hard to get off of it. Too many negative emotions about the self-determined, independent position of Russia had accumulated during the Yugoslav crisis. And sooner or later the international community would let us know this. Thus, when the operation in Chechnya began, I immediately understood that the moment of truth for our relations with the West had come. Now they would really try to push our backs to the wall.

When he returned in early November from an international conference in Oslo, where the Chechen topic had been actively discussed, Putin told me about a funny episode. In farewell, Clinton had said, "See you soon at the summit in Istanbul, Vladimir!"

"No, we won't be meeting in Istanbul," Putin explained. "Boris Nikolayevich will be going there."

"Oh, Lord, that's all we need!" said Clinton, grabbing his head in mock distress.

Putin laughed when he retold this story, then glanced at me curiously. Some hard times awaited us in Istanbul. Was I mentally and, more important, physically ready for them? Just in case, Putin began to prepare for the trip. Still, both of us knew that I was the one who should go.

Clinton didn't really feel like meeting me in Istanbul. The Western countries were preparing an extremely tough statement on Chechnya. Everyone knew about it all too well. In essence, a new stage in the isolation of Russia was beginning. This had to be prevented no matter what.

Day after day I prepared myself for the trip. I thought about Istanbul all the time. I imagined the hall, the faces, the atmosphere. It was all so familiar. I could easily imagine the setting.

One of the most important elements during these visits is the president's speech. We sometimes work on the text until the last minute.

I knew that writing the Istanbul speech would be extremely difficult. The overall task—to defend Russia against unfair criticism over Chechnya—was one thing, and the specific words were another. I have always liked to depart from my text, not to be limited by what's on the paper. And this was the case now.

I was ruthless in rewriting the first draft that had been prepared for me. I inserted the toughest and sharpest formulations. When the text was returned to me, it had been softened, smoothed, and polished. My international affairs aides feared a confrontation with our Western partners. I read their latest version, then called Voloshin in the middle of the night and yelled, "Why are you making a mockery of me, Aleksandr Stalyevich?" I threatened to fire everyone. Still, I knew my aides were right about some things. There was no sense in going overboard. I needed a sharp, tough tone but no threats. The speech had to be rational, dry, and stripped of any sentiment. And our position on Chechnya was simple: We were saving the world from international terrorism. We were saving Russia from the threat of dissolution.

Three days before the flight, I told my "understudy," Putin, that it had been decided. I was going.

I continued to revise the text of the speech on the flight to Istanbul. I inserted another handwritten correction: "Nobody has the right to criticize us for Chechnya." I gave the text to Igor Ivanov, the foreign

minister, and my aide, Sergei Prikhodko, for a final going-over. They
tried to persuade me to change the addition. I took the text back from
them and read it again. "Go away. I'll think about it for a while," I said.
The next morning, I reread the text and left the phrase in. I had to deliver the speech with the handwritten insertion.

A lot depended on the speech, but not everything. From my many
meetings with Clinton, I knew that he was a lively, open person,
though he can turn on the chill and be stern when necessary. Personal
contact can have an enormous influence on him. From the first seconds of the summit, Clinton sensed that I would be sharp. Disregarding protocol, he walked through the wrong doors and passed through
the entire hall, about 100 meters, stopping to greet everyone and smile,
letting us all know that he was the boss in the room. I pointed to my
watch. "You're late, Bill!" He smiled. That was a good sign.

The hall was scattered with shards of distrust and misunderstanding. I could almost feel it in my skin when I rose to speak. I began to
read my speech, putting the utmost into every word. Each word was
right on target. Animated faces and eyes were watching me, some condemning, some expressing total approval.

Chirac and Schröder sat with long faces. They hadn't expected such
intensity. Germany and France had taken the toughest positions regarding the Chechen problem. I understood that both leaders were
forced to heed public opinion in their home countries. They did not
like my words.

After the meeting, Chirac approached me and asked if the three of
us—Schröder, he, and I—could speak for half an hour. It was their last
chance to extract some concessions from Russia. "No," I said firmly.
"We won't have time."

The final resolution of the Istanbul meeting did not contain the
condemnation of our position in Chechnya as originally planned.
Chirac didn't look happy during the signing. I had rejected even a five-
minute meeting with him. I thought it wasn't the right time; I wanted
to let him think about his position.

The summit was an important international victory for Russia.

I flew out of Istanbul with mixed feelings. On the one hand, I was overjoyed that the job was done and that I had done it. On the other hand, I felt empty and sad. It was probably my last summit meeting.

My decade, the "Yeltsin decade" in international politics, was over. In that decade Russia's diplomatic relations had grown far closer and more confiding. They were reinforced with personal relationships. I was able to incorporate the new term *multipolar world* into diplomatic language. Relations with Japan, India, South Korea, and other Asian countries were raised to a new level. I am especially pleased that we developed a very trusting tone in our relations with our Chinese friends.

Yet the events of the past year, 1999, in Yugoslavia and the Caucasus had led relations between Russia and the West in the wrong direction. Unfortunately, this is an objective reality. We can't do anything about it. Still, in the greater scheme of things, our overall relations with the West had improved fundamentally. Russia is gradually becoming part of a united Europe. This can be seen in politics, economics, and everyday life. We are already a component of the common European market and the common European home. We do not intend to fight for military superiority. We will not maintain a huge army beyond the boundaries of our country. We will not build our diplomacy on force.

This is all quite different than it was only ten years ago. But there are still serious opponents to this process. They are here in Russia and in the United States and in Europe.

The North Atlantic strategy of NATO, which is trying to turn the bloc into an instrument of political pressure, still ignores Russia's national interests. This problem can be resolved in various ways. Russia can become integrated into NATO and fit into European security as an equal partner. But NATO is not expecting us. This resolution is hardly realistic for the coming years. The second option is to construct a new, powerful defense system on our own borders and, in the future, on the military bases of CIS countries, which we would rent for a high price. But the position of the former Soviet republics is a major stumbling block. NATO and others are trying to cut the republics off from Russia and its influence by establishing a system of special relationships with NATO, among others.* Meanwhile, millions of residents of the former Soviet republics now live and work in Russia. Their economies obtain constant subsidies from us in the form of commodities, energy, tax, and customs preferences. Such a double standard regarding Russia is absolutely impermissible.

Perhaps these options are not mutually exclusive, but we can find our way only by engaging in constant political dialogue, not isolation. Isolation cannot be permitted, no matter the circumstances. Unfortunately, I will not resolve this problem but leave it to the new Russian leader.

As I flew home from Istanbul, I took the text of my summit speech out of my suit jacket pocket. I no longer needed it. The plane was descending, bound for Vnukovo Airport outside Moscow. That was it. It was over. Yes, it was a little sad.

I believe that Putin will not lose sight of Russia's bearings; the uniqueness of its role in the world; and along with that, the importance of its total integration into the world community. As God is my witness, I never lost those bearings.

---

* "Special relationships" is apparently a reference to some of the East and Central Europe countries placed on a fast-track to get into NATO and other European institutions. —Trans.

· 24 ·

The Party of the Center: Unity

Throughout his presidency, Yeltsin wrestled with an angry and
antagonistic Communist parliament. He vows not to let Putin
suffer the same fate. A new, energetic, and democratic "party
of power" must be created, both to counterbalance the Communists in the Duma and to carry Putin to victory in the presidential elections of 2000. That party is called Unity.

· ·

AFTER VLADIMIR PUTIN was appointed acting prime minister and
confirmed by the Duma, I began to think through my next main political problem: winning the elections. Putin's ratings were steadily ris-
ing. But the situation could change after the parliamentary elections,
which political analysts predicted would be won by the Communist
Party and the Luzhkov-Primakov bloc, Fatherland–All Russia. Without a really centrist, conservative party close to his heart, Vladimir
Putin risked giving huge odds to his rivals in these Duma elections.
And the parliamentary elections could strongly influence the outcome
of the presidential elections.

Regardless of the elections, the future president would need some
real support in the Duma. How would he build a normal economic
policy and normal laws if he was constantly fighting an unbridled, embittered parliament? Judging from the furious media campaign they
had been waging in recent months, our opponents were willing to

play dirty. I couldn't let Putin suffer under their attacks as I had for so many years. A party to support him was needed. As the newspapers that supported Luzhkov and Primakov wrote, it would be the "next party of power."

During the first Duma elections in 1993, the president's interests were represented by a party called Russia's Choice organized by Yegor Gaidar and his supporters, the first-wave democrats. Back then it seemed quite logical that there would be a strong anti-Communist reaction after the unsuccessful coup of October 1993. But anticommunism had already exhausted itself as a ruling ideology. People needed some kind of positive program, something reliable. Unfortunately, Gaidar's reforms were extremely unpopular and, more important, Gaidar himself was not a charismatic leader. Everybody knew that. But we didn't have another alternative for the president.

In 1995 Viktor Chernomyrdin headed up a new "party of power" called Our Home Is Russia. It bet on centrism with a moderate-liberal ideology emphasizing the priorities of the state. Of course it relied on state people—the major economic managers, governors, and bureaucrats. It was a complete failure. A political party that is called upon to reflect the interests of large social groups cannot be built so obviously on a government-style vertical chain of command. Chernomyrdin's party, like the Gaidar party in 1993, ended up in the clear minority in parliament. This result was very bad for the authority of the government, the economy, and the entire system of civil society. Instead of a political dialogue, we would suffer through years of fierce battles between the red Duma and the president.

Looking back, I think that it wasn't specific leaders or circumstances or the political battles of the moment that were to blame for these failures. Or to be more accurate, those weren't the only factors. It was also me and my attitude toward the Duma. I understood that the parliament was theoretically a most important instrument of democracy. But in practice, beginning with Gorbachev's Congress of People's Deputies of 1989, I saw a parliament full of Communists. At endless sessions I would be surrounded by all those painfully familiar faces. I saw the obvious hatred, unconcealed even for the sake of decency, directed toward reform and change. That initial impression of our parliament as unwaveringly Communist in orientation never left me.

Even so, I thought that reforms could be moved forward with a push of political will. But year after year I watched as the Duma, which among the population provoked only laughter—laughter mixed with tears—contrived to negatively influence the situation in the country. Laws that were extremely important for the country or fundamental for the development of the economy were not passed. The most important decisions of the government were blocked. Year after year the deputies drew up unrealistic budgets that hung like a heavy weight over the economy. I had to correct this mistake, if only at the very end of my second presidential term.

First, I asked my aides to commission a study. Whom do people trust in their own regions? Whom do they consider a leader? What politicians or public figures have high moral authority in their local area, territory, or republic? Whom, to put it bluntly, do the people like or consider just a nice, decent person? I wasn't talking about people from the Moscow beau monde but local and regional leaders.

The sociologists replied that it was probably impossible to conduct such a poll—love and decency were hard to measure in statistics—but that they would try to calculate the credibility of various leaders.

Their findings proved to be quite interesting. In many regions they found local heroes, popular people who had enormous authority and who were also fairly well known in the rest of the country. But most significant, these local leaders were absolutely clean in the political sense. For example, in Kalmykia such a person was the anchor on a new Channel One program, a likable and lovely young woman, Aleksandra Buratayeva. In Novosibirsk it was the legendary athlete and repeated world and Olympic wrestling champion Aleksandr Karelin.

And I realized that people really are tired of the same old faces, the same old professional politicians. New leaders who have not gone through the route of politics but who have a real interest in defending the concerns of their fellow citizens have an enormous chance. They are a kind of protective layer hidden deep within the country's soul. They are Russia's hope.

The idea of a new party to be known as Unity was not born immediately, of course. Many people, both from my 1996 election campaign and from Putin's own campaign headquarters, took part in its development. The hardest thing was to find a leader, a person to head the movement. Sergei Shoigu, minister for emergencies, who helped people survive through catastrophes, floods, and earthquakes, was our greatest star and the most famous person on our entire list of the hopes of Russia. But for a long time we didn't dare approach him, because he was heading up a difficult ministry, was busy at work, and really loved his job. He didn't want to go into politics at all.

But here's what it means to be a team player: When Shoigu finally agreed to head the movement, he plunged into the political maelstrom with all his passion, desperately and sincerely. Now he was fired up with the idea of creating a new party of the center, not a "party of power," as it was previously understood—a party of bosses and chiefs —but a party of apolitical people who would go into politics in order to bring it closer to the interests of ordinary Russians and to make it morally cleaner, more transparent, and more understandable.

The wrestling champion, Aleksandr Karelin, was the number two in Unity. The number three was a former investigator, a police general called Aleksandr Gurov, who in the 1980s was the first to speak about organized crime and the mafia in our country. I thought this was a brilliantly composed troika. The courageous Shoigu, a rescuer and a really romantic figure, embodied the idealism of the new generation. He was supposed to attract youth and, by virtue of his charm, women. Karelin was counting on the support of the male population. Gurov spoke the language near and dear to middle-aged and older people.

But it seemed to me that Unity's main asset was the way in which it incorporated the spirit of a new conservatism and bet on the whole of society, not just the political elite. An original political technique played a role as well. Other parties would put the Muscovites and the political functionaries on their federal party list but leave the regional chapters to work with the local electorate on the regional lists. Unity, however, put the people who were trusted in the regions on its federal list. This was a smart move.

But soon I ceased to have anything to do with this work. From the outset it was clear to me that this party of social optimism should not be associated with my name or, for that matter, the name of any other famous politician of the previous generation. The peculiarity of the new movement, as I said, consisted of its absolute freshness and apolitical nature.

I didn't care that Unity distanced itself from me, sometimes criticizing the previous political era and even my specific policies and decisions. For me, the party's main priorities were much more important: defending the interests of the state, defending business and liberal freedoms, and defending civil rights.

Putin had far more trouble. There was a real split in his campaign headquarters. The old warriors who had headed the campaign in 1996, such as Aleksandr Oslon, Gleb Pavlovsky (head of the Fund for Effective Policy), and other veterans of the campaign battles, insisted that Putin indicate his political preferences and support Unity. Their opponents within Putin's campaign claimed the opposite, arguing that Putin shouldn't gamble his entire political stock on such an unknown and inexperienced political party: "He should remain above the fray," they said. "He is the future president of all citizens and not just some of them. If he supports Unity, his credibility rating by March won't be 50 percent but 5."

Vladimir Putin decided it in his own way. During a television interview, he very briefly answered a reporter's question about what party he would vote for in the parliamentary elections. "There is only one party that clearly and definitely supports our course. That's Unity," said the prime minister.

I spent election day, December 19, worrying. Although we drank champagne in anticipation of Unity's victory, I was tired from the agitations of the day. The vote totals flickering on the television screen kept changing. Late at night, almost falling asleep, I kept thinking and comparing and analyzing. What had happened?

In the morning I woke up with the feeling that something very important had happened. The results of the vote confirmed what I had thought all these weeks: Vladimir Putin has an enormous reserve of credibility. That December people were essentially already voting for the new president and "his" bloc, even though he wasn't its leader and had just extended a hand to this new movement. Putin's thirty seconds on the air were long enough to assure the new bloc's resounding success: a solid 23 percent! No one could have expected such a significant showing for the new party.

In the end the Communists overtook Unity, but only by 1 percent. The new "party of hope" would need at least another six months to take root in the regions and ultimately become the dominating political movement in the country. The special vote in Moscow also played a role.* Muscovites gave Unity about 10 percent, whereas voters in other regions gave it 20 to 30 percent.

We now had a very new picture: The leftist forces had ceased to be a majority in parliament. A large group of independent deputies were elected; the right-wing forces and the Primakov-Luzhkov bloc got another 7–8 percent; and the Liberal Democratic Party of Russia (Zhirinovsky's party) and Yabloko (Yavlinsky's party) got a little less. It was a victory.

So what will become of Russian parliamentarianism? What is its destiny? I think Russia will develop a normal, working parliament. If the leaders of Unity do not rest on their laurels and do not become totally lost in the Duma madness but continue to work on the creation of an all-Russian movement, they will definitely build the kind of conservative, centrist party that many developed countries have. I'm thinking of the Conservatives in England, the Republicans in the United States, the Christian Democrats in Germany, and the Liberal Democrats in Japan. To some extent Unity will be the "party of power," though it will not claim an exceptional status in society or any political monopoly.

---

* This may be a reference to the strong support Muscovites gave Mayor Luzhkov. — Trans.

In almost all these countries, the conservatives have political opponents of the social democratic persuasion. We will have them here, too. For that to happen, some intelligent politicians from the ranks of the Communist Party will have to give up the slogans of yesterday and become more selective in their choice of allies. If they do not find the courage to disassociate themselves from the unbridled leftist radicals, their place will be occupied by others, such as the Fatherland–All Russia Party.

These are only forecasts, and I don't like to make empty predictions. I'm not a political scientist but a politician. It's an entirely different profession. I can offer only one firm prediction: The modernization of the Duma began with the year that was so difficult and dramatic for us, 1999. With each passing year and with each new election, Russia will get a more viable, contemporary, and decent parliament.

· 25 ·

Presidential Guarantees

With his own resignation from office looming ahead, Yeltsin thinks back over his somewhat troubled relationship with former president Mikhail Gorbachev. He also discusses the rather touchy issue of presidential guarantees, those powers and privileges—a pension, a dacha, medical care, car service, security—bestowed upon retiring presidents.

. .

THE TIME HAD COME to make the last, perhaps most important decision. Several days before the elections, to get ahead of the curve, I had met with Vladimir Putin. Our conversation had reinforced my decision to resign. I could no longer get in Putin's way. I had to step down and clear the path.

I would be resigning before the end of the presidential term. This had happened one other time, when the first and last president of the USSR, Mikhail Sergeyevich Gorbachev, left office in December 1991.

My thoughts often return to that terrible and dangerous time in the late 1980s and early 1990s when Russia's political system changed so radically. A new country replaced the Soviet Union, with new borders, alternative political institutions, another system of government, and different priorities in foreign and domestic policies. I realized what a difficult, painful process this would be.

Gorbachev realized it as well. During our last meetings in the

Kremlin in the fall of 1991, when we discussed the new ministers to be appointed immediately after the August coup attempt, the danger of the regime's collapse hung unspoken in the air. Could something that had been established with such difficulty, over the course of decades, be destroyed so abruptly? From Gorbachev's expression, I could see that it was not possible.

Images of the 1991 putsch floated before my eyes: tanks and armored personnel carriers on the streets; Gorbachev's comrades, who had decided to violate the country's laws. I thought that if Gorbachev's so-called generals, his obedient enforcers such as Yazov, Kryuchkov, and Pugo, could decide on a putsch, then things had come to an end.* If these representatives of the mightiest power ministries, whose very positions obliged them to protect the state from upset, could rise up against the president, then the system was no longer viable. These generals were in command of a country equipped with nuclear weapons! I simply did not have the right to give them the chance to stage another coup. Moreover, Soviet power was lying in wait, and Gorbachev was afraid of destroying it. He was almost panicking. It was extremely dangerous to put one's faith in the system. There was no way to save it from collapse.

We needed to make immediate and fundamental political changes in order to prevent the Soviet generals from organizing another coup and creating a bloodbath. Here I have to give Mikhail Gorbachev his due. Despite our persistent disagreements and our troublesome personal relations, he clearly understood the logic of the political process and didn't try to complicate the situation. He didn't struggle for personal power. After the coup he clearly understood that it was irrevocably lost.

In those November and December days, both Gorbachev and I were troubled by the same question: How smoothly could we shift the levers of power? Given our difficult relationship, how could we secure the transition from one political system to another, from a bu-

---

* Yazov was the Soviet minister of defense, Kryuchkov chair of the KGB, and Pugo minister of the interior. — Trans.

reaucratic "party democracy" to a true democracy supported by real freedom?

In this situation the document signed in the November 1991 Belovezh Forest by the leaders of the three Slavic states—Russia, Ukraine, and Belarus—was the only political maneuver possible. The Communists wouldn't anticipate such an abrupt and decisive turn of events. The new political status of the Soviet Union's republics knocked the main weapon from the Communists' hands: the old Soviet administrative system. They suddenly found themselves in a new situation, a new reality. They needed a good deal of time to organize and gather forces. And this time they didn't have the support of a huge state machine. I described the circumstances surrounding the signing of this treaty in my previous book, *The Struggle for Russia.*

I considered the question of personal guarantees for Gorbachev and his family. The question would seem to be of a personal nature. But in the case of our country and our history, it went far beyond the president's personal needs. For Russia, it was a question of historic importance. This peaceful transition was an accomplishment of sorts for Russia. Never before had a ruler willingly given up power. Authority in Russia had always been transferred through natural death, conspiracy, or revolution. The tsar ceased to rule only after his death or after a coup. It was exactly the same with the general secretary of the Communist Party. I suppose the Communist regime inherited the inability to transfer power painlessly.

And the fact that the 1964 coup against the Soviet premier occurred in a seemingly peaceful manner and that Khrushchev remained alive does not change the essence of what happened. Khrushchev was forcibly removed from the political scene and placed under house arrest. For the Soviet Union's vast population, it was as though the living, thinking man who had been their leader just twenty-four hours earlier had disappeared forever. He couldn't participate in the life of the country; he couldn't travel anywhere without permission. Years later, his death was announced in a tiny, obscure notice in the newspaper.

If the August 1991 coup had succeeded and the junta of the Soviet

generals had come to power, the same fate probably would have be-
fallen Gorbachev, although events could have taken a far more tragic
turn. Now Gorbachev and I faced a hard question: the fate of the former president and the new Russia. It was necessary to establish a
precedent for the respectful, dignified treatment of a major political
figure who was leaving the political scene. I did everything I could in
this respect, not for anyone personally but for the country.

Gorbachev was given a state residence for lifetime use: the presidential dacha known as Moscow River–5. He liked it so much that he
had requested it. He and his family were also provided with security,
car service, medical care, and a pension. Later a lot of caustic things
were said about how, in response to Gorbachev's impudence, I supposedly took away his security detail, his car, and his dacha. This is untrue.

The 1991 decree on Gorbachev's guarantees contained several
other important points. Most important, it ensured that Gorbachev
could engage in new civic and political activities by helping to set up
the Gorbachev Foundation, which it presented with a large complex of
buildings in the center of Moscow. The Gorbachev Foundation leased
a portion of its space. It's true that we transferred this space legally to
a different institution, a university of the humanities, but we didn't do
this for political reasons. Associates at the foundation said that rental
income was necessary for the foundation, but commercial use of the
foundation space would have violated the essence of the decree.

I realize that in the eight years since his resignation, Mikhail
Sergeyevich has strengthened his popularity as the person who
brought down the iron curtain. I have received numerous memoranda
about Gorbachev's highly critical comments in speeches abroad and in
his books about the politics of the new Russia. These memoranda indicate that Gorbachev tries to gain points by criticizing me. There have
been people who have urged me to punish the former president. But I
cut such conversations short.

And yet, frankly, it wasn't easy to cope during the first years of Gorbachev's retirement. I would rage inside when I heard what Gorbachev was saying about me and about Russian domestic affairs.
Strangely enough, I was the sole guarantor of Gorbachev's immunity.

At that time it would have been very easy to have made Gorbachev into a scapegoat or to portray him as a wanted criminal. Many democrats of the so-called first wave in the early days of reform were unable to forgive Gorbachev for his vacillations, for his darting from one side to the other. For the average person at the time, he embodied the evil of the Communist Party *nomenklatura*. He was seen as the cause of all our misfortunes and crises. The usual logic of bureaucracy heaps the sins of the past upon one's predecessor. Thus Gorbachev became one of the most unpopular figures in the country.

Nevertheless, I constantly tried to rein in my feelings and forget about our personal relations. (I don't want to deal with this subject here. In my previous books I have spoken about how Gorbachev criticized me and how he attempted to interfere in my every political act.) I understand full well that regardless of our mutual resentments, Gorbachev's ability to live his own life, to speak his mind, and to participate in the 1996 campaign was as important for Russia and for the new democracy as it was for Gorbachev.

After 1996, when one of my assistants sought my signature on an invitation to Gorbachev for some gala event, I suddenly noticed the absence of the usual internal protest. I felt instead a sense of relief that we would have something to talk about. Toward the end of my second presidential term, I finally understood that I had been right to hold back my sense of resentment and not give full rein to my emotions. The resentment and the emotion passed, and the goal was achieved. We had wanted to establish the precedent of an open, unfettered, and peaceful life for an ex–head of state, and this we accomplished for the first time in Russian history. We did it despite all obstacles.

Still, even up to Putin's inauguration, Gorbachev didn't once respond to my invitations. And yet almost eight years had passed since we had last seen each other. Eight years!

The last contact our family had with the Gorbachevs occurred in unquestionably sad circumstances, after the death of Raisa Maksimovna Gorbacheva, Gorbachev's wife. I didn't know whether it made sense for me to attend the funeral. I wanted very much to express my condolences; at the same time, I understood that my presence might cause unnecessary distress and add to Gorbachev's bitterness. So Naina went to the funeral alone. She spent nearly an hour with Gorbachev. Their meeting after the long hiatus was sincere and warm.

Opinion about Gorbachev has now changed. Gorbachev has been forgiven for many things. The untimely death of Raisa Maksimovna facilitated this. For the first time in many years, regular people experienced ordinary, warm feelings for the former head of state; they felt sympathy and understanding.

One would suppose that in considering my decision to retire, I would try to anticipate what would happen to me afterward. What sort of relationships would I have with others? I had no illusions. No one was going to love or worship me. I even had some doubts. For example, what if I were to show up in a public place such as a theater and people started jeering me? Clearly, after a certain period of time, people would come to understand much of what I had done. But what would my own feelings be? How would I live immediately after stepping down, when, according to the old Russian tradition, all misfortunes and sins are heaped upon the outgoing leader?

You already know how my doubts and reflections played out that December. In the first weeks and months that Vladimir Putin was in power, there was, in my opinion, one rather questionable decision. I would like to mention it in connection with the president's resignation. I am speaking about the guarantees that Putin granted me.

I have never asked anyone about the guarantees. I flatly refused to discuss the subject. Before I retired, negotiators, including representatives from the Communist Party, came to see me several times, seeking "consultation" on a law regarding the guarantees to be granted an outgoing president. But I always said, "You want to adopt such a law? Go ahead. This is not my affair." And so no such law was adopted.

Voloshin later explained to me that lawyers from the administration insisted that a decree be hastily issued. They believed that it was impermissible to wait for a law in the state Duma because a legal vacuum could form. And with respect to the legal status of the outgoing president, such a temporary vacuum was impermissible. The constitution stipulated that in the absence of a law, the president is obliged to fill the legal vacuum by means of decree. When I resigned on December 31, there was no law. Nevertheless, even for the sake of these high-level legal materials, it made no sense to hurry. Having said all that, I do understand Putin's actions.

There are any number of rumors and theories in our country and abroad about the content of the decree. People say that every member of my family is now exempt from any responsibility before the law. They assume that we have been granted unthinkable privileges, or that the decree is some special deal between Putin and myself. Supposedly Putin granted me immunity, and in exchange I vacated my space in the Kremlin ahead of time. This last hypothesis is especially ridiculous. No decree can secure any kind of immunity. Only a profoundly naive person who is ignorant of politics could believe that decrees or laws can provide any kind of guarantee to a country's past leader. If Russian society is sick and embittered, it will find a guilty party for its misfortunes, and then I will be accused of every mortal sin. In this case no decree, let alone law, is going to help. But if our country develops in a democratic and civilized manner, the resulting healthy society will be the main guarantor of immunity for me, an outgoing president.

Now, as for the decree itself, this is how the point about immunity reads: "The president of the Russian Federation, having completed his duties in office, shall enjoy immunity. . . . He is not subject to criminal or administrative procedure, detention, or arrest; he is not subject to search of his premises, interrogation, or search of his person." This decree was written with only a single goal in mind: to prevent the spread of political accusations. Immunity has not been conferred upon my family. There are no legal hurdles to investigating any matter concerning the circle surrounding the president. This is a myth dreamed up by the press. Maybe the time will come when the question of legal immunity will fade away of its own accord.

The decree speaks about certain ordinary guarantees the state gives the president, which I would describe as related to past public office. These are the right to auto transportation and security protection; the right to use special reception halls at airports and train stations reserved for officials and delegations; and the right to make use of government telecommunications. There is a point in the decree regarding a state dacha provided to the president for lifetime use. There is another on medical care. In other words, it includes nothing sensational.

But in fact, at the time, at the end of December, I knew nothing about this decree and was thinking about something else entirely. I was completely focused on what would happen after December 31. What kind of life would it be?

· 26 ·

A Different Life

Yeltsin reflects on retirement. It's an entirely different life. He travels and spends time with his growing family. He takes Naina to the theater and to restaurants for the first time in years. He teaches himself how to relax. Of course there are moments of depression, when the retired president realizes there are no major decisions to be made, no decrees to be signed. But now he can work on his "midnight diaries," sorting through the notes and memories of his remarkable political life.

.   .

DURING THE first days of January 2000, I had an amazing feeling. I felt as if I had been dropped into a different life. It was almost a physical sensation, as though the heavy burdens of the last weeks, months, and years were falling from my shoulders. It's difficult to put this sensation into words. There wasn't the slightest hint of depression or the emptiness that I had so feared and that I had tried to prepare myself for bit by bit in advance. It was just the opposite. I was filled with positive emotions. I was in a happy, steady mood.

On January 1 Vladimir Putin and his wife, Lyudmila, came to visit us. Vladimir Vladimirovich gave a memorable New Year's toast to me. With satisfaction, he and I clinked our glasses of champagne—and it wasn't just in celebration of the New Year. From that day on, Putin was absolutely free to do everything—to chose his priorities, his economic programs, and the people he would have on his new team. Both he and I understood full well that a totally new life had begun for him. And for me.

Then a week out of a fairy tale began. Right after New Year's, I went on a trip to Israel with Naina and my daughters. We were going to Bethlehem to celebrate 2,000 years of Christianity. We flew through very bad weather—rain, wet snow, wind, and lightning. When we arrived at the airport, I asked the person who met us whether the famous star of Bethlehem had already risen. He was embarrassed and replied that because of the rain nothing was visible. But I had to see this star over Bethlehem! The beginning of the new millennium for Christianity was also my rebirth.

Israel amazed us with its atmosphere of simple, ordinary miracles. The blue Mediterranean air was suffused with myth, mystery, and ancient history. You sensed it immediately, as soon as you set foot on the land of Israel.

I met with President Ezer Weizman and we discussed the issues of our bilateral relations. The visit had been prepared before my resignation was announced, and I had studied all the necessary documents. At the end of the meeting, I caught myself saying my customary, "All right, we're agreed," and I had to force myself to say, "I will definitely pass your message along to Vladimir Vladimirovich." Old habits die hard.

On the way to Yasir Arafat's residence, our car was suddenly stopped on the highway. Four minutes passed in confusion. I wasn't afraid, but Anatoly Kuznetsov, chief of security, was very tense—terrorist acts aren't a rare occurrence in Israel. But it turned out that while we were waiting on the road, Palestinian guards were being bused up to Arafat's palace at breakneck speed. Arafat had decided to receive me with special honors. Of course I was flattered by such a cordial welcome.

Incidentally, Kuznetsov is one of the people who has been practically inseparable from me throughout all the long years of my presidency. He's a cheerful, good-natured, smart fellow. How did he feel now that he was no longer guarding the current president? Outwardly, nothing had changed; the wrestler's solid figure was still by my side. I think nothing had changed inwardly either. Anatoly is an amazingly devoted and reliable person.

In addition to these official meetings, I got together in Israel with some old classmates and friends from Sverdlovsk, Arnold Lavochkin and Anya Lvova, whom I hadn't seen in God knows how many years. Nolik and Anya had moved to Israel a few years ago.* Naina phoned ahead, and we met in the hotel room. As we sat there, Nolik slapped my knee and exclaimed, "Borka! Who would have thought!" Anya told us all about life in Israel. With the sea, the sun, the fresh fruits, and the wonderful social security system, pensioners had it pretty good here. Of course I couldn't live in Israel—there's the terrible heat in the summer, and home is simply better—but Nolik had no complaints. "It's different here, Borka," he said. "It's a different life!"

Jerusalem is full of huge crowds—on every street and at every crossroad. I felt this especially keenly when I visited the patriarchate in Jerusalem. The security service had to hold the crowd back with their elbows and bodies. Inside the patriarchy, the presidents of Orthodox countries were given the Star of the Knights of the Order of the Lord's Tomb. My longtime colleagues Kuchma, Lukashenko, Shevardnadze, and Luchinski stood near me. They all seemed a little at a loss in this unfamiliar setting. The hall was noisy, packed with jostling journalists, politicians, and priests. The quiet Jerusalem patriarchy was overflowing with guests that day.

Finally, the time came for my speech, but I set the prepared text aside. The setting was such that I couldn't read from my paper. I said that some day in this city a common international document of peace would be signed and that I would put all my efforts into it. It would be a new charter of peace. When the hall quieted back down, I could distinctly hear someone exclaiming in Russian, "Good for you, Grandpa!"

The next day, after several official visits, we went to the Bethlehem Basilica of the Birth of Christ, wending our way through the narrow streets and between the houses. I felt an incredible surge of emotion when I glimpsed the ancient stones. The entryway to the basilica was

* Nolik is the diminutive of Arnold.—Trans.

very low, almost waist-high. There were ancient, gray patriarchs, as in the Bible; semidarkness; the flickering of candles. The basilica was terribly stuffy.

People filled the basilica. At the altar they sang praises to the Savior in all the languages of the Orthodox peoples. Below the altar, in a cave where Mary and Joseph had hidden, people were quietly praying. There were pilgrims sleeping right on the ground, exhausted from their long travels. I was very excited. I had been baptized as a child, but like the overwhelming majority of Soviet people, I didn't observe the church rituals, and there was no one to teach me about them. You weren't allowed to cross yourself or go to church or pray. It seems that people in our country have turned back to God only in recent years. But when I came out of the cathedral, numerous pilgrims spoke to me in Russian. "Greetings, Boris Nikolayevich! How are you feeling? We're with you; we're concerned about you! Merry Christmas!" I hadn't expected that here, so far from home, I would hear so much of my native tongue and see so many native faces.

I flew home somewhat stunned, full of emotion. It was, after all, my first trip since my resignation.

On January 7 Naina, Tanya, and I were scheduled to appear at the Bolshoi Theatre for the annual Triumph Prize. Frankly, I wanted to beg off because of my health. Besides that, I was worried. It was my next test in my new life—my first public appearance—and this time it was before a Russian audience.

Tanya kidded me a little bit about it. "Papa, what are you afraid of?" she said. "I guarantee that, at a minimum, people won't whistle."*

It was a clear, snowy New Year's night in Moscow, with stinging, frozen air. The famous square in front of the Bolshoi Theatre was lit up with stage lights and advertisements. They were waiting for me at the back entrance. I climbed up the stairs to the loge and made my

* Russian audiences commonly show their disapproval with whistles.—Trans.

way to my seat. At first I blinked in the darkness. Then suddenly the whole audience was on its feet, applauding. To be honest, I hadn't expected such a reception. I hadn't expected that after eight years of crisis and severe political struggle, people's reaction would be so warm. It was truly stunning.

The Triumph Prize is a major cultural event in Russia. It is also a marvelous Christmas celebration at the Bolshoi Theatre.* I saw all the celebrities of Russia—the poets Bella Akhmadullina and Andrei Voznesensky, the satirist Mikhail Zhvanetsky, the mime Aleksandr Polunin, the playwright Aleksandr Volodin, and many, many others. And the fact that they came up to wish me a merry Christmas was both an honor for me and, if you will, a most important psychological test. A nation's strong support for its retired president seems to me an indication of its unity. That evening, for the first time, I really felt that I was coping with the job of being the "first president of Russia," as I was now called. I felt people's warmth and support.

Everything was going smoothly. A day or two passed. I rested and relaxed. Then one day I was struck with that very sense of emptiness that I had known before but had not wanted to believe I would encounter again.

It happened on January 10. That morning I got up early as always and went to my office. Usually there is a pile of documents waiting for me. For many years, day in and day out, this pile of marked papers was my life. It occupied my mind. I would read the dry words and contemplate the difficult problems, relations, and governmental issues that hid behind them. That pile of papers used to give me a shot of adrenaline every morning. Now the desk was empty.

I went to the desk and took the special communications telephone from the control panel. There was no dial tone. The telephone wasn't working. I had absolutely nothing to do in this office. I sat in the chair for a while and then got up and left.

---

* Russian Orthodox Christmas is on January 7. —Trans.

The whole day I felt an engulfing emptiness. I was filled with loneliness, even grief. I didn't want to impose my feelings on the people
around me, but I suppose that I seemed more withdrawn than in the
previous days. It was probably noticeable. Lena, Tanya, and Naina
watched me carefully. I went for a walk, had lunch, and then took a little nap. At the end of the day, I decided to find out what had happened
to the console and why the phone had been shut off. I was told that the
network was down and that everything would be in order the next
morning. It was merely a technical problem. I just hadn't realized it
right away. Was every trivial thing going to drive me nuts? How would
I live? How would I get used to this? I looked out the window and reflected hard on my new life.

But finally, gradually, I was able to adapt to the retired life. I really
had to take myself back to everything that I had missed all these last
years—the reflections, the calm, the satisfaction in every minute, the
simple human pleasures, the joy of music, theater, and reading. Besides, I was still responsible for the people I had mentored and worked
with. I was not responsible as president, of course, but as a person ac-
countable for the political process and for the path that Russia had
taken. Anyone, including the new president of Russia, could come to
me today, pose his most painful questions, and ask my opinion. I was
obliged to answer without pretending to have the final truth. Yes, this
was important. I had to restrain my reflex to decide, established over
many years of leadership, and instead become an interlocutor for all
these people. I had to listen and to offer my opinions. This was an extremely serious mission.

Then there was another task: There were my midnight diaries, my
thoughts, my impressions, my emotions, my various notes. Now I
could rightly give my political memoir as much time as I wanted. Perhaps readers will like my book. Even if they don't, it will still be one of
the most important documents upon which I have worked.

It was good that I hadn't told anybody about my unsettled
thoughts and had struggled through my quandary by myself. Such a
day must happen in the life of any person who has worked hard and
then suddenly gone into retirement. With these thoughts, I fell asleep.

The next morning I woke calm, refreshed, and full of strength. On that morning my "different life," with its own new, fairly strict schedule, really began.

What does a typical day in my new retired life look like? Just as before, I get up around 6:00 A.M. You can't change your biorhythms. I drink tea and go to my office. The presidential service prepares reading materials and sends them here, to Gorki-9. I get memos about the results of public opinion polls, analyses of the latest events, press digests. I read the reports. Lately I've been working on the manuscript of this book as well. But more and more frequently, I sit down with a tape recorder to do some dictation. If I'm tired of dictating in the office, I go out into the garden and walk along the paths, speaking into the tape recorder, which I was given for my birthday. It fits neatly into the palm of my hand. At first it was strange hearing my own voice, as if it weren't me.

Sometimes, early in the morning or during the day at the dacha, I go out to the stables to visit the horses. I've received dozens of horses as gifts from official visitors, and I usually gave them away to breeders. But one Akhaltekin stallion, given to me by Kazakhstan's President Nursultan Nazarbayev, was so handsome and fine that I decided to keep him. And so that he wouldn't get bored, I added a pair of tame mares. I thought that my daughters and my grandchildren would learn to ride—it's already too late for me—but nothing has come of this project yet. Everyone is too busy. Tanya helps me with my work; Lena is wrapped up in her new duties as a young grandmother; Katya is a young mother; Masha has graduated from high school and has entered Moscow State Institute of International Relations; Borya is far away, studying abroad. But the horses remain. I visit them, touching their warm muzzles and looking into their intelligent eyes. I feed them by hand. My mood immediately improves as soon as I see them.

Often the younger generation, four-year-old Gleb and two-year-old Vanka, drags me to the pool. They love to splash around with Grandpa, to play, horse around, and do somersaults. To be honest, I get a lot of satisfaction from all this, too.

Then I go back to my office. I should control myself, but despite retirement I have a reflex to work. In fact, the day largely remains a workday for me. The phone rings, or I call people. The special phone to communicate with important callers is still in my office, as it was before.

Noon is the time for scheduled visits. I met with Vladimir Putin several times during the first few months after my resignation. We discussed the elections and talked about the Chechen problem particularly often. For the same reason—Chechnya and the army—there were also several meetings with the defense minister, Marshal Igor Sergeyev; the chief of the general staff, Anatoly Kvashnin; and the interior minister, Vladimir Rushailo. Chechnya is a painful topic for me. But I really believe that peace will be established this year.

I also had several meetings with the new prime minister, Mikhail Kasyanov. I like him. He is calm, assured, and competent. On the whole, a strong team has come together in the government, including the other power ministers: Shoigu, minister of emergencies; Konstantin Totsky, head of the Border Service; and Vladimir Matyukhin, director of the Federal Communications Agency. I met a number of times with Yury Krapivin, head of the Federal Guard Service. It was too bad that several months after my resignation Krapivin decided to leave as well. I always liked the way he worked: unnoticed but absolutely steadily and reliably, the way the head of such a special service should work. He and I have developed very good personal relations. So we now get together in a different capacity. We have a lot to reminisce and talk about.

In recent months my circle of personal contacts has widened significantly. I invite people over to visit much more frequently now that I have the opportunity. It was hard before. I had to pay a heavy price for my political career—the loss of my health, the loss of my childhood friends. Almost all of those old friends live in Sverdlovsk, but I hardly saw even those who live in Moscow. There wasn't time or energy. Even now most of my thoughts are confined to the invisible world of the political life, its struggles and passions.

At 1:00 P.M. I have lunch. My inclination for simple, uncomplicated food has only increased. I didn't make any particular culinary discoveries during my presidential trips. I didn't like to eat at official receptions because of the tension and the negotiations. I always had my presidential menu, tested by the Federal Guard Service. There was nothing fancy. I do remember one incident in Beijing when Tanya and Naina decided to try the famous Peking duck. They ordered it through room service late at night, so that no one could prevent them from eating untested food. I woke up and came into the room in my bathrobe. "What are you eating? I want to try it, too!" But that was the exception.

Furthermore, I'm now trying to take some weight off. Tanya has purchased electronic scales for me. It's almost like being an athlete in training, dieting and weighing myself every day. Tanya and I are competing to see who will reach the planned weight goal first. I give her valuable advice. She laughs and says that the scales will determine the winner.

I eat little. For dinner, I usually drink a glass of kefir and that's it. On the weekends our extended family always gets together. It's a tradition I established. During the week I host government officials for dinner.

What else do I do? I've been listening to a lot of music lately, mostly classical music—Mozart, Vivaldi, Tchaikovsky, the famous operas—in various performances and variations. Recently, I have come to like contemporary musicals as well. I listen to Andrew Lloyd Webber's works, such as *Phantom of the Opera*. I also like the French musical *Notre Dame de Paris*. But as soon as I learn a song's rhythm and discover its musical theme (after listening two or three times), I lose interest. Then I beg Tanya or Lena to bring me something brand new.

There has also been so much new literature about World War II—new facts and new ideas—that I want to read it all. I'm also understandably interested in memoirs. I'm trying to understand the specific nature of this genre better.

I've acquired some new habits: I now have a television in my life. I watch the news, but I don't like the political programs. Sometimes I'll watch a movie, although the good films are usually shown after midnight, and I go to sleep early. At my request Tanya ordered all the films of Vladimir Motyl from the State Film Fund. I know his *White Sun of the Desert* practically by heart. I got great satisfaction from rewatching some of his old movies and seeing some new ones, including *Zhenya, Zhenyechka and Katyusha; The Stars of Captivating Fortune;* and *The Forest.* I want to invite this great director out to dinner.

And that's my daily agenda.

Of course, there are variations in my schedule. In late March our family went on a theater kick. First we went to my favorite theater, the Sovremennik, to see *Pygmalion.* The play's director, Galina Borisovna Volchek, is my favorite. She is an amazing woman with very subtle humor. I don't know if there is a comparable theatrical atmosphere anywhere else in Moscow, with such a clear understanding and empathy, such contact between the stage and the audience. And what performers there are—Marina Neyelova, Yelena Yakovleva, Liya Akhedzhakova, Valentin Gaft, Igor Kvasha. I can't even name them all.

The very next day Tanya invited me to a modern musical, *Metro,* in the operetta theater. Naina said, "Why are we going to the theater so often? Are we making up for lost time?" And Tanya replied, "Mama, this is the most fashionable show in Moscow. You must see it!" So I said, "Let's go! I won't miss the most modern, youthful play for anything."

The car stopped on the old Pushkinskaya Street. As I got out, I was startled by the deafening screams of a group of girls. It turns out that young people, fans of the musical, gather by the theater before the show. When they saw the real-life Yeltsin, they decided to offer me their own style of ceremonial welcome. Of course their exuberance could largely be explained by one thing—their age—but there was also some sincere feeling behind it.

I realized this later in the theater, when a girl reached up, almost coming out of her high heels—we were sitting in the loge—and stretched her program to me, saying, "Please, give me your autograph, Boris Nikolayevich!" I said, "I'm sorry, but I don't have a pen." She said, "Take my lipstick, Boris Nikolayevich!" Well, my women weren't about to let me sign my autograph with a stranger's lipstick, so they found a pen. It's a funny little detail, but it's pleasant to recall somehow.

The musical simply amazed me with its energy; its clear, bright vocals; and its decibels. They really could turn the volume down a little. But the actors were amazing kids who used very contemporary language, style, and movement on the stage. At one point the actor who plays the role of a cynical producer talks to an important boss—on his cell phone. Of course he answers, "Yes, Boris Nikolayevich!" The audience chuckled at the joke. My grandson Borya was sitting in the sixth row with three of his friends; I think they found it interesting. It was too bad I had to leave a little early to make it to another meeting that evening. But I did like the show.

In February I went to the Kremlin for the first time after a long break. Of course it's hard to return to an old workplace you have just recently left. I was there to meet with my presidential pool of journalists. These were the people who had flown with me on all my trips since 1996— Tanya Malkina, Natasha Timakova, Veronika Kutsylo, Svetlana Babayeva, Vyacheslav Terekhov, and many others. Our reunion took place in one of the offices of the Great Kremlin Palace, so as not to bother the people in the "working" buildings. It was very touching. Even the acidic Aleksei Venediktov of the radio program *Ekho Moskvy* was congenial and polite. I presented each guest with a presidential watch and gave bouquets of flowers to the women. But that was not the end of it. I didn't want to say good-bye. Somebody—I think it was Tanya Malkina—asked, "How will you spend your birthday, Boris Nikolayevich?"

"How else?" I said. "I'll spend it at home. Will you come?"

And they said, "Will you invite us?"

"Of course, I'll invite you!" I answered.

My birthday was very festive. Poor Naina didn't sleep half the night before, as she was up baking cakes to treat all the journalists. The girls from *Kommersant* presented me with a very valuable gift: a special issue of their newspaper with all the best *Kommersant* articles that had been written about me. Several days later they got up the nerve to call and asked me to send them back just one autographed copy.

The excitement about the elections grew throughout February and March. I was absolutely certain of Putin's victory. Both my own intuition and the whole spectrum of public opinion (confirmed by the diagnoses of sociologists) pointed to victory. Then there was the fact that there was no real alternative to Putin.

I waited for March 26 in a calm, cheerful, upbeat mood. Still, I became rather nervous and agitated on the day of the elections. I learned the preliminary results on the telephone. I called the governors of all the regions and territories where the elections were taking place and asked them how it was going. Tanya tried to talk some sense into me. "Papa, why are you worried?" she asked. "He's going to win anyway."

"I know that myself. I just want to learn the results faster," I said.

When the first published figures of the votes came out and Nikolai Svanidze began to announce them, I called everyone in. "Bring in the champagne! Faster!" Everyone was upbeat. I couldn't sit still for the excitement. Perhaps it was my greatest victory. Lord, how long had I waited for this.

Lena took her little son, my grandson Vanka, with her to vote. Vanka, disregarding the law against electioneering, began to demand loudly that everyone vote for Putin. When they announced the results, Lena said, "See, Vanka, your candidate has won. Do you know who he's going to work as now?"

"I know!" cried Vanka.

"Who?"

"Yeltsin!"

March 14 was Naina's birthday. My daughters and I tried to think of what to give her. Jewelry? A dress? Then we remembered that Naina had recently mentioned that she might take up sewing. A sewing machine would be the perfect gift. Tanya drove to the store and spent a long time picking out the latest model. When I saw this sewing machine, I could hardly believe my eyes. It was totally electronic. You could press some buttons, and it would select from hundreds of stitches and dozens of loops. It was some kind of computer. You got the impression that you could stick a piece of material into this sewing machine and out would pop a ready-made suit.

Early in the morning the three of us rolled a table with the sewing machine–computer into Naina's room. As I've already mentioned, we've kept this tradition for years—the birthday person wakes up to find the whole family gathered with flowers and presents. Only this time, on this morning, I wasn't in a hurry. I stood watching for a long time as Naina exclaimed over the machine. "What am I going to do with this wealth?" she asked.

"For starters," I said, "You could sew me some initials on my handkerchiefs."

Naina and I had gone out so rarely over all these years. We never went to the theater or to restaurants. Now we were able to explore and entertain. We invited Dr. Sergei Mironov, the head of my medical consulting team for many years, to visit. Then we decided that all of us would go to a Georgian restaurant, Suliko. It was wonderful. The manager of the restaurant tried to close it down so that we could have a private party, but I asked him not to do that. Instead, we enjoyed a noisy and gay Georgian evening. There was real Georgian food and Aleksandrouli wine, specially ordered from Tbilisi. Dr. Mironov's wife, Julie, has a marvelous, deep voice. She sang along with the Georgian male choir. And when the rhythmic Georgian songs began to play, I tried to beat time with spoons.

Journalists have often laughed at my passion for spoons. Well, what can you do? When I was young, there were no fancy percussion instruments as there are now. We learned to beat a rhythm using spoons. And rhythm is in my blood. I'm a rhythmic person, although in my own way. I love to take sharp turns, pauses, and transitions in conversation, but I always keep the rhythm going. I can't stand monotony.

.   .   .

In April the former prime minister of Japan, Ryutaro Hashimoto, flew to Moscow. I invited him to my favorite residence in Zavidovo. We continued our fishing tradition. Tanya drove us in a golf cart to the pond, which is full of trout and mirror carp.

In all that time since Krasnoyarsk, Ryu still had not learned how to cast his line with a fly. And from the shore you simply can't cast a baited line. But Ryu wasn't overly concerned about catching fish. What he really wanted was to learn about Putin. Did I truly trust the new president? Would Russia stay on its political course? Ryu didn't want to lose what we had achieved in Krasnoyarsk. And I assured him that I absolutely trusted Putin. The new president of Russia would continue the path of partnership with Japan. I think that the new Japanese prime minister, Yoshiro Mori, who unfortunately took up his post under tragic circumstances, will agree to keep the same course, especially because of his special, personal relationship to Russia.*

As Ryu and I returned from our fishing trip, I had an interesting idea: We could create a world club of former presidents and prime ministers. Powerful figures who had set the tone on the world political scene—leaders like Kohl, Bush, Thatcher, Clinton, Hashimoto, Walesa, Mandela—couldn't just retreat into private life. I knew how hard it was to begin retired life. And a club of "elders" could exert some moral influence on the whole international climate. When I finish my book, I will definitely return to that idea.

Bill Clinton came to Moscow for an official visit in June 2000. After negotiations with Putin and the rest of his official program, he came to see me at Gorki-9. Bill and I hadn't seen each other in a long time and, frankly, I even missed him. We flung the gates open, and the U.S. president and his escort drove into our yard.

I expected Bill to come by himself, but the entire American delegation arrived with him. These were the people who had helped Bill and

---

* That spring Japan's prime minister, Obuchi Keizo, fell ill and died suddenly. —Trans.

worked closely with our administration. They all wanted to shake my hand and wish me well. It was nice.

I turned to Clinton and asked him how many times we had met. He smiled. It was hard to say. Time always flies, but politics runs at a pace of its own. During the worst crises, time can slow to a crawl, while at other periods it rushes forward. But over the course of several ordinary, human years, Bill and I had managed to become friends. We were fond of each other.

"How do you like Putin?" I asked.

"He's a good, strong leader," Bill replied seriously. "I know that he has enormous authority in Russia. But he's just taking his first steps, and in order to become a great politician, he needs to trust his heart more and trust his feelings."

I asked Clinton how he felt the talks about the antimissile defense systems had gone. Clinton didn't give a direct reply but said there were philosophical, political, and technical aspects to antimissile defense. The military people should define the mechanisms for our agreements. I reminded him that together we had found a way out of the most impossible situations, even where our experts had been unable to come to an agreement. Clinton thought for a moment. I realized that he wanted to resolve the antimissile defense problem before he left office. He didn't want to leave it for the next president. How would the dialogue between our two countries continue? What could the world expect? Only through compromise could we preserve our disarmament achievements and help make the twenty-first century a century of peace.

I asked Bill how his wife, Hillary, was doing. He told me about a radio show he had done the previous day. It was a live Russian call-in show. "There was a funny question," Bill said. "What would I think if Hillary were to become president of the United States? How would I feel in the role of the president's husband? And I said, that would be O.K. I'd serve her tea!"

I always liked Bill's good-natured openness and his free and easy style of communicating. Once I sat next to him for a long time at a state function. He said to me, "We're almost the same height, Boris." I asked him, "Bill, what size shoe do you wear? Let's compare." He laughed, and I started taking off my shoes. It turned out that although we were the same height, his shoes were at least one size larger.

Finally, I stood up in order to see the guests off. In parting, Bill looked at me and said, "You wanted to change your country, Boris, and you did."

"And you changed your country, too, Bill," I replied. I don't think these were just clichés.

We walked out of the house. It was a wonderful summer day. Tanya and Naina had themselves photographed with the president of the United States. He waved and headed toward his car. The officer with the nuclear suitcase walked ahead of him. He was wearing gloves, even in the heat.

When Bill left, I looked at the photograph he had given me. He and I were sitting in the famous wicker Roosevelt chairs. We were looking ahead into a blue sky. Two presidents. Two ordinary men. It's a great photograph.

The May holidays were upon us. Just days remained before Vladimir Putin's inauguration. I was getting more and more excited. Aleksandr Voloshin, head of the presidential administration, brought me a preliminary plan for the inauguration. There were two options for its location: the Palace of Congresses, where my inauguration of 1996 had taken place, or the Great Kremlin Palace. I had unpleasant memories associated with my 1996 inaugural ceremony, so it was hard for me to judge. I told them to decide for themselves. I was very glad when they chose the newly restored hall of the old Kremlin and not the glass and concrete Soviet Palace of Congresses.

The inauguration of the new president of Russia was to take place on May 7 in the Andrei Hall of the Great Kremlin Palace. These halls, the halls of George, Andrei, and Aleksandr, had witnessed the coronations of the tsars. They preserved the memory of those historical events. There is nothing wrong with making such analogies. Our great Russian history demands love and respect.

Here's an interesting footnote: The planners knew how many seats could fit in the Palace of Congresses. But how many people would fit in the halls of the Great Kremlin Palace? No one knew. In order to solve the problem, they brought soldiers in from the barracks, lined them up along the carpeted runway, and counted.

I had doubts about my role in the inauguration ceremony. Should I go out on the stage together with Putin? Should I give a speech? Finally, I realized that my role would not be decided by the whim of some stage manager but by history itself. Still, I became very agitated when I began to work on my speech. After all, from the beginning until the very end, I had never had an easy minute in the Kremlin. I had been in power in Russia for eight years. For eight years, I had tried to keep the country from upheavals, and I had been forced to take some very difficult and unpopular measures. For eight years, I had suffered some hellish tension. There are no apt analogies in world political practice for what I did over the last quarter of a century. What could I say about this on one page of text?

I got up early in the morning, as usual. Tanya asked what suit I would be wearing. "I don't know. What do you suggest?" I asked. Tanya suggested the dark blue suit. I thought that black would be more serious. We argued, as we often do. Finally the whole family came out to see me off beyond the gates.

The Great Kremlin Palace was filled with about 1,500 people, representatives of the entire Russian elite, waiting in tense anticipation. There were politicians, officials, journalists, businessmen, and cultural figures. There were clergy from all faiths without exception. The first and last president of the USSR, Mikhail Gorbachev, was also present.

The daylight reflected off the enormous crystal chandeliers. Gilded velvet ropes kept the audience off the new president's path to the stage. Right on schedule, at 12:00 noon, the automobile and motorcycle escort approached the Kremlin, where the audience for the inauguration was already waiting in the hall. Putin began his procession past everyone who watched him—and who would be watching his every move and step for the next four years. How long those few minutes must have lasted for him.

The inauguration kept to the strict state rituals, but it was a magnificent spectacle. CNN and other major Western television companies broadcast it live throughout the whole world. Naturally, the three federal TV channels broadcast it on Russian television. Every detail had been planned, and it was no wonder that the whole country was glued to their TV sets on May 7. Only one thing went wrong: The bright stage lights suddenly began to flicker just as I was trying to read the lines of my speech on the teleprompter screen. For a moment, I could see only the occasional word, but the problem was quickly fixed. Thank God this mishap didn't detract from the overall celebration.

After the ceremony, Vladimir Vladimirovich and I went out to Cathedral Square. A light wind was blowing, and a pale sun was shining. I had waited for this moment for so many years and had prepared for it for such a long while. Still, I felt sad. A regiment of Kremlin guards marched past our stage. It seemed as if I were watching all this from the wings, as if it were a movie. The cannons fired from the banks of the river. And the entire great epoch of changes and upheavals—an era in which I had been a main actor—disappeared into the air with a roar.

I got up in the middle of the night. I wondered if everything was accurate in my book. I am the type of person who can speak only in the first person and write only what I know and feel myself. Yes, I was president for many years, and much of what happened in Russia depended on my actions, right or wrong. But in the end history is not written by individuals. There are greater, sometimes mysterious patterns in the lives of nations.

Have I been too self-confident? Have I taken too much upon myself? I don't think so. I am obliged to report absolutely everything I thought and felt, and why I behaved in this or that way. But one question remains. What next—who am I now?

I feel like a runner who has just completed a supermarathon of 40,000 kilometers. I gave it my all. I put my whole heart and soul into running my presidential marathon. I honestly went the distance. If I have to justify anything, here is what I will say: If you think you can do it better, just try. Run those 40,000 kilometers. Try to do it faster, better, more elegantly, or more easily. Because I did it.

Epilogue

IT'S 4:00 A.M. I'm in my office. Once again I'm sitting up with the manuscript. I can't sleep, and the book is essentially done. Still, I have a feeling I haven't said everything. I suppose it's impossible to say everything. It's an unrealistic hope.

The nights are short in the summer, and it's almost dawn. A fog has settled around the trees in the backyard. Damp air wafts into my room. How to end this book?

In these pages I've deliberately avoided any kind of official tone. I have refrained as much as possible from quoting documents, decrees, and statements. Instead, this is my view on current events. It's totally subjective. In some sense, these are my personal notes.

But there is one document that I do want to cite, right here at the end of the book, because it is a very unusual document, unusually charged with emotion. Each word comes from the heart. It is also a personal letter, not to one person but to everyone. It is my last speech as president to the citizens of Russia. I have it before me:

Dear Russians!

There is just a little time left before a magic date in our history. The year 2000 is approaching, a new century and a new millennium.

We have all tried this date out on ourselves. When we were children, and later when we were more grown-up, we tried to calculate how old we would be in the year 2000, how old our mothers would be, how old our children would be. It once seemed too far away, this unusual New Year's Eve. Now this day is here.

My dear friends! My dear ones! Today I am giving you my New Year's greetings for the last time. But that's not all. Today I am speaking to you for the last time as the president of Russia. I have made a decision. I have thought about it long and hard. Today, on the last day of the outgoing century, I am stepping down from office.

I have often heard it said that Yeltsin would cling to power by any means possible and would never give it up. That's a lie. And it's not the point. I have always said that I would not depart from the constitution be even a single step, and that the Duma elections must take place within the time allotted by the constitution. That has happened. I also wanted the presidential elections to take place on schedule, in June 2000. This is very important for Russia. We are creating a most important precedent for the civilized, voluntary transfer of power, power from one president of Russia to another, elected anew. But I have nonetheless made a different decision. I am leaving. I am leaving before the end of my term.

I realize that I must do this. Russia must enter the new millennium with new politicians, with new faces, with new, intelligent, strong, energetic people. And we who have been in power for many years must step down.

When I saw how people voted with such faith and hope for a new generation of politicians during the Duma elections, I realized that I had achieved my life's main goal: Russia would no longer return to the past. Now Russia will always move only ahead. And I must not get in the way of this natural course of history. Why should I hang on to power for another half year when there is such a strong person in the country who is worthy of becoming president and with whom practically every Russian links his or her hopes for the future? Why should I get in the way? Why wait another six months? That's not like me. It's not my nature.

Today, on this unusually important day for me, I want to say a few words that are more personal than the ones I generally employ.

I want to ask your forgiveness. I want to apologize for not making many of our dreams come true. What had seemed easy turned out to be extremely difficult. I apologize for not justifying some of the expectations of people who believed that we could jump in one swoop from the gray, stagnant, totalitarian past to the bright, prosperous, civilized future. I believed in it myself. It seemed that if we could just make one jump, we would overcome everything.

But the one jump didn't work. I was too naive about some things. In some areas the problems turned out to be far too complicated. We slogged ahead through these mistakes, through these failures. Many people experienced upheavals during this difficult time.

But I want you all to know something that I have never said and that is important for me to say today: The pain each of you experienced was reflected by pain in my own heart—sleepless nights, torturous suffering over what must be done so that people would have lives that were just a little bit easier and better. But I had a more important task.

I am leaving. I did everything that I could. A new generation is coming to take my place, a generation that will do it bigger and better.

In accordance with the constitution, I am resigning. I have signed the decree on the appointment of chair of the government, Vladimir Vladimirovich Putin, as acting president. Under the constitution, elections for president must take place within three months.

I have always believed in the amazing wisdom of Russians. Therefore, I have no doubt what choice you will make at the end of March 2000.

In wishing you farewell, I would like to say to each of you, be happy. You deserve happiness. You deserve happiness and peace.

Happy New Year! Happy new century, my dear Russians!

Index

Yeltsin family members are listed under the familiar names that appear in the text.